# THE KALENDARIUM

## OF NICHOLAS OF LYNN

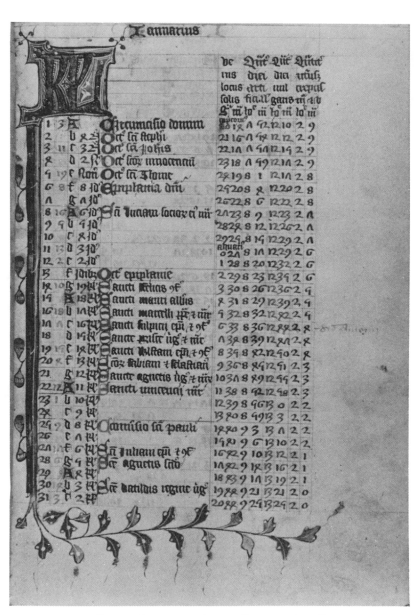

Bodleian Library, Laud Miscellaneous 662, f. 2r

# THE KALENDARIUM
## OF NICHOLAS OF LYNN

EDITED BY
### SIGMUND EISNER

TRANSLATION BY
GARY MAC EOIN AND
SIGMUND EISNER

THE CHAUCER LIBRARY

THE UNIVERSITY OF GEORGIA PRESS
ATHENS

Copyright © 1980 by the University of Georgia Press
Athens, Georgia 30602

All rights reserved

Set in VariTyper Bembo
Printed in the United States of America

Library of Congress Cataloging in Publication Data

Nicholas, of Lynne, fl. 1386.
  The kalendarium of Nicholas of Lynn.
  English and Latin.
  Part of the Chaucer library.
  Includes bibliographical references.
    I. Almanacs, Latin—England.  I. Eisner, Sigmund,
1920-  II. Chaucer library.  III. Title.
AY751.Z7 1979          529'.4          78-3532
              ISBN 0-8203-0449-2

The publication of this book was supported in part by a
grant from the Andrew W. Mellon Foundation, admin-
istered by the American Council of Learned Societies.
The University of Georgia Press gratefully acknowledges this assistance.

DEDICATED WITH LOVE TO THE FOLLOWING:

NFE· 23 Libre 17 Kalendas Novembris
KSE 3 Leonis 7 Kalendas Augusti
KKE 8 Arietis 5 Kalendas Aprilis
SNKE 4 Sagittarii 6 Kalendas Decembris
CME 17 Tauri 8 Idus Mayi
KLE 11 Leonis 2 Nonas Augusti
NKE 25 Aquarii 16 Kalendas Marcii
VAE 24 Libre 15 Kalendas Novembris
HHE 28 Cancri 12 Kalendas Augusti
PCJ 15 Virginis 6 Idus Septembris
CFE 6 Aquarii 7 Kalendas Februarii

# CONTENTS

# FOREWORD

The English poet Geoffrey Chaucer (ca. 1343-1400), like most other medieval writers at a time when the notion of "authority" was quite different from the current notion, made use of the works of classical and earlier medieval authors, but there are no editions of these works in versions that would have been available to Chaucer and his contemporaries in the late Middle Ages. Present editions, unless they are facsimiles, attempt to reconstruct an author's original or the closest thing to that original, but before the invention of printing, when texts were reproduced by hand, a classical or medieval work would have been altered, often greatly, by each successive copying. The purpose of the Chaucer Library, therefore, since its creation in 1946, has been to present the works that Chaucer knew, translated, or made use of in his writings in versions that are as close as possible to those that were in existence, circulating, and being read by Chaucer and his contemporaries. These versions were, of course, not critical editions—they were filled with readings that the original authors did not write, with additions and omissions, and sometimes with glosses and commentaries—and to have a true understanding of the ways in which classical and medieval texts were perceived by medieval readers, it is necessary to reproduce such nonoriginal material. This the Chaucer Library has done, as in the previous volume published by the University of Georgia Press, Pope Innocent III's *De Miseria Condicionis Humane,* and will continue to do, while at the same time striving to present readable texts, with punctuation and capitalization modernized, abbreviations expanded, some letters regularized, and accompanied by English translations.

At the same time, however, there are, and will be, a few works in the Chaucer Library that, because of their special nature, do not warrant this kind of presentation. Nicholas of Lynn's *Kalendarium,* the subject of the present volume, is one of these. It is clear that Chaucer knew and used the *Kalendarium,* as Professor Eisner demonstrates in his Introduction, but the verbal evidence is too limited to determine Chaucer's text precisely and to choose thereby a manuscript to be printed in its entirety; moreover, the *Kalendarium* has never been printed before. In this case, and in cases like it, the Chaucer Library Committee believes that it would be more useful to publish a critical edition, prepared according to whatever editorial method is most appropriate, than to follow slavishly its traditional policy. The present volume, as Professor Eisner describes it, is "a conservative critical edition"—that is, a base manuscript emended in a limited number of places with readings from other extant manuscripts. Given the genre and subject matter of the *Kalendarium* and the date of Chaucer's use of it, one can feel confident that the text printed here is very close to Nicholas's presumed original as well as to Chaucer's manuscript of it. It is with great pleasure, therefore, that the Committee now adds Nicholas of Lynn's *Kalendarium,* a work of importance for students both of Chaucer and of medieval science, to the list of books in Chaucer's library.

Robert E. Lewis
General Editor and Chairman

For the Chaucer Library Committee:
Albert C. Baugh
Morton W. Bloomfield
Martin M. Crow
Ruth J. Dean
John H. Fisher
Albert C. Friend
Robert A. Pratt
Siegfried Wenzel

# ACKNOWLEDGMENTS

There have been many who have given me help and encouragement in this study, and I would be remiss if I did not express my gratitude here. In 1972 I was awarded both a grant from the University of Arizona Gràduate College for Faculty Research Support in the Humanities and Social Sciences and a year's sabbatical from my duties at the University of Arizona, enabling me to examine, in England, the surviving manuscripts of the *Kalendarium* of Nicholas of Lynn.

The authorities of the six libraries which hold the manuscripts of the *Kalendarium* have graciously given permission for me to examine, to copy on microfilm, to quote, and to describe their manuscripts. These libraries are as follows: the Bodleian Library of Oxford University, Manuscripts Laud Miscellaneous 662, Digby 41, Ashmole 5, Rawlinson C.895, Ashmole 370, and Ashmole 319; the British Library, Manuscripts Sloane 1110, Arundel 347, Additional 15209, Arundel 207, and Sloane 3285; the Bibliothèque Royale Albert I$^{er}$ of Brussels, Manuscript 4862/69; the Society of Antiquaries of London, Manuscript 8; the Bayerische Staatsbibliothek of Munich, Codex Latinus Monacensis 10661; and the Cambridge University Library, Manuscript Gg. 5.37. In addition the staffs of other libraries have been diligently helpful. In particular I wish to mention the personnel of the following: the Library of the University of Arizona; the Bancroft Library of the University of California at Berkeley; the Huntington Library of San Marino, California; the Library of London University; and the New York Public Library in New York City.

Many individuals graciously offered both time and expertise, each in his or her own specialized area: Professor Morton W. Bloomfield of Harvard University; Professor Alan K. Brown of Ohio State University; Dr. Curt Bühler of the Pierpont Morgan Library of New York, who not only loaned me one of his own fourteenth-century manuscripts but courageously shipped it across the American continent so that I could see it; Professor Roger Dahood of the University of Arizona; Mr. C. St.J. H. Daniel of the National Maritime Museum in London; Professor E. Talbot Donaldson of Indiana University; Professor Emeritus Albert C. Friend of the City College of New York; Professor Edward Grant of Indiana University; Professor Richard Hosley of the University of Arizona; Professor Richard C. Jensen of the University of Arizona; Dr. Manfred Kudlek of the *Institut für Informatik,* Hamburg, Germany; Professor Robert E. Lewis of Indiana University, the general editor of the Chaucer Library; Professor Michael Masi of Loyola University of Chicago; Professor J. D. North of the Museum of the History of Science in Oxford; Professor Robert A. Pratt of the University of Pennsylvania, chairman of the Chaucer Library Committee; Mr. Harold N. Saunders of Bude, Cornwall, a craftsman and a maker of astrolabes; Dr. D. Justin Schove of St. David's College, Beckenham, Kent; Miss Cornelia Starks of the Bodleian Library of Oxford; and Professor Siegfried Wenzel of the University of Pennsylvania. And of course nothing could have been done without the sympathetic and careful help of the members of the secretarial staff of the English Department of the University of Arizona and the aid of Mr. Ian Frederick, a graduate student at the University of Arizona, who proofread the entire study.

Dr. Gary Mac Eoin, who is listed on the title page as the chief translator of this study, is that and much, much more. Not only is he a linguist, a scholar, and above all a humanitarian, but he has been graciously helpful in every major scholarly effort I have made over the last twenty-five years. It is with the utmost pleasure that here again I am able to acknowledge my gratitude.

Finally my wife, Nancy Fereva Eisner, as always, has patiently read, corrected, and reread all that is said here.

# INTRODUCTION

Nicholas of Lynn was a Carmelite friar who flourished at Oxford in the late fourteenth century. In 1386 he composed a *Kalendarium* to begin in 1387 and run through 1462. Geoffrey Chaucer, who died in 1400, said in his *Treatise on the Astrolabe* that he knew and used the *Kalendarium* of Nicholas of Lynn.[1]

Nicholas is no more garrulous about himself than is any medieval writer. In the prologue to the *Kalendarium* he identifies himself as a Carmelite brother at Oxford, unworthy and least among readers of sacred theology. He dates the composition of his *Kalendarium* as 1386 and says it is to replace a similar work by Walter of Elvedene, whom he calls a great teacher. Completing his contemporary references, he dedicates his *Kalendarium* to John of Gaunt, addressing him not only as an illustrious prince and Duke of Lancaster but also as King of Castile and Leon, which latter appellation is of some interest in dating Nicholas's *Kalendarium*. In 1372 John of Gaunt married Constance of Castile and after his marriage styled himself as King of Castile. His claim came to little until April 1386, when King Richard II of England placed a symbolic crown of Castile on John's head. John then headed an unsuccessful expedition to Castile, and in 1387 he renounced his claim to that kingship.[2] So, at the very time when John, with the support of the English crown, was attempting to conquer Castile, Nicholas, at home in Oxford, was writing his *Kalendarium*.

Nicholas is apparently remembered more as a mathematician and an explorer than as a writer of a calendar. John Bale, who died in 1563, calls him "philosophus, cosmographus, et astronomus inter omnes sui temporis celeberrimus."[3] Gerardus Mercator, who died in 1594, quotes James Knox of Bolduc, "who reporteth that a certaine English friar, minorite of Oxford, a Mathematician, hath seen and composed the lands lying about the Pole, and measured them with an astrolabe, and described them by a Geometrical instrument." Richard Hakluyt, who died in 1616, expands the Mercator statement as follows:

Touching the description of the North parts, I have taken the same out of the voyage of James Cnoyen of Hartzeban Bushe [James Knox of Bolduc?], which alleageth certaine conquests of Arthur king of Britaine: and the most part, and chiefest things among the rest, he learned of a certaine priest in the king of Norwayes court, in the yeere 1364. This priest was descended from them which king Arthur had sent to inhabite these Islands, and he reported that in the yeere 1360, a certaine English Frier, a Franciscan, and a Mathematician of Oxford, came into those Islands, who leaving them, and passing further by his Magicall Arte, described all those places that he sawe, and tooke the height of them with his Astrolabe, according to the forme that I (Gerard Mercator)

2

have set downe in my mappe, and as I have taken it out of the aforesaid James Cnoyen. Hee sayd that those four Indraughts were drawne into an inward gulfe or whirlepoole, with so great a force, that the ships which once entred therein, could by no means be driven backe again, and that there is never in those parts so much winde blowing, as might be sufficient to drive a Corne mille.[4]

Hakluyt adds the testimony of John Dee, an English mathematician who died in 1608, that in 1360 an Oxford friar visited the uncharted north and charted it in a book called *Inventio Fortunata,* which he presented to King Edward III of England. Then this adventuresome friar made five more voyages to the far north, leaving each time from the harbor of Lynn.[5] The voyages described by Mercator and Dee were assumed by Hakluyt to have been made by Nicholas of Lynn, possibly because the voyager was an Oxford friar and possibly because he sailed from the port of Lynn (since 1537: King's Lynn). In 1748 Thomas Tanner says in his *Bibliotheca Britannico-Hibernica* that Nicholas was the author of a calendar which Chaucer praised, a voyager to northern islands previously unknown to Europeans, and also the author of not only the *Inventio Fortunata* but also a number of astronomical works. Tanner adds that Nicholas died at Lynn, from where he came, and there he was buried with his fellow Carmelites.[6]

The expanding pseudo-biography of Nicholas had run its course by 1923 when R. T. Gunther labeled Hakluyt's identification of the peregrinating priest of 1360 as a confusion.[7] Gunther is probably right. There is no solid evidence to connect the astrolabe-owning Franciscan who sailed, or was reported to have sailed, to the northern islands with the Carmelite Nicholas of Lynn. Presumably many an Oxford Nicholas has owned an astrolabe, including the hero of Chaucer's Miller's Tale. One voice, however, does stand against these conclusions. M. C. Seymour writes that he owns a fragmentary copy of the *Inventio Fortunata,* which describes "what is now Long Island."[8] But even if the *Inventio Fortunata* should prove to be genuine, no proof has risen so far to identify its author with Nicholas of Lynn.[9]

On occasion Nicholas of Lynn's name appears in print with a letter symbolizing the sound [k] instead of the sound [n] for the final consonant. In 1748 Tanner refers to him as "Nicholaus Linnensis (de Leuca),"[10] and Thorndike and Kibre in 1963 quote: "Nicholas de Lunica (Lynn?), Canones super calendarium," from Brussels, Bibliothèque Royale, MS. 4862/69.[11] In each case, I think, someone has misread the manuscript presentation of Nicholas's name. Normally Nicholas's name is spelled in the manuscripts *Nicholaus* or *Nicholai de Lennea* or *Linea.* In Oxford MS. Laud Miscellaneous 662, folio 14, the name appears as *Nicholaus de Lenea.* The letter *n* consists of two minims, joined at neither the top nor the bottom. The letter *e* is exactly the same as a *c* except that the *e* has a light diagonal stroke, a distinction that is not always clear. Therefore, in Laud Miscellaneous 662, it is quite possible to read *Lenea* as *Leuca,* and probably Tanner or his source did exactly that. Thorndike and Kibre cite Brussels, Bibliothèque Royale Albert Ier, 4862/69. On folio 41v of that manuscript the following appears: "Expliciunt canones super kalendarium fratris Nicholai de Linnea ordinis Carmelitarum." The word *Linnea* consists of the initial *L* followed by five minims and *ea.* If again the *e* is read as *c,* and the line signifying the dot over the *i* is ignored, the name could appear as *Lunica.* In a recent and excellent study Professor J.A.W. Bennett[12] carries the alleged [k] sound in Nicholas's name even further. He suggests that Nicholas of Lynn could be the mysterious *Leyk,* whom Dr. Derek J. Price, using an ultra-violet light, discovered in *The Equatorie of the Planetis,* which survives in Peterhouse (Cambridge) MS. 75.9.[13] Dr. Price thinks that *Leyk* might be either an error for the name [John of] Linières or a transliteration of an Arabic name. Professor Bennett says that *Leyk* might also be an error for *Lynne,* and cites Oxford MS. "Laud 662" as mentioning Nicholas as *Nicholas de Leuka.* But Oxford, Bodleian Library, MS. Laud Miscellaneous 662, as I said above, spells the name *Lenea,* not *Leuca* nor *Leuka,* and I cannot agree that Nicholas's name appears as *Leyk* in *The Equatorie of the Planetis* or anywhere else. Again an inviting speculation about Nicholas's identity must be disregarded.

There is no proof, but it seems likely that Nicholas was associated with the School of Astronomy at Oxford's Merton College. During the fourteenth century Merton was the hub of English, and even European, scientific inquiry.[14] The thirteenth-century Spanish Alfonsine astronomical tables had been readjusted for Oxford and reproduced by the Merton scholars. Bishop William Rede (or Reed) of the Merton College School of Astronomy, who died in 1385, set the latitude of Oxford at 51° 50', a figure which Nicholas uses. The actual latitude of Oxford is 51° 46'. Also, at Merton a longitudinal difference between Oxford and Toledo was established to be 16', with Oxford lying toward the east. Oxford is actually 2° 44' east of Toledo. These errors are probably responsible for some errors in Nicholas's eclipse and lunar tables. Few of Nicholas's tables have great errors, but few are exact. Because Nicholas uses the information provided by Merton College, I suggest that he probably was associated with that college.

This, then, we know about Nicholas of Lynn: he flourished at Oxford in the late fourteenth century, he was a Carmelite friar, and he wrote a calendar. Beyond these bare facts we can say with some assurance that he walked in an environment conducive to his own expertise. Anything beyond these assertions is speculation, and so far as I have been able to judge, most of these speculations are still unprovable.

## THE MEDIEVAL *KALENDARIUM*

The European medieval *Kalendarium*, which modern readers would call an almanac, combined Greco-Roman attempts to record the days of the year with Greco-Arabic mathematics, astronomy, and medicine. The Greeks were the first in the western world to equate 235 lunations with nineteen solar years. The early Romans contributed a system of months based originally on new and full moons and added a public record of important festivals. Later, in the first century B.C., Julius Caesar reformed the Roman calendar into a new calendar which, although faulty, survived without successful challenge for sixteen centuries.

In the fifth century B.C., Meton, an Athenian who may have been following Babylonian observations, declared that nineteen years to the day after a given new moon another new moon would occur. In that period about 235 lunations would take place. Thus he gave his world a means of time measurement resting on both a solar and lunar base. This system was useful but not exact. Others tried without much success to improve it by multiplying a variety of numbers and adding or subtracting one or more days so that in a very long period solar and lunar observations would be the same.[15] The number of a given year in its Metonic cycle was known as the golden number, possibly, as Archer suggests, because the fifth-century Athenians were so proud of their discovery that they emblazoned the Metonic number of the current year with figures of gold into a prominent place in the agora.[16] The concept of the golden number survived into Christian Europe: for any year the golden number may be obtained by dividing the number of the year by 19 and adding one to the remainder. For instance, 1979 divided by 19 yields 104 and a remainder of 3. Add 1 to that remainder, and we have 4, which is the golden number for 1979.

The pre-Julian Roman calendar, which was in use in the third century B.C., was based on a year of twelve months, each averaging one lunation of twenty-nine and a half days, totalling 354 days. The discrepancy between that short year and the actual year was made up with the insertion of an intercalary month which was slipped in whenever the College of Pontiffs thought necessary. On the first day of the Roman month, which was the first day of a lunation (the day of a new moon),[17] a convocation was called. The early Latin *kalo* meant "I convoke," and the first day of each Roman month came to be known as the *kalendae* or *kalends*. The Romans indicated not only the time of the new moon but also the time of the full moon, which was given the name *idus* or *ides,* a word which earlier had meant "bright." The ninth day before the ides or the day of the quarter moon was called *nonae* or the *nones*. The ides fell on the fifteenth day of March, May, Quinctilis (July), and October, and on the thirteenth day of the other months, with the nones always nine days earlier. By the end of the fourth century B.C., the Romans were posting calendars in public places along with *fasti* or lists of feast and lawful business days, thus looking forward to the Christian calendar and its list of saints' festivals.

By the time of Julius Caesar there was no correlation between the Roman lunar month and the actual phases of the moon. Caesar, aided by the Alexandrian astronomer Sosigenes, based his revision of the calendar on a solar year, which he trustingly believed to be exactly 365.25 days long. Caesar added one intercalary day to each fourth year. To do so he doubled the sixth kalends of March, which was 24 February, and thus a year so lengthened by one day came to be called a bissextile year.

During the Christian era the practice rose of assigning to each day of the year an alphabetical letter between *a* and *g* inclusive. The first of January was an *a*, 2 January a *b,* 7 January a *g;* and on 8 January the cycle would recur with an *a*.Thus a given saint's day on a certain date would always have the same dominical, or Sunday, letter, as these letters came to be called. Also, when 1 January was a Sunday, the dominical letter *a* was assigned to the entire year; if 1 January was a Monday, the letter for the year was a *b,* etc. In a bissextile year the do-minical letter of the year dropped on 24 February to one less in the alphabetical order. A knowledge of both the golden number and the dominical letter, and a table like Nicholas's in his *Kalendarium* (pp. 178–79), enabled one to determine the date of Easter or any other movable feast. At the Council at Nicaea in A.D. 325, the date of the vernal equinox was fixed on 21 March, and the complexities of arriving at the proper date of Easter were established.

The political expansion of Islam brought an influx of Arabic learning to the Christian world. The Arabs, who had absorbed Greek medicine, astronomy, and mathematics and who offered a means of arithmetic of their own, passed much information into the Christian calendars, changing them from calendars as the Romans knew them to almanacs as we know them.[18] The word *almanac* itself derives from an Arabic word meaning "the weather." Nicholas of Lynn cites an Arab whom he calls Haly as a commentator on the *Centiloquium*, which was either by or said to be by the second-century Greek, Claudius Ptolemy (p. 207).

In 1267 Roger Bacon used the word *almanac* in his *Opus Majus* to mean a book which includes the (apparent) motions of the heavenly bodies. Within the next century or two the use of almanacs had spread throughout Europe. Almanacs included calendars inherited from the Greeks and Romans, astronomical data inherited from the Greeks and Arabs, lists of ecclesiastical and other anniversaries inherited from the Roman *fasti* and bolstered by the popularity of the Christian saints, and medical information, much of which was transmitted from the Greeks by the Arabs. Almanacs were useful to astronomers, physicians, and members of the ecclesiastical orders. Nicholas's *Kalendarium* is actually such an almanac, but the meanings of the two words overlapped.

Because the Julian calendar assumed a year of 365.25 days and the actual year is 365.2425 days, there was a cumulative error of about one day in 130 years.[19] By the thirteenth century both Roger Bacon and Robert Grosseteste called for a calendar reform, and in the early fourteenth century the Avignonese popes, John XXII and Clement VI, although more eager than effectual, assigned to their subordinates the task of drawing up a new calendar.[20] These attempts at reform came to nothing, and in the late fourteenth century Nicholas of Lynn, also aware of the calendar error, offered a corrective table (p. 180) in his own *Kalendarium*. The vernal equinox was then 12 March. In 1582, almost two centuries after the time of Nicholas, Pope Gregory XIII successfully recorrected the Julian calendar so that the vernal equinox would again be 21 March. He eliminated three bissextile years every four centuries to prevent the error from recurring. The Gregorian calendar was adopted by Catholic Europe very quickly and by the rest of Europe over the next three and a half centuries.[21]

Normally a medieval calendar or almanac gives information discussed above, including saints' days with the dominical letters, sunrises and sunsets throughout the year, twilights, new and full moons, solar and lunar eclipses, some planetary information, dates of movable feasts, medical information including proper times for phlebotomy or bloodletting, and astrological information pertaining to all of the above. The calendar may be spiced with fascinating illuminated drawings: attractive blue and gold sketches of eclipses; a drawing of a man showing which parts of his body belong to the various signs of the zodiac; or once in a while a volvelle, which shows the phases of the moon by means of a circular piece of perforated vellum pivoting over a page in the manner of our modern foreign language verb wheels. When calendars became obsolete, because the specific years for all the new and full moons (and of course eclipses) had passed, the folios were sometimes scraped clean and re-inked with the same information brought up to date. Parts of calendars on occasion developed an interest of their own and were copied separately. For instance, a portion of Nicholas's calendar containing only medical information was copied for the use of physicians in 1470, eight years after the calendar became obsolete. The language of the calendars was Latin, and usually they were written in what has come to be known in England as a university book hand, although calendars were copied in a variety of European handwritings well beyond the time of the introduction of printing.

Besides the Oxford *Kalendarium* of Nicholas of Lynn, the Oxford *Kalendarium* of John Somer is an additional example of such a calendar. It was mentioned by Chaucer as one of his sources in the same sentence as the *Kalendarium* of Nicholas of Lynn,[22] and was, according to Somer's own testimony, composed in 1380 at the request of Thomas Kingsbury, a provincial minister of the Franciscan order, and dedicated to Joan, Princess of Wales, Duchess of Cornwall, Countess of Chester, widow of the Black Prince, and mother of King Richard II. Somer's *Kalendarium* was designed to run for the same four Metonic cycles as that of Nicholas of Lynn, from 1387 through 1462. Tables which are from Somer's *Kalendarium* survive in the same Peterhouse manuscript which contains *The Equatorie of the Planetis*.[23] Somer himself, so far as is known, was a Franciscan friar associated with Oxford.[24] No legend of marvellous adventures was ever created for him as was for Nicholas.

As far as I have seen, Somer's *Kalendarium* also survives all or in part in the following manuscripts: Oxford, Bodleian Library, Digby 5, Rawlinson D.238, Ashmole 391, Ashmole 789, and Savile 39; British Library, Royal 2 B.viii, Royal 12 E.xvi, Sloane 2250, Sloane 282, and Harley 321; Cambridge, Trinity College Library, R.15.18 and R.15.21; Biblioteca Apostolica Vaticana, Regina Sueviae 155; and No. 12 in the private collection of Dr. Curt F. Bühler of the Pierpont Morgan Library of New York City.[25] Some fragments from Somer's *Kalendarium* are dovetailed into British Library, MS. Additional 15209, which is essentially a Nicholas of Lynn manuscript, and one drawing appears in the Nicholas of Lynn manuscript, Bodleian Library, MS. Ashmole 370. Bodleian Library, MS. Ashmole 391 also contains one canon by Nicholas.

Somer's *Kalendarium* begins with a prologue and a chart of movable feasts. The month-to-month section consists of one page for each month, each page containing the Metonic cycles of new moons, sunrises, a single column with the order of the Metonic cycles, a column of dominical letters, a Roman calendar, and a saints' calendar in the middle of the page. Next, as in Nicholas's *Kalendarium*, is a section of tables and charts giving solar and lunar information, a table for determining Easter, a zodiac man, a human figure showing the proper places for bleeding, sometimes a volvelle, sometimes a chart showing the various colors of urine, and figures of eclipses. The

*Kalendarium* ends with a number of canons explaining the preceding.

Somer's and Nicholas's *Kalendaria* were confused from the beginning. Some manuscripts, i.e., those labeled Ad, As[2], and As[3] in this study, include portions from both *Kalendaria*. Dr. Bühler's manuscript of John Somer's *Kalendarium* is labeled "Nicholas of Lynn" and is so described by Faye and Bond.[26] In addition Bodleian MSS. Ashmole 789 and Savile 39 are called, in error, "Nicholas of Lynn, Astronomical calendar."[27] They are both copies of John Somer's *Kalendarium,* although both they and Dr. Bühler's manuscript omit from the prologue the few lines that give John Somer's name. Presumably because Bodleian MS. Ashmole 391 contains a small portion from the work of Nicholas of Lynn (As[3] in this study), the entire *Kalendarium* in Ashmole 391 has been incorrectly labeled as one by Nicholas.[28]

Some of the confusion about John Somer was built into his *Kalendarium*. Gunther in 1923 copied, almost verbatim, the 1898 article about John Somer in the *Dictionary of National Biography*.[29] When Gunther ventured away from the *DNB,* he said that the *Kalendarium* of John Somer was to run from 1387, the year of the birth of King Richard II, until 1507. King Richard, of course, was born in 1367; otherwise he would have quelled the Peasants' Rebellion six years before he was born. The source of Gunther's confusion is that John Somer gives a table showing the dominical letters from the year 1367, which he accurately designates as the year of the birth of King Richard II, until the year 1507. But only this table extends so far. The *Kalendarium* is designed, as I said above, from 1387 through 1462.

On at least one occasion Somer and Nicholas share an error, and the suggestion may be made that the error was in their common source. Both *Kalendaria* list a lunar eclipse for 21 January 1450. The actual eclipse occurred on 28 January 1450. Errors of a few minutes are common, but this error of a full week is unusual and leads to the supposition that both composers shared at least one common source, possibly an earlier calendar composed at Merton College.

John Somer's *Kalendarium* is made up of material common to most astronomical writing of his time. It contains nothing unique, and therefore it is very difficult to say that in any place Chaucer was using Somer's *Kalendarium* and that of no one else. It contains more medical information than Nicholas's but less astronomical material.

## THE *KALENDARIUM* OF NICHOLAS OF LYNN

The *Kalendarium* of Nicholas of Lynn survives in greater or lesser completeness in fifteen extant manuscripts. Not one of these contains the entire composition by Nicholas, and at least twelve of them show some evidence that Chaucer could not have used them. The very best of the manuscripts is Bodleian Library, MS. Laud Miscellaneous 662, which is used as a base manuscript in this edition, where it is known as L. Where L has a missing folio I have taken the information from British Library, Sloane 1110, S[1] in this edition, and from British Library, Arundel 347, A[1] in this edition. Using L as so emended one may reconstruct with some assurance the *Kalendarium* as Nicholas composed it. The corpus of Nicholas's *Kalendarium* is in four parts: the prologue, the months of the year, a series of astronomical tables and charts, and a set of canons or rules explaining all of the preceding.

In the prologue Nicholas says that he is of the Order of the Blessed Mary Mother of God, of Mount Carmel; that he is least and unworthy (*minimus et indignus*) among readers of sacred theology; and that he has written the *Kalendarium* at the request and friendly interest of John of Gaunt, whom he addresses as Duke of Lancaster and King of Castile and Leon. He says that he is writing the *Kalendarium* in the year 1386 for use during the four Metonic or nineteen-year cycles beginning in 1387 and extending through 1462. The *Kalendarium* is to replace that of his reverend teacher Walter of Elvedene,[30] whose calendar expired at the end of 1386. Nicholas's *Kalendarium* is computed for the longitude and latitude of Oxford, and, he adds, according to the custom of astrologers, a given day begins at noon on the previous day.

After he establishes who he is, where he is, what he is doing, and who John of Gaunt is, Nicholas gets down to the business of the contents of the *Kalendarium*. For each day of the year, he promises, he will show for his latitude the position of the sun in the zodiac, the extent of daylight hours with their twilights, new and full moons as they occur, and the following times in clock hours: midnight until sunrise, sunset until midnight, noon until sunset, sunrise until noon, and the same times to and from the dark edge of twilight. Next he says he will offer tables so that by measuring the shadow of a six-foot man or any other six-foot perpendicular object, one may tell the clock time for every daylight hour of the year. Following the list of calendar months, there will appear both tables and charts of solar and lunar eclipses during the four Metonic cycles, including the times of starting, full occultation, and duration, along with the magnitude of each eclipse. Then he promises six other tables: the first will be for discovering the ascendants and the beginnings of the celestial houses; the second will show the dignities and strengths of the planets; the third will demonstrate what hour of the day or night a planet reigns or is dominant; the fourth will determine in what sign of the zodiac and degree of that sign the moon may be at any time; the fifth will show one how to establish the dates of the movable feasts for any year; and the sixth will show the continuation of the motion of the sun, that is, the perennial slippage of the Julian calendar. Finally, he promises to complete the *Kalendarium* with a set of canons or rules which not only will explain all of the foregoing but also will give the proper and safe times for such medical activities as bloodletting, purging and receiving medicine.

### THE MONTH-BY-MONTH CALENDAR

Each page or half-folio of the month-by-month calendar is arranged in vertical columns with a horizontal line to indicate each day of the given month. On the left edge of each page, or half-folio, is a column of numbers running from 1 to 28, 30, or 31, depending on the month. This column is labeled **Numerus dierum** or "the number of the days." The first half-folio of each month shows, after the days of the month, a narrow column to indicate the order in which the moon returns to the position it held in the nineteenth year before a given year. Each of these numbers stands for a year in the Metonic cycle. For instance, 23 January is labeled "1" and stands for the first year in the Metonic cycle, or in this calendar, 1387, 1406, 1425, and 1444. The twelfth of January is labeled "2" and accordingly stands for 1388, 1407, 1426, and 1445. The next column again is a narrow one and shows the dominical letter for each day.

The following column is a Roman calendar. The first of each month is the kalends of that month and is so indicated by a very large and often illuminated *KL*. The second of the month is between the fourth and sixth day before the nones, which is the ninth day before the ides. The ides is on the fifteenth day of March, May, July, and October, and on the thirteenth of other months. After the ides is the day of either the seventeenth or nineteenth kalends of the succeeding month. For instance, the fourteenth day of January is the nineteenth kalends of February.

The Roman calendar is followed by a wide column showing many of the saints' days, the sign of the zodiac on the first of the month, and the day on which the succeeding sign of the zodiac begins. After the saints' days is a double column labeled **Verus locus solis** or "True position of the sun." It shows for noon on each day the degrees and minutes of a degree of the sun in a given sign of the zodiac during the year 1385. For instance, 1 January is labeled Capricorn 20° 14′. The eleventh of January is labeled Aquarius 0° 27′. Actually 1 January 1385 at noon was Capricorn 19° 53′, a difference of twenty-one minutes from Nicholas's figure, and 11 January 1385 at noon was Aquarius 0° 3′, a difference of twenty-four minutes from Nicholas's figure. These differences are not great. Nicholas is perfectly aware that because of

11

the error in the Julian calendar the figures he gives would change from year to year. In the canons he gives directions for computing the same information for any year other than 1385.

The next column is double and is labeled **Quantitates diei artificialis** or "The lengths of the artificial day." An artificial day is the time from sunrise until sunset, and these lengths are given in hours and minutes of the hour. The next column is also double and labeled **Quantitates diei vulgaris** or "The lengths of the vulgar day." A vulgar day is the artificial day plus the morning and evening twilights, and the vulgar days are also given in hours and minutes. The last column on the folio is double and is labeled **Quantitates utriusque crepusculorum matutini et vespertini** or "The lengths of both the morning and evening twilights." These are also given in hours and minutes. Obviously on any day the sum of the length of the artificial day plus twice the length of the twilight equals the vulgar day.

The second half-folio of each month shows the new and full moons for the first, second, and third Metonic cycles or for the periods of 1387-1405, 1406-24, and 1425-43. The third half-folio of each month begins after the column of days with the six columns of the fourth cycle, that is, 1444–62. It is followed by four sets of double columns, each scaled in hours and minutes. The first double column is labeled **Quantitates a noctis medio ad auroram** or "The lengths [of time] from midnight until dawn." By "dawn" Nicholas means the beginning of the morning twilight, which to Nicholas is a solar altitude of about -20°. The second double column is labeled **Quantitates a noctis medio ad solis ortum** or "The lengths [of time] from midnight until sunrise." The third double column is labeled **Quantitates a meridie ad solis occasum** or "The lengths [of time] from noon until sunset." The last double column of this series is labeled **Quantitates a meridie ad noctem obscuram** or "The lengths [of time] from noon until the end of twilight."

The remaining pages or half-folios in a given month are concerned with Nicholas's unique shadow scale. In many manuscripts there is enough space on the third half-folio for the shadow scale to begin there, and the economical scribe, unwilling to waste vellum, acted accordingly. In this edition, where precious vellum is not a consideration, the shadow scale begins on its own page. The length of the shadow scale, and accordingly the space it occupies in the manuscripts, varies. In the summer months, when there is more daylight, it is longer than it is during the winter months. There is a heading over the entire shadow scale for each month, but it is complete only in the summer months and somewhat shortened in the winter months. The heading occupies the first line of all the pages together and in its complete form is as follows: **Altitudines solis et longitudines umbrarum cuius-libet hominis stature sex pedum in horis equalibus distantibus a meridie et a media nocte 51 graduum et 50 minutorum** or "The altitudes of the sun and the lengths of the shadows of any man six feet high in hours of equal distance from noon and from midnight at [a latitude of] 51 degrees, 50 minutes." By "hours of equal distance" Nicholas means equal or clock hours as opposed to unequal hours, which indicate for each day the time from sunrise until sunset divided by twelve. The second line of all the pages gives the morning hours and is properly marked "a.m." at the end. The third line gives the afternoon hours and is marked "p.m." In Nicholas's world, where there was no standard time and where every community considered noon to be the time when the sun reached the local zenith, the same information for 11:00 A.M. would apply to 1:00 P.M.; for 10:00 A.M. to 2:00 P.M., etc. Thus the columns of the shadow scale are grouped under 5/7, 6/6, 7/5, 8/4, 9/3, 10/2, 11/1, and 12/0. Each of these columns is divided into **altitudines solis** and **umbre hominis** or "the altitudes of the sun" and "the shadows of a man." The solar altitudes are given in two columns marked **g** and **m** or degrees and minutes of a degree. The lengths of the shadows are given in **pedes** and **partes** or "feet" and "parts" of feet. Each part of a foot is one sixtieth of a foot; therefore five parts equals one inch. The information is generally accurate. On the January table one reads that at noon on 31 January the sun is 23° 32′ high and the length of the shadow of a six-foot man is thirteen feet and forty-seven parts. This information is exact, as anyone may determine by multiplying six by cotangent 23° 32′. But when the sun is less than 1° high, all accuracy vanishes. The manuscripts which give this information fall into two groups. The manuscripts which I believe are earlier and closer to what Nicholas actually wrote are very specific, although inaccurate about shadow lengths. The other group, which I think was copied later, alters the shadow lengths into round numbers. For instance, on 5 January at 8:00 A.M. or 4:00 P.M., according to Nicholas, the sun is 0° 6′ high and the shadow of a six-foot man is 3439 feet and twenty-six parts long. The manuscripts which I assume to be copied later give the shadow at 3600 feet even. The fact is that if such a shadow could exist (which it could not, because it would go to a cone long before stretching so far), it would be 3529 feet and twenty-five parts long. In order to show these contrasts I have put into Appendix A supplementary pages which show the contrast among Nicholas's information, the information of assumed later copiers, and actual fact, for each day and hour when the sun is below 1°.

After the December shadow scale Nicholas begins the many tables and charts which he promises in the prologue. The first set of tables and charts concerns eclipses. Nicholas gives a table of the solar eclipse, figures of the solar eclipse, a table of the lunar eclipse, and figures of the lunar eclipse.

The solar eclipse table on pages 142–143 of this edition is divided into four sections, each for one of the four Metonic cycles. Each section has a heading telling what it is. The first Metonic cycle is headed as follows: **Tabula eclipsis solis pro primo ciclo cuius principium est annus Christi 1387 finis 1396** or "Table of the eclipse of the sun for the first cycle whose beginning is the year of Christ 1387, ending 1396." The information below the heading is divided into columns with one subheading sufficing for each column continued through all four cycles. The first subheading is **Ciclus,** and the column under it tells the number of the year in the Metonic cycle. The second subheading is **Anni Christi,** and the actual years are listed under it. The third subheading is **Menses,** and the names of the months are listed under it. The fourth subheading is **Conjuncciones vise,** or "Seen conjunctions." It is divided into days, hours, minutes, and seconds. The fifth subheading is **Punctus eclipsis** or "Point of the eclipse," which means magnitude. A magnitude of twelve is 100% occultation, and it is possible for the moon to be near enough to the earth so that the percentage of occultation rises a bit over 100%. The *Punctus* itself is divided into magnitude, minutes, and seconds, with 60″ to a minute and 60′ to the magnitude. The sixth subheading is **Tempus casus** or "The time of fall." It gives the hours, minutes, and seconds from the beginning of occultation until the midpoint or point of greatest occultation of the eclipse. The seventh and last subheading is **Duracio** or "Duration" and gives the time in hours, minutes, and seconds. The *Duracio* is the time from the beginning until the end of occultation and accordingly is twice the *Tempus casus.*

Nicholas follows his table of the solar eclipse with folios entitled **Figure eclipsis solis** or "Figures of the solar eclipse." These, which in this edition are on pages 144–149, are illuminations of the eclipsed sun and are, in the better illuminated manuscripts, among the most striking pages in the *Kalendarium.* Each figure is of a gold sun with the occulted part of the sun at the moment of fullest occultation in blue. The gold is pressed gold leaf, and the blue is painted. This edition of the *Kalendarium* offers paltry black and white sketches that in no way do justice to the original. The Latin inscription above each sketch tells the date and time of the beginning of the eclipse. For instance, above the first solar eclipse in the *Kalendarium* is written **Hec est solis incipiens anno Domini 1387 in Junio ante meridiem ƒ qui est 16 Kalendas Julii 2 hore 26 minute 29 secunda.** This means "This is [the eclipse] of the sun beginning in the year of the Lord 1387 in June before noon [dominical letter] ƒ, which is the 16th Kalends of July at 2 hours, 26 minutes, 29 seconds." Several points should be noted: The date "16th Kalends of July" is 16 June, on which date the dominical letter is ƒ, as one may see by looking at the first page of the month of June in the *Kalendarium.* The time **ante meridiem . . . 2 hore, 26 minute, 29 secunda** does not, of course, refer to a time in the early morning but 2 hours, 26 minutes, 29 seconds before noon or 9:33:31 on the morning of June sixteenth. Nicholas, who starts his day at noon on the previous day, would have it 21:33:31. Looking at Nicholas's table of the eclipse, one sees that the point of conjunction that morning is 22:3:40 and the time between the beginning of the eclipse and point of greatest occultation, that is the **Tempus casus,** is 0:30:9. By subtracting the *Tempus casus* from the point of conjunction one obtains the time 21:33:31, which is the beginning time on the figure. The eclipse actually began that morning at 21:41:44, local Oxford time, that is 9:41:44 by our way of telling time, about eight minutes after the time Nicholas says it did.[31]

TABLE OF THE LUNAR ECLIPSE

Nicholas's table of the lunar eclipse on pages 150–153 is almost the same as his table of the solar eclipse. The main heading and first three columns, which show the cycles, years, and months, are the same. The fourth column has a subheading of **Vere opposiciones,** or "True oppositions," for a lunar eclipse happens only when there is a full moon. The fifth column, **Punctus eclipsis,** is the same as its equivalent in the solar table and shows the magnitude of the eclipse. Since the shadow of the earth may be larger than the moon, magnitudes greater than 100% may occur, as one does in May 1389. The sixth column **Tempus casus** is also the same as its solar equivalent. In the lunar table, however, a column headed by the word **Mora** appears between the *Tempus casus* and the *Duracio. Mora* means "Delay" and refers to half of the time when the eclipse is total. Thus in the table of lunar eclipses the term **Duracio** refers to twice the sum of the *Tempus casus* and the *Mora.*

FIGURES OF THE LUNAR ECLIPSE

Nicholas's lunar eclipse figures on pages 154–163 are similar to his solar eclipse figures. Over each figure of an eclipse is written the necessary information concerning it. Over the figure of the lunar eclipse dated

15

September 1392 is written: **Hec est incipiens anno Domini 1392 in Septembri post mediam noctem precedens _g_ 4 nonas Septembris 0 hore 58 minute 26 secunda,** or "This is [the eclipse of the moon] beginning in the year of our Lord 1392 in September preceding [the dominical letter] _g_, the fourth nones of September, at 0 hours, 58 minutes, 26 seconds after midnight." The fourth nones of September is, as one may see from the first page of September in the *Kalendarium,* 2 September, when the dominical letter is _g_. The time 0 hours 58 minutes 26 seconds after midnight is 0:58:26 A.M., or 12:58:26, as Nicholas would have it. Then, according to the figure, the eclipse begins. Nicholas says in his table of lunar eclipses that the moment of opposition is 14:26:36, or 2:26:36 A.M. The *Duracio* is 3:36:20. Half of that amount is 1:48:10. Subtract that from 14:26:36, and the result is 12:38:26, which is the time Nicholas says in his table that the eclipse begins, although it begins in the figure at 12:58:26, twenty minutes later. So one sees that the eclipse information in the table does not necessarily coincide with the eclipse information in the figure. The eclipse actually began that Oxford morning at 13:4:1 or 1:4:1 A.M.

Nicholas's eclipse information is fairly accurate but not completely so. Actually there were twenty-eight partial or total solar eclipses visible at Oxford from 1 January 1387 through 31 December 1462. Nicholas mentions twenty-six of these, but he adds two which were not visible at Oxford. Furthermore Nicholas, apparently oblivious to the opaque nature of the earth, does on occasion begin eclipses before sunrise or end them after sunset. A similar situation occurs with his table of the lunar eclipse. From 1 January 1387, through 31 December 1462, sixty-nine partial or total lunar eclipses were visible at Oxford. Nicholas mentions fifty-one of these and adds nine that were not visible at Oxford. Since the possibility, or rather probability, exists that Nicholas was using the Spanish Alfonsine tables readjusted for Oxford, it seems likely that his errors in calculating future eclipses may be blamed on an improper alteration of the Spanish tables. For those who wish to compare Nicholas's eclipse tables with actual solar and lunar eclipses visible at Oxford during the period of the *Kalendarium,* I have added Appendix B, which shows, in the manner of Nicholas, the exact information.[32]

Next Nicholas gives the six other tables which he promises in the prologue.

ASCENDANT AND BEGINNINGS OF THE CELESTIAL HOUSES

The first table, on page 164, is, as Nicholas says in the prologue, designed for discovering, for each degree of each sign of the zodiac, the ascendant and the beginnings of the celestial houses. For each sign

16

of the zodiac this table is divided into four major columns. The first is headed **Gradus ascendentis et locus solis** or "The degree of the ascendant and the place of the sun." It contains numbers 1 through 30, as there are thirty degrees in each sign of the zodiac. The second column is labeled **Ascenciones Arietis** (or whatever sign is pertinent) **in circulo directo** or "The ascensions of Aries" (or whatever sign) "in the direct circle," which is that circle formed by the two lines of longitude exactly 90° east and 90° west of that line of longitude passing through the observer. This column is divided into degrees and minutes of degrees. The third column is labeled **Ascenciones Arietis** (or whatever) **in latitudine 51 graduum 50 minutorum,** which is the latitude Nicholas accepted for Oxford. The last column is labeled **Equaciones domorum ad latitudinem 51 graduum et 50 minutorum** or "Equations of houses at a latitude of 51 degrees 50 minutes." The third column is concerned with ascension of the first visible celestial house; the last column is concerned with the ascensions of the second through sixth visible houses. Accordingly it has five divisions, each labeled with the sign and degrees of sign of the zodiac then ascending. The sequence of Aries is repeated for each of the other eleven signs of the zodiac from Taurus through Pisces.

### THE REIGN OF EACH PLANET

In most manuscripts the table which Nicholas mentions in his prologue as the third of the six additional tables appears right after the table for finding the ascension of houses, and accordingly it is so placed in this edition on pages 176–177. The heading of this table is **Tabula ad sciendum pro qualibet hora diei vel noctis quis planeta regnat** or "Table for finding, for any hour of the day or night, which planet reigns." This chart is based on the twenty-four hours in each day of the week. The first column is marked **Hore** and contains the twenty-four hours of the day. The next seven columns are headed by the seven planets which stand for the seven days of the week: **Solis, Lune, Martis, Mercurii, Jovis, Veneris, Saturni.** Under these headings for each hour of the day one may see which planet reigns. For instance, on Sunday at the tenth hour Mercury reigns, and on Friday at the twentieth hour Mars reigns. To the right of this table is another entitled **Incipiendo diem ab ortu solis** or "By beginning the day from sunrise." Under the heading are four boxes. The first is split between the first through the third hour and the twenty-second through the twenty-fourth hour. It is labeled **Calidus et humidus sanguis movetur** or "Hot and moist blood moves along." The second, from the fourth hour through the ninth hour, is labeled **Calida et sicca colera dominatur** or "Hot and dry choler dominates." The third, from the tenth hour through the

17

fifteenth hour, is labeled **Frigida et sicca melencolia regnat** or "Cold and dry melancholy reigns." The fourth, from the sixteenth hour through the twenty-first, is labeled **Frigida et humida fleuma habundat** or "Cold and moist phlegm abounds." These labels refer to the four conditions of the body: moist, dry, hot, and cool; the four humors or bodily fluids: blood, choler or yellow bile, melancholy or black bile, and phlegm or white bile; and the resulting combinations. Each humor, as can be seen from the chart, refers to certain hours of the day and to certain bodily conditions. Under the chart appears this information: **Jupiter atque Venus boni sunt. Saturnus Mars que maligni. Sol et Mercurius cum Luna sunt mediocres** or "Jupiter and Venus are good. Saturn and Mars [are] malignant. The sun and Mercury with the moon are indifferent." Below that is a brief table combining the four powers of the body, attraction, digestion, retention, and expulsion, with the four elements, fire, air, earth, and water, each with three signs of the zodiac. All of this information was of great value to the medieval physician, who had to know what planet dominated what humors and when, and which elements, conditions, and powers of the body were associated with which signs of the zodiac.

### TABLE OF MOVABLE FEASTS

The fifth table Nicholas mentions in the prologue usually appears third in the manuscripts and on pages 178–179 in this edition. This is the very complex table for determining movable feasts: Septuagesima Sunday, which is seven weeks before Easter; Easter itself; and Pentecost, which is seven weeks after Easter. Obviously the establishment of the date of each feast depends upon the establishment of the date of Easter.

The accepted method for determining the date of Easter was set at the Council at Nicaea in A.D. 325. Easter occurs on the first Sunday following the fourteenth day of the paschal full moon, which itself is the first full lunar cycle of twenty-eight or twenty-nine days, beginning with a new moon, of which the fourteenth day falls on or after 21 March, a date which in 325 (as now) marked the vernal equinox. Thus the earliest possible Easter is 22 March, and the latest is 25 April. Note that although by the fourteenth century the vernal equinox had dropped back to 12 March, the date of 21 March was still used for determining Easter. If a paschal moon is known in a given year, the next paschal moon on that date will be in twenty years. The fifth paschal moon on that date will recur in one hundred years. The twelfth paschal moon on that date will recur in one thousand years. Thus the heading at the top of the table for determining movable feasts states: **Prima viginti quinta centum duodena que mille** or "The first to twenty, the fifth to one hundred, and the twelfth to one

18

thousand." Adding to that information, a second heading says: **Si pro preteritis scandas descende futuris** or "If for the past you ascend, descend for the future," meaning that one should work backward to determine a paschal moon for the past and forward to determine one for the future.

To the right of the chart on the same page are two statements over a small chart. Together they give a means for discovering the dominical letter for any past or future year. The chart is labeled on the left **Ciclus solaris** or "solar cycle." Nicholas explains that the first year of the solar cycle is 1381, for in the statement over the chart he says: **Hec parva subsequens tabula pro littera dominicali invenienda incipit anno Christi 1381 anno cicli solaris primo cicli vero decennovenali 14** or "This following little table for discovering the dominical letters begins in the year of Christ 1381, the first year of the solar cycle, the true Metonic cycle 14." That means that in the first row of the chart, in the first year or 1381, the dominical letter is *f;* in 1382 *e,* in 1383 *d,* and in 1384, which being a leap year occupies not one but two columns, *c* and *b.* The second row is headed with a 5 and refers to the years 1385 through 1388; the third row headed with a 9 refers to 1388 through 1392; and so on until the seventh row, which ends with 1408. With this chart one may tell the dominical letter for any year from 1381 through 1408. To find the dominical letter for any other year, one should arrange the dominical letters in the following sequence: *f, a, c, e, g, b, d.* Then if one counts from the initial given letter ahead for four letters in the same sequence, one has the dominical letter for the 100th year. For instance, if one wishes to know the dominical letter for 1481 and does know that *f* is the dominical letter for 1381, one counts ahead four letters from *f,* that is *a, c, e, g,* and *g* is the dominical letter for 1481. If one wishes to know the dominical letter for either twenty or a thousand years into the future, count ahead five. To go into the past, count backwards. Nicholas gives this information: **Centum quarta tenet viginti mille ve quinta. Si pro preteritis scandas descende futuris** or "One hundred holds the fourth, twenty or a thousand, the fifth. If for the past you ascend [the table], for the future descend." For instance, supposing one wishes to know the dominical letter for the year 395, one looks at the table on the lower right and learns that the letter for 1395 is *c.* Then one counts backwards on the above sequence, *a, f, d, b, g,* and the fifth letter or *g* should be the dominical letter for the year 395, as indeed it is.

If one knows the paschal moon, one may determine Easter according to the rules set down by the Council at Nicaea. After one knows Easter, he can discover Septuagesima Sunday by counting back seven weeks and Pentecost by counting ahead seven weeks. But knowledge

19

of the paschal moon is not necessary with Nicholas's chart. All one needs to know is the number of the year in the Metonic cycle and the dominical letter of the year. The number of the year in the Metonic cycle may be found by dividing the actual number of the year itself by nineteen. The remainder plus one is the Metonic number of the year. For instance 1381 divided by nineteen yields seventy-two with a remainder of thirteen. Thus fourteen is the Metonic number for 1381. The method of finding the dominical letter of the year has been stated above. Nicholas's chart gives the Metonic cycles on the left and the movable feasts, three for each dominical letter, at the top. Under the names are two rows of abbreviations for the months. In the manuscript the first row is red, and red numbers in the chart indicate the use of a month from the top row. Should one wish to discover the date of Easter, and the date is revealed to be between the twenty-sixth and the thirty-first of a month, that month would have to be March, for Easter never falls after 25 April. In a like manner if the date is between the first and the twenty-first of a month, that month must be April, for Easter never falls before 22 March. If a date is between the twenty-second and the twenty-fifth of the month, the month could be either March or April. Such dates are infrequent. In the fifth cycle, *e* and *f*, the references are to March. In the eighth cycle, *a, b,* and *g,* the references are to April. In the eleventh cycle, *g,* the reference is to April. In the thirteenth cycle, *g,* the reference is to March. In the sixteenth cycle, *d, e, f, g,* the references are to March. In the nineteenth cycle, *a, b, g,* the references are to April. With such information, one may determine a movable feast for any time in Nicholas's Julian calendar. In 1394 the Metonic number is 8, and the dominical letter is *d.* Thus Easter, according to Nicholas's chart, falls on the nineteenth of the month, which must be April because 19 March is too early for Easter. And so it does. Sunday, 19 April 1394, was Easter.

Below the chart for movable feasts Nicholas gives the following information: **Quis planeta quem humorem proicit. Saturnus melencoliam et egritudines melencolias. Mars coleram et egritudines coleras. Jupiter Sol et Venus sanguinem et eius egritudines. Luna fleuma et eius egritudines. Mercurius omnis equaliter prout est communitus,** or "Which planet projects which humor. Saturn, melancholy and the sicknesses of melancholy. Mars, choler and the sicknesses of choler. Jupiter, the sun, and Venus, blood and its sicknesses. The moon, phlegm and its sicknesses. Mercury, all equally [and] accordingly is the same for all."

### THE MOTION OF THE SUN AND THE DIGNITIES OF THE PLANETS

The next page or half-folio, on pages 180–181 in this edition, holds two of the six tables which Nicholas mentions in his prologue: number six, the continuation of the motion of the sun, and number two, the dignities of the strengths of the planets in the signs of the zodiac.

The table labeled **Tabula continuacionis motus solis** or "Table of the continuation of the motion of the sun" demonstrates the continuing error in the Julian calendar. Using the year 1385 as a base, Nicholas shows for each four years an average slippage of about 1′ 45″, which may be contrasted with the actual average of 1′ 53″. He explains in the canons that these figures are to be used to determine the true position of the sun at any future date.

On the same page is Nicholas's second table labeled, **Tabula ad inveniendum dignitates planetarum in signis,** or "The table for discovering the dignities of the planets in their signs." This table is divided into five major columns. The first is headed **Signa** and lists the names of the twelve signs of the zodiac. The second is labeled **Domini domorum** or "The lords of the houses" and shows which planet occupies the primary position of influence when the sun is in a given sign. The third column is headed **Domini exaltacionum** or "The lords of the exaltations." The exaltation of a planet is the time of the year, expressed by a given degree of a given sign of the zodiac, when the planet has especial strength. As indicated on the chart, those times are as follows: sun, Aries 19° or 30 March; moon, Taurus 3° or 15 April; Jupiter, Cancer 15° or 29 June; Mercury, Virgo 15° or 30 August; Saturn, Libra 21° or 6 October; Mars, Capricorn 28° or 9 January; and Venus, Pisces 27° or 9 March. In addition Gemini 3° or 16 May is marked **Caput,** while Sagittarius 3° or 17 November is marked **Cauda.** These words indicate the Head and Tail of the Dragon for the year 1385. The Head of the Dragon, *Caput draconis,* is the ascending node of the moon or the point in the moon's orbit when the moon crosses the ecliptic. It is considered a most fortunate day and varies on the zodiac by nineteen degrees each year. Derek Price says that one Head of the Dragon was 31 December 1392.[33] Accordingly, by simple arithmetic it may be established that the Head of the Dragon in 1385, the year on which Nicholas bases many of his computations, is Gemini 3° or 16 May. The Tail of the Dragon, the descending node of the moon and a most unfortunate day, is exactly opposite on the zodiac and in 1385 was Sagittarius 3° or 17 November. Children born of a liaison under the Tail of the Dragon come to no good, for instance Edmund in *King Lear,* who in Act II, scene ii, lines 124—25 admits: "My father compounded with my mother under the Dragon's Tail."

The fourth column is labeled **Domini triplicitatum** or "The lords of the triplicities." The triplicities are trios of planets having special significance to each zodiacal sign. The fifth column is labeled **Termini planetarum in signis secundum Egypcios et dicuntur esse hermetis** or "The terms of the planets in signs according to the Egyptians and they are said to be from the desert." The Egyptian terms are as old as, if not older than, Ptolemy. Each of five planets, Mercury, Venus, Mars, Jupiter, Saturn, holds a dominance during some degrees of each sign. The number of degrees during which each planet holds its dominance is indicated on the table. For instance, during the thirty degrees of Aries, Jupiter dominates for six degrees, then Venus for six degrees, then Mercury for eight degrees, Mars for five degrees, and Saturn for five degrees. The sixth and last column is headed **Domini facierum** or "The lords of the faces." Each face is ten degrees of the zodiac or one third of a sign, and each face is governed by a different planet. According to the entire chart, at any given time most of the planets in one way or another are governing, with varying importance, any day of the year.

### WHICH SIGN THE MOON IS IN EACH DAY

Nicholas's fourth chart appears last in the *Kalendarium* on pages 182–183 of this edition. Its purpose is to discover for every day of the year in which sign and degree of sign the moon is according to its average rate of motion. The table is headed **Tabula ad sciendum in quo signo et in quo gradu signi luna fuerit omni die secundum motum** or "Table for discovering in what sign and in what degree of sign the moon may have been on every day according to its motion." The usage of the table is as follows. One must know the day and time of the most recent new moon prior to the day in question. The number of days between a new moon and any point before the next new moon is called the age of the moon. The ages of the moon are in the column to the left. The sign of the sun at the time of the most recent new moon must be taken from the first line under the title. Find the sign of the sun and look down the column to the age of the moon. Then on that line look to the right hand column to discover how many degrees and minutes must be added to the information already known. For instance, one may wish to know the sign of the moon on 25 April 1387. In his tables of new moons Nicholas shows that in 1387, the first year of the first Metonic cycle, there is a new moon on 19 April 1387, at 4 hours and 3 minutes. The sun on that day is at Taurus 7° 40′. One must look at the first row in the table and find Taurus. On 25 April the age of the moon is six days. The sign under Taurus for six days is Cancer, which is two signs beyond Taurus. Looking at the right column one sees that when the moon is six days old one must add 19° 3′ to the existing figure. In this case one adds 19° 3′ to Cancer 7° 40′, which is two signs ahead of Taurus 7° 40′. The result is Cancer 26° 43′, which is the place Nicholas says the moon is on 25 April 1387. Actually on 19 April 1387, the new moon, according to Nicholas's method of beginning a given day at noon on the previous day, is not at 4 hours and 3 minutes but at 5 hours and 26 minutes. On 25 April, again as Nicholas would determine the time, the moon is at Cancer 27° 44′, an error of about 1° of the zodiac. Nicholas is commendably close when we remember that on a given day the moon moves between 10° and 14° on the zodiac. Second example: on 3 December 1975, the sun was at Sagittarius 11°, and there was a new moon, which was also at Sagittarius 11°. With that information one might find the sign of the moon on 17 December 1975. On 17 December the moon was fourteen days old. On the table one finds Sagittarius in the first line and then looks down fourteen days to discover Gemini. On the right one finds 4° 28′, which must be added to Gemini 11°, yielding Gemini 15° 28′. That, according to the system of Nicholas of Lynn, was the true place of the moon on 17 December 1975. Actually the true place of the moon for the day of 17 December was between Gemini 13° and Gemini 26°. For a given moment on that day the information provided by Nicholas was quite correct.[34] Accordingly, the moon was demonstrably in Gemini for all of 17 December 1975, and this information would have been not merely interesting but vital to a person believing in the medical information provided by Nicholas. In the canons concerned with phlebotomy he says that if one bleeds a part of the body and the moon is in the very sign of the zodiac pertaining to that part of the body, a hemorrhage will ensue. Gemini controls the shoulders, arms and hands, and Nicholas, had he been present to do so, would have advised strongly against bleeding any part of the arm on 17 December 1975, or any other time while the moon was in Gemini. One would have had to wait a few days until the moon moved to Cancer before instigating such an operation.

Below the last row of signs on these pages appears information which tells which parts of the body are controlled by each sign. This information rightfully appears on the same page as a chart to determine the sign of the moon because, as said above, a part of the body must not be bled when the moon is in the sign controlling that part. Under Aries appears **Habet capud et faciem** or "[Aries] controls the head and face"; under Taurus **Habet collum et gutturis nodum** or "[Taurus] controls the neck and the knot of the throat [i.e., Adam's apple]"; under Gemini **Habet humeros brachios et manus** or "[Gemini] controls the shoulders, arms, and hands"; under Cancer **Habet cor pectus et pulmonem** or "[Cancer] controls the heart, chest, and lungs"; under Leo **Habet latus dorsum et stomacum** or "[Leo] controls the sides, back and stomach"; under Virgo **Habet epartem et intestina** or "[Virgo] controls the liver and intestines"; under Libra **Habet lumbos renes et hancas** or "[Libra] controls the loins, the kidneys, and the buttocks"; under Scorpio **Habet basa seminaria et**

23

**femorem** or "[Scorpio] controls the [blood] vessels, the semen, and the thigh"; under Sagittarius **Habet coxas et femoralia** or "[Sagittarius] controls the hips and the genitalia"; under Capricorn **Habet genua** or "[Capricorn] controls the knees"; under Aquarius **Habet tibias et crura** or "[Aquarius] controls the shins and the legs"; and under Pisces **Habet pedes** or "[Pisces] controls the feet."

THE CANONS

The last part of the *Kalendarium* is the group of promised canons in which Nicholas offers a series of rules to explain all of the foregoing material.

The first canon, which begins on page 185 in this edition, explains the daily zodiacal positions of the sun given in the *Kalendarium*. Nicholas says that the figures in the *Kalendarium* are adjusted to the year 1385, a convenient year because it is one year after leap year and immediately precedes (or could conceivably be) the year in which he was working. For any given year two adjustments must be made. First the distance of the year in question from leap year must be established. If the year in question is the first year after leap year, as is 1385, no adjustment here is necessary. If it is the second year after leap year, 1° 15′ of the zodiac must be deducted. If it is the third year after leap year, 30′ must be subtracted. In the Julian leap year the sixth kalends of March, that is the sixth day before 1 March, is doubled so that 24 February lasts for two days, giving rise to the name *bissextile* for leap year. Nicholas explains that in leap year during the days between 1 January and 24 February inclusive, 45′ must be deducted. From 25 February, the Feast of St. Matthew in leap year, through 31 December, 15′ must be added. The second adjustment is concerned with the table for the continuation of the motion of the sun. For the year in question, if it follows 1385, the minutes and seconds of 1° of the zodiac listed in this table must be added. The table is for every four years beginning in 1385. To discover the necessary addition for the years between these one must interpolate. For instance, should one wish to know the true position of the sun on 25 October 1400, the day of Chaucer's death, one must turn to the first October page of the *Kalendarium* and note that on 25 October the true position of the sun is Scorpio 10° 35′. Because 1400 is a leap year and the date is after 24 February, one must add 15′ of a zodiacal degree, giving Scorpio 10° 50′. By 1397 the motion of the sun is 5′ 14″; by 1401 it is 6′ 57″. Interpolation gives a figure of 6′ 31″ for 1400. This figure must be added to Scorpio 10° 50′, giving a result of Scorpio 10° 56′ 31″, the true position of the sun according to Nicholas on the day of Chaucer's death. Actually on that dark day the true position of the sun was Scorpio 11° 3′ 58″, an insignificant 7′ 27″ of a zodiacal degree from what Nicholas says it is.

The second canon tells where to find the lengths of the artificial and vulgar days and of the evening and morning twilights for the latitude of Oxford. In most manuscripts this information may be found on the first page of each month. The term *artificial day,* as used by Nicholas and Chaucer among others, means the time from sunrise until sunset. The vulgar day is the artificial day and the two twilights. Twilight today has three definitions. Civil twilight is the time when the sun has an elevation between 0° and –6°. The end of civil evening twilight in the British Isles is lighting-up time. Nautical twilight is the time when the sun has an elevation between 0° and –12°. Astronomical twilight is the time when the sun has an elevation between 0° and –18°. Nicholas's twilight is even more than that: the time when the sun has an elevation between 0° and –20°. In the latitude of Oxford during the fourteenth century twilight lasted all night between 12 May and 14 July inclusive, that is, for about a month on either side of the summer solstice, which in 1385 was on 13 June.

The third canon informs one how to find the new and full moons to the minute of the clock during the four Metonic cycles of the *Kalendarium*. Each of the four cycles is divided into six columns. The first column in each cycle is labeled **Ciclus conjunccionis** or "The cycle of the conjunction" and shows the year in which the new moon appears on a given day. Each year in a cycle bears a number. For instance: 1387, the first year in the first cycle, is 1; 1388 is 2; and 1405 is 19. When a number appears opposite a given day, on that day of the month in the very year signified by the number will be a new moon. On 3 January the number is 8, telling the reader that on 3 January 1394 there is a new moon. The next two columns, which are labeled **Tempus vere conjunccionis** or "The time of the true conjunction [i.e., new moon]," tell in hours and minutes the very moment of the new moon. On 3 January the time is given as 5 hours, 24 minutes. Since Nicholas begins each day at noon on the previous day, we must reinterpret his figure to read that on 2 January at 5:24 P.M. (that is, 5 hours and 24 minutes after noon on 2 January) there is a new moon. Actually there was a new moon over Oxford on 2 January 1394, at 5:50 P.M. The full moons are managed in the same way. The fourth column in each cycle is labeled **Ciclus opposicionis,** or "The cycle of the opposition," meaning the number within its cycle of the year which has the full moon under consideration. The next two columns are labeled **Tempus vere opposicionis,** or "The time of the true opposition," meaning the very time in hours and minutes that the sun and the moon are opposite to each other or that the moon is full. On 7 January, Nicholas tells us, there is a full moon in the ninth year of the first cycle at the 10th hour and 41st minute. That means there is a full moon on 6 January 1395 at 10:41 P.M., when the time is adjusted to Nicholas's practice of beginning his day at noon on the previous day. Actually, on 6 January 1395, at 10:45 P.M., a full moon shone on the good citizens of London, which had a five-minute time difference from Oxford.

In the fourth canon Nicholas discusses the clock time of sunrise, sunset, and the beginnings and endings of twilight. These figures are found on the third page of each month after the fourth Metonic cycle of new and full moons.

In the fifth canon Nicholas explains the unique shadow scale which distinguishes his *Kalendarium* from all other known medieval *kalendaria*. The tables of the shadow scale are the last pages of each month. To Nicholas noon is always the time when the sun is at its zenith. The time from noon until noon is divided by twenty-four, and each of those divisions is called an equal or clock hour. The unequal hours, on the other hand, are determined by dividing the period from sunrise until sunset by twelve, just as they are in the Bible (Matt. 20:1-16). In this section Nicholas explains the use of the tables to determine the time in clock hours and minutes by measuring the shadow of a six-foot man or any object of similar height. In doing so he gives a tortured explanation of interpolation, which in the fourteenth century must have been in its springtime of development.

In the sixth canon he analyzes the unequal hours by means of a plumb line and more shadows, adding the calculations for leap year and each of the three succeeding years and explaining how the unequal hours vary if one strays to the north or south of Oxford. If one wants excellent accuracy, he advises, one should go elsewhere for a set of tables compounded for the place which is to the north or south of Oxford.

The seventh canon explains the tables and figures of the solar and lunar eclipses. Nicholas is not completely accurate. In the years 1387-1462 inclusive twenty-eight solar eclipses were visible from Oxford. Nicholas mentions twenty-six of these, eliminating an eclipse of seventy-eight per cent totality on 29 October 1399 and one of thirty-six per cent totality which began before dawn on 26 April 1446. In addition he adds two, neither actually visible at Oxford but possible somewhere in the world, one on 28 July 1394 and one on 19 November 1416. He acknowledges that both of these have a very low percentage of totality and that each lasts less than an hour. In Appendix B, as I said above, is a table entitled "Actual Solar Eclipses Calculated in the Manner of Nicholas." Nicholas also ignores seventeen lunar eclipses that could have been seen from Oxford between 1387 and 1462. He does add nine to his list, but these did not occur at Oxford. Again in Appendix B see the table entitled "Actual Lunar Eclipses Calculated in the Manner of Nicholas."

The eighth canon is concerned with the times of ascendance of the great astrological houses. In the world of Nicholas, and also that of today's astrologers, the sky both below and above a spherical world is divided like an orange into twelve segments, each extending from the north point of an observer's horizon to the south point. The terrestrial observer may see only six houses because the others are below the horizon. Each object in the sky passes through each of the twelve houses in a twenty-four hour period, and in each house each celestial object has a different effect on the welfare of man.

The ninth canon tells which sign of the zodiac the moon is in at any time. This information was very important to medieval physicians, because, Nicholas tells us, if a patient is bled with the moon in an inauspicious sign, he will hemorrhage and die.

The tenth canon is concerned with the computations of the movable feasts, as described above. Nicholas, never dreaming that in time his Julian calendar would be replaced by the Gregorian calendar, tells how to compute the movable feasts for the next millennium.

In the eleventh canon Nicholas turns to the duties of a physician and explains the regulations for bleeding. Nicholas here says that he depends upon the *Centiloquium* of Ptolemy, as interpreted by Haly, and on the works of Campanus. Claudius Ptolemy lived in the second century and allegedly wrote a book known as the *Centiloquium*. Haly may have been the tenth-century physician Haly Abbas, the eleventh-century Ali ben Ridhwan, who wrote a commentary on Galen, or the eleventh-century astrologer Ali ibn Abí Al-Rajjál.[35] Campanus may have been Campanus of Novara, who lived in Italy in the thirteenth century but who apparently said nothing that Nicholas says he said.[36] Bloodletting or phlebotomy was perhaps the principal cure for almost everything. According to Ptolemy and Haly as reported by Nicholas, bloodletting depends on the direction of flow of the humors, and that, like the tides of the sea, depends on the moon. During the first and third quarters of the moon, we learn, the humors flow from the interior of the body to the exterior. During the second and fourth quarters, of course, they flow back. When the humors are flowing to the exterior, bloodletting is rather risky, for the physician may start something he cannot stop. But when the moon is safe and the humors are flowing back toward the center, a little bloodletting hurts no one and probably does some good. But also be aware, we are warned, that every part of the body is associated with one of the signs of the zodiac. And if one touches a given part of the body with iron, the moon being in the zodiacal sign of that part of the body, then one has real trouble, for the humors tend to rush to that part of the body which has the moon in its sign. So the tiniest prick of a knife, under such conditions, is likely to start a hemorrhage. Humors also flow toward an injury: Campanus is quoted as saying that if the skin receives a blow from a stick or a stone, and the skin is not broken, all the humors of the body will flow toward the injury, causing swelling and discoloration. Never, however, casually bleed any part of the body without checking the moon. Campanus says that he saw a man with an injured arm. Gemini controls the arm, and that day the moon was in Gemini. The poor man, being ignorant of astronomy, bled himself in the arm and, although he had no sign of trouble aside from his injury, was dead within a week.

In the twelfth canon Nicholas considers the giving and receiving of medicine, mainly laxatives. Today physicians do not hesitate to prescribe laxatives when needed. But when the medieval patient needed a laxative, his physician had to weigh many other matters. First he had to know that within the body of man, in addition to the four humors, are four powers: attraction, retention, digestion, and expulsion. Each of these powers is closely related to the humors within the body and to all of the conditions outside the body, especially to signs of the zodiac. Depending on the time of the year, one of the powers is strong. Further, any medicine, including a laxative, has a stronger effect when the ascendant is in the same sign as one of the four bodily powers. And the physician was obligated to remember that the date of compounding the medicine had to depend upon the zodiacal positions of heavenly bodies. There were, of course, dangers if precautions were not observed. Ptolemy says that no one should give laxatives when the moon and Jupiter are together at the zenith. Haly explains that Jupiter is a friend to all nature and does not enjoy seeing the body purged. Therefore it was wiser to give a laxative when Jupiter was out of sight, that is, below the horizon, and could not be offended. If a medicine was given at the wrong time, the best that could be expected was that the patient would vomit and be nauseated. The worst was that he would die. But if the doctor wished the patient to vomit, he had to avoid giving an emetic when the moon was in Leo. If people vomited when the moon was in Leo, they would vomit blood. Nicholas concludes the medical canons, and the *Kalendarium* itself, with the rather sensible admonition that, no matter what the pattern of the heavenly bodies, some people are going to be sick while at the same time others will enjoy good health.

Apparently the medical canons by Nicholas were treasured apart from the rest of the *Kalendarium*. Four manuscripts contain only these canons. Three of the four look as if they were written in a late fifteenth- or early sixteenth-century hand, and one is firmly dated 1470. One may guess from the evidence of the extant manuscripts that even after the *Kalendarium* was obsolete, and after Nicholas and his contemporaries were long in their graves, the medical information remained valuable and in demand.[37]

## CHAUCER'S USE OF NICHOLAS'S *KALENDARIUM*

We know that Chaucer used Nicholas's *Kalendarium* because Chaucer says he did.[38] In the Prologue to the *Treatise on the Astrolabe* Chaucer says, "The thirde partie shal contene diverse tables of longitudes and latitudes of sterres fixe for the Astrelabie, and tables of the declinacions of the sonne, and tables of longitudes of citees and townes; and tables as well for the governaunce of a clokke, as for to fynde the altitude meridian; and many anothir notable conclusioun after the kalenders of the reverent clerkes, Frere J. Somer and Frere N. Lenne" (77-86). The "Frere N. Lenne" is, of course, Nicholas of Lynn. But the problems are that either Chaucer did not write the Third Part to the *Treatise on the Astrolabe* or the Third Part did not survive, and that the information which Chaucer said he would put into the Third Part does not appear in Nicholas's *Kalendarium.* Nicholas has neither stellar tables nor terrestrial longitudes, although he does give some commonplace information about the sun, the clock, and the meridian, items that were discussed by just about everyone who wrote on astronomy. Nor is there any more evidence of the use of Nicholas's *Kalendarium* in Chaucer's promise concerning the missing Fourth Part of the *Treatise on the Astrolabe,* where Chaucer says that he will offer a table of the motion of the moon, a table not appearing in Nicholas's *Kalendarium* but common in other medieval astronomical treatises. In his statement about the missing Fifth Part, however, Chaucer does say, "In which fifthe partie shalt thou fynden tables of equaciouns of houses after the latitude of Oxenforde; and tables of dignitees of planetes, . . ." (103-6). Nicholas does give tables of the equations of houses and the dignities of planets. John Somer's *Kalendarium* does not have a table of the equations of houses, and although he has a table of what hour a planet reigns, he does not have a table devoted solely to the dignities of the planets in their signs. The assumption must be that Chaucer planned to use Nicholas's *Kalendarium* in the unwritten or lost fifth part. But an assumption concerning a non-extant text is not enough; we must look elsewhere.

Chaucer does use Nicholas's *Kalendarium,* especially his unique shadow scale, in at least three places in the *Canterbury Tales.* Knowing Nicholas's *Kalendarium,* we may, I think, learn more about what Chaucer intends. Also, as we shall see shortly, an awareness of

29

Nicholas's *Kalendarium* raises some new problems in our knowledge of Chaucer's intentions.

Early in the *Canterbury Tales*, in the Introduction to The Man of Law's Tale, the Host makes two observations concerning the time. First he says that the sun has risen one quarter of the artificial day plus half an hour plus a bit more. Then he notices that shadows are just as long as the objects which cause them, and since he knows that the date is 18 April, he concludes that the time is 10:00 A.M.

> Oure Hooste saugh wel that the brighte sonne
> The ark of his artificial day hath ronne
> The ferthe part, and half an houre and moore,
> And though he were nat depe ystert in loore,
> He wiste it was the eightetethe day
> Of Aprill, that is messager to May;
> And saugh wel that the shadwe of every tree
> Was as in lengthe the same quantitee
> That was the body erect that caused it.
> And therfore by the shadwe he took his wit
> That Phebus, which that shoon so clere and brighte,
> Degrees was fyve and fourty clombe on highte;
> And for that day, as in that latitude,
> It was ten of the clokke, he gan conclude, . . .(*CT,* II, 1-14)

The second observation is far more direct and therefore easier to handle. The Host knows that on 18 April shadows at 10:00 A.M. are just as long as the objects which cause them. The Host is right here; his statement agrees with Nicholas's shadow scale.[39] I also know that the Host is right because on one 27 April, our Gregorian equivalent to Chaucer's Julian 18 April, standing in the rare sunshine of Chaucer's island and latitude, I too measured a shadow and discovered that at 10:00 A.M. it was just as long as the object which caused it. Quod erat demonstrandum.

But the first observation by the Host presents a problem. According to Nicholas the sun rises on that day at 4:47 A.M. and sets at 7:13 P.M. The artificial day, which means the time from sunrise until sunset, is 14 hours and 26 minutes long. One fourth of the artificial day is 3 hours and 36 minutes. Add that to 4:47, which is sunrise, and we have 8:23 A.M. Add half an hour to that and we have 8:53. Chaucer's words "and moore" take us to 9:00 A.M. or a little after, unless by "and moore" Chaucer means an unlikely 1 hour 7 minutes. Robinson in his edition of Chaucer states that one fourth of that particular artificial day plus half an hour plus a bit more comes close to 10:00 A.M.[40] Robinson is depending on the nineteenth-century scholar, Andrew Edmund Brae, who in 1851 assumes that by "artificial day" Chaucer really means the azimuthal day, which is determined by observing the direction of the sun from the observer.[41] The sun rose on 18 April, as Nicholas says, at 4:47 A.M., and Brae determines its direction to be ENE, or 22° 30′ north of the east point of the horizon, giving an azimuthal day of about 224°. Actually the sun on that day, when one computes with Nicholas's *Kalendarium* as a base, rose at 24° 26′ 15″ north of the east point of the horizon. If one doubles that figure because the sun must pass an equivalent amount after passing the west point, and then adds the 180° between the east and west points, the sum or the azimuthal day is 228° 52′ 30″. One fourth of that amount is 57° 13′ 7.5″. After one fourth of the azimuthal day passes, the direction of the sun will move south 57° 13′ 7.5″, appearing at that moment at 32° 46′ 52.5″ south of the east point. The time at that moment is not 9:20 A.M. as Brae declares but 9:04 A.M. The Host's "half an houre" moves the time to 9:34, and the words "and moore" have to signify an inappropriately long stretch to bring the time to 10:00 A.M. Therefore the azimuthal date does not fit the particular situation. Brae's conclusion that Chaucer confuses the artificial and the azimuthal day is endorsed by Skeat, who approximates the problem with a globe and a string.[42] Robinson, without explaining the difference between the artificial and azimuthal arcs, follows Brae;[43] and Chauncey Wood, explaining, however, the difference between the two arcs, does the same.[44] Hamilton Smyser, also, has no quarrel with this conclusion.[45]

On the other hand, I do. Not only does a computation of the azimuthal day fail to solve the problem, but Chaucer knows exactly what an artificial day is and says so in the *Treatise on the Astrolabe*, II, 7.[46] Nicholas, also, is very specific about the artificial day, and because Chaucer uses Nicholas's shadow scale in the very passage, we must accept that he knew Nicholas's use of the term. Accordingly, I cannot accept a conclusion that depends upon Chaucer's ignorance of astronomical terminology. It is, I think, a mistake to charge Chaucer with errors made by his characters. If anyone offers a faulty computation here, it is the Host himself, who, as Chaucer tells us, is not "depe ystert in loore."

In the Nun's Priest's Tale there is another use of Nicholas's shadow scale. On the morning of the day that the fox seizes Chauntecleer, 3 May,[47] a singularly unlucky day when mentioned by Chaucer,[48] Chauntecleer promenades through his barnyard and tells from the sun's position that the time is prime, or 9:00 A.M.

> Whan that the month in which the world bigan,
> That highte March, whan God first maked man,
> Was compleet, and passed were also,
> Syn March bigan, thritty dayes and two,

Bifel that Chauntecleer in al his pryde,
His sevene wyves walkynge by his syde,
Caste up his eyen to the brighte sonne,
That in the signe of Taurus hadde yronne
Twenty degrees and oon, and somwhat moore,
And knew by kynde, and by noon oother loore,
That it was pryme, and crew with blisful stevene.
"The sonne," he seyde, "is clomben up on hevene
Fourty degrees and oon, and more ywis." (*CT,* VII, 3187-99)

Chauntecleer is quite correct. On 3 May, according to Nicholas, the sun is at Taurus 21° 6'. At prime, or 9:00 A.M., on that day the altitude of the sun is 41° 5' or Chauntecleer's "fourty degrees and oon, and more ywis." If Chauntecleer used a bit more of the knowledge that comes to him "by kynde," he would know that if at that moment a six-foot man appeared in the barnyard, his shadow would be six feet ten inches long. Chaucer undoubtedly received this information from Nicholas of Lynn and not from John Somer. Nicholas, as I said above, begins his astronomical day at noon on the previous day, but John Somer begins his later; in John Somer's *Kalendarium* 3 May is labeled as Taurus 22°.

At the beginning of the Prologue to the Parson's Tale Chaucer makes another observation concerning the time. He says that the sun is just less than 29° and sinking, that his shadow is about eleven feet, and that the time is 4:00 P.M.

By that the Maunciple hadde his tale al ended,
The sonne from the south lyne was descended
So lowe that he nas nat, to my sighte,
Degreës nyne and twenty as in highte.
Foure of the clokke it was tho, as I gesse,
For ellevene foot, or litel moore or lesse,
My shadwe was at thilke tyme, as there,
Of swiche feet as my lengthe parted were
In sixe feet equal of proporcioun.
Therwith the moones exaltacioun,
I meene Libra, alwey gan ascende, . . . (*CT,* X, 1-11)

This passage, which so obviously depends on Nicholas's shadow scale, swirls with difficulties. Most of these have been considered before. The first is that the Manciple begins his tale in the morning. Now it is 4:00 P.M. In many manuscripts, however, the time is given as "ten of the clokke." The modern emendation to "foure of the clokke," in spite of the morning hour of the Manciple's Tale, seems justified. After all, the sun is not sinking at 10:00 in the morning and is not there at all at 10:00 P.M. In medieval handwritings a Roman *ten* and an Arabic *four* are similar: the Roman *ten* was, and is, an x; the Arabic *four* was an x closed by an arc over the top. Thus a *four* with part of the ink rubbed away could easily be copied as a *ten*. Much more convincing evidence comes from Nicholas. Were the time really 10:00 and the sun at the elevation stated, the date would be pushed back to 2 March, and the final tale of the Canterbury Pilgrimage would be told some six or seven weeks before the Pilgrims leave Southwark.[49]

The second problem is that Libra is not the moon's exaltation but Saturn's. Libra at 4:00 P.M. in mid-April is rising. Skeat, about a century ago, suggested that Chaucer made a mistake.[50] In this particular case he probably did, and there is evidence that he did. Nicholas of Lynn in his table of the dignities of the planets in their signs makes it clear that the exaltation of Libra is Saturn. The third problem is one of dates. At 4:00 P.M., the passage tells us, the sun is less than 29° high. According to Nicholas, at 4:00 P.M. on 17 April the sun is at 28° 57′, and on 18 April it is 29° 11′.[51] This means that the passage can apply only to 17 April or earlier. Robinson's suggestion of 20 April[52] must be incorrect. Presumably we may read here that Libra is in its first few degrees of ascendency over the horizon. If the date is the latest possible, 17 April, the sun according to Nicholas is at Taurus 5°, and Libra according to my own (and undoubtedly Chaucer's) astrolabe, is exactly 3° in ascension.

All of these calculations fit properly for the Prologue to the Parson's Tale, but we now are led into the fourth and final problem: the date, 17 April. How can we be at the end of the Canterbury Pilgrimage on 17 April when the Introduction to the Man of Law's Tale, which is traditionally placed early in the pilgrimage,[53] is dated 18 April? J. D. North of Oxford, who considers this matter, concludes no more than that in Chaucer's mind the pilgrimage takes place in April, as we learn from the first three words of the *Canterbury Tales*.[54] But Chaucer normally has a meaning assigned to each date and time. The 10:00 A.M. time on 18 April is used, one may guess, because, according to Nicholas, that is the only moment during the month of the Canterbury Pilgrimage when the sun is at 45°, the shadow of a six-foot man is exactly six feet, and the time of day is an hour unaccompanied by fractions of an hour or minutes.[55] Now I wish to reoffer an unsubstantiated suggestion.[56] Because every identifiable date in the *Canterbury Tales* takes place between January and July and between 1387 and 1394,[57] it would seem that these dates, rather than presenting a chronological sequence for the *Canterbury Tales* and their links, are useful only for symbolic purposes. Thus the 17 April date following the 18 April date is not significant. But consider: the tone of the Parson's Tale is fitting for Good Friday. The joyous arrival in Canterbury would be fitting for Easter. In 1394 Good Friday was 17 April.

To sum up, Chaucer does use the *Kalendarium* of Nicholas of Lynn, not in the *Treatise on the Astrolabe,* where he mentions it, but in the *Canterbury Tales.* He does not, however, use it to give a final chronological organization to the *Canterbury Tales.* He uses it instead as a source of information concerning specific hours and days which are necessary for his entire artistic scheme: he is content to use Nicholas's *Kalendarium* as a time and date-telling device, and after all, that is what a calendar is for.

## MANUSCRIPTS

Parts of Nicholas's *Kalendarium* survive in fifteen manuscripts of various quality. No manuscript has a title. I have given each manuscript a sigil and have arranged them in descending order of importance to students of both Nicholas and Chaucer. The first four, L, S[1], A[1], and D, could have been seen by Chaucer. Internal evidence suggests that the others were copied after Chaucer's death in 1400. The last four, M, S[2], Gg, and As[3], appear to have been copied after the 1462 expiration of the *Kalendarium.* With each of the fifteen manuscripts I shall comment where relevant on the following:

1) The location of the manuscript, the name of the collection where appropriate, and the number within the collection.

2) The number and size of the folios of the manuscript.

3) The handwriting.

4) Omissions from the *Kalendarium,* based on the text as reconstructed in this edition.

5) Additions to the *Kalendarium,* based on the text as reconstructed in this edition.

6) The Metonic or lunar cycles. Note: in some manuscripts these cycles, which are normally calculated for the four nineteen-year periods between 1387 and 1462, have been scraped clean and recalculated for Metonic cycles occurring after 1462.

7) The date of the manuscript if it is known.

8) Examples of specific evidence, where it exists, that Chaucer could or could not have seen the manuscript under consideration.

9) Other material, if any, bound with the manuscript.

The descriptions of the manuscripts follow.

**L,** Oxford, Bodleian Library, MS. Laud Miscellaneous 662, consists of forty-two folios, each about 198 by 139 millimeters. The handwriting is a university book hand. L is complete except for some figures scraped from the first page of April and one folio which is missing between folios 32 and 33. The recto of the missing folio would have shown the figures of the twenty lunar eclipses from 1 March 1439 until 12 June 1462 inclusive. The verso would have shown the ascensions and equations of houses for both Aries and Taurus. There are no additions to L, and the Metonic cycles are correctly indicated for the periods of 1387 through 1462. The date is agreed by all to be late fourteenth century.[58] There is no specific evidence that Chaucer did not see L. No other material is bound with the manuscript.

S[1], British Library, MS. Sloane 1110, has forty folios, each about 180 by 132 millimeters. The handwriting is a university book hand. Omitted from the prologue is the reference to St. Augustine's first homily on the Gospel of John and the statement that the canons are at the end of the *Kalendarium*. One folio, which apparently followed folio 40, is missing. On a blank folio following folio 40 is written in a modern hand, "The portion wanting may be found in MS. Arundel 347. F. M." Presumably the initials are those of Sir Frederic Madden. The only additions to S[1] are titles to the fifth, sixth, seventh, ninth, tenth, and eleventh canons. The Metonic cycles, however, are incomplete. Missing are the indications for the full moons of the fourth cycle, which is 1444-62 inclusive. The date is undoubtedly fourteenth century.[59] There is no specific evidence that Chaucer did not see S[1], and no other material is bound with the manuscript.

A[1], British Library, MS. Arundel 347, has forty-six folios, each about 214 by 144 millimeters. The handwriting is a university book hand. There are no serious omissions from A[1], other than (1) the statement in the prologue that the canons are to be found at the end of the *Kalendarium* and (2) certain Metonic cycles to be discussed below. The manuscript has three additions. At the beginning, before the prologue, there is a table which gives the Julian date of Easter for any year between 1387 and 1918 inclusive. Second, at the very end of the manuscript there is a passage explaining for each sign of the zodiac the qualities of wetness, dryness, heat and cold pertaining to fortune or misfortune in bleeding. Third, the table of the continuation of the motion of the sun is extended beyond the normal 1469 until 1529. Apparently somebody proposed extending the usefulness of this manuscript beyond the 1462 terminal date of the *Kalendarium*. To have done so one would have altered all the figures for both new and full moons and for both solar and lunar eclipses to figures which would be proper for Metonic cycles which follow 1462. Metonic cycles after that date begin in the years 1463, 1482, 1501, 1520, etc. In A[1] the solar and lunar eclipses are unaltered, but the figures in the tables of full and new moons are completely missing for the months of January through September inclusive. For the month of October figures are offered under the headings *Ciclus conjunccionis* and *Ciclus opposicionis* in each of the

35

first three cycles. No figures appear under *Tempus vere conjunccionis* or *Tempus vere opposicionis* in the first three cycles, and no figures appear at all in the fourth cycle. The figures which do appear in the first cycle are proper for the Metonic period beginning in 1453; in the second cycle, proper for the Metonic period beginning in 1482; and in the third cycle, proper for the Metonic period beginning in 1501. The lunar cycles for November have been treated in the same way. The first three cycles for each month give full information for Metonic periods beginning in 1463, 1482, and 1501. The fourth cycle for November and December is unaltered; it begins with the year 1444, as it normally does in the other manuscripts. The names of the saints in $A^1$ correspond very closely with those in $S^1$, suggesting a close relationship between these manuscripts. I see no reason to date $A^1$ any later than 1400, and there is no specific evidence that Chaucer did not see it. No other material is bound with the manuscript.

   **D** is folios 57r–90v of Oxford, Bodleian Library, MS. Digby 41, which in its entirety contains 104 folios. The size of each folio is about 188 by 115 millimeters. The handwriting is a university book hand. Omitted from the *Kalendarium* are the following: the prologue, the months of January through March inclusive, the month of April through the lengths of the twilights, the figures of the solar eclipses, the table of the lunar eclipses, the figures of the lunar eclipses, the table of the ascendants and the beginnings of the house for Aries and Taurus, and the table for the continuation of the motion of the sun. Added to the *Kalendarium* is a table for determining the Julian date of Easter from 1387 through 1918, identical to the extraneous table in $A^1$. Also, additional astrological information in a handwriting of a later century has been added to the pages containing the table for the dignities of the planets and the table for discovering the dominical letters of past or future years. The full and new moon information for the first Metonic cycle has been altered to give the same information for the years 1520–31, which is the first twelve of the nineteen years of the fourth Metonic cycle after the 1462 expiration of the *Kalendarium*. The alteration is in a later hand; for instance, the number 7 is depicted as we know it today and not as the conventional lambda or inverted V of the fourteenth century. To make these alterations someone scraped away the proper figures for the first cycle. But in a few places, where the scraping was not performed thoroughly, one may still see the original figures from the first cycle. D was probably copied in the fourteenth century,[60] for it contains no clear-cut evidence that in its original form it was copied after Chaucer's death. Apart from the *Kalendarium*, the folios contain the following: Latin medical directions for the twelve months of the year; an English reply of Daw Topias to

*The Complaint of Jack Uplond;* a moral Latin allegory of Alanus de Insulis entitled "Anti-Claudianus sive de officio boni viti"; a Latin piece on prices for travelers; a Latin note on the translation of the body of St. Cuthbert; a Latin note on the elections of the antipopes Clement VII and Benedict XIII; Latin words and musical notations to some Old Testament prayers; a Latin catalogue of church relics; a Latin philosophical poem in the form of a dialogue; a Latin note on Saints Edmund of Abington and Thomas of Canterbury; and a Latin fragment of some examples of Greek mythology.

**B** is the first forty-one of the ninety-eight folios of Brussels, Bibliothèque Royale Albert Ier, MS. 4862/69. Each folio is about 224 by 146 millimeters. The handwriting is a university book hand. Omitted from the *Kalendarium* is the prologue. The only additions to B are titles to the ninth, tenth, eleventh, and twelfth canons. The Metonic cycles are correctly indicated for the periods of 1387 through 1462. There is fairly good evidence that Chaucer did not see this manuscript, for although it has been dated about 1400,[61] I think the folios containing the *Kalendarium* were copied later. On folio 5r on the list of saints for the date 27 March appear the words *Resureccio domini* or "The Resurrection of the Lord," signifying, presumably, that Easter was on 27 March during the year that either this version of the *Kalendarium* or its source was copied. The first year that Easter was 27 March after the 1386 composition of the *Kalendarium* was 1407, and Easter fell on that date also in 1418, 1429, 1440, and 1502. The nearest 27 March Easter before the *Kalendarium* was composed was 1345, some forty-one years before Nicholas tried his hand at a calendar. Therefore, the year 1407 must stand as a *terminus a quo* for the *Kalendarium* folios of B, and Chaucer could not have seen them. Besides Nicholas's *Kalendarium,* B contains the following: a medical treatise attributed to Hippocrates beginning *Incipit tractatus cuiusdam sapientissimi philosophi Ypocratis;* a set of tables beginning *Incipiunt tabule de modo graduandi sive calculandi medicinas,* by Arnaud de Villeneuve or Arnoldus de Villa Nova (Chaucer's Arnold of the Newe Toun, *Canterbury Tales* VIII, 1428), who died in 1314; a treatise on blood-letting beginning *Hoc est flebotomie speculum per quod qui sanguinem minuere voluerit;* another passage on blood-letting beginning *Dicta de fleobotomia iam dicendum est de ventosis et primo propter quas intenciones fiunt ut patebit in capitulo subsequenti;* another medical passage entitled *Electio horarum ad medicinas dandas;* a passage attributed to Galen on anatomy; and last an untitled copy of Chaucer's *Treatise on the Astrolabe.*[62]

**So,** Society of Antiquaries of London, MS. 8, consists of nineteen folios, each about 186 by 133 millimeters. The first two folios, which are badly stained, have nothing to do with the *Kalendarium* but are prayers in various hands later than the rest of the manuscript. The *Kalendarium* itself begins with the prologue on folio 3r and runs through the end of the month of July on folio 19v. The handwriting is a university book hand. The prologue is complete although the promise of the sixth and last table is in a marginal gloss. Omitted from the *Kalendarium* are the months after July, all the figures and tables, and all of the canons. Added right after the prologue (the scribe must have wondered what to do with half a sheet of blank vellum) is a square multiplication table from one through ten. The Metonic cycles are unaltered. Where the manuscripts so far discussed were meticulous, albeit not entirely accurate, about the shadow lengths caused by solar altitudes of less than 1°, So continually gives the less accurate approximations, which were discussed above in the description of the *Kalendarium* and are recorded in detail in Appendix A. There is no positive way to tell whether Nicholas of Lynn in his calculations used the meticulous or the approximate shadow lengths. Because the manuscripts which use the approximate lengths are less accurate in many ways, have more omissions, and have more additions than the manuscripts which use the meticulous lengths, I suggest that the approximations are the work of a later scribe and that the meticulous lengths are those set out by Nicholas of Lynn. This suggestion cannot be proved, although it seems likely, especially when we see that as in B, the words *Resureccio domini* are given on the list of saints for the date 27 March. Again the implication is that a *terminus a quo* for So must be 1407,[63] and Chaucer could not have seen it. No other material is bound with the manuscript.

**As¹**, Oxford, Bodleian Library, ms. Ashmole 5, contains forty-two folios, each about 140 by 96 millimeters. The handwriting is a university book hand. Omissions from the prologue include the mention of John of Gaunt as King of Castile and Leon, part of the promise of times from midnight and noon until sunrise and sunset, the description of the tables of eclipses, the promise of six other tables, the description of the first table, the description of the sixth table, and the statement that the canons are at the end of the *Kalendarium*. Some of the statements in the prologue have been moved and occasionally rewritten. Missing from the charts and figures is only the sixth table, the continuation of the motion of the sun. Missing from the canons are part of the first canon, the daily position of the sun; part of the second canon, the lengths of the artificial and vulgar days and twilights; part of the sixth canon, the unequal hours; part of the ninth canon, the zodiacal position of the moon; part of the tenth canon, the movable feasts; and part of the twelfth canon, the receiving of medicine. An addition to the manuscript is the figure of a human body showing which parts are affected by the various signs of the zodiac. Also added to As[1] are titles to all of the canons except the second. The Metonic cycles appear to be unaltered, except that the full moons of the fourth cycle, as they are in S[1], are missing. Pächt and Alexander date this manuscript in the fourteenth century, although they offer no more evidence than the obvious *terminus a quo* of 1387.[64] Approximations for shadow lengths caused by low solar altitudes are given. No other material is bound with the manuscript.

**R,** Oxford, Bodleian Library, MS. Rawlinson C.895, contains thirty-two folios, each about 238 by 153.5 millimeters. The handwriting is a university book hand. Omitted from R are the following: the mention in the prologue of the table of the continuation of the motion of the sun, the table of the solar eclipses, the figures of the solar eclipses, the table of the lunar eclipses, the figures of the lunar eclipses, the table of the ascensions and equations of houses, the table of the continuation of the motion of the sun, the table for discovering the dignities of the planets in their signs, and the table for discovering the sign and degree of sign of the moon. The canons, which only in this manuscript are placed directly after the prologue, have the following omissions: from the sixth canon of the unequal hours, the means of discovering the given information if one is away from Oxford, and the entire twelfth canon, which is concerned with receiving medicine. Added to R are titles to all of the existing canons except the first. The Metonic cycles of this manuscript have been altered by a hand other than the copier of the manuscript as follows: the first cycle, 1387–1405, has been changed to the second Metonic cycle after the expiration of the *Kalendarium,* 1482–1500; the second cycle, 1406–24, has been changed to 1501–19; the third cycle, 1425–43, has been altered to 1520–38. The fourth cycle, which like the fourth cycle in S[1] shows only full moons, has been left unchanged. Approximations are given for low solar altitudes, thus suggesting a later copiest and a fifteenth-century date.[65] No other material is bound with the manuscript.

**Ad,** British Library, MS. Additional 15209, has fifty-nine folios, each about 183 by 120 millimeters. The handwriting is a university book hand. Omitted from the prologue are the statement from St. Augustine's homily on the Gospel according to John, the promise of times from midnight and noon until sunrise and sunset, the descriptions of tables of eclipses, the promise of six other tables, the descriptions of the first, second, and sixth tables, the promise of the canons, and the statement that the canons are at the end of the *Kalendarium.* The month-by-month part of the *Kalendarium* has no alterations other than those described below. Omitted from the charts and tables are the table of solar eclipses, the table of lunar eclipses, the table of ascensions and equations of houses, the table of the continuation of the motion of the sun, and the table for discovering the dignities of the planets in their signs. Omitted from the canons are part of the first canon, the daily zodiacal position of the sun; all of the second canon, the lengths of the artificial and vulgar days and the twilights; all of the fourth canon, the clock times of sunrise, sunset, and twilight; part of the fifth canon, the shadow scale; all of the seventh canon, the solar and lunar eclipses; all of the eighth canon, the ascensions of houses; part of the ninth canon, the zodiacal signs of the moon; and part of the tenth canon, the movable feasts. There are many additions to this manuscript: tables of lunar and solar eclipses appear, but the information on them is not from Nicholas of Lynn. The author of the tables of eclipses in Ad consistently has his eclipses, both solar and lunar, begin one full day before Nicholas has his eclipses begin. The only explanation is that where Nicholas begins his day at noon on the previous day, the author of these tables begins his day at noon on the day in question. On folios 32r–35v the scribe of Ad gives solar and lunar eclipse tables and figures completely unlike Nicholas's and quite similar to the eclipse tables and figures found in the *Kalendarium* of John Somer. Interestingly enough, Nicholas's eclipse figures appear on folios 55v–57v at the end of Ad, after the canons. Ad also offers more material which is found in the manuscripts of John Somer's *Kalendarium*. On folio 36r is a circular drawing of the Ptolemaic universe with the outer circle labeled *Primum mobile* and the inner circle labeled *Infernus*. The order of the spheres is Prime Mover, Stars, Saturn, Jupiter, Mars, Sun, Venus, Mercury, Moon, Fire, Air, Water, Earth, Hell. One can hardly be more complete than that. On folio 36v is a table of the signs of the zodiac and bits of information pertaining to each sign: Aries, for example, is masculine, eastern, hot, dry, fiery, choleric, good for bleeding, and important to one's head. On folio 37r appears a volvelle that demonstrates different phases of the moon. On folio 37v is a circular calendar, emphasizing movable feasts and dates on a Roman calendar. On folio 38r is a physician's urine chart consisting of a ring of urinals, each colored and labeled in such a way as to instruct a physician to match the color of a patient's urine with a given medical disorder. On folio 38v the figure of a man bears indications where he should be bled in order to relieve an excess of a given humor or other disorder. On folio 39r appears a circular diagram referring to the planets and other significant bits of information such as how to avoid sickness and death. The next drawing, on folio 39v, is of the conventional zodiac man, quite similar to the drawing in As[1]. The canons include additional material explaining the additional charts and tables. The Metonic cycles in Ad are unaltered for the full moons of the period covered by the *Kalendarium*. The new moon tables, however, have been altered in a way to make them meaningless. The first column, *Ciclus conjunccionis,* which tells the years of the new moons, is unchanged. The second and third columns, which show the hours and minutes, have been altered to conform with the four Metonic cycles which follow the 1462 expiration of the *Kalendarium*. Since the very day of each new moon is for a year seventy-six years in the past, the figures for the hours and minutes have no value when one cannot know the day of the new moon. A proper alteration would have changed the figures in the first column as well as those in the second and third. The date is probably fifteenth century.[66] There is specific information in Ad that whatever manuscript Chaucer used, he did not use this one. In the prologue to the Man of Law's Tale in the *Canterbury Tales,* Chaucer has the Host remark that the length of every shadow is the same as the object which causes it, that the date is 18 April, and that therefore the time must be 10:00 A.M. Such information, as was discussed above, comes right out of Nicholas of Lynn's shadow scale for April. The length of the shadow of a six-foot man at 10:00 A.M. and at 2:00 P.M. between 4 April and 18 April runs from six feet and fifty-nine parts to six feet and no parts. For every place where the number 6 is required, the scribe of Ad writes an 8. Since neither Nicholas nor Chaucer is talking about an eight-foot man, Ad gives incorrect information, and Chaucer's information is exactly correct. Therefore, Chaucer did not use Ad. The lengths of shadows cast by a low-altitude sun are incorrect approximations. Nothing other than the *Kalendarium* is contained in Ad. This manuscript is apparently a compilation of the *Kalendaria* of Nicholas of Lynn, John Somer, and perhaps one or more other authors whose names we do not know.

**A²,** British Library, Arundel 207, has thirty-six folios, each about 170 by 127 millimeters. The handwriting is a university book hand. Omitted from the prologue are the mention of John of Gaunt as King of Castile and Leon; part of the promises of times from midnight and noon until sunrise and sunset; the description of the tables of eclipses; the promise of six other tables; the descriptions of the first, second, and sixth tables; and the statement that the canons are at the end of the *Kalendarium*. In A² the prologue is placed after the canons and is glossed *Nicholaus de Linea 1386.* Omitted from the tables and charts are the table of solar eclipses, the entire table of ascensions and beginnings of houses, the table of the continuation of the motion of the sun, and the table for discovering the dignities of the planets in their signs. Omitted from the canons are the part of the first canon which explains how to make corrections for the true place of the sun; the entire second canon concerning the lengths of the artificial days, the vulgar days, and the twilights; the entire sixth canon concerning the unequal hours; the entire eighth canon concerning the ascension of houses; most of the ninth canon concerning the zodiacal signs of the moon; all of the eleventh canon of bleeding and purges; and all of the twelfth canon of receiving medicine. Brief titles are added to the canons in A². At the beginning is a statement in a modern hand explaining that the canons are abridged and signed "F. M." (presumably Sir Frederic Madden). At the end there is a brief statement that the manuscript has thirty-six folios, signed by "R.P.S.," and dated 1884. Folios 34v–36v contain in what may be a late-fifteenth- or sixteenth-century hand some astrological directions for each month. Certain days in A², i.e., 25 January, 1 March, 10 April, 20 April, 3 May, 25 May, 11 June, 13 July, 1 August, 30 August, 3 September, 3 October, 22 October, 5 November, 28 November, 12 December, and 22 December are labeled *dies egritudinis* or "a day of ill health," which is undoubtedly the equivalent of "unlucky day." Prominent evenings of vigils are indicated. The Metonic cycles are unaltered except that, as in S¹, the full moon figures for the fourth cycle are omitted. The date is probably fifteenth century.[67] Shadow lengths at low solar altitudes are approximations. A² contains the same error in the shadow scale as Ad; therefore Chaucer did not use it. No additional material is bound with this manuscript.

**As²** is the first twenty-nine folios of Oxford, Bodleian Library, MS. Ashmole 370. Each folio is about 201.5 by 121.6 millimeters. The handwriting is a university book hand. Omitted is the entire prologue, the first and second Metonic cycles in the month-by-month section, the shadow scale for July, the entire tables and figures of the solar eclipses, the tables and figures of the lunar eclipses through the year 1419, the table of ascensions and beginnings of houses, the table of movable feasts, the table of the continuation of the motion of the sun, the table for discovering the dignities of the planets in their signs, and all of the canons. Only two Metonic cycles are given: the third cycle from 1425 through 1443 and the fourth cycle from 1444 through 1462, suggesting a *terminus a quo* of 1425 for this manuscript.[68] Shadow lengths at low solar altitudes are approximations. Like B and So, As² offers the words *Resureccio domini* on the saints' list for 27 March, again postulating an early fifteenth-century *terminus a quo*. The saints in As² correspond very closely to those in R, thus suggesting a close relationship. In addition to the above, Ashmole 370 contains the following: an English-language volvelle, the figure of a zodiac man with a description in English, the beginning of a circular astronomical drawing, an English-language recital of some important events including the Battle of Agincourt in 1415, and some more English-language astrological information. The passages in English are in a vernacular hand. This manuscript appears to be a copy of what remained pertinent of the *Kalendarium* after the first quarter of the fifteenth century. Chaucer could not have seen it.

**M,** folios 71r through the first column of folio 72r of Munich, Bayerische Staatsbibliothek, Codex Latinus Monacensis 10661, contains the eleventh canon on bleeding and purges, and the twelfth canon on the receiving of medicine. Each folio is about 173 by 118 millimeters. The handwriting is a court hand. At the end of the passage appears the date 1470. Prior to the passage by Nicholas in this manuscript are the following: a passage on judicial astrology by Arnold of Villanova, a section on celestial motion by one Amotra son of Ametri, an essay on quadrants said to be by Thebit, a passage from a computation of the Jews, a translation by John Hispalensi from Arabic into Latin concerning Alkabitus on judicial astrology, John Delmeriis on the prime mover, and a theory of planets. Succeeding the passage by Nicholas are the following: John of Saxony's canons of the Alfonsine tables, a composition by Almonach, an astronomical table, directions for making a quadrant and a cursor, John Delmeriis on bleeding, an Italian description of Ptolemy on cosmography, a table of regional longitudes, a work on the armillary, and Raymond Julius (or Lullius) on general arts.

**S²,** folios 70v through 73r of British Library, MS. Sloane 3285, contains only the eleventh canon, bleeding and purges, and part of the twelfth canon, the receiving of medicine. Each folio is about 192 by 129 millimeters. The handwriting is like a vernacular hand. Added are titles to the canons. The date appears to be fifteenth century.[69] Bound with the folios from the *Kalendarium* are the following: a letter concerning the plague in the eighth year of King Henry VI (1430), Hippocrates' book purportedly sent to "the Emperor Caesar," the influence of heavenly bodies on human bodies, a list of English parish churches, a list of perilous days, further rules for bleeding, and information about medicine for horses.

**Gg,** folios 160v through 161v of Cambridge University Library, MS. Gg.5.37, contains only the eleventh canon on bleeding and purges, and part of the twelfth canon on the receiving of medicine. Each folio is about 211 by 146 millimeters. The date is fifteenth century.[70] The handwriting is like a vernacular hand. Bound with these folios are the following: a collection of letters dated 1475–80 and a passage concerning urine.

**As³** is on folios 4v and 5r of the fifth of six books of Oxford, Bodleian Library, MS. Ashmole 391. It contains the eleventh canon on bleeding and purges. The size of each folio is about 242 by 162 millimeters. The handwriting is a university book hand. The surviving parts of this manuscript are quite similar to corresponding parts in Ad and also contain paragraphs and drawings not by Nicholas of Lynn but similar not only to those in Ad but also to those in manuscripts of John Somer's *Kalendarium*. I think the date of As[3] is fifteenth century.[71] The first book in Ashmole 391 is a sixteenth-century treatise on astronomy. The second is a calendar which appears to be a post-1440 copy of John Somer's *Kalendarium*. It is possible that the second book contains those folios missing from the John Somer *Kalendarium* which occupies most of the fifth book. The third book is a printed astronomical prediction dating perhaps from the very late fifteenth century and containing a curious woodcut on almost every page. The fourth book is a Nativity handwritten in the sixteenth century. The fifth is mostly from the *Kalendarium* of John Somer but omits the month-by-month section and does contain the small amount from Nicholas mentioned above. The sixth book is a water-damaged handwritten fifteenth-century copy of Chaucer's *Treatise on the Astrolabe*.

From the fifteen manuscripts listed above one had to be chosen to serve as a base manuscript. The ideal requirements for this base manuscript were that it be complete or nearly so, that it contain nothing contrary to Chaucer's known use of the *Kalendarium,* and that so far as can be ascertained it be as close as possible to the *Kalendarium* written by Nicholas of Lynn in 1386. Although some of the fifteen manuscripts listed above were altered after they were written, we must take them as we find them and consider them according to their surviving merits. In the preceding description of the manuscripts each was placed, so far as I was able, in an order of descending importance to the purpose of an accurate reconstruction of the *Kalendarium.* I wish now to consider them here in ascending importance so that the last one considered will be manifestly the best candidate. In doing so I believe I can offer reasonable justification why fourteen of the manuscripts may be eliminated from consideration, thus leaving L as the best possible surviving text.

A[3] offers eight per cent of the canons, Gg and S[2] offer thirty-one per cent of the canons, M contains forty-four per cent of the canons; and none of these offers any of the rest of the *Kalendarium.* As[2] eliminates all of the canons and everything else of any significance before the year 1419. In addition, the shadow lengths at low solar altitudes offered in As[2] are approximations (see Appendix A), thus suggesting that it was copied either by a careless scribe or from another manuscript copied by an equally careless scribe. A[2] eliminates most of the tables, offers the approximate shadow lengths, and contains only twenty per cent of the canons. Finally, A[2] indicates that the length of the shadow of a six-foot man at 10:00 A.M. on 18 April is eight feet. Since Chaucer correctly stated that this particular shadow length was six feet, he did not use $A^2$ and we may be sure that $A^2$ was incorrectly copied. Ad eliminates much of what Nicholas wrote, offers the approximate shadow lengths, and adds material written by John Somer. More important, Ad contains the same error in shadow length that $A^2$ does, thus demonstrating evidence of incorrect copying. R lacks most of the tables and about half of the canons. It offers the approximate shadow lengths and has altered the figures in the first three Metonic cycles. $As^1$ lacks many of the tables and about a quarter of the canons. It too offers the approximate shadow lengths. Manuscript So is incomplete, ending in July, and in addition, it has the approximate shadow lengths. B omits the prologue. Since all of the above manuscripts are far from complete and since $A^2$ and Ad show evidence of being miscopied in that they contain misinformation in the very place where Chaucer uses correct information, not one of them deserves consideration as a base manuscript.

Four manuscripts remain for consideration: D, $A^1$, $S^1$, and L. None shows any serious evidence of being miscopied, and all have meticulous shadow lengths. D, however, begins in the middle of April, contains Metonic cycles altered for periods after the expiration of the *Kalendarium,* and eliminates a number of the tables. On the day it was copied D might have been pristine, but in its current condition it is far too mutilated to serve as a base manuscript. $A^1$ is also mutilated, but not as much so as D. In $A^1$ the numbers of the Metonic cycles have been scraped away, and new ones for later years have been partially inserted. $S^1$ lacks the numbers of the full moons in the fourth Metonic cycle and the final third of the canons. Thus by elimination, only L remains. It is not perfect, lacking one folio, but it is the best we have; and therefore it has been chosen as a base manuscript. $S^1$ was selected to fill in the gaps in L because it is the second most useful manuscript. $A^1$, which contains more accurate eclipse drawings than does $S^1$, is used to supplement $S^1$ when necessary. All of these substitutions are carefully documented in the textual notes.

Certain similarities and dissimilarities among the manuscripts are worthy of attention so that my selection of the order of presentation of the manuscripts, both in the preceding part of this introduction and in the corpus of variants, may be justified and so that the relationships among the manuscripts may be further understood. These are correspondences in the saints' lists and variants from L in the prologue and the canons.

Correspondences among lists of saints may be made among all manuscripts which contain saints' lists, but may, of course, be made only for the parts of the manuscripts which are extant. For instance, when comparing $S^1$ with $A^1$, one has access to all twelve months of the calendar. But when comparing So, which offers only the months January through July, or D, which offers only the months May through December, one must use the corresponding months in another manuscript. No two manuscripts have one hundred per cent exactness in the lists of saints, and no two manuscripts drop below thirty per cent. An examination of these percentages reveals that some of the manuscripts appear to fall into clusters. The saints' names in L have a ninety per cent exactness with those in R and $As^2$. The saints' names in $S^1$ have a ninety-five per cent exactness with those in $A^1$, eighty-nine per cent with those in D, eighty-eight per cent with those in $As^1$, and eighty-six per cent with those in Ad. $A^2$ has only about half the number of saints' names that the others have. Of the saints in $A^2$ eighty per cent appear in R and $As^2$. The clusters, therefore, group in the following manner: first cluster, L, R, $A^2$, and $As^2$; second cluster, $S^1$, $A^1$, $As^1$, and Ad. D, B, and So appear to have equal parallels to manuscripts in both clusters but belong in neither. A given list of saints, however, could have been taken from another copy of Nicholas's *Kalendarium* or from some other source. Accordingly, the saints' lists suggest relationships but offer no visible proof that any given manuscript derives from any other.

One may examine the substantive variants of the prologue, which is offered in eight manuscripts: L, $S^1$, $A^1$, So, $As^1$, R, Ad, and $A^2$. These variants are defined in the editorial principles of this introduction and are listed in the corpus of variants. The quantities of substantive prologue variants from L are as follows: R, five variants; $A^1$, eight variants; So, eight variants; $S^1$, nine variants; Ad, twenty variants; $A^2$, twenty-five variants; and $As^1$, twenty-seven variants. As do the saints' lists, the variants of the prologue force the manuscripts into clusters, the first of which includes L, $S^1$, $A^1$, So, and R, and the second of which includes $As^1$, Ad, and $A^2$. There are few surprises here. $S^1$ and $A^1$ have already been established to have close correspondences with the base manuscript. R has been noted to have a saints' list similar to that of L. Probably R was copied from a manuscript quite similar to L. The scribe of So probably copied the prologue from a manuscript which, if we had it, could be placed in the same group with L. $As^1$ and Ad have saints' lists dissimilar to that in L. Ad and $A^2$ have been shown to be in part miscopied.

The substantive variants of the canons are also defined in the editorial principles and are listed in the corpus of variants. The manuscripts which contain all or parts of the canons are L, $S^1$, $A^1$, D, B, $As^1$, R, Ad, $A^2$, M, $S^2$, Gg, and $As^3$. Some manuscripts contain fewer than the 456 lines of the canons, but the number of variants from them can be expanded proportionally. The number of variants from L, once the proportional expansions have been effected, are as follows: $S^1$, 96; $A^1$, 100; D, 125; B, 151; Ad, 188; $As^3$, 222; $S^2$, 252; $As^1$, 257; Gg, 262; R, 340; M, 376; and $A^2$, 383. Note that $S^1$, $A^1$, D, and B, which have the fewest variants from L, are also those manuscripts which contain the more meticulous shadow lengths. Ad, $As^1$, R, and $A^2$, which have a greater number of variants, also have the approximate shadow lengths. $As^3$, $S^2$, Gg, and M do not have the shadow scale.

## EDITORIAL PRINCIPLES

Out of fifteen surviving manuscripts, the best, L (so chosen for reasons given in the previous section), has been selected as a base manuscript for this edition. It is somewhat less than perfect if one wishes as a finished product a reproduction of the very *Kalendarium* which Nicholas completed in 1386. In places where L contains substantive variants such as lacunae or obvious mistakes such as the use of *Susuper* for *Insuper* (canon, line 462) a few additions and emendations are necessary so that the text presented here will be a conservative critical edition of Nicholas's presumed original. The additions and emendations in the charts and diagrams are identified and explained in the textual notes. Those emendations which appear in the prologue and in the canons are noted with an asterisk in the corpus of variants and an indication that the reading comes from a manuscript or manuscripts other than L. Certain minor errors such as the incorrect placement of a saint's name are recorded in this edition the way they are found in L, but these errors are noted in both the corpus of variants and the textual notes. Thus L may be recovered completely by a combination of the text, the textual notes, and the corpus of variants.

The major additions to L are as follows: on the first folio of April certain numbers are missing from the lunar cycle column and from the column showing the numbers of the nones and the ides. Missing from the lunar cycle column are 8 (for 5 April), 16 (for 6 April), and 5 (for 7 April); from the nones column 4 (for 2 April), 3 (for 3 April), and 2 (for 4 April); from the ides column 8 (for 6 April), 7 (for 7 April), 6 (for 8 April), 5 (for 9 April), and 4 (for 10 April). All of these numbers have been supplied from $S^1$. Also on the same page the words *Aries* and *Taurus* are missing from their proper places and are supplied from $S^1$. Between folios 32 and 33 of L one folio is missing. The recto of this folio would show the figures of the twenty lunar eclipses from 1 March 1439 to 12 June 1462 inclusive and a small amount of text describing each figure. The figures have been supplied from $A^1$, because the artist who drew the eclipses on A¹ more accurately portrayed the *punctus eclipsis,* or magnitude of the occultation, than did the artist of S¹. The text which pertains to each figure, however, has been supplied from S¹ because the information which it gives conforms more closely to the information given on the eclipse tables of L than does the information offered by A¹. The verso of the missing folio of L would show the ascensions and the equations of houses for both Aries and Taurus. This information is supplied from S¹.

A number of emendations have been made to the figures and tables. These usually replace the incorrect numbers recorded only by the scribe of L and are indicated in the textual notes because the variants of the figures and tables are not recorded in the corpus of variants.

The emendations to the prologue and canons are kept to an absolute minimum. In most situations where L differs from the other manuscripts yet is in readable and logical fourteenth-century Latin consistent with the context, I have judged no emendation to be required. In a few places in the prologue and more in the canons they are necessary. Each is marked with an asterisk in the corpus of variants.

In this edition the lines of both the Latin prologue and the Latin canons are numbered consecutively, with the numbers appearing every five lines. Each of the canons is numbered with an Arabic numeral, and because this system of numbering does not appear in any of the manuscripts, it appears in this edition in square brackets. In addition titles are offered for the prologue and for each of the canons. These are not contained in L but do appear in several other manuscripts and are so noted in the corpus of variants. The titles are not counted in the line numbers of the prologue or canons.

In addition to the above, certain alterations are consistently used in this edition. The letters *i/j* and *u/v* are regularized; *i* and *u* are used for vowels and *j* and *v* are used for consonants. When *w* means *vu* as in *wlgaris,* the *w* is regularized as in *vulgaris.* Punctuation and capitalization of the Latin prose passages are modernized and conform as closely as possible with the English translation, although the Latin particles are not set off by commas. Dominical letters in the canons are lower case and italicized. Certain scribal misspellings such as *corespondente* are retained because they are consistent throughout almost all texts. For capitalization of names of saints and their descriptions I have followed the usage of the modern edition of Butler.[72] The saints' names are given in Latin in the genitive because the word *festivitas* is implied.

Manuscript abbreviations are expanded silently except on some charts where limitations of space make abbreviations necessary. Because in such cases the manuscript abbreviations would be difficult to reproduce, the following modern abbreviations have been substituted for the medieval forms: a.m. for ante meridiem; Apr. for Aprilis; Aquar. for Aquarius; Canc. for Cancer; Capr. for Capricornus; d. for dies; Feb. for Februarius; Gem. for Gemini; ° for gradus, graduum; g. for gradus, graduum; h. for hora, hore; Jan. for Januarius; Jun. for Junius; Kl. for Kalendas, Kalendis; Mar. for Marcius; ' for minuta, minute, minutorum; m. for minuta, minute, minutorum; Pisc. for Piscis; p.m. for post meridiem; pt. for punctus; Sag. for Sagittarius; " for secundus, secunda; s. for secundus, secunda; Scorp. for Scorpio; Taur. for Taurus.

The following principles apply to the use of numbers in the text and translation. Numbers of one or two digits are spelled out in both Latin and English, whether the digits form parts of words or stand alone: e.g., the manuscript *7triones* is expanded silently to *septentriones;* the manuscript 6° is expanded silently to *sexto.* The ordinals *one hundredth* and *one thousandth* are also spelled out. There are certain exceptions to this policy: all numbers except for ordinals on tables and charts are Arabic, as are the numbers of the propositions of Ptolemy's *Centiloquium.* Aside from direct quotations, the numbers which appear in longitudes and latitudes, Metonic cycles, degrees of the signs of the zodiac, degrees of altitude, and both equal and unequal hours of time are given in Arabic numerals, including the minutes and seconds when necessary.

None of the scribes is particularly consistent with the use of the letters *c* or *t* before *i* and another vowel. Because the use of *c* appears much more frequently than the use of *t,* I have attempted to normalize this procedure by consistently using *c* in such words as *conjunccionem* or *eciam.* Occasionally when a letter is omitted from its normal place I insert it silently and indicate the change in the corpus of variants: e.g., *conjunccio* (from L *conjuccio*) canon, line 235. The insertion is indicated in the corpus of variants with an asterisk so that L may be recovered completely by a combination of text and variants.

The corpus of variants, which is offered for the prologue, the listed saints in the *Kalendarium,* and the canons, conforms generally with the practice of the Chaucer Library. The principal objective is to record substantive variants, by which I mean readings which change the meaning: i.e., omissions, additions, or alterations of words or numbers. Minor variants in spelling such as *arcum* and *archum* are not recorded, nor are variants in common words which have the same meaning such as *vel* and *sive* or *eciam* and *autem.* A few interesting variants in the spelling of proper names such as *Tholomei* and *Ptolomei* are, however, included. For each variant in the prologue and the canons the following is noted: line number; boldface reading in L, the base manuscript (or in the case of the prologue and canon headings the manuscript as noted); an italicized direction if needed; the variant reading; and the sigil or unpunctuated sigils of the manuscript or manuscripts where the variant may be found. The order of the manuscripts is always that given in the manuscript descriptions above; that is, after L appear in sequence S[1], A[1], D, B, So, As[1], R, Ad, A[2], As[2], M, S[2], Gg, and As[3]. Punctuation within the variants is omitted although I have retained capitalization. Each separate variant is separated by a semicolon, and the end of each entire entry is followed by a period. The italicized directions are *om,* for "omit"; *add,* meaning that the variant follows the lemma; *(1st)* or *(2nd),* indicating which of two identical words in a line is the lemma under consideration; *expunged,* meaning that a manuscript word was written and then crossed out; *after,* meaning that the variant follows a given line; and other indications (such as *from* As[1]) which are self-explanatory.

There is no corpus of variants for the pages which consist of columns of numbers, for the tables, or for the charts. Major alterations in the above to manuscripts other than L are noted in the introduction or the textual notes.

The prologue to the *Kalendarium* appears in L and the following: S[1], A[1], So, As[1], R, Ad, and A[2]. The order of the paragraphs is not the same in all manuscripts, and these differences are recorded in the textual notes.

The corpus of variants for the listed saints is organized into paragraphs, one for each month. Within the month, the day is given without the reading in L. Then follows the other information as listed above. Variants in the listed saints are given for the months January through December from S[1], A[1], B, As[1], R, Ad, A[2], and As[2], for the months January through July from So, and for the months May through December from D.

L includes the entire body of canons, lines 1–456. The lines of the canons included in the other manuscripts are as follows: S[1], 1–299; A[1], 1–456; D, 1–456; B, 1–456; As[1], 1–18, 36–38, 49–102, 142–79, 197–320, 321–97; R, 1–43, 49–102, 142–293; Ad, 1–18, 49–54, 62–70, 95–141, 178–91, 195–205, 213–20, 239–456; A[2], 1–18, 49–94, 142–52, 178–79, 197–230, 231–55; M, 256–456; S[2], 256–397; Gg, 256–397; and As[3], 256–93.

The translation of the prologue and canons is designed to follow the Latin as closely as possible. Occasionally words are added to produce more readable English, but these words are always in square brackets. For example see lines 302–4 of the canons: *et proxima primacio erit primacio vicesimi anni sequentis; et quinta primacio centesimi anni. . . .* The translation of this passage is "and the next paschal moon [on that date] will be the paschal moon of the twentieth year following; and the fifth paschal moon [will be that] of the hundredth year. . . ."

# NOTES TO INTRODUCTION

1. All citations to Chaucer, unless otherwise noted, are from F. N. Robinson, ed., *The Works of Geoffrey Chaucer,* 2nd ed. (Boston: Houghton Mifflin Co., 1957), hereafter cited as *Works.* All lines are numbered according to Robinson's edition.

2. Sidney Leed, ed., *The Dictionary of National Biography,* vol. 19 (London: Smith, Elder & Co., 1891), p. 419. Hereafter cited as *DNB.*

3. A. B. Emden, *A Biographical Register of the University of Oxford to A. D. 1500,* vol. 2 (Oxford: The Clarendon Press, 1957-59), p. 1194. Bale also ascribes to Nicholas a study on the astrolabe. See E.G.R. Taylor, *Tudor Geography 1485-1583* (1930; rpt. New York: Octagon Books, 1968), pp. 3, 165.

4. *Mercator's Atlas* (1636; rpt. Amsterdam: Theatrum Orbis Terrarum, 1968), p. 44. For more about Mercator, Nicholas, and "the mythic age of northern cartography" see A. E. Nordenskiöld, *Facsimile-Atlas to the Early History of Cartography,* tr. Johan Adolf Ekelöf and Clements R. Markham (1889; rpt. New York: Kraus Reprint Corp., 1961), pp. 57, 64-65, 95.

5. Richard Hakluyt, *Voyages,* vol. 1, Everyman Library, no. 264 (London: J. M. Dent & Sons, 1907), pp. 99-101. See also Taylor, pp. 133-34. Dee's statement appears in his unpublished "Famous and Rich Discoveries," surviving in British Library, Cotton MS. Vitellius C. VII.

6. Thomas Tanner, *Bibliotheca Britannico-Hibernica* (London: William Bowyer, 1748), p. 546.

7. R. T. Gunther, *Early Science in Oxford,* vol. 2 (1923; rpt. London: Dawsons of Pall Mall, 1967), pp. 62-63.

8. M. C. Seymour, *The Metrical Version of Mandeville's Travels* (London: Oxford University Press, 1973), p. 126.

9. For others who ponder this question see Lynn Thorndike, *A History of Magic and Experimental Science during the First Thirteen Centuries of Our Era,* vol. 3 (1923; rpt. New York: Columbia University Press, 1938), pp. 523-24; George Sarton, "The Mysterious Arctic Traveller of 1360, Nicholas of Lynn?," *Isis* 29 (1938): 98-99; Aubrey Diller, "The Mysterious Arctic Traveller of 1360. Nicholas of Lynn," *Isis* 30 (1939): 277-78; George Sarton, *Introduction to the History of Science,* vol. 3 (Washington: Carnegie Institution of Washington, 1948), p. 1501; John J. D. Gangi, "Chaucer's 'Hende Nicholas': A Possible Identification," *American Notes and Queries* 13 (1974): 50-51.

10. Tanner, loc. cit. See also Henricus O. Coxe, *Catalogi Codicum Manuscriptorum Bibliothecae Bodleianae* (Oxford, 1858), part 2, section 480, where the error is continued.

11. Lynn Thorndike and Pearl Kibre, *A Catalogue of Incipits of Mediaeval Scientific Writings in Latin* (Cambridge, Massachusetts: The Mediaeval Academy of America, 1963), section 652.

12. J.A.W. Bennett, *Chaucer at Oxford and Cambridge* (Toronto: University of Toronto Press, 1974), pp. 76-77.

13. Derek J. Price, *The Equatorie of the Planetis* (Cambridge: Cambridge University Press, 1955), pp. 47, 165-66.

14. Bennett, pp. 58-85, gives a superb description of the scientific activi-

ties at Merton College during the fourteenth century. See also Gunther, vol. 2, pp. 42–65.

15. P. W. Wilson, *The Romance of the Calendar* (New York: W. W. Norton & Co., 1937), p. 89.

16. Peter Archer, S.J., *The Christian Calendar and the Gregorian Reform* (New York: Fordham University Press, 1941), p. 4.

17. Wilson points out that the accuracy of these arrangements was questionable. Ennius, a third-century B.C. Roman, refers to a solar eclipse occurring on 5 June. Five days after a new moon a solar eclipse is impossible. See op. cit., p. 109.

18. W. T. Sedgwick and H. W. Tyler, *A Short History of Science*, rev. H. W. Tyler and R. P. Bigelow (New York: The Macmillan Co., 1939), p. 211.

19. So observed Bacon in the twelfth century. See Sedgwick and Tyler, pp. 209f.

20. George Sarton, *Introduction to the History of Science*, vol. 3 (Baltimore: The Carnegie Institute of Washington, 1947), part 1, p. 115, part 2, p. 1111.

21. Wilson, pp. 142–56.

22. *Treatise on the Astrolabe*, Prologue, line 86, *Works*, p. 546.

23. Bennett, p. 76.

24. Gunther, vol. 2, pp. 60–61. See also *DNB*, ed. Sidney Lee, vol. 53 (1898), pp. 218–19. For a discussion and printed version of the month-by-month section of the *Kalendarium* of John Somer see Francis Wormald, *English Benedictine Kalendars after A.D. 1100*, 1, Henry Bradshaw Society, vol. 77 (London: Harrison and Sons, 1939), pp. 145–60.

25. For a brief description of this manuscript see Curt F. Bühler, "A New Manuscript of the Middle English Tract on Proportions (Sometimes attributed to Chilston)," *Speculum* 21 (1946): 229–33, and especially note 5 on pp. 229–30. I am grateful for the kindness and trust of Dr. Bühler, who shipped this manuscript across the American continent so that I might look at it.

26. *Supplement to the Census of Medieval and Renaissance Manuscripts in the United States and Canada*, originated by C. U. Faye, continued and edited by W. H. Bond (New York: The Bibliographic Society of America, 1962), p. 389.

27. Otto Pächt and J.J.G. Alexander, *Illuminated Manuscripts in the Bodleian Library Oxford*, vol. 3 (Oxford: The Clarendon Press, 1973), p. 62.

28. See Harry Bober, "The Zodiacal Miniature of the *Très Riches Heures* of the Duke of Berry—Its Sources and Meaning," *Journal of the Warburg and Courtauld Institutes* 11 (1948): 25, plates 9a, 9b.

29. *Early Science in Oxford*, vol. 2, pp. 60–62.

30. For more information concerning Walter of Elvedene see Bennett, pp. 76–77; Lynn Thorndike, "Eclipses in the Fourteenth and Fifteenth Centuries," *Isis* 48 (1957): 53; A. B. Emden, *A Biographical Register of the University of Cambridge to 1500* (Cambridge: Cambridge University Press, 1963), pp. 210–11.

31. When the eclipse figures show a P.M. time, such as the eclipse in July 1394, the date of the eclipse is given one day earlier on the figure than on the table. The reason, one may surmise, is that the original compiler of the information on the figures did not begin his astronomical day at noon on the previous day.

32. Dr. Manfred Kudlek of the *Institut für Informatik*, Hamburg, very kindly made for me a computerized list of all solar and lunar eclipses, including every detail of each eclipse, which could have been seen from Oxford between the years 1308 and 2038. Dr. Kudlek's kindness has made possible accurate comparisons between Nicholas's eclipses and actual eclipses.

33. Price, pp. 72–73.

34. Lunar and solar tables pertaining to both of these examples are available in Bryant Tuckerman, *Planetary, Lunar and Solar Positions A.D. 2 to A.D. 1649 at Five-Day and Ten-Day Intervals* (Philadelphia: The American Philosophical Society, 1964); William D. Stahlman and Owen Gingerich, *Solar and Planetary Longitudes for Years −2500 to +2000 by 10-Day Intervals* (Madison: The University of Wisconsin Press, 1963); and *The American Ephemeris and Nautical Almanac for the Year 1975,* ed. Capt. Edward A. Davidson et al. (Washington: U.S. Govt. Printing Office, 1972).

35. For Haly Abbas see C. H. Talbot, *Medicine in Medieval England* (London: Oldbourne Book Co., 1967), pp. 28–30. For the others see Walter Clyde Curry, *Chaucer and the Medieval Sciences,* 2nd ed. (New York: Barnes and Noble, 1960), p. 321, n. 44. Chaucer mentions a Haly (*CT,* I, 431), whom Robinson, following Curry, discusses briefly, *Works,* p. 622. See also Michael Masi, "Chaucer, Messahala and Bodleian Selden Supra 78," *Manuscripta* 19 (1975): 36–47. Professor Masi points out that MS. Selden Supra 78 contains the *Centiloquium* or *Centum Verba* of Ptolemy with a commentary by Haly, and he argues that this manuscript probably was at Oxford in the mid-fourteenth century and therefore available to Nicholas of Lynn. The *Centiloquium,* Professor Masi suggests in correspondence to me, is probably a post-Ptolemaic digest of material which Ptolemy set down in his *Almagest.*

36. Francis S. Benjamin, Jr., and G. J. Toomer, eds. and trans., *Campanus of Novara and Medieval Planetary Theory* (Madison, Wisconsin: The University of Wisconsin Press, 1971), pp. 23–24. Gg, with more wisdom than usual, notes in the margin of folio 160v, line 28, the words *non narrat,* indicating to all who might care that Campanus said no such thing.

37. For more about the medieval physician and his duties see Talbot, chapters X and XI.

38. The following material appears in essence elsewhere. See Sigmund Eisner, "Chaucer's Use of Nicholas of Lynn's Calendar," *Essays and Studies 1976,* vol. 29, n.s., collected for the English Association by E. Talbot Donaldson (London: John Murray, 1976), pp. 1–22. The matter which is used here appears with the gracious permission of the Secretary of the English Association.

39. That is, Nicholas says so in L, S¹, A¹, D, B, So, As¹, R, and As². In Ad and A², the length of the shadow of a six-foot man is given as eight feet, an impossibility with the sun at 45°. M, S², Gg, and As³ do not have the shadow scale.

40. *Works,* p. 690. Robinson errs when he says that when the sun is 56° from the south point, the time is 9:20. Actually it is about an hour earlier.

41. Andrew Edmund Brae, ed., *A Treatise on the Astrolabe of Geoffrey Chaucer* (London: John Russell Smith, 1870), pp. 68–71.

42. W. W. Skeat, ed., *A Treatise on the Astrolabe Addressed to His Son Lowys by Geoffrey Chaucer, A. D. 1391,* Chaucer Society Publications, no. 29 (London: N. Trübner & Co., 1872), pp. l-lii.

43. *Works,* p. 690.

44. Chauncey Wood, *Chaucer and the Country of the Stars* (Princeton: Princeton University Press, 1970), pp. 272-73, note 1.

45. Hamilton M. Smyser, "A View of Chaucer's Astronomy," *Speculum* 45 (1970): 360.

46. *Works,* p. 552.

47. That date is 3 May because the sun is at Taurus 21°, which, according to Nicholas, is 3 May. Professor Pratt emends "Syn March bigan" on line 3190 to "Syn March was gon," making much more sense of the passage. See *The Tales of Canterbury,* ed. Robert A. Pratt (Boston: Houghton Mifflin, 1947), p. 244.

48. Cf. *CT,* I, 1462-63, and *Troilus and Criseyde,* II, 56, *Works,* pp. 31, 402. The scribe of A² very cautiously labels 3 May *dies egritudinis.*

49. For another opinion see Edward S. Cohen, "The Sequence of *The Canterbury Tales,*" *Chaucer Review* 9 (1974): 190-94. Mr. Cohen suggests that Chaucer moved The Parson's Tale from 4:00 P.M. to 10:00 A.M. of the last day but neglected to remove the reference to the sinking sun.

50. Skeat, op. cit., p. lxiv.

51. Nicholas's solar times are designed for the first year after leap year. For other years he offers two slight adjustments: one based on the differences among the first, second, and third year after leap year and leap year itself; the other based on the *motus solis,* or the yearly change in the Julian calendar. Both of the adjustments are so slight that Nicholas advises the user of the *Kalendarium* to take little notice of them unless he is projecting many years to the future. There was no reason for Chaucer to avoid Nicholas's advice. Even with these adjustments, however, the latest date to fit the conditions here is 17 April, except in the leap year itself, when it is 16 April.

52. *Works,* p. 765.

53. Fragment II (B¹) of *CT* contains no reference that specifically places it before or after another fragment. It is found after The Cook's Tale in the manuscripts, and certainly no one has ever suggested that it could possibly follow the Introduction to The Parson's Tale.

54. J. D. North, "Kalenderes Enlumyned Ben They," *Review of English Studies,* n.s., 20, no. 78 (1969): 129-54; no. 79 (1969): 257-83; no. 80 (1969): 411-44. See especially no. 80, 422-26.

55. On 29 March at noon and on 23 August at 11:00 and 1:00 the sun is given at 44° 59 parts, and the shadow is given as six feet even. On 28 June at 11:00 and 1:00 the sun is given at 45° even, and the shadow is six feet even.

56. For the first offer, see Eisner, loc. cit.

57. North, *passim.*

58. Thorndike and Kibre, sections 1131 and 1214. See also Pächt and Alexander, 3, 72; and Coxe, loc. cit.

59. Thorndike and Kibre, section 1131. See also *A Catalogue of the Manu-*

*scripts Preserved in the British Museum* by Samuel Ayscough, Clerk (London: John Rivington Jun., 1782), vol. 1, p. 410.

60. So agree Thorndike and Kibre, section 1131. See also Pächt and Alexander, vol. 3, p. 62, and Gulielmus D. Macray, *Catalogi Codicum Manuscriptorum Bibliothecae Bodleianae Pars Nona, Codices a Viro Clarissimo Kenelm Digby, EQ. AUR., Anno 1634, Complectens: Adiecto Indice Nominum et Rerum* (Oxford, 1883), section 38.

61. P. Pintelon, *Chaucer's Treatise on the Astrolabe: MS. 4862–4869 of the Royal Library in Brussels* (Antwerp: Martinus Nijhoff, 1940), p. 42.

62. For a further description see ibid., pp. 40–41.

63. N. R. Ker, however, dates this manuscript as late fourteenth or early fifteenth century. See *Medieval Manuscripts in British Libraries,* vol. 1 (Oxford: The Clarendon Press, 1969), p. 296.

64. Loc. cit. See also William Henry Black, *Descriptive, Analytical, and Critical Catalogue of the Manuscripts Bequeathed unto the University of Oxford by Elias Ashmole, esq., M.D., F.R.S.* (Oxford: The University Press, 1845), sections 3, 4.

65. The catalogue description of R suggests, however, that it is a fourteenth-century manuscript. See Gulielmus D. Macray, *Catalogi Codicum Manuscriptorum Bibliothecae Bodleianae Partis Quintae Fasciculus Secundus Viri Munificentissimi Ricardi Rawlinson J.C.D. Codicum Classem Tertiam, In Qua Libri Theologici atque Miscellanei, Complectens; Accedit in Uniuscujusque Classis Codicum Contenta Index Locupletissimus* (Oxford, 1857), sections 467–68.

66. Thorndike and Kibre, sections 1131, 1214. See also *Catalogue of Additions to the Manuscripts in the British Museum in the Years MDCCCXLI–MDCCCXLV* (London: 1850), p. 111.

67. Thorndike and Kibre, section 1131. See also *Catalogue of the Manuscripts of the British Museum,* n.s. (London, 1834), p. 57.

68. Black dates it 1424, op. cit., section 286. Pächt and Alexander agree but add a question mark, op. cit., p. 76.

69. Thorndike and Kibre, section 1231. See also *A Catalogue of the Manuscripts Preserved in the British Museum,* vol. 1, p. 277; vol. 2, pp. 558, 606, 611, 614, 646.

70. Thorndike and Kibre, section 1231.

71. Black, op. cit., section 298, and Thorndike and Kibre, op. cit., section 1231, suggest the fourteenth century but give no evidence. My own opinion is based on the apparent derivation of As³ from Ad, the lack in As³ of any part of Nicholas's *Kalendarium* except the eleventh canon (the rest of the *Kalendarium* must have been obsolete), and the fifteenth-century and even post-fifteenth-century material bound with As³.

72. *Butler's Lives of the Saints,* ed. Herbert Thurston, S.J., and Donald Attwater, 4 vols. (New York: P. J. Kenedy & Sons, 1963).

# KALENDARIUM
## DE NICHOLAI DE LENNEA

# PROLOGUE

For Jesus Christ, the mediator of God and men, by his own testimony is Alpha and Omega, the beginning and the end, who is, who was, and who is to come. First chapter of the Apocalypse. From him, according to the blessed Augustine in his first homily on John, all created things take their origin and beginning, and to him, as to their end, all things should be directed and led back. For that reason, to the glory and splendor both of him and of his blessed mother, Mary the chaste virgin, the special patroness of our order, as well as at the request and friendly interest of the most illustrious prince, Lord John, King of Castile and Leon and Duke of Lancaster, did I, Brother Nicholas of Lynn of the Order of the Blessed Mary Mother of God, of Mount Carmel, unworthy and least among readers of sacred theology, compose the present calendar in the year of our same Lord Jesus Christ 1386, for the four Metonic cycles immediately following. And this calendar will begin with the ending of the calendar of the Reverend Teacher Walter of Elweden, namely in the year of Christ 1387, on the first day of the month of January, this being the first year of the Golden Cycle. And it will last for seventy-six years, namely until the year of our Lord 1463. This calendar, moreover, is made for the longitude and latitude of the city of Oxford, in which, according to the practice of astrologers, the natural day is computed from noon of the preceding day until noon of the following day. And it shows the way to find the degree of the sun and its minute for any day of the year; the lengths of the artificial and vulgar days and the twilights of morning and evening; also the lengths of the times from midnight until the beginning of dawn; and from the beginning of the dark of night until midnight; and from midnight until sunrise; and from sunset until midnight. Furthermore it tells the

*Title to Prologue (from A²) om* LS¹A¹SoAs¹RAd. 3-7 **A quo . . . reduci** *om* S¹Ad. 8 **sue** *om* S¹. **beate** *om* SoAs¹RAdA². 11 **Regis . . . Legionis** *om* As¹A². 13 **Lenea** Linea SoAdA². 13-15 **Ordinis . . . indignus** inter lectores sacre theologie minimus et indignus Ordinis Beate Dei Genetricis Marie de Monte Carmeli As¹. 20 \***luna** *(from* S¹SoAs¹RAdA²*)* prima LA¹. 22 **1463** 1462 As¹. 26 \***subsequentis** *(from* S¹A¹SoAs¹RAd*)* subsequent L. 28 **vulgarium** vulgaria Ad. **et** *(1st) om* S¹A¹Ad. 29 **quantitates** conjunciones eciam solis et lune et opposiciones quantitates As¹A². **eciam** *om* Ad. 30 **aurore** aurorem As¹A². 30-31 **inicium . . . noctem** *om* As¹A². 32-33 **ab . . . temporum** *om*

# PROLOGUS

Quia Christus Jesus, mediator dei et hominum, ipso attestante est Alpha et Omega, principium et finis, qui est, qui erat, et qui venturus est. Apocalypsis Primo. A quo, secundum beatum Augustinum super Johannem omelia prima, omnia creata originem sumunt et prin- 5
cipium, et ad quem, tanquam ad finem, universa ordinari debent et reduci. Hinc est quod, ad eius laudem et magnificenciam et genitricis sue beate, Marie intemerate virginis, nostri ordinis patrone specialis, necnon ad peticionem et complacenciam illustrissimi principis, 10
Domini Johannis, Regis Castelle et Legionis et Ducis Lancastrie, presens kalendarium ego, Frater Nicholaus de Lenea Ordinis Beate Marie Genitricis Dei, de Monte Carmeli, inter lectores sacre theologie minimus et indignus, composui anno eiusdem Domini Nostri Jesu 15
Christi 1386, pro quatuor ciclis decennovenalibus immediate sequentibus. Et incipiet istud kalendarium terminato kalendario Reverendi Magistri Walteri Elwedene, videlicet anno Christi 1387, primo die mensis Januarii, luna currente per unum. Et durabit per sextos 20
et septuagesimos annos, videlicet usque ad annum Domini 1463. Factum est autem istud kalendarium ad longitudinem et latitudinem civitatis Oxoniensis, in quo, juxta morem astrologorum, dies naturalis a meridie diei precedentis computatur usque ad meridiem 25
diei subsequentis. Et docet invenire gradum solis et eius minutum pro quolibet die anni; quantitates dierum artificialium vulgarium et crepusculorum matutini et vespertini; quantitates eciam temporum a media nocte usque ad aurore inicium; et a principio noctis obscure 30
usque ad mediam noctem; et a noctis medio usque ad ortum solis; et ab eius occasu usque ad mediam noctem.

lengths of the times from noon until sunset, and from sunrise until noon, and from noon until the end of evening twilight, and from the beginning of dawn until noon. Next it shows by means of the altitude of the sun and the shadow of a man, or even that of any thing set up perpendicularly, what may be the hour of the clock and the minute at any time of the artificial day. It also shows how to determine the ascendants and the beginnings of the twelve houses for any hour of the day. It also sets out clearly the conjunctions of the sun and the moon and the oppositions; the eclipses, their beginnings, durations, endings, diagrams or lengths of time of occultation. Moreover at the end of this are put tables of the eclipse of the sun and moon for the four Metonic cycles with the non-completed years, the months, and the days of Christ: specifically in the lunar table, with the true opposition and the magnitude of the eclipse with the times of starting, and the interval from start until maximum occultation, and its duration. In the table of the solar eclipse is written the observed conjunction, the magnitude of the eclipse, the interval from start until maximum occultation, and the duration of the eclipse. Above the diagrams of the solar and lunar eclipses are written the non-completed years and months of Christ in which eclipses will occur and the time of their beginnings. After this are put six other tables: the first for finding the ascendant and the beginnings of the rest of the houses, the second for investigating the dignities and strengths of the planets in the signs, the third for knowing for each hour of the day and night which planet is dominant or reigns, the fourth for discovering for every day of the year in what sign and degree of that sign the moon was according to its average rate of motion, the fifth for determining the movable feasts for any past or

As¹A². 32-36 **et ab . . . meridiem** *om* Ad. 35 **finem . . . vespertini** noctem obscuretatem As¹; noctis obscuretatem A². 35-36 **et ab . . . meridiem** *om* As¹A². 37 **umbram** umbra Ad. 38 **cuiuscumque** cuiuslibet A². 39 **et . . . minutum** *om* Ad. **minutum . . . tempore** *om* A². 40 **eciam** in As¹. **accipere ascenciones** *om* A². **ascenciones** ascendens A¹. 40-41 **Docet . . . diei** *om* Ad. 41-42 *****Conjuncciones** (*from* S¹A¹SoRAd) Conjucciones L; *om* As¹A². 42 **eciam** *om* As¹A². **opposiciones eclipses** *om* As¹A². **eclipses** eclipsium A¹. 43 **incepciones . . . duraciones** incepciones earum et duraciones As¹A²; et earum Ad. **fines** ac As¹A². **fines figuras** *om* Ad. 43-44 **seu quantitates** *om* As¹AdA². 44-51 **In . . . solis** *om* As¹AdA². 44-61 **In . . . quinta** *om* Ad. 45 **eclipsis** eclipsium A¹. 48 **eclipsis** vero S¹. 50 **visa** vera R. 51 **eclipsis** (*1st*) eclipsium S¹A¹. **eclipsis** (*2nd*) eclipsium A¹SoR. 51-56 **et** (*2nd*) **. . . secunda** *om* As¹. 54 **pro** *om* S¹A¹. 56 **ad investigandum** alia inveniendum As¹. **et**

Declarat eciam quantitates temporum a meridie usque
ad solis occasum, et ab eius ortu usque ad meridiem, et
a meridie usque ad finem crepusculi vespertini, et ab    35
aurore inicio usque ad meridiem. Consequenter osten-
dit per altitudinem solis et umbram hominis, ac eciam
cuiuscumque rei perpendiculariter erecte, que sit hora
de clok et quantum minutum omni tempore diei artificialis. Docet eciam accipere ascenciones et principia    40
duodecim domorum pro qualibet hora diei. Conjuncciones eciam solis et lune et opposiciones; eclipses,
incepciones earum, duraciones, fines, figuras seu quantitates aperte demonstrat. In fine autem eiusdem ponuntur tabule eclipsis solis et lune pro quatuor ciclis    45
decemnovenalibus cum annis Christi, mensibus, et diebus imperfectis: in tabula vero lune cum vera oppo-
sicione et punctis eclipsis cum temporibus casus, et
dimidie more, et duracione eius. In tabula eclipsis solis
scribitur visa conjunccio, punctus eclipsis, tempus ca-   50
sus, et duracio eclipsis. Supra figuras eclipsis solis et
lune scribuntur anni Christi et menses imperfecti in
quibus erunt eclipses et tempus incepcionum earum.
Post quas ponuntur sex alie tabule: prima pro ascendente et ceterarum domorum iniciis inveniendis; se-      55
cunda ad investigandum dignitates et fortitudines planetarum in signis; tercia ad cognoscendum pro qualibet
hora diei vel noctis quis planeta dominatur seu regnat;
quarta ad inveniendum pro quolibet die anni in quo
signo et gradu signi luna fuerit secundum eius motum    60
medium;  quinta  pro  festis  mobilibus  inveniendis

fortitudines *om* As¹. 57–58 **qualibet . . . regnat** similiter quis planeta
dominatur in omni hora diei vel noctis Ad. 58 **regnat** *add* Explicit A²; *end of
Prologue in* A². 59 **quarta** alia As¹A²; similiter Ad. 61 **medium** et Ad. **quinta**

future time, the sixth and last for the continuation of the motion of the sun. Finally, to complete the entire work the canons are inserted by means of which, using the altitude of the sun and an almanac, one may choose the proper time for bloodletting, and purging, and receiving medicines. Further, the explanations of the foregoing are placed at the end of this calendar.

**pro** Ponuntur eciam in fine quedam tabule pro As[1]; Ponuntur eciam quedam tabule pro A[2]. 62 **futuro** *end of Prologue in* Ad. 62–63 **sexta . . . solis** *in marginal gloss* So; *om* R. **sexta . . . Postea** *om* As[1]. 63 **ultima** *add* tabula S[1]A[1]. 62–68 **sexta . . . kalendarii** *om* AdA[2]. 67 **vero** *add* punctorum SoR. 67–68

pro quolibet tempore preterite vel futuro; sexta et ultima pro continuacione motus solis. Postea pro complemento tocius operis ponuntur canones per quos, mediante altitudine solis et almanak, eligi potest tempus aptum pro minucionibus, et purgacionibus, ac medicinis recipiendis. Declaraciones vero precedencium ponuntur in fine huius kalendarii. 65

**Declaraciones . . . kalendarii** *om* S¹A¹As¹. 68 **fine** secundo folio A²; tabula ad investigandum dignitates planetarum in signis in fine As¹.

**Numerus dierum**

# JANUARIUS

| 1 | 3 | a | **KL** | Circumcisio Domini |
|---|---|---|---|---|
| 2 | | b | 4 Nonas | Octava Sancti Stephani |
| 3 | 11 | c | 3 Nonas | Octava Sancti Johannis |
| 4 | | d | 2 Nonas | Octava Sanctorum innocencium |
| 5 | 19 | e | Nonis | Octava Sancti Thome |
| 6 | 8 | f | 8 Idus | Epiphania Domini |
| 7 | | g | 7 Idus | |
| 8 | 16 | a | 6 Idus | Sancti Inciani sociorum eius martyrum |
| 9 | 5 | b | 5 Idus | |
| 10 | | c | 4 Idus | |
| 11 | 13 | d | 3 Idus | |
| 12 | 2 | e | 2 Idus | |
| 13 | | f | Idibus | Octava Epiphanie |
| 14 | 10 | g | 19 Kl. | Sancti Felicis confessoris |
| 15 | | a | 18 Kl. | Sancti Mauri abbatis |
| 16 | 18 | b | 17 Kl. | Sancti Marcelli pape et martyris |
| 17 | 7 | c | 16 Kl. | Sancti Sulpicii episcopi et confessoris |
| 18 | | d | 15 Kl. | Sancte Prisce virginis et martyris |
| 19 | 15 | e | 14 Kl. | Sancti Wulfstani episcopi et confessoris |
| 20 | 4 | f | 13 Kl. | Sanctorum Fabiani et Sebastiani |
| 21 | | g | 12 Kl. | Sancte Agnetis virginis et martyris |
| 22 | 12 | a | 12 Kl. | Sancti Vincencii martyris |
| 23 | 1 | b | 10 Kl. | |
| 24 | | c | 9 Kl. | |
| 25 | 9 | d | 8 Kl. | Conversio Sancti Pauli |
| 26 | | e | 7 Kl. | |
| 27 | 17 | f | 6 Kl. | Sancti Juliani episcopi et confessoris |
| 28 | 6 | g | 5 Kl. | Sancte Agnetis secunde |
| 29 | | a | 4 Kl. | |
| 30 | 14 | b | 3 Kl. | Sancte Batildis regine et virginis |
| 31 | 3 | c | 2 Kl. | |

Variant readings for this month are listed on p. 136.

| Numerus dierum | Verus locus solis | | Quantitates diei artificialis | | Quantitates diei vulgaris | | Quantitates utriusque crepusculorum matutini et vespertini | |
|---|---|---|---|---|---|---|---|---|
| | g. | m. | h. | m. | h. | m. | h. | m. |
| | Capricornus | | | | | | | |
| 1 | 20 | 14 | 7 | 52 | 12 | 10 | 2 | 9 |
| 2 | 21 | 16 | 7 | 54 | 12 | 12 | 2 | 9 |
| 3 | 22 | 17 | 7 | 57 | 12 | 15 | 2 | 9 |
| 4 | 23 | 18 | 7 | 59 | 12 | 17 | 2 | 9 |
| 5 | 24 | 19 | 8 | 1 | 12 | 17 | 2 | 8 |
| 6 | 25 | 20 | 8 | 4 | 12 | 20 | 2 | 8 |
| 7 | 26 | 22 | 8 | 6 | 12 | 22 | 2 | 8 |
| 8 | 27 | 23 | 8 | 9 | 12 | 23 | 2 | 7 |
| 9 | 28 | 24 | 8 | 12 | 12 | 26 | 2 | 7 |
| 10 | 29 | 25 | 8 | 15 | 12 | 29 | 2 | 7 |
| | Aquarius | | | | | | | |
| 11 | 0 | 27 | 8 | 17 | 12 | 29 | 2 | 6 |
| 12 | 1 | 28 | 8 | 20 | 12 | 32 | 2 | 6 |
| 13 | 2 | 29 | 8 | 23 | 12 | 35 | 2 | 6 |
| 14 | 3 | 30 | 8 | 26 | 12 | 36 | 2 | 5 |
| 15 | 4 | 31 | 8 | 29 | 12 | 39 | 2 | 5 |
| 16 | 5 | 32 | 8 | 32 | 12 | 42 | 2 | 5 |
| 17 | 6 | 33 | 8 | 36 | 12 | 44 | 2 | 4 |
| 18 | 7 | 34 | 8 | 39 | 12 | 47 | 2 | 4 |
| 19 | 8 | 35 | 8 | 42 | 12 | 50 | 2 | 4 |
| 20 | 9 | 36 | 8 | 45 | 12 | 51 | 2 | 3 |
| 21 | 10 | 37 | 8 | 49 | 12 | 55 | 2 | 3 |
| 22 | 11 | 38 | 8 | 52 | 12 | 58 | 2 | 3 |
| 23 | 12 | 39 | 8 | 56 | 13 | 0 | 2 | 2 |
| 24 | 13 | 40 | 8 | 59 | 13 | 3 | 2 | 2 |
| 25 | 14 | 40 | 9 | 3 | 13 | 7 | 2 | 2 |
| 26 | 15 | 41 | 9 | 6 | 13 | 10 | 2 | 2 |
| 27 | 16 | 42 | 9 | 10 | 13 | 12 | 2 | 1 |
| 28 | 17 | 42 | 9 | 14 | 13 | 16 | 2 | 1 |
| 29 | 18 | 43 | 9 | 17 | 13 | 19 | 2 | 1 |
| 30 | 19 | 44 | 9 | 21 | 13 | 21 | 2 | 0 |
| 31 | 20 | 44 | 9 | 25 | 13 | 25 | 2 | 0 |

Translations of Latin headings are to be found in the introduction, pp. 11-25.

# JANUARIUS

| | Primus Ciclus | | | | Secundus Ciclus | | | | Tercius | |
|---|---|---|---|---|---|---|---|---|---|---|
| Numerus dierum | Ciclus Conjunccionis | Tempus vere conjunccionis | Ciclus Opposicionis | Tempus vere opposicionis | Ciclus Conjunccionis | Tempus vere conjunccionis | Ciclus Opposicionis | Tempus vere opposicionis | Ciclus Conjunccionis | Tempus vere conjunccionis |
| | | h. m. | | h. m. | | h. m. | | h. m. | | h. m. |
| 1 | 19 | 21 46 | 15 | 4 20 | | | 15 | 18 16 | 19 | 23 49 |
| 2 | | | 4 | 13 51 | 19 | 14 27 | 4 | 14 22 | | |
| 3 | 8 | 5 24 | 12 | 21 18 | 8 | 6 22 | 12 | 21 57 | | |
| 4 | 16 | 13 47 | | | 16 | 13 23 | | | 8 | 3 58 |
| 5 | | | 1 | 16 37 | | | 1 | 7 3 | 16 / 5 | 13 57 / 20 52 |
| 6 | 5 | 13 24 | | | 5 | 1 14 | 9 | 20 22 | | |
| 7 | | | 9 | 10 41 | 13 | 16 24 | | | 13 | 6 43 |
| 8 | 13 | 8 12 | | | | | 17 | 13 12 | | |
| 9 | | | 17 | 5 36 | | | | | 2 | 10 31 |
| 10 | 2 | 13 9 | | | 2 | 2 37 | 6 | 22 53 | | |
| 11 | 10 | 23 26 | 6 | 6 41 | 10 | 18 17 | | | 10 | 5 27 |
| 12 | | | 14 / 3 | 15 31 / 22 47 | | | 14 | 12 52 | 18 | 22 40 |
| 13 | 18 / 7 | 7 11 / 15 52 | | | 18 | 6 20 | 3 | 22 37 | | |
| 14 | | | 11 | 9 54 | 7 | 14 7 | | | 7 | 15 7 |
| 15 | 15 | 4 54 | | | 15 | 22 24 | 11 | 5 59 | 15 | 22 12 |
| 16 | | | 19 | 0 45 | 4 | 21 29 | 19 | 15 33 | | |
| 17 | 4 | 13 48 | | | | | 8 | 18 40 | 4 | 9 36 |
| 18 | | | 8 | 10 53 | 12 | 16 9 | | | | |
| 19 | 12 | 7 19 | | | | | 16 | 13 37 | 12 | 0 32 |
| 20 | | | 16 | 2 58 | 1 | 21 37 | | | 1 | 10 40 |
| 21 | 1 | 0 40 | 5 | 16 21 | | | 5 | 15 18 | | |
| 22 | 9 | 7 52 | 13 | 23 18 | 9 | 8 4 | | | 9 | 2 40 |
| 23 | 17 | 15 5 | | | 17 | 15 55 | 13 | 0 13 | 17 | 14 54 |
| 24 | | | 2 | 13 21 | | | 2 | 7 21 | 6 | 22 50 |
| 25 | 6 | 9 4 | | | 6 | 0 22 | 10 | 18 14 | | |
| 26 | | | 10 | 5 37 | 14 | 13 6 | | | 14 | 6 57 |
| 27 | 14 | 2 46 | | | | | 18 | 8 49 | | |
| 28 | 3 | 11 26 | 18 | 0 14 | 3 | 21 42 | | | 3 | 5 26 |
| 29 | | | 7 | 6 15 | | | 7 | 18 50 | | |
| 30 | 11 | 0 7 | 15 | 17 1 | 11 | 15 22 | | | 11 | 0 3 |
| 31 | 19 | 9 16 | | | | | 15 | 11 8 | 19 | 18 38 |

# Ciclus     Quartus Ciclus

| Ciclus Opposicionis | Tempus vere opposicionis | Ciclus Conjunccionis | Tempus vere conjunccionis | Ciclus Opposicionis | Tempus vere opposicionis | Quantitates a noctis medio ad auroram | Quantitates a noctis medio ad solis ortum | Quantitates a meridie ad solis occasum | Quantitates a meridie ad noctem obscuram |
|---|---|---|---|---|---|---|---|---|---|
|  | h. m. |  | h. m. |  | h. m. | h. m. | h. m. | h. m. | h. m. |
| 15 | 2 21 | 19 | 7 53 |  |  | 5 55 | 8 4 | 3 56 | 6 5 |
|  |  |  |  | 4 | 21 14 | 5 54 | 8 3 | 3 57 | 6 6 |
| 4 | 9 43 | 8 | 18 6 |  |  | 5 53 | 8 2 | 3 58 | 6 7 |
| 12 | 21 22 |  |  | 12 | 14 11 | 5 52 | 8 1 | 3 59 | 6 8 |
| 1 | 4 57 | 16 | 9 24 |  |  | 5 52 | 8 0 | 4 0 | 6 8 |
| 9 | 13 24 | 5 | 21 31 | 1 | 5 55 | 5 50 | 7 58 | 4 2 | 6 10 |
|  |  |  |  | 9 | 12 56 | 5 49 | 7 57 | 4 3 | 6 11 |
| 17 | 0 56 | 13 / 2 | 4 31 / 20 7 | 17 | 20 28 | 5 49 | 7 56 | 4 4 | 6 11 |
|  |  |  |  | 6 | 16 12 | 5 47 | 7 54 | 4 6 | 6 13 |
| 6 | 8 2 | 10 | 13 3 |  |  | 5 46 | 7 53 | 4 7 | 6 14 |
|  |  |  |  | 14 | 10 18 | 5 46 | 7 52 | 4 8 | 6 14 |
| 14 | 2 23 | 18 | 7 53 |  |  | 5 44 | 7 50 | 4 10 | 6 16 |
| 3 | 23 2 |  |  | 3 | 18 7 | 5 43 | 7 49 | 4 11 | 6 17 |
|  |  | 7 | 12 33 |  |  | 5 42 | 7 47 | 4 13 | 6 18 |
| 11 | 6 43 | 15 | 22 38 | 11 | 5 57 | 5 41 | 7 46 | 4 14 | 6 19 |
| 19 | 13 42 |  |  | 19 | 14 39 | 5 39 | 7 44 | 4 16 | 6 21 |
|  |  | 4 | 5 37 | 8 | 22 0 | 5 38 | 7 42 | 4 18 | 6 22 |
| 8 | 4 33 | 12 | 15 12 |  |  | 5 37 | 7 41 | 4 19 | 6 23 |
| 16 | 21 14 |  |  | 16 | 9 17 | 5 35 | 7 39 | 4 21 | 6 25 |
|  |  | 1 | 18 29 |  |  | 5 35 | 7 38 | 4 22 | 6 25 |
| 5 | 7 3 |  |  | 5 | 16 0 | 5 33 | 7 36 | 4 24 | 6 27 |
| 13 | 21 16 | 9 | 13 26 |  |  | 5 31 | 7 34 | 4 26 | 6 29 |
|  |  |  |  | 13 | 10 26 | 5 30 | 7 32 | 4 28 | 6 30 |
| 2 | 7 21 | 17 / 6 | 6 48 / 23 47 | 2 | 7 38 | 5 29 | 7 31 | 4 29 | 6 31 |
| 10 | 14 38 |  |  | 10 | 15 26 | 5 27 | 7 29 | 4 31 | 6 33 |
| 18 | 23 59 | 14 | 6 54 | 18 | 22 23 | 5 25 | 7 27 | 4 33 | 6 35 |
|  |  | 3 | 17 55 |  |  | 5 24 | 7 25 | 4 35 | 6 36 |
|  |  |  |  | 7 | 12 46 | 5 22 | 7 23 | 4 37 | 6 38 |
| 7 | 2 34 | 11 | 8 34 |  |  | 5 21 | 7 22 | 4 38 | 6 39 |
| 15 | 21 30 |  |  | 15 | 5 11 | 5 20 | 7 20 | 4 40 | 6 40 |
|  |  | 19 | 2 24 |  |  | 5 18 | 7 18 | 4 42 | 6 42 |

# JANUARIUS

Altitudines solis et longitudines umbrarum cuiuslibet

| Numerus dierum | 8 4 altitudines solis g. m. | 8 4 umbre hominis pedes | 8 4 umbre hominis partes | 9 3 altitudines solis g. m. | 9 3 umbre hominis pedes | 9 3 umbre hominis partes |
|---|---|---|---|---|---|---|
| 1 | 0 0 | 0 | 0 | 6 20 | 54 | 21 |
| 2 | 0 0 | 0 | 0 | 6 29 | 53 | 7 |
| 3 | 0 0 | 0 | 0 | 6 38 | 51 | 53 |
| 4 | 0 0 | 0 | 0 | 6 46 | 50 | 47 |
| 5 | 0 6 | 3439 | 26 | 6 56 | 49 | 25 |
| 6 | 0 15 | 1375 | 10 | 7 6 | 48 | 15 |
| 7 | 0 25 | 825 | 0 | 7 16 | 47 | 14 |
| 8 | 0 35 | 589 | 15 | 7 28 | 46 | 0 |
| 9 | 0 45 | 458 | 17 | 7 39 | 44 | 53 |
| 10 | 0 56 | 368 | 15 | 7 50 | 43 | 45 |
| 11 | 1 7 | 323 | 40 | 8 2 | 42 | 34 |
| 12 | 1 17 | 295 | 1 | 8 14 | 41 | 36 |
| 13 | 1 30 | 257 | 46 | 8 27 | 40 | 33 |
| 14 | 1 41 | 226 | 15 | 8 40 | 39 | 30 |
| 15 | 1 52 | 194 | 44 | 8 52 | 38 | 32 |
| 16 | 2 6 | 166 | 5 | 9 6 | 37 | 30 |
| 17 | 2 18 | 154 | 37 | 9 19 | 36 | 40 |
| 18 | 2 32 | 141 | 15 | 9 32 | 35 | 49 |
| 19 | 2 45 | 128 | 49 | 9 46 | 34 | 55 |
| 20 | 2 59 | 115 | 27 | 10 1 | 33 | 58 |
| 21 | 3 13 | 108 | 17 | 10 15 | 33 | 14 |
| 22 | 3 27 | 101 | 36 | 10 31 | 32 | 24 |
| 23 | 3 42 | 94 | 26 | 10 46 | 31 | 37 |
| 24 | 3 56 | 87 | 46 | 11 2 | 30 | 47 |
| 25 | 4 11 | 82 | 41 | 11 17 | 30 | 7 |
| 26 | 4 25 | 78 | 39 | 11 33 | 29 | 25 |
| 27 | 4 41 | 74 | 3 | 11 50 | 28 | 40 |
| 28 | 4 57 | 69 | 27 | 12 7 | 27 | 58 |
| 29 | 5 14 | 65 | 54 | 12 23 | 27 | 22 |
| 30 | 5 29 | 63 | 2 | 12 40 | 26 | 44 |
| 31 | 5 45 | 59 | 58 | 12 57 | 26 | 6 |

hominis stature sex pedum in horis de clok

| 10 | | | 11 | | | 12 a.m. | | |
| 2 | | | 1 | | | 0 p.m. | | |
| altitudines solis | umbre hominis | | altitudines solis | umbre hominis | | altitudines solis | umbre hominis | |
| g. m. | pedes | partes | g. m. | pedes | partes | g. m. | pedes | partes |
|---|---|---|---|---|---|---|---|---|
| 11 36 | 29 | 17 | 14 58 | 22 | 27 | 16  8 | 20 | 45 |
| 11 47 | 28 | 47 | 15  9 | 22 | 10 | 16 19 | 20 | 31 |
| 11 56 | 28 | 24 | 15 19 | 21 | 55 | 16 29 | 20 | 18 |
| 12  6 | 28 |  0 | 15 29 | 21 | 40 | 16 39 | 20 |  5 |
| 12 15 | 27 | 40 | 15 39 | 21 | 26 | 16 48 | 19 | 53 |
| 12 26 | 27 | 15 | 15 50 | 21 | 10 | 16 59 | 19 | 39 |
| 12 37 | 26 | 51 | 16  1 | 20 | 54 | 17 11 | 19 | 25 |
| 12 50 | 26 | 22 | 16 14 | 20 | 37 | 17 24 | 19 |  9 |
| 13  0 | 25 | 59 | 16 26 | 20 | 22 | 17 36 | 18 | 55 |
| 13 12 | 25 | 36 | 16 38 | 20 |  6 | 17 49 | 18 | 40 |
| 13 25 | 25 | 11 | 16 50 | 19 | 50 | 18  2 | 18 | 25 |
| 13 37 | 24 | 48 | 17  3 | 19 | 34 | 18 15 | 18 | 12 |
| 13 50 | 24 | 23 | 17 17 | 19 | 18 | 18 29 | 17 | 57 |
| 14  3 | 23 | 59 | 17 31 | 19 |  1 | 18 43 | 17 | 43 |
| 14 16 | 23 | 38 | 17 44 | 18 | 46 | 18 56 | 17 | 29 |
| 14 31 | 23 | 12 | 18  0 | 18 | 27 | 19 11 | 17 | 15 |
| 14 45 | 22 | 49 | 18 15 | 18 | 12 | 19 26 | 17 |  1 |
| 15  0 | 22 | 23 | 18 30 | 17 | 56 | 19 42 | 16 | 46 |
| 15 15 | 22 |  1 | 18 46 | 17 | 39 | 19 59 | 16 | 30 |
| 15 30 | 21 | 39 | 19  1 | 17 | 25 | 20 14 | 16 | 17 |
| 15 46 | 21 | 16 | 19 17 | 17 | 10 | 20 30 | 16 |  4 |
| 16  3 | 20 | 52 | 19 34 | 16 | 54 | 20 48 | 15 | 48 |
| 16 19 | 20 | 31 | 19 52 | 16 | 37 | 21  5 | 15 | 34 |
| 16 35 | 20 | 10 | 20  9 | 16 | 21 | 21 23 | 15 | 20 |
| 16 51 | 19 | 49 | 20 26 | 16 |  7 | 21 40 | 15 |  7 |
| 17  7 | 19 | 29 | 20 42 | 15 | 53 | 21 57 | 14 | 53 |
| 17 25 | 19 |  8 | 21  1 | 15 | 37 | 22 16 | 14 | 40 |
| 17 42 | 18 | 48 | 21 20 | 15 | 22 | 22 34 | 14 | 27 |
| 18  1 | 18 | 26 | 21 38 | 15 |  8 | 22 53 | 14 | 13 |
| 18 18 | 18 |  8 | 21 56 | 14 | 54 | 23 11 | 14 |  1 |
| 18 37 | 17 | 49 | 22 14 | 14 | 41 | 23 32 | 13 | 47 |

# FEBRUARIUS

| | | | | |
|---|---|---|---|---|
| 1 | | *d* | **KL** | Sancti Ignacii episcopi |
| 2 | 11 | *e* | 4 Nonas | Purificacio Beate Marie |
| 3 | 19 | *f* | 3 Nonas | Sancti Blasii episcopi et martyris |
| 4 | 8 | *g* | 2 Nonas | |
| 5 | | ᴀ | Nonis | Sancte Agathe virginis et martyris |
| 6 | 16 | *b* | 8 Idus | Sanctorum Vedasti et Amandi |
| 7 | 5 | *c* | 7 Idus | |
| 8 | | *d* | 6 Idus | |
| 9 | 13 | *e* | 5 Idus | |
| 10 | 2 | *f* | 4 Idus | Sancte Scolastice virginis non martyris |
| 11 | | *g* | 3 Idus | |
| 12 | 10 | ᴀ | 2 Idus | |
| 13 | | *b* | Idibus | |
| 14 | 18 | *c* | 16 Kl. | Sancti Valentini martyris |
| 15 | 7 | *d* | 15 Kl. | |
| 16 | | *e* | 14 Kl. | Sancte Juliane virginis et martyris |
| 17 | 15 | *f* | 13 Kl. | |
| 18 | 4 | *g* | 12 Kl. | |
| 19 | 19 | ᴀ | 11 Kl. | |
| 20 | 12 | *b* | 10 Kl. | |
| 21 | 1 | *c* | 9 Kl. | |
| 22 | | *d* | 8 Kl. | Cathedra Sancti Petri |
| 23 | 9 | *e* | 7 Kl. | |
| 24 | | *f* | 6 Kl. | Sancti Mathie apostoli |
| 25 | 17 | *g* | 5 Kl. | |
| 26 | 6 | ᴀ | 4 Kl. | |
| 27 | | *b* | 3 Kl. | |
| 28 | 14 | *c* | 2 Kl. | |

Variant readings for this month are listed on p. 136.

| Numerus dierum | Verus locus solis | | Quantitates diei artificialis | | Quantitates diei vulgaris | | Quantitates utriusque crepusculorum matutini et vespertini | |
|---|---|---|---|---|---|---|---|---|
| | g. | m. | h. | m. | h. | m. | h. | m. |
| | Aquarius | | | | | | | |
| 1 | 21 | 45 | 9 | 28 | 13 | 28 | 2 | 0 |
| 2 | 22 | 45 | 9 | 32 | 13 | 22 | 2 | 0 |
| 3 | 23 | 46 | 9 | 36 | 13 | 34 | 1 | 59 |
| 4 | 24 | 47 | 9 | 40 | 13 | 38 | 1 | 59 |
| 5 | 25 | 47 | 9 | 44 | 13 | 42 | 1 | 59 |
| 6 | 26 | 47 | 9 | 47 | 13 | 45 | 1 | 59 |
| 7 | 27 | 48 | 9 | 51 | 13 | 49 | 1 | 59 |
| 8 | 28 | 48 | 9 | 55 | 13 | 51 | 1 | 58 |
| 9 | 29 | 48 | 9 | 59 | 13 | 55 | 1 | 58 |
| | Pisces | | | | | | | |
| 10 | 0 | 49 | 10 | 3 | 13 | 59 | 1 | 58 |
| 11 | 1 | 49 | 10 | 7 | 14 | 3 | 1 | 58 |
| 12 | 2 | 49 | 10 | 11 | 14 | 7 | 1 | 58 |
| 13 | 3 | 49 | 10 | 15 | 14 | 11 | 1 | 58 |
| 14 | 4 | 49 | 10 | 19 | 14 | 15 | 1 | 58 |
| 15 | 5 | 50 | 10 | 23 | 14 | 19 | 1 | 58 |
| 16 | 6 | 50 | 10 | 27 | 14 | 21 | 1 | 57 |
| 17 | 7 | 50 | 10 | 31 | 14 | 25 | 1 | 57 |
| 18 | 8 | 50 | 10 | 35 | 14 | 29 | 1 | 57 |
| 19 | 9 | 50 | 10 | 39 | 14 | 33 | 1 | 57 |
| 20 | 10 | 50 | 10 | 43 | 14 | 37 | 1 | 57 |
| 21 | 11 | 50 | 10 | 47 | 14 | 41 | 1 | 57 |
| 22 | 12 | 49 | 10 | 51 | 14 | 45 | 1 | 57 |
| 23 | 13 | 49 | 10 | 55 | 14 | 49 | 1 | 57 |
| 24 | 14 | 49 | 10 | 59 | 14 | 53 | 1 | 57 |
| 25 | 15 | 48 | 11 | 3 | 14 | 57 | 1 | 57 |
| 26 | 16 | 48 | 11 | 7 | 15 | 1 | 1 | 57 |
| 27 | 17 | 48 | 11 | 11 | 15 | 5 | 1 | 57 |
| 28 | 18 | 47 | 11 | 15 | 15 | 11 | 1 | 58 |

Translations of Latin headings are to be found in the introduction, pp. 11-25.

# FEBRUARIUS

| Numerus dierum | Primus Ciclus | | | | Secundus Ciclus | | | | Tercius | |
|---|---|---|---|---|---|---|---|---|---|---|
| | Ciclus Conjunccionis | Tempus vere conjunccionis | Ciclus Opposicionis | Tempus vere opposicionis | Ciclus Conjunccionis | Tempus vere conjunccionis | Ciclus Opposicionis | Tempus vere opposicionis | Ciclus Conjunccionis | Tempus vere conjunccionis |
| | | h. m. | | h. m. | | h. m. | | h. m. | | h. m. |
| 1 | 8 | 16 18 | 4 | 0 7 | 19 / 8 | 5 55 / 16 32 | | | 4 | 1 1 |
| 2 | | | 12 | 9 8 | 16 | 23 40 | 12 | 7 57 | 8 | 16 35 |
| 3 | 16 | 2 51 | | | | | 1 | 21 30 | | |
| 4 | | | 1 | 10 48 | 5 | 17 6 | | | 16 / 5 | 0 33 / 8 43 |
| 5 | 5 | 8 15 | | | | | 9 | 13 31 | 13 | 21 12 |
| 6 | | | 9 | 5 44 | 13 | 10 35 | | | | |
| 7 | 13 | 2 57 | 17 | 23 36 | | | 17 | 8 1 | | |
| 8 | | | | | 2 | 19 32 | | | 2 | 5 32 |
| 9 | 2 | 1 54 | 6 | 18 16 | | | 6 | 14 28 | 10 | 23 20 |
| 10 | 10 | 10 6 | | | 10 | 8 27 | | | | |
| 11 | 18 | 17 4 | 14 / 3 | 1 35 / 11 26 | 18 | 17 50 | 14 | 1 31 | 18 | 14 7 |
| 12 | 7 | 5 56 | | | | | 3 | 8 40 | | |
| 13 | 15 | 21 38 | 11 | 1 19 | 7 | 0 46 | 11 | 17 29 | 7 | 1 8 |
| 14 | | | 19 | 18 33 | 15 | 11 4 | | | 15 | 8 10 |
| 15 | | | | | 4 | 15 57 | 19 | 5 34 | | |
| 16 | 4 | 7 44 | | | | | 8 | 13 25 | 4 | 1 0 |
| 17 | 12 | 22 56 | 8 | 3 47 | 12 | 10 42 | | | 12 | 8 18 |
| 18 | | | 16 | 17 4 | | | 16 | 7 27 | | |
| 19 | 1 | 10 38 | | | 1 | 10 19 | | | 1 | 3 30 |
| 20 | 9 | 17 37 | 5 | 2 2 | 9 | 18 36 | 5 | 2 42 | 9 | 16 41 |
| 21 | | | 13 | 9 36 | | | 13 | 10 7 | | |
| 22 | 17 | 2 12 | | | 17 | 1 35 | 2 | 19 35 | 17 | 2 14 |
| 23 | | | 2 | 5 36 | 6 | 13 55 | | | 6 | 9 8 |
| 24 | 6 / 14 | 2 27 / 21 15 | 10 | 23 45 | | | 10 | 9 10 | 14 | 19 12 |
| 25 | | | 18 | 18 34 | 14 | 5 19 | | | | |
| 26 | | | | | 3 | 15 26 | 18 | 2 10 | 3 | 23 21 |
| 27 | 3 | 1 35 | 7 | 18 58 | | | 7 | 11 37 | | |
| 28 | 11 | 11 31 | | | 11 | 6 52 | | | 11 | 18 18 |

Ciclus     Quartus Ciclus

| Ciclus Opposicionis | Tempus vere opposicionis (h. m.) | Ciclus Conjunccionis | Tempus vere conjunccionis (h. m.) | Ciclus Opposicionis | Tempus vere opposicionis (h. m.) | Quantitates a noctis medio ad auroram (h. m.) | Quantitates a noctis medio ad solis ortum (h. m.) | Quantitates a meridie ad solis occasum (h. m.) | Quantitates a meridie ad noctem obscuram (h. m.) |
|---|---|---|---|---|---|---|---|---|---|
| 4 | 23 43 | | | 4 | 15 6 | 5 16 | 7 16 | 4 44 | 6 44 |
| | | 8 | 10 51 | | | 5 14 | 7 14 | 4 46 | 6 46 |
| 12 / 1 | 8 49 / 15 52 | 16 | 23 21 | 12 | 4 35 | 5 13 | 7 12 | 4 48 | 6 47 |
| | | | | 1 | 16 1 | 5 11 | 7 10 | 4 50 | 6 49 |
| 9 | 2 30 | 5 | 7 30 | 9 | 23 13 | 5 9 | 7 8 | 4 52 | 6 51 |
| 17 | 16 49 | 13 | 15 27 | | | 5 8 | 7 7 | 4 53 | 6 52 |
| | | 2 | 13 17 | 17 | 8 21 | 5 6 | 7 5 | 4 55 | 6 54 |
| | | | | 6 | 10 20 | 5 5 | 7 3 | 4 57 | 6 55 |
| 6 | 2 31 | 10 | 7 51 | | | 5 3 | 7 1 | 4 59 | 6 57 |
| 14 | 19 13 | | | 14 | 5 17 | 5 1 | 6 59 | 5 1 | 6 59 |
| | | 18 | 2 29 | | | 4 59 | 6 57 | 5 3 | 7 1 |
| 3 | 9 36 | | | 3 | 8 3 | 4 57 | 6 55 | 5 5 | 7 3 |
| 11 | 16 32 | 7 | 1 7 | 11 | 17 20 | 4 55 | 6 53 | 5 7 | 7 5 |
| | | 15 | 9 9 | | | 4 53 | 6 51 | 5 9 | 7 7 |
| 19 | 0 18 | 4 | 17 5 | 19 | 0 36 | 4 51 | 6 49 | 5 11 | 7 9 |
| 8 | 21 20 | | | 8 | 10 41 | 4 50 | 6 47 | 5 13 | 7 10 |
| | | 12 | 5 14 | | | 4 48 | 6 45 | 5 15 | 7 12 |
| 16 | 15 42 | | | 16 | 0 43 | 4 46 | 6 43 | 5 17 | 7 14 |
| 5 | 22 33 | 1 | 13 12 | | | 4 44 | 6 41 | 5 19 | 7 16 |
| | | | | 5 | 10 25 | 4 42 | 6 39 | 5 21 | 7 18 |
| 13 | 9 51 | 9 | 7 10 | | | 4 40 | 6 37 | 5 23 | 7 20 |
| 2 | 17 8 | 17 | 22 12 | 13 / 2 | 3 10 / 18 5 | 4 38 | 6 35 | 5 25 | 7 22 |
| | | 6 | 9 38 | | | 4 36 | 6 33 | 5 27 | 7 24 |
| 10 | 1 45 | 14 | 16 39 | 10 | 1 2 | 4 34 | 6 31 | 5 29 | 7 26 |
| 18 | 13 32 | | | 18 | 8 38 | 4 32 | 6 29 | 5 31 | 7 28 |
| | | 3 | 8 50 | | | 4 30 | 6 27 | 5 33 | 7 30 |
| 7 | 20 59 | | | 7 | 5 0 | 4 28 | 6 25 | 5 35 | 7 32 |
| | | 11 | 1 55 | 15 | 23 14 | 4 25 | 6 23 | 5 37 | 7 35 |

# FEBRUARIUS

## Altitudines solis et longitudines umbrarum cuiuslibet

| Numerus dierum | 7 / 5 altitudines solis g. m. | umbre hominis pedes | umbre hominis partes | 8 / 4 altitudines solis g. m. | umbre hominis pedes | umbre hominis partes | 9 / 3 altitudines solis g. m. | umbre hominis pedes | umbre hominis partes |
|---|---|---|---|---|---|---|---|---|---|
| 1  | 0 0  | 0 | 0  | 6 2   | 56 | 49 | 13 15 | 25 | 30 |
| 2  | 0 0  | 0 | 0  | 6 18  | 54 | 37 | 13 32 | 24 | 58 |
| 3  | 0 0  | 0 | 0  | 6 35  | 52 | 17 | 13 50 | 24 | 23 |
| 4  | 0 0  | 0 | 0  | 6 51  | 50 | 6  | 14 8  | 23 | 51 |
| 5  | 0 0  | 0 | 0  | 7 9   | 47 | 57 | 14 26 | 23 | 21 |
| 6  | 0 0  | 0 | 0  | 7 26  | 46 | 13 | 14 45 | 22 | 49 |
| 7  | 0 0  | 0 | 0  | 7 44  | 44 | 22 | 15 3  | 22 | 19 |
| 8  | 0 0  | 0 | 0  | 8 1   | 42 | 39 | 15 21 | 21 | 52 |
| 9  | 0 0  | 0 | 0  | 8 20  | 41 | 7  | 15 40 | 21 | 24 |
| 10 | 0 13 | 1586 | 38 | 8 38  | 39 | 40 | 15 59 | 20 | 56 |
| 11 | 0 31 | 665 | 15 | 8 56  | 38 | 12 | 16 19 | 20 | 31 |
| 12 | 0 48 | 429 | 39 | 9 14  | 36 | 59 | 16 38 | 20 | 6  |
| 13 | 1 6  | 326 | 32 | 9 33  | 35 | 45 | 16 57 | 19 | 41 |
| 14 | 1 23 | 277 | 49 | 9 50  | 34 | 40 | 17 16 | 19 | 19 |
| 15 | 1 41 | 226 | 15 | 10 10 | 33 | 30 | 17 36 | 18 | 55 |
| 16 | 1 58 | 177 | 33 | 10 28 | 32 | 33 | 17 57 | 18 | 31 |
| 17 | 2 16 | 156 | 32 | 10 46 | 31 | 37 | 18 17 | 18 | 9  |
| 18 | 2 34 | 139 | 20 | 11 5  | 30 | 39 | 18 36 | 17 | 50 |
| 19 | 2 53 | 121 | 11 | 11 24 | 29 | 48 | 18 57 | 17 | 28 |
| 20 | 3 11 | 109 | 14 | 11 44 | 28 | 55 | 19 17 | 17 | 10 |
| 21 | 3 29 | 100 | 39 | 12 3  | 28 | 7  | 19 37 | 16 | 51 |
| 22 | 3 47 | 92 | 3   | 12 21 | 27 | 27 | 19 57 | 16 | 32 |
| 23 | 4 6  | 84 | 7   | 12 41 | 26 | 42 | 20 17 | 16 | 15 |
| 24 | 4 25 | 78 | 39  | 13 0  | 25 | 59 | 20 37 | 15 | 58 |
| 25 | 4 43 | 73 | 29  | 13 20 | 25 | 21 | 20 59 | 15 | 39 |
| 26 | 5 2  | 68 | 12  | 13 40 | 24 | 42 | 21 20 | 15 | 22 |
| 27 | 5 20 | 64 | 45  | 13 59 | 24 | 6  | 21 40 | 15 | 7  |
| 28 | 5 39 | 61 | 7   | 14 18 | 23 | 34 | 22 0  | 14 | 51 |

hominis stature sex pedum in horis de clok 51 graduum

| | 10 | | | 11 | | | 12 a.m. | |
| | 2 | | | 1 | | | 0 p.m. | |
| altitudines solis | umbre hominis | | altitudines solis | umbre hominis | | altitudines solis | umbre hominis | |
| g. m. | pedes | partes | g. m. | pedes | partes | g. m. | pedes | partes |
|---|---|---|---|---|---|---|---|---|
| 18 55 | 17 | 30 | 22 33 | 14 | 27 | 23 51 | 13 | 34 |
| 19 13 | 17 | 13 | 22 53 | 14 | 13 | 24 10 | 13 | 22 |
| 19 32 | 16 | 56 | 23 14 | 13 | 59 | 24 30 | 13 | 10 |
| 19 52 | 16 | 37 | 23 34 | 13 | 45 | 24 51 | 12 | 58 |
| 20 11 | 16 | 20 | 23 54 | 13 | 32 | 25 11 | 12 | 46 |
| 20 30 | 16 | 4 | 24 14 | 13 | 20 | 25 32 | 12 | 34 |
| 20 50 | 15 | 47 | 24 34 | 13 | 8 | 25 52 | 12 | 23 |
| 21 9 | 15 | 31 | 24 55 | 12 | 55 | 26 13 | 12 | 11 |
| 21 29 | 15 | 15 | 25 15 | 12 | 44 | 26 34 | 12 | 0 |
| 21 49 | 15 | 0 | 25 36 | 12 | 32 | 26 56 | 11 | 48 |
| 22 9 | 14 | 45 | 25 57 | 12 | 20 | 27 17 | 11 | 38 |
| 22 29 | 14 | 30 | 26 18 | 12 | 8 | 27 38 | 11 | 28 |
| 22 51 | 14 | 14 | 26 41 | 11 | 56 | 28 1 | 11 | 17 |
| 23 12 | 14 | 0 | 27 2 | 11 | 46 | 28 23 | 11 | 7 |
| 23 33 | 13 | 46 | 27 25 | 11 | 34 | 28 46 | 10 | 56 |
| 23 55 | 13 | 31 | 27 47 | 11 | 24 | 29 7 | 10 | 47 |
| 24 15 | 13 | 19 | 28 9 | 11 | 13 | 29 30 | 10 | 37 |
| 24 35 | 13 | 7 | 28 30 | 11 | 4 | 29 52 | 10 | 27 |
| 24 58 | 12 | 54 | 28 53 | 10 | 53 | 30 15 | 10 | 17 |
| 25 20 | 12 | 41 | 29 16 | 10 | 43 | 30 39 | 10 | 8 |
| 25 41 | 12 | 29 | 29 38 | 10 | 33 | 31 1 | 9 | 59 |
| 26 1 | 12 | 17 | 30 0 | 10 | 23 | 31 23 | 9 | 50 |
| 26 22 | 12 | 6 | 30 22 | 10 | 15 | 31 46 | 9 | 41 |
| 26 45 | 11 | 54 | 30 46 | 10 | 5 | 32 9 | 9 | 33 |
| 27 7 | 11 | 43 | 31 8 | 9 | 56 | 32 33 | 9 | 24 |
| 27 29 | 11 | 32 | 31 30 | 9 | 48 | 32 56 | 9 | 15 |
| 27 50 | 11 | 22 | 31 53 | 9 | 39 | 33 20 | 9 | 7 |
| 28 12 | 11 | 12 | 32 16 | 9 | 30 | 33 43 | 8 | 59 |

# MARCIUS

| | | | | |
|---|---|---|---|---|
| 1 | 3 | *d* | **KL** | Sancti Davidi confessoris |
| 2 | | *e* | 6 Nonas | |
| 3 | 11 | *f* | 5 Nonas | |
| 4 | | *g* | 4 Nonas | |
| 5 | 19 | A | 3 Nonas | |
| 6 | 8 | *b* | 2 Nonas | |
| 7 | | *c* | Nonis | Sanctarum Perpetue et Felicitatis virginum |
| 8 | 16 | *d* | 8 Idus | Sancti Felicis confessoris |
| 9 | 5 | *e* | 7 Idus | |
| 10 | | *f* | 6 Idus | |
| 11 | 13 | *g* | 5 Idus | |
| | | | | |
| 12 | 2 | A | 4 Idus | Sancti Gregorii pape |
| 13 | | *b* | 3 Idus | |
| 14 | 10 | *c* | 2 Idus | |
| 15 | | *d* | Idibus | |
| 16 | 18 | *e* | 17 Kl. | |
| 17 | 7 | *f* | 16 Kl. | |
| 18 | | *g* | 15 Kl. | Sancti Edwardi regis et martyris |
| 19 | 15 | A | 14 Kl. | |
| 20 | 4 | *b* | 13 Kl. | |
| 21 | | *c* | 12 Kl. | Sancti Benedicti abbatis |
| 22 | 12 | *d* | 11 Kl. | |
| 23 | 1 | *e* | 10 Kl. | |
| 24 | | *f* | 9 Kl. | |
| 25 | 9 | *g* | 8 Kl. | Annunciacio Sancte Marie |
| 26 | | A | 7 Kl. | |
| 27 | 17 | *b* | 6 Kl. | |
| 28 | 6 | *c* | 5 Kl. | |
| 29 | | *d* | 4 Kl. | |
| 30 | 14 | *e* | 3 Kl. | |
| 31 | 3 | *f* | 2 Kl. | |

Variant readings for this month are listed on pp. 136–37.

| Numerus dierum | Verus locus solis | | Quantitates diei artificialis | | Quantitates diei vulgaris | | Quantitates utriusque crepusculorum matutini et vespertini | |
|---|---|---|---|---|---|---|---|---|
| | g. | m. | h. | m. | h. | m. | h. | m. |
| | Pisces | | | | | | | |
| 1 | 19 | 47 | 11 | 19 | 15 | 15 | 1 | 58 |
| 2 | 20 | 46 | 11 | 23 | 15 | 19 | 1 | 58 |
| 3 | 21 | 46 | 11 | 27 | 15 | 23 | 1 | 58 |
| 4 | 22 | 45 | 11 | 31 | 15 | 27 | 1 | 58 |
| 5 | 23 | 45 | 11 | 35 | 15 | 31 | 1 | 58 |
| 6 | 24 | 44 | 11 | 39 | 15 | 37 | 1 | 59 |
| 7 | 25 | 43 | 11 | 43 | 15 | 41 | 1 | 59 |
| 8 | 26 | 43 | 11 | 47 | 15 | 45 | 1 | 59 |
| 9 | 27 | 42 | 11 | 51 | 15 | 49 | 1 | 59 |
| 10 | 28 | 41 | 11 | 55 | 15 | 53 | 1 | 59 |
| 11 | 29 | 40 | 11 | 59 | 15 | 59 | 2 | 0 |
| | Aries | | | | | | | |
| 12 | 0 | 39 | 12 | 3 | 16 | 3 | 2 | 0 |
| 13 | 1 | 38 | 12 | 7 | 16 | 7 | 2 | 0 |
| 14 | 2 | 37 | 12 | 11 | 16 | 13 | 2 | 1 |
| 15 | 3 | 36 | 12 | 15 | 16 | 17 | 2 | 1 |
| 16 | 4 | 35 | 12 | 19 | 16 | 23 | 2 | 2 |
| 17 | 5 | 34 | 12 | 23 | 16 | 27 | 2 | 2 |
| 18 | 6 | 33 | 12 | 27 | 16 | 31 | 2 | 2 |
| 19 | 7 | 32 | 12 | 31 | 16 | 37 | 2 | 3 |
| 20 | 8 | 31 | 12 | 35 | 16 | 41 | 2 | 3 |
| 21 | 9 | 29 | 12 | 39 | 16 | 47 | 2 | 4 |
| 22 | 10 | 28 | 12 | 43 | 16 | 51 | 2 | 4 |
| 23 | 11 | 27 | 12 | 47 | 16 | 57 | 2 | 5 |
| 24 | 12 | 26 | 12 | 51 | 17 | 3 | 2 | 6 |
| 25 | 13 | 24 | 12 | 54 | 17 | 6 | 2 | 6 |
| 26 | 14 | 23 | 12 | 58 | 17 | 12 | 2 | 7 |
| 27 | 15 | 22 | 13 | 2 | 17 | 16 | 2 | 7 |
| 28 | 16 | 20 | 13 | 6 | 17 | 22 | 2 | 8 |
| 29 | 17 | 19 | 13 | 10 | 17 | 28 | 2 | 9 |
| 30 | 18 | 17 | 13 | 14 | 17 | 34 | 2 | 10 |
| 31 | 19 | 16 | 13 | 18 | 17 | 38 | 2 | 10 |

Translations of Latin headings are to be found in the introduction, pp. 11-25.

# MARCIUS

| | Primus Ciclus | | | | Secundus Ciclus | | | | Tercius | |
|---|---|---|---|---|---|---|---|---|---|---|
| Numerus dierum | Ciclus Conjunccionis | Tempus vere conjunccionis | Ciclus Opposicionis | Tempus vere opposicionis | Ciclus Conjunccionis | Tempus vere conjunccionis | Ciclus Opposicionis | Tempus vere opposicionis | Ciclus Conjunccionis | Tempus vere conjunccionis |
| | | h. m. | | h. m. | | h. m. | | h. m. | | h. m. |
| 1 | 19 | 19 2 | 15 | 3 28 | 19 | 18 32 | 15 | 1 9 | | |
| 2 | | | 4 | 10 50 | | | 4 | 10 27 | 19 | 11 17 |
| 3 | 8 | 4 2 | 12 | 22 10 | 8 | 2 0 | 12 | 17 53 | 8 | 2 58 |
| 4 | 16 | 17 7 | | | 16 | 10 21 | | | 16 | 9 55 |
| 5 | | | | | | | 1 | 13 13 | 5 | 21 34 |
| 6 | | | 1 | 4 57 | 5 | 9 58 | | | | |
| 7 | 5 | 2 20 | 9 | 23 17 | | | 9 | 7 12 | 13 | 12 56 |
| 8 | 13 | 19 39 | | | 13 | 4 40 | | | | |
| 9 | 2 | 12 17 | 17 | 15 3 | | | 17 | 2 2 | 2 | 22 58 |
| 10 | 10 | 19 18 | 6 | 3 53 | 2 | 9 33 | | | | |
| 11 | | | 14 | 10 47 | 10 | 19 42 | 6 | 3 3 | 10 | 14 40 |
| 12 | 18 | 2 35 | | | | | 14 / 3 | 11 43 / 18 56 | | |
| 13 | 7 | 21 7 | 3 | 1 16 | 18 / 7 | 3 20 / 11 59 | | | 18 | 2 34 |
| 14 | | | 11 | 17 40 | | | 11 | 5 58 | 7 | 10 16 |
| 15 | 15 | 14 49 | | | 15 | 0 55 | 19 | 20 43 | 15 | 18 25 |
| 16 | | | 19 | 12 15 | | | | | 4 | 17 21 |
| 17 | 4 | 23 7 | | | 4 | 9 40 | | | | |
| 18 | | | 8 | 17 45 | | | 8 | 6 41 | 12 | 11 58 |
| 19 | 12 | 11 27 | | | 12 | 3 8 | 16 | 22 41 | | |
| 20 | 1 | 19 32 | 16 | 4 18 | 1 | 20 25 | | | 1 | 17 19 |
| 21 | | | 5 | 11 14 | | | 5 | 12 4 | | |
| 22 | 9 | 3 27 | 13 | 20 20 | 9 | 3 31 | 13 | 18 57 | 9 | 3 44 |
| 23 | 17 | 14 6 | 2 | 22 20 | 17 | 10 39 | | | 17 | 11 31 |
| 24 | 6 | 19 43 | | | | | 2 | 8 49 | 6 | 19 50 |
| 25 | | | 10 | 17 9 | 6 | 4 30 | | | | |
| 26 | 14 | 14 17 | | | 14 | 21 59 | 10 | 0 55 | 14 | 8 25 |
| 27 | | | 18 | 10 52 | | | 18 | 19 23 | | |
| 28 | 3 | 12 46 | | | 3 | 6 37 | | | 3 | 16 50 |
| 29 | 11 | 20 45 | 7 | 4 58 | 11 | 19 15 | 7 | 1 24 | | |
| 30 | | | 15 | 12 11 | | | 15 | 12 13 | 11 | 10 29 |
| 31 | 19 | 3 37 | 4 | 22 12 | 19 | 4 25 | 4 | 19 14 | | |

Ciclus    Quartus Ciclus

| Ciclus Opposicionis | Tempus vere opposicionis | Ciclus Conjunccionis | Tempus vere conjunccionis | Ciclus Opposicionis | Tempus vere opposicionis | Quantitates a noctis medio ad auroram | Quantitates a noctis medio ad solis ortum | Quantitates a meridie ad solis occasum | Quantitates a meridie ad noctem obscuram |
|---|---|---|---|---|---|---|---|---|---|
| | h. m. | | h. m. | | h. m. | h. m. | h. m. | h. m. | h. m. |
| 15 | 15 7 | 19 | 20 44 | | | 4 23 | 6 21 | 5 39 | 7 37 |
| 4 | 11 1 | | | | | 4 21 | 6 19 | 5 41 | 7 39 |
| 12 | 18 30 | | | 4 | 6 29 | 4 19 | 6 17 | 5 43 | 7 41 |
| | | 8 | 0 43 | 12 | 18 2 | 4 17 | 6 15 | 5 45 | 7 43 |
| 1 | 3 37 | 16  5 | 10 31  17 22 | 1 | 1 9 | 4 15 | 6 13 | 5 47 | 7 45 |
| 9 | 16 53 | | | 9 | 9 53 | 4 12 | 6 11 | 5 49 | 7 48 |
| | | 13 | 3 11 | 17 | 21 22 | 4 10 | 6 9 | 5 51 | 7 50 |
| 17 | 9 39 | | | | | 4 8 | 6 7 | 5 53 | 7 52 |
| | | 2 | 6 56 | | | 4 6 | 6 5 | 5 55 | 7 54 |
| 6 | 19 16 | | | 6 | 4 23 | 4 4 | 6 3 | 5 57 | 7 56 |
| | | 10 | 1 45 | 14 | 22 32 | 4 1 | 6 1 | 5 59 | 7 59 |
| 14 | 9 5 | 18 | 18 55 | | | 3 59 | 5 59 | 6 1 | 8 1 |
| 3 | 18 46 | | | 3 | 19 12 | 3 57 | 5 57 | 6 3 | 8 3 |
| | | 7 | 11 12 | | | 3 54 | 5 55 | 6 5 | 8 6 |
| 11 | 2 4 | 15 | 18 13 | 11 | 2 47 | 3 52 | 5 53 | 6 7 | 8 8 |
| 19 | 11 32 | | | 19 | 9 42 | 3 49 | 5 51 | 6 9 | 8 11 |
| 8 | 14 30 | 4 | 5 33 | | | 3 47 | 5 49 | 6 11 | 8 13 |
| | | 12 | 20 21 | 8 | 0 29 | 3 45 | 5 47 | 6 13 | 8 15 |
| 16 | 9 20 | | | 16 | 16 59 | 3 42 | 5 45 | 6 15 | 8 18 |
| | | 1 | 6 21 | | | 3 40 | 5 43 | 6 17 | 8 20 |
| 5 | 10 58 | 9 | 22 18 | 5 | 2 36 | 3 37 | 5 41 | 6 19 | 8 23 |
| 13 | 19 50 | | | 13 | 16 50 | 3 35 | 5 39 | 6 21 | 8 25 |
| | | 17 | 10 29 | | | 3 32 | 5 37 | 6 23 | 8 28 |
| 2 | 2 54 | 6 | 18 23 | 2 | 2 55 | 3 29 | 5 35 | 6 25 | 8 31 |
| 10 | 13 38 | | | 10 | 10 7 | 3 27 | 5 33 | 6 27 | 8 33 |
| | | 14 | 2 22 | 18 | 19 20 | 3 24 | 5 31 | 6 29 | 8 36 |
| 18 | 4 4 | | | | | 3 22 | 5 29 | 6 31 | 8 38 |
| | | 3 | 0 34 | 7 | 21 39 | 3 19 | 5 27 | 6 33 | 8 41 |
| 7 | 13 54 | 11 | 19 3 | | | 3 16 | 5 25 | 6 35 | 8 44 |
| | | | | 15 | 16 27 | 3 13 | 5 23 | 6 37 | 8 47 |
| 15  4 | 6 10  20 8 | 19 | 13 33 | | | 3 11 | 5 21 | 6 39 | 8 49 |

# MARCIUS

Altitudines solis et longitudines umbrarum cuiuslibet hominis stature

| Numerus dierum | 6 / 6 altitudines solis g. m. | umbre hominis pedes | partes | 7 / 5 altitudines solis g. m. | umbre hominis pedes | partes | 8 / 4 altitudines solis g. m. | umbre hominis pedes | partes |
|---|---|---|---|---|---|---|---|---|---|
| 1 | 0 0 | 0 | 0 | 5 58 | 57 | 28 | 14 38 | 23 | 1 |
| 2 | 0 0 | 0 | 0 | 6 16 | 54 | 54 | 14 56 | 22 | 30 |
| 3 | 0 0 | 0 | 0 | 6 35 | 52 | 17 | 15 16 | 22 | 0 |
| 4 | 0 0 | 0 | 0 | 6 54 | 49 | 41 | 15 36 | 21 | 30 |
| 5 | 0 0 | 0 | 0 | 7 13 | 47 | 32 | 15 56 | 21 | 1 |
| 6 | 0 0 | 0 | 0 | 7 32 | 45 | 36 | 16 16 | 20 | 35 |
| 7 | 0 0 | 0 | 0 | 7 51 | 43 | 39 | 16 36 | 20 | 9 |
| 8 | 0 0 | 0 | 0 | 8 10 | 41 | 56 | 16 54 | 19 | 45 |
| 9 | 0 0 | 0 | 0 | 8 30 | 40 | 19 | 17 14 | 19 | 21 |
| 10 | 0 0 | 0 | 0 | 8 48 | 38 | 51 | 17 34 | 18 | 58 |
| 11 | 0 0 | 0 | 0 | 9 7 | 37 | 26 | 17 54 | 18 | 34 |
| 12 | 0 13 | 1586 | 38 | 9 25 | 36 | 16 | 18 13 | 18 | 14 |
| 13 | 0 31 | 665 | 15 | 9 44 | 35 | 3 | 18 33 | 17 | 53 |
| 14 | 0 49 | 420 | 54 | 10 2 | 33 | 55 | 18 52 | 17 | 33 |
| 15 | 1 7 | 323 | 40 | 10 20 | 32 | 58 | 19 11 | 17 | 15 |
| 16 | 1 26 | 269 | 14 | 10 40 | 31 | 55 | 19 30 | 16 | 57 |
| 17 | 1 44 | 217 | 39 | 10 58 | 30 | 59 | 19 50 | 16 | 39 |
| 18 | 2 3 | 168 | 57 | 11 16 | 30 | 10 | 20 9 | 16 | 21 |
| 19 | 2 21 | 151 | 45 | 11 35 | 29 | 19 | 20 28 | 16 | 5 |
| 20 | 2 41 | 132 | 39 | 11 55 | 28 | 26 | 20 48 | 15 | 48 |
| 21 | 2 58 | 116 | 24 | 12 13 | 27 | 44 | 21 6 | 15 | 33 |
| 22 | 3 16 | 106 | 51 | 12 30 | 27 | 6 | 21 25 | 15 | 18 |
| 23 | 3 34 | 98 | 15 | 12 48 | 26 | 26 | 21 44 | 15 | 4 |
| 24 | 3 52 | 89 | 40 | 13 7 | 25 | 46 | 22 2 | 14 | 50 |
| 25 | 4 11 | 82 | 41 | 13 25 | 25 | 11 | 22 21 | 14 | 36 |
| 26 | 4 29 | 77 | 30 | 13 44 | 24 | 35 | 22 40 | 14 | 22 |
| 27 | 4 46 | 72 | 37 | 14 1 | 24 | 3 | 22 58 | 14 | 9 |
| 28 | 5 4 | 67 | 49 | 14 19 | 23 | 33 | 23 17 | 13 | 57 |
| 29 | 5 22 | 64 | 22 | 14 38 | 23 | 1 | 23 35 | 13 | 45 |
| 30 | 5 40 | 60 | 55 | 14 54 | 22 | 34 | 23 54 | 13 | 32 |
| 31 | 5 57 | 57 | 40 | 15 12 | 22 | 5 | 24 11 | 13 | 22 |

sex pedum in horis de clok 51 graduum et quinquaginta minutorum

| 9 | | | 10 | | | 11 | | | 12 a.m. | | |
|---|---|---|---|---|---|---|---|---|---|---|---|
| 3 | | | 2 | | | 1 | | | 0 p.m. | | |
| alti-tudines solis | umbre hominis | | alti-tudines solis | umbre hominis | | alti-tudines solis | umbre hominis | | alti-tudines solis | umbre hominis | |
| g. m. | pedes | partes | g. m. | pedes | partes | g. m. | pedes | partes | g. m. | pedes | partes |
| 22 20 | 14 | 37 | 28 33 | 11 | 2 | 32 39 | 9 | 22 | 34 6 | 8 | 52 |
| 22 40 | 14 | 22 | 28 55 | 10 | 52 | 33 1 | 9 | 14 | 34 29 | 8 | 44 |
| 23 1 | 14 | 7 | 29 17 | 10 | 42 | 33 24 | 9 | 6 | 34 52 | 8 | 37 |
| 23 24 | 13 | 52 | 29 40 | 10 | 32 | 33 48 | 8 | 58 | 35 16 | 8 | 29 |
| 23 44 | 13 | 39 | 30 2 | 10 | 23 | 34 12 | 8 | 50 | 35 40 | 8 | 21 |
| 24 4 | 13 | 26 | 30 23 | 10 | 14 | 34 35 | 8 | 42 | 36 4 | 8 | 14 |
| 24 25 | 13 | 13 | 30 46 | 10 | 6 | 34 58 | 8 | 35 | 36 28 | 8 | 7 |
| 24 46 | 13 | 1 | 31 8 | 9 | 56 | 35 21 | 8 | 27 | 36 51 | 8 | 0 |
| 25 7 | 12 | 48 | 31 30 | 9 | 48 | 35 44 | 8 | 20 | 37 14 | 7 | 54 |
| 25 28 | 12 | 36 | 31 52 | 9 | 39 | 36 8 | 8 | 13 | 37 39 | 7 | 46 |
| 25 48 | 12 | 25 | 32 13 | 9 | 31 | 36 31 | 8 | 6 | 38 2 | 7 | 40 |
| 26 9 | 12 | 13 | 32 36 | 9 | 23 | 36 53 | 7 | 59 | 38 25 | 7 | 34 |
| 26 30 | 12 | 2 | 32 58 | 9 | 15 | 37 17 | 7 | 53 | 38 49 | 7 | 27 |
| 26 50 | 11 | 51 | 33 20 | 9 | 7 | 37 40 | 7 | 46 | 39 12 | 7 | 21 |
| 27 11 | 11 | 41 | 33 42 | 9 | 0 | 38 4 | 7 | 39 | 39 36 | 7 | 15 |
| 27 31 | 11 | 32 | 34 3 | 8 | 53 | 38 26 | 7 | 34 | 40 0 | 7 | 9 |
| 27 51 | 11 | 22 | 34 25 | 8 | 46 | 38 49 | 7 | 27 | 40 24 | 7 | 3 |
| 28 11 | 11 | 12 | 34 47 | 8 | 39 | 39 11 | 7 | 22 | 40 46 | 6 | 58 |
| 28 31 | 11 | 3 | 35 8 | 8 | 31 | 39 34 | 7 | 16 | 41 9 | 6 | 52 |
| 28 52 | 10 | 54 | 35 30 | 8 | 25 | 39 58 | 7 | 10 | 41 34 | 6 | 46 |
| 29 12 | 10 | 45 | 35 52 | 8 | 18 | 40 20 | 7 | 4 | 41 56 | 6 | 41 |
| 29 31 | 10 | 36 | 36 12 | 8 | 11 | 40 41 | 6 | 59 | 42 18 | 6 | 36 |
| 29 51 | 10 | 27 | 36 33 | 8 | 5 | 41 4 | 6 | 53 | 42 42 | 6 | 30 |
| 30 11 | 10 | 19 | 36 54 | 7 | 59 | 41 27 | 6 | 48 | 43 5 | 6 | 25 |
| 30 31 | 10 | 11 | 37 14 | 7 | 54 | 41 49 | 6 | 43 | 43 27 | 6 | 20 |
| 30 51 | 10 | 3 | 37 37 | 7 | 47 | 42 12 | 6 | 37 | 43 51 | 6 | 15 |
| 31 11 | 9 | 55 | 37 59 | 7 | 41 | 42 34 | 6 | 32 | 44 14 | 6 | 10 |
| 31 30 | 9 | 48 | 38 19 | 7 | 35 | 42 56 | 6 | 27 | 44 37 | 6 | 5 |
| 31 49 | 9 | 40 | 38 39 | 7 | 30 | 43 18 | 6 | 22 | 44 59 | 6 | 0 |
| 32 8 | 9 | 33 | 39 0 | 7 | 24 | 43 40 | 6 | 17 | 45 20 | 5 | 56 |
| 32 27 | 9 | 26 | 39 20 | 7 | 19 | 44 1 | 6 | 13 | 45 42 | 5 | 52 |

# APRILIS

| | | | | |
|---|---|---|---|---|
| 1 | | *g* | **KL** | |
| 2 | 11 | A | 4 Nonas | |
| 3 | | *b* | 3 Nonas | Sancti Ricardi episcopi et confessoris |
| 4 | 19 | *c* | 2 Nonas | Sancti Ambrosii doctoris |
| 5 | 8 | *d* | Nonis | |
| 6 | 16 | *e* | 8 Idus | Sancti Sixti pape |
| 7 | 5 | *f* | 7 Idus | |
| 8 | | *g* | 6 Idus | |
| 9 | 13 | A | 5 Idus | |
| 10 | 2 | *b* | 4 Idus | |
| 11 | | *c* | 3 Idus | |
| 12 | 10 | *d* | 2 Idus | |
| 13 | | *e* | Idibus | |
| 14 | 18 | *f* | 18 Kl. | Sancti Tyburcii martyris |
| 15 | 7 | *g* | 17 Kl. | |
| 16 | | A | 16 Kl. | |
| 17 | 15 | *b* | 15 Kl. | |
| 18 | 4 | *c* | 14 Kl. | |
| 19 | | *d* | 13 Kl. | Sancti Alphegi archiepiscopi |
| 20 | 12 | *e* | 12 Kl. | |
| 21 | 1 | *f* | 11 Kl. | |
| 22 | | *g* | 10 Kl. | |
| 23 | 9 | A | 9 Kl. | Sancti Georgii martyris |
| 24 | | *b* | 8 Kl. | Sancti Melliti episcopi |
| 25 | 17 | *c* | 7 Kl. | Sancti Marci ewangeliste |
| 26 | 6 | *d* | 6 Kl. | Sancti Cleti pape |
| 27 | | *e* | 5 Kl. | |
| 28 | 14 | *f* | 4 Kl. | Sancti Vitalis martyris |
| 29 | 3 | *g* | 3 Kl. | Translacio Sancti Edmundi regis |
| 30 | | A | 2 Kl. | |

Variant readings for this month are listed on p. 137.

| Numerus dierum | Verus locus solis | | Quantitates diei artificialis | | Quantitates diei vulgaris | | Quantitates utriusque crepusculorum matutini et vespertini | |
|---|---|---|---|---|---|---|---|---|
| | g. | m. | h. | m. | h. | m. | h. | m. |
| | Aries | | | | | | | |
| 1 | 20 | 14 | 13 | 22 | 17 | 44 | 2 | 11 |
| 2 | 21 | 12 | 13 | 26 | 17 | 50 | 2 | 12 |
| 3 | 22 | 11 | 13 | 30 | 17 | 56 | 2 | 13 |
| 4 | 23 | 9 | 13 | 33 | 18 | 1 | 2 | 14 |
| 5 | 24 | 7 | 13 | 37 | 18 | 7 | 2 | 15 |
| 6 | 25 | 6 | 13 | 41 | 18 | 13 | 2 | 16 |
| 7 | 26 | 4 | 13 | 45 | 18 | 19 | 2 | 17 |
| 8 | 27 | 2 | 13 | 49 | 18 | 25 | 2 | 18 |
| 9 | 28 | 0 | 13 | 53 | 18 | 31 | 2 | 19 |
| 10 | 28 | 58 | 13 | 56 | 18 | 36 | 2 | 20 |
| 11 | 29 | 56 | 14 | 0 | 18 | 42 | 2 | 21 |
| | Taurus | | | | | | | |
| 12 | 0 | 54 | 14 | 4 | 18 | 48 | 2 | 22 |
| 13 | 1 | 53 | 14 | 8 | 18 | 56 | 2 | 24 |
| 14 | 2 | 50 | 14 | 11 | 19 | 1 | 2 | 25 |
| 15 | 3 | 48 | 14 | 15 | 19 | 7 | 2 | 26 |
| 16 | 4 | 46 | 14 | 19 | 19 | 15 | 2 | 28 |
| 17 | 5 | 44 | 14 | 22 | 19 | 20 | 2 | 29 |
| 18 | 6 | 42 | 14 | 26 | 19 | 26 | 2 | 30 |
| 19 | 7 | 40 | 14 | 30 | 19 | 34 | 2 | 32 |
| 20 | 8 | 37 | 14 | 33 | 19 | 41 | 2 | 34 |
| 21 | 9 | 35 | 14 | 37 | 19 | 47 | 2 | 35 |
| 22 | 10 | 33 | 14 | 40 | 19 | 54 | 2 | 37 |
| 23 | 11 | 30 | 14 | 44 | 20 | 2 | 2 | 39 |
| 24 | 12 | 28 | 14 | 47 | 20 | 9 | 2 | 41 |
| 25 | 13 | 26 | 14 | 51 | 20 | 17 | 2 | 43 |
| 26 | 14 | 23 | 14 | 54 | 20 | 24 | 2 | 45 |
| 27 | 15 | 21 | 14 | 57 | 20 | 31 | 2 | 47 |
| 28 | 16 | 18 | 15 | 1 | 20 | 39 | 2 | 49 |
| 29 | 17 | 16 | 15 | 4 | 20 | 48 | 2 | 52 |
| 30 | 18 | 13 | 15 | 7 | 20 | 55 | 2 | 54 |

Translations of Latin headings are to be found in the introduction, pp. 11–25.

# APRILIS

| Numerus dierum | Primus Ciclus | | | | Secundus Ciclus | | | | Tercius | |
|---|---|---|---|---|---|---|---|---|---|---|
| | Ciclus Conjunccionis | Tempus vere conjunccionis | Ciclus Opposicionis | Tempus vere opposicionis | Ciclus Conjunccionis | Tempus vere conjunccionis | Ciclus Opposicionis | Tempus vere opposicionis | Ciclus Conjunccionis | Tempus vere conjunccionis |
| | | h. m. | | h. m. | | h. m. | | h. m. | | h. m. |
| 1 | 8 | 16 44 | | | 8 | 11 21 | | | 19 / 8 | 0 57 / 11 35 |
| 2 | | | 12 | 12 10 | 16 | 21 42 | 12 | 4 6 | 16 | 18 38 |
| 3 | 16 | 8 30 | | | | | | | | |
| 4 | | | 1 | 21 45 | | | 1 | 5 25 | 5 | 11 44 |
| 5 | 5 | 18 26 | | | 5 | 2 47 | | | | |
| 6 | | | 9 | 14 23 | 13 | 21 22 | 9 | 0 12 | 13 | 5 2 |
| 7 | 13 / 2 | 9 24 / 20 49 | | | | | 17 | 18 3 | | |
| 8 | | | 17 / 6 | 3 26 / 12 10 | 2 | 20 36 | | | 2 | 13 58 |
| 9 | 10 | 3 45 | 14 | 19 43 | | | 6 | 12 52 | | |
| 10 | 18 | 12 22 | | | 10 | 4 42 | 14 | 20 10 | 10 | 2 55 |
| 11 | | | 3 | 15 55 | 18 | 11 36 | 3 | 5 44 | 18 | 12 16 |
| 12 | 7 | 12 46 | | | 7 | 0 4 | 11 | 19 21 | 7 | 19 6 |
| 13 | | | 11 | 10 2 | 15 | 15 33 | | | | |
| 14 | 15 | 7 29 | | | | | 19 | 12 21 | 15 | 5 13 |
| 15 | | | 19 | 4 42 | | | | | 4 | 9 39 |
| 16 | 4 | 11 28 | | | 4 | 1 28 | 8 | 21 34 | | |
| 17 | 12 | 21 14 | 8 | 4 46 | 12 | 16 44 | | | 12 | 4 17 |
| 18 | | | 16 | 13 7 | | | 16 | 10 55 | | |
| 19 | 1 | 4 3 | 5 | 20 29 | 1 | 4 40 | 5 | 20 2 | 1 | 4 13 |
| 20 | 9 | 13 42 | | | 9 | 11 32 | | | 9 | 12 31 |
| 21 | | | 13 | 7 50 | 17 | 19 55 | 13 | 3 26 | 17 | 19 26 |
| 22 | 17 | 2 56 | 2 | 14 36 | | | 2 | 22 51 | | |
| 23 | 6 | 11 56 | | | 6 | 19 36 | | | 6 | 7 19 |
| 24 | | | 10 | 8 47 | | | 10 | 16 46 | 14 | 22 27 |
| 25 | 14 | 4 59 | | | 14 | 14 13 | | | | |
| 26 | 3 | 21 30 | 18 | 0 24 | 3 | 18 49 | 18 | 11 29 | | |
| 27 | | | 7 | 13 3 | | | 7 | 12 15 | 3 | 8 21 |
| 28 | 11 | 4 29 | 15 | 19 54 | 11 | 4 50 | 15 | 20 49 | 11 | 23 53 |
| 29 | 19 | 11 41 | | | 19 | 12 25 | | | | |
| 30 | | | 4 | 10 24 | 8 | 21 1 | 4 | 3 59 | 19 / 8 | 11 36 / 19 13 |

Ciclus          Quartus Ciclus

| Ciclus Opposicionis | Tempus vere opposicionis | Ciclus Conjunccionis | Tempus vere conjunccionis | Ciclus Opposicionis | Tempus vere opposicionis | Quantitates a noctis medio ad auroram | Quantitates a noctis medio ad solis ortum | Quantitates a meridie ad solis occasum | Quantitates a meridie ad noctem obscuram |
|---|---|---|---|---|---|---|---|---|---|
|  | h. m. |  | h. m. |  | h. m. | h. m. | h. m. | h. m. | h. m. |
|  |  |  |  | 4 | 18 44 | 3 8 | 5 19 | 6 41 | 8 52 |
| 12 | 3 0 | 8 | 11 41 |  |  | 3 5 | 5 17 | 6 43 | 8 55 |
| 1 | 16 15 | 16 | 19 34 | 12 / 1 | 3 50 / 10 47 | 3 2 | 5 15 | 6 45 | 8 58 |
|  |  | 5 | 3 35 | 9 | 21 14 | 3 0 | 5 14 | 6 46 | 9 0 |
| 9 | 8 4 | 13 | 15 48 |  |  | 2 57 | 5 12 | 6 48 | 9 3 |
|  |  |  |  | 17 | 11 19 | 2 54 | 5 10 | 6 50 | 9 6 |
| 17 | 2 24 | 2 | 22 51 |  |  | 2 51 | 5 8 | 6 52 | 9 9 |
|  |  |  |  | 6 | 20 59 | 2 48 | 5 6 | 6 54 | 9 12 |
| 6 | 8 54 | 10 | 17 36 |  |  | 2 45 | 5 4 | 6 56 | 9 15 |
| 14 | 19 59 |  |  | 14 | 13 29 | 2 42 | 5 2 | 6 58 | 9 18 |
|  |  | 18 | 8 25 |  |  | 2 39 | 5 0 | 7 0 | 9 21 |
| 3 | 3 8 | 7 | 19 33 | 3 | 4 4 | 2 36 | 4 58 | 7 2 | 9 24 |
| 11 | 11 46 |  |  | 11 | 10 57 | 2 32 | 4 56 | 7 4 | 9 28 |
| 19 | 23 35 | 15 | 2 33 | 19 | 18 32 | 2 30 | 4 55 | 7 5 | 9 30 |
|  |  | 4 | 18 52 |  |  | 2 27 | 4 53 | 7 7 | 9 33 |
| 8 | 7 3 |  |  | 8 | 15 4 | 2 23 | 4 51 | 7 9 | 9 37 |
|  |  | 12 | 11 57 |  |  | 2 20 | 4 49 | 7 11 | 9 40 |
| 16 | 1 1 | 1 | 21 7 | 16 | 9 14 | 2 17 | 4 47 | 7 13 | 9 43 |
| 5 | 20 36 |  |  | 5 | 16 12 | 2 13 | 4 45 | 7 15 | 9 47 |
|  |  | 9 | 10 21 |  |  | 2 10 | 4 44 | 7 16 | 9 50 |
| 13 | 4 0 | 17 | 20 0 | 13 | 3 36 | 2 7 | 4 42 | 7 18 | 9 53 |
| 2 | 13 9 |  |  | 2 | 10 54 | 2 3 | 4 40 | 7 20 | 9 57 |
|  |  | 6 | 2 49 | 10 | 19 18 | 1 59 | 4 38 | 7 22 | 10 1 |
| 10 | 2 24 | 14 | 12 36 |  |  | 1 56 | 4 37 | 7 23 | 10 4 |
| 18 | 19 8 |  |  | 18 | 6 47 | 1 52 | 4 35 | 7 25 | 10 8 |
|  |  | 3 | 16 21 |  |  | 1 48 | 4 33 | 7 27 | 10 12 |
|  |  |  |  | 7 | 13 46 | 1 45 | 4 32 | 7 28 | 10 15 |
| 7 | 4 32 | 11 | 11 3 |  |  | 1 41 | 4 30 | 7 30 | 10 19 |
| 15 | 18 14 |  |  | 15 | 7 52 | 1 36 | 4 28 | 7 32 | 10 24 |
| 4 | 3 46 | 19 | 4 0 |  |  | 1 33 | 4 27 | 7 33 | 10 27 |

Altitudines solis et longitudines umbrarum cuiuslibet hominis
a media nocte

| Numerus dierum | 5 / 7 altitudines solis g. m. | umbre hominis pedes | partes | 6 / 6 altitudines solis g. m. | umbre hominis pedes | partes | 7 / 5 altitudines solis g. m. | umbre hominis pedes | partes | 8 / 4 altitudines solis g. m. | umbre hominis pedes | partes |
|---|---|---|---|---|---|---|---|---|---|---|---|---|
| 1 | 0 0 | 0 | 0 | 6 14 | 55 | 10 | 15 29 | 21 | 40 | 24 30 | 13 | 10 |
| 2 | 0 0 | 0 | 0 | 6 31 | 52 | 50 | 15 46 | 21 | 16 | 24 47 | 13 | 0 |
| 3 | 0 0 | 0 | 0 | 6 48 | 50 | 31 | 16 4 | 20 | 50 | 25 5 | 12 | 49 |
| 4 | 0 0 | 0 | 0 | 7 6 | 48 | 15 | 16 21 | 20 | 28 | 25 22 | 12 | 40 |
| 5 | 0 0 | 0 | 0 | 7 22 | 46 | 37 | 16 38 | 20 | 6 | 25 40 | 12 | 29 |
| 6 | 0 0 | 0 | 0 | 7 39 | 44 | 53 | 16 54 | 19 | 45 | 25 58 | 12 | 19 |
| 7 | 0 0 | 0 | 0 | 7 55 | 43 | 15 | 17 10 | 19 | 26 | 26 14 | 12 | 11 |
| 8 | 0 0 | 0 | 0 | 8 12 | 41 | 46 | 17 27 | 19 | 6 | 26 31 | 12 | 1 |
| 9 | 0 0 | 0 | 0 | 8 29 | 40 | 23 | 17 43 | 18 | 47 | 26 48 | 11 | 52 |
| 10 | 0 0 | 0 | 0 | 8 46 | 39 | 1 | 18 1 | 18 | 26 | 27 5 | 11 | 44 |
| 11 | 0 0 | 0 | 0 | 9 3 | 37 | 41 | 18 17 | 18 | 9 | 27 22 | 11 | 36 |
| 12 | 0 16 | 1289 | 15 | 9 18 | 36 | 43 | 18 32 | 17 | 54 | 27 38 | 11 | 28 |
| 13 | 0 34 | 606 | 35 | 9 33 | 35 | 45 | 18 48 | 17 | 37 | 27 54 | 11 | 20 |
| 14 | 0 49 | 420 | 54 | 9 48 | 34 | 47 | 19 3 | 17 | 23 | 28 9 | 11 | 13 |
| 15 | 1 4 | 332 | 15 | 10 4 | 33 | 49 | 19 18 | 17 | 9 | 28 25 | 11 | 6 |
| 16 | 1 20 | 286 | 25 | 10 19 | 33 | 2 | 19 34 | 16 | 54 | 28 41 | 10 | 59 |
| 17 | 1 37 | 237 | 43 | 10 35 | 32 | 11 | 19 50 | 16 | 39 | 28 57 | 10 | 51 |
| 18 | 1 51 | 197 | 36 | 10 49 | 31 | 27 | 20 4 | 16 | 26 | 29 11 | 10 | 45 |
| 19 | 2 6 | 166 | 5 | 11 4 | 30 | 41 | 20 18 | 16 | 14 | 29 26 | 10 | 38 |
| 20 | 2 21 | 151 | 45 | 11 18 | 30 | 4 | 20 32 | 16 | 2 | 29 40 | 10 | 32 |
| 21 | 2 37 | 136 | 28 | 11 33 | 29 | 25 | 20 48 | 15 | 48 | 29 56 | 10 | 25 |
| 22 | 2 51 | 123 | 5 | 11 47 | 28 | 47 | 21 1 | 15 | 37 | 30 10 | 10 | 19 |
| 23 | 3 6 | 111 | 37 | 12 1 | 28 | 11 | 21 15 | 15 | 26 | 30 24 | 10 | 14 |
| 24 | 3 20 | 104 | 56 | 12 15 | 27 | 40 | 21 29 | 15 | 15 | 30 38 | 10 | 8 |
| 25 | 3 34 | 98 | 15 | 12 29 | 27 | 9 | 21 42 | 15 | 5 | 30 52 | 10 | 3 |
| 26 | 3 48 | 91 | 35 | 12 42 | 26 | 40 | 21 55 | 14 | 55 | 31 7 | 9 | 56 |
| 27 | 4 2 | 85 | 16 | 12 55 | 26 | 11 | 22 8 | 14 | 45 | 31 20 | 9 | 51 |
| 28 | 4 15 | 81 | 32 | 13 8 | 25 | 44 | 22 21 | 14 | 36 | 31 31 | 9 | 47 |
| 29 | 4 28 | 77 | 48 | 13 21 | 25 | 19 | 22 33 | 14 | 27 | 31 44 | 9 | 42 |
| 30 | 4 40 | 74 | 20 | 13 33 | 24 | 56 | 22 45 | 14 | 19 | 31 56 | 9 | 38 |

stature sex pedum in horis equalibus distantibus a meridie et
51 graduum

| 9 | | | 10 | | | 11 | | | 12 a.m. | | |
| 3 | | | 2 | | | 1 | | | 0 p.m. | | |
| altitudines solis | umbre hominis | | altitudines solis | umbre hominis | | altitudines solis | umbre hominis | | altitudines solis | umbre hominis | |
| g. m. | pedes | partes | g. m. | pedes | partes | g. m. | pedes | partes | g. m. | pedes | partes |
|---|---|---|---|---|---|---|---|---|---|---|---|
| 32 47 | 9 | 19 | 39 41 | 7 | 14 | 44 25 | 6 | 8 | 46 6 | 5 | 47 |
| 33 5 | 9 | 13 | 40 0 | 7 | 9 | 44 44 | 6 | 3 | 46 27 | 5 | 43 |
| 33 23 | 9 | 6 | 40 21 | 7 | 4 | 45 5 | 5 | 59 | 46 49 | 5 | 38 |
| 33 42 | 9 | 0 | 40 40 | 6 | 59 | 45 26 | 5 | 55 | 47 10 | 5 | 34 |
| 34 1 | 8 | 53 | 41 0 | 6 | 54 | 45 48 | 5 | 50 | 47 33 | 5 | 29 |
| 34 20 | 8 | 47 | 41 21 | 6 | 49 | 46 10 | 5 | 46 | 47 56 | 5 | 25 |
| 34 37 | 8 | 42 | 41 40 | 6 | 45 | 46 30 | 5 | 42 | 48 16 | 5 | 21 |
| 34 55 | 8 | 36 | 41 59 | 6 | 40 | 46 50 | 5 | 38 | 48 37 | 5 | 17 |
| 35 12 | 8 | 30 | 42 18 | 6 | 36 | 47 10 | 5 | 34 | 48 57 | 5 | 14 |
| 35 30 | 8 | 25 | 42 38 | 6 | 31 | 47 32 | 5 | 30 | 49 19 | 5 | 10 |
| 35 49 | 8 | 18 | 42 57 | 6 | 27 | 47 54 | 5 | 25 | 49 41 | 5 | 5 |
| 36 6 | 8 | 13 | 43 16 | 6 | 23 | 48 13 | 5 | 22 | 50 0 | 5 | 2 |
| 36 23 | 8 | 8 | 43 33 | 6 | 19 | 48 31 | 5 | 18 | 50 20 | 4 | 58 |
| 36 39 | 8 | 3 | 43 51 | 6 | 15 | 48 51 | 5 | 15 | 50 41 | 4 | 54 |
| 36 54 | 7 | 59 | 44 8 | 6 | 11 | 49 9 | 5 | 11 | 50 59 | 4 | 51 |
| 37 12 | 7 | 54 | 44 27 | 6 | 7 | 49 30 | 5 | 8 | 51 20 | 4 | 48 |
| 37 29 | 7 | 49 | 44 44 | 6 | 3 | 49 49 | 5 | 4 | 51 40 | 4 | 45 |
| 37 44 | 7 | 45 | 45 0 | 6 | 0 | 50 5 | 5 | 1 | 51 57 | 4 | 42 |
| 38 0 | 7 | 40 | 45 18 | 5 | 56 | 50 24 | 4 | 58 | 52 17 | 4 | 38 |
| 38 15 | 7 | 36 | 45 34 | 5 | 53 | 50 41 | 4 | 54 | 52 35 | 4 | 35 |
| 38 31 | 7 | 32 | 45 52 | 5 | 50 | 51 0 | 4 | 51 | 52 55 | 4 | 32 |
| 38 46 | 7 | 28 | 46 7 | 5 | 47 | 51 19 | 4 | 48 | 53 13 | 4 | 29 |
| 39 0 | 7 | 24 | 46 24 | 5 | 43 | 51 36 | 4 | 45 | 53 30 | 4 | 26 |
| 39 15 | 7 | 21 | 46 40 | 5 | 40 | 51 52 | 4 | 43 | 53 48 | 4 | 23 |
| 39 30 | 7 | 17 | 46 56 | 5 | 37 | 52 9 | 4 | 40 | 54 6 | 4 | 21 |
| 39 45 | 7 | 13 | 47 11 | 5 | 34 | 52 27 | 4 | 37 | 54 24 | 4 | 18 |
| 40 0 | 7 | 9 | 47 27 | 5 | 31 | 52 44 | 4 | 34 | 54 42 | 4 | 15 |
| 40 12 | 7 | 6 | 47 41 | 5 | 28 | 52 58 | 4 | 31 | 54 57 | 4 | 13 |
| 40 25 | 7 | 3 | 47 56 | 5 | 25 | 53 14 | 4 | 29 | 55 13 | 4 | 10 |
| 40 38 | 7 | 0 | 48 10 | 5 | 22 | 53 29 | 4 | 27 | 55 28 | 4 | 8 |

# MAYUS

| | | | | |
|---|---|---|---|---|
| 1 | 11 | *b* | **KL** | Apostolorum Philippi et Jacobi |
| 2 | | *c* | 6 Nonas | Sancti Athanasii episcopi |
| 3 | 19 | *d* | 5 Nonas | Sancti Blasii episcopi et martyris |
| 4 | 8 | *e* | 4 Nonas | Sancti Quiriaci episcopi et martyris |
| 5 | | *f* | 3 Nonas | |
| 6 | 16 | *g* | 2 Nonas | |
| 7 | 5 | A | Nonis | |
| 8 | | *b* | 8 Idus | |
| 9 | 13 | *c* | 7 Idus | |
| 10 | 2 | *d* | 6 Idus | Sanctorum Gordiani et Epimachi martyrum |
| 11 | | *e* | 5 Idus | |
| 12 | 10 | *f* | 4 Idus | Sanctorum Nerrei et Achillei martyrum |
| 13 | | *g* | 3 Idus | |
| 14 | 18 | A | 2 Idus | |
| 15 | 7 | *b* | Idibus | |
| 16 | | *c* | 17 Kl. | |
| 17 | 15 | *d* | 16 Kl. | |
| 18 | 4 | *e* | 15 Kl. | |
| 19 | | *f* | 14 Kl. | Sancti Dunstani |
| 20 | 12 | *g* | 13 Kl. | |
| 21 | 1 | A | 12 Kl. | |
| 22 | | *b* | 11 Kl. | |
| 23 | 9 | *c* | 10 Kl. | |
| 24 | | *d* | 9 Kl. | |
| 25 | 17 | *e* | 8 Kl. | Sancti Urbani pape |
| 26 | 6 | *f* | 7 Kl. | Sancti Augustini primi Anglorum archiepisc |
| 27 | | *g* | 6 Kl. | |
| 28 | 14 | A | 5 Kl. | |
| 29 | 3 | *b* | 4 Kl. | |
| 30 | | *c* | 3 Kl. | |
| 31 | 11 | *d* | 2 Kl. | |

Variant readings for this month are listed on p. 137.

| Numerus dierum | Verus locus solis | | Quantitates diei artificialis | | Quantitates diei vulgaris | | Quantitates utriusque crepusculorum matutini et vespertini | |
|---|---|---|---|---|---|---|---|---|
| | g. | m. | h. | m. | h. | m. | h. | m. |
| | Taurus | | | | | | | |
| 1 | 19 | 11 | 15 | 10 | 21 | 4 | 2 | 57 |
| 2 | 20 | 8 | 15 | 14 | 21 | 14 | 3 | 0 |
| 3 | 21 | 6 | 15 | 17 | 21 | 23 | 3 | 3 |
| 4 | 22 | 3 | 15 | 20 | 21 | 32 | 3 | 6 |
| 5 | 23 | 1 | 15 | 23 | 21 | 43 | 3 | 10 |
| 6 | 23 | 58 | 15 | 26 | 21 | 54 | 3 | 14 |
| 7 | 24 | 56 | 15 | 29 | 22 | 7 | 3 | 19 |
| 8 | 25 | 53 | 15 | 32 | 22 | 18 | 3 | 23 |
| 9 | 26 | 50 | 15 | 35 | 22 | 33 | 3 | 29 |
| 10 | 27 | 48 | 15 | 38 | 22 | 50 | 3 | 36 |
| 11 | 28 | 45 | 15 | 40 | 23 | 10 | 3 | 45 |
| 12 | 29 | 42 | 15 | 43 | 24 | 0 | 0 | 0 |
| | Gemini | | | | | | | |
| 13 | 0 | 40 | 15 | 46 | 24 | 0 | 0 | 0 |
| 14 | 1 | 37 | 15 | 48 | 24 | 0 | 0 | 0 |
| 15 | 2 | 34 | 15 | 51 | 24 | 0 | 0 | 0 |
| 16 | 3 | 31 | 15 | 53 | 24 | 0 | 0 | 0 |
| 17 | 4 | 29 | 15 | 56 | 24 | 0 | 0 | 0 |
| 18 | 5 | 26 | 15 | 58 | 24 | 0 | 0 | 0 |
| 19 | 6 | 23 | 16 | 0 | 24 | 0 | 0 | 0 |
| 20 | 7 | 20 | 16 | 3 | 24 | 0 | 0 | 0 |
| 21 | 8 | 17 | 16 | 5 | 24 | 0 | 0 | 0 |
| 22 | 9 | 14 | 16 | 7 | 24 | 0 | 0 | 0 |
| 23 | 10 | 11 | 16 | 9 | 24 | 0 | 0 | 0 |
| 24 | 11 | 8 | 16 | 11 | 24 | 0 | 0 | 0 |
| 25 | 12 | 5 | 16 | 12 | 24 | 0 | 0 | 0 |
| 26 | 13 | 3 | 16 | 14 | 24 | 0 | 0 | 0 |
| 27 | 14 | 0 | 16 | 16 | 24 | 0 | 0 | 0 |
| 28 | 14 | 57 | 16 | 17 | 24 | 0 | 0 | 0 |
| 29 | 15 | 54 | 16 | 19 | 24 | 0 | 0 | 0 |
| 30 | 16 | 51 | 16 | 20 | 24 | 0 | 0 | 0 |
| 31 | 17 | 48 | 16 | 22 | 24 | 0 | 0 | 0 |

Translations of Latin headings are to be found in the introduction, pp. 11-25.

# MAYUS

<table>
<thead>
<tr><th rowspan="2">Numerus dierum</th><th colspan="4">Primus Ciclus</th><th colspan="4">Secundus Ciclus</th><th colspan="2">Tercius</th></tr>
<tr><th>Ciclus Conjunccionis</th><th>Tempus vere conjunccionis<br>h. m.</th><th>Ciclus Opposicionis</th><th>Tempus vere opposicionis<br>h. m.</th><th>Ciclus Conjunccionis</th><th>Tempus vere conjunccionis<br>h. m.</th><th>Ciclus Opposicionis</th><th>Tempus vere opposicionis<br>h. m.</th><th>Ciclus Conjunccionis</th><th>Tempus vere conjunccionis<br>h. m.</th></tr>
</thead>
<tbody>
<tr><td>1</td><td>8</td><td>6 11</td><td></td><td></td><td></td><td></td><td>12</td><td>15 0</td><td></td><td></td></tr>
<tr><td>2</td><td>16</td><td>23 51</td><td>12</td><td>2 44</td><td>16</td><td>9 56</td><td></td><td></td><td>16</td><td>3 23</td></tr>
<tr><td>3</td><td></td><td></td><td></td><td></td><td></td><td></td><td>1</td><td>21 14</td><td></td><td></td></tr>
<tr><td>4</td><td></td><td></td><td>1</td><td>12 21</td><td>5</td><td>18 34</td><td></td><td></td><td>5</td><td>2 19</td></tr>
<tr><td>5</td><td>5</td><td>7 59</td><td></td><td></td><td></td><td></td><td>9</td><td>15 32</td><td>13</td><td>20 48</td></tr>
<tr><td>6</td><td>13</td><td>20 9</td><td>9</td><td>2 34</td><td>13</td><td>11 52</td><td></td><td></td><td></td><td></td></tr>
<tr><td>7</td><td>2</td><td>4 14</td><td>17<br>6</td><td>12 57<br>19 53</td><td></td><td></td><td>17</td><td>7 21</td><td></td><td></td></tr>
<tr><td>8</td><td>10</td><td>12 5</td><td></td><td></td><td>2</td><td>5 5</td><td>6</td><td>20 43</td><td>2</td><td>2 0</td></tr>
<tr><td>9</td><td>18</td><td>22 41</td><td>14</td><td>4 57</td><td>10</td><td>12 10</td><td></td><td></td><td>10</td><td>12 20</td></tr>
<tr><td>10</td><td></td><td></td><td></td><td></td><td>18</td><td>19 14</td><td>14<br>3</td><td>3 32<br>17 22</td><td>18</td><td>20 2</td></tr>
<tr><td>11</td><td></td><td></td><td>3</td><td>6 53</td><td>7</td><td>12 58</td><td></td><td></td><td></td><td></td></tr>
<tr><td>12</td><td>7</td><td>3 12</td><td></td><td></td><td></td><td></td><td>11</td><td>9 23</td><td>7</td><td>4 20</td></tr>
<tr><td>13</td><td>15</td><td>22 41</td><td>11</td><td>1 35</td><td>15</td><td>6 26</td><td></td><td></td><td>15</td><td>16 50</td></tr>
<tr><td>14</td><td></td><td></td><td>19</td><td>19 8</td><td></td><td></td><td>19</td><td>3 46</td><td></td><td></td></tr>
<tr><td>15</td><td>4</td><td>21 2</td><td></td><td></td><td>4</td><td>14 50</td><td></td><td></td><td>4</td><td>1 8</td></tr>
<tr><td>16</td><td></td><td></td><td>8</td><td>13 15</td><td></td><td></td><td>8</td><td>9 39</td><td>12</td><td>18 39</td></tr>
<tr><td>17</td><td>12</td><td>5 0</td><td>16</td><td>20 23</td><td>12</td><td>3 27</td><td>16</td><td>20 21</td><td></td><td></td></tr>
<tr><td>18</td><td>1</td><td>12 50</td><td></td><td></td><td>1</td><td>11 48</td><td></td><td></td><td>1</td><td>12 35</td></tr>
<tr><td>19</td><td></td><td></td><td>5</td><td>6 21</td><td>9</td><td>19 28</td><td>5</td><td>3 23</td><td>9</td><td>19 45</td></tr>
<tr><td>20</td><td>9</td><td>0 51</td><td>13</td><td>20 13</td><td></td><td></td><td>13</td><td>12 11</td><td></td><td></td></tr>
<tr><td>21</td><td>17</td><td>16 29</td><td></td><td></td><td>17</td><td>5 45</td><td></td><td></td><td>17</td><td>2 44</td></tr>
<tr><td>22</td><td></td><td></td><td>2</td><td>5 40</td><td></td><td></td><td>2</td><td>13 22</td><td>6</td><td>19 41</td></tr>
<tr><td>23</td><td>6</td><td>2 20</td><td>10</td><td>22 10</td><td>6</td><td>10 40</td><td></td><td></td><td></td><td></td></tr>
<tr><td>24</td><td>14</td><td>17 9</td><td></td><td></td><td></td><td></td><td>10</td><td>8 3</td><td>14</td><td>12 53</td></tr>
<tr><td>25</td><td></td><td></td><td>18</td><td>11 9</td><td>14</td><td>5 12</td><td></td><td></td><td></td><td></td></tr>
<tr><td>26</td><td>3</td><td>4 40</td><td>7</td><td>20 0</td><td>3</td><td>4 18</td><td>18<br>7</td><td>1 47<br>20 40</td><td>3</td><td>21 39</td></tr>
<tr><td>27</td><td>11</td><td>11 33</td><td></td><td></td><td>11</td><td>12 28</td><td></td><td></td><td></td><td></td></tr>
<tr><td>28</td><td>19</td><td>20 4</td><td>15</td><td>3 28</td><td>19</td><td>19 17</td><td>15</td><td>3 55</td><td>11</td><td>10 33</td></tr>
<tr><td>29</td><td></td><td></td><td>4</td><td>23 31</td><td></td><td></td><td>4</td><td>13 24</td><td>19</td><td>20 0</td></tr>
<tr><td>30</td><td>8</td><td>20 18</td><td></td><td></td><td>8</td><td>7 42</td><td></td><td></td><td>8</td><td>2 48</td></tr>
<tr><td>31</td><td></td><td></td><td>12</td><td>17 31</td><td>16</td><td>23 0</td><td>12</td><td>2 54</td><td>16</td><td>12 50</td></tr>
</tbody>
</table>

Ciclus    Quartus Ciclus

| Ciclus Opposicionis | Tempus vere opposicionis h. m. | Ciclus Conjunccionis | Tempus vere conjunccionis h. m. | Ciclus Opposicionis | Tempus vere opposicionis h. m. | Quantitates a noctis medio ad auroram h. m. | Quantitates a noctis medio ad solis ortum h. m. | Quantitates a meridie ad solis occasum h. m. | Quantitates a meridie ad noctem obscuram h. m. |
|---|---|---|---|---|---|---|---|---|---|
| 12 | 11 1 | 8 | 20 10 | 4 | 4 11 | 1 28 | 4 25 | 7 35 | 10 32 |
|  |  |  |  | 12 / 1 | 11 43 / 20 28 | 1 23 | 4 23 | 7 37 | 10 37 |
| 1 | 5 41 | 16 / 5 | 3 8 / 14 27 |  |  | 1 19 | 4 22 | 7 38 | 10 41 |
| 9 | 23 24 |  |  | 9 | 9 22 | 1 14 | 4 20 | 7 40 | 10 46 |
|  |  | 13 | 5 13 |  |  | 1 9 | 4 19 | 7 41 | 10 51 |
| 17 | 18 7 |  |  | 17 | 1 48 | 1 3 | 4 17 | 7 43 | 10 57 |
|  |  | 2 | 15 5 |  |  | 0 57 | 4 16 | 7 44 | 11 3 |
| 6 | 19 36 |  |  | 6 | 11 22 | 0 51 | 4 14 | 7 46 | 11 9 |
|  |  | 10 | 6 54 |  |  | 0 44 | 4 13 | 7 47 | 11 16 |
| 14 | 4 25 | 18 | 18 56 | 14 | 1 25 | 0 35 | 4 11 | 7 49 | 11 25 |
| 3 | 11 26 |  |  | 3 | 11 24 | 0 25 | 4 10 | 7 50 | 11 35 |
| 11 | 22 6 | 7 | 2 51 | 11 | 18 34 | 0 0 | 4 9 | 7 51 | 0 0 |
|  |  | 15 | 10 48 |  |  | 0 0 | 4 7 | 7 53 | 0 0 |
| 19 | 12 27 |  |  | 19 | 3 44 | 0 0 | 4 6 | 7 54 | 0 0 |
| 8 | 22 10 | 4 | 8 54 |  |  | 0 0 | 4 5 | 7 55 | 0 0 |
|  |  |  |  | 8 | 5 56 | 0 0 | 4 4 | 7 56 | 0 0 |
| 16 | 14 18 | 12 | 3 20 |  |  | 0 0 | 4 2 | 7 58 | 0 0 |
|  |  | 1 | 9 2 | 16 | 0 39 | 0 0 | 4 1 | 7 59 | 0 0 |
| 5 | 4 17 | 9 | 19 43 | 5 | 2 47 | 0 0 | 4 0 | 8 0 | 0 0 |
| 13 | 11 6 |  |  | 13 | 11 54 | 0 0 | 3 59 | 8 1 | 0 0 |
|  |  | 17 | 3 38 | 2 | 18 48 | 0 0 | 3 58 | 8 2 | 0 0 |
| 2 | 0 15 | 6 | 11 35 |  |  | 0 0 | 3 57 | 8 3 | 0 0 |
| 10 | 15 57 | 14 | 23 42 | 10 | 5 9 | 0 0 | 3 56 | 8 4 | 0 0 |
|  |  |  |  | 18 | 19 9 | 0 0 | 3 55 | 8 5 | 0 0 |
| 18 | 10 11 |  |  |  |  | 0 0 | 3 54 | 8 6 | 0 0 |
|  |  | 3 | 7 34 |  |  | 0 0 | 3 53 | 8 7 | 0 0 |
| 7 | 16 34 |  |  | 7 | 4 41 | 0 0 | 3 52 | 8 8 | 0 0 |
|  |  | 11 | 1 17 | 15 | 21 4 | 0 0 | 3 52 | 8 8 | 0 0 |
| 15 / 4 | 3 38 / 10 50 | 19 | 15 59 |  |  | 0 0 | 3 51 | 8 9 | 0 0 |
| 12 | 19 23 |  |  | 4 | 12 4 | 0 0 | 3 50 | 8 10 | 0 0 |
|  |  | 8 | 3 14 | 12 | 18 36 | 0 0 | 3 49 | 8 11 | 0 0 |

## Altitudines solis et longitudines umbrarum cuiuslibet hominis nocte 51

| Numerus dierum | 4 / 8 altitudines solis g. m. | umbre hominis pedes | umbre hominis partes | 5 / 7 altitudines solis g. m. | umbre hominis pedes | umbre hominis partes | 6 / 6 altitudines solis g. m. | umbre hominis pedes | umbre hominis partes | 7 / 5 altitudines solis g. m. | umbre hominis pedes | umbre hominis partes |
|---|---|---|---|---|---|---|---|---|---|---|---|---|
| 1 | 0 0 | 0 | 0 | 4 53 | 70 | 36 | 13 45 | 24 | 33 | 22 57 | 14 | 10 |
| 2 | 0 0 | 0 | 0 | 5 6 | 67 | 26 | 13 57 | 24 | 10 | 23 11 | 14 | 1 |
| 3 | 0 0 | 0 | 0 | 5 18 | 65 | 8 | 14 9 | 23 | 49 | 23 22 | 13 | 53 |
| 4 | 0 0 | 0 | 0 | 5 30 | 62 | 50 | 14 21 | 23 | 29 | 23 33 | 13 | 46 |
| 5 | 0 0 | 0 | 0 | 5 43 | 60 | 21 | 14 32 | 23 | 11 | 23 44 | 13 | 39 |
| 6 | 0 0 | 0 | 0 | 5 54 | 58 | 14 | 14 44 | 22 | 50 | 23 56 | 13 | 31 |
| 7 | 0 0 | 0 | 0 | 6 6 | 56 | 16 | 14 54 | 22 | 34 | 24 6 | 13 | 25 |
| 8 | 0 0 | 0 | 0 | 6 16 | 54 | 54 | 15 4 | 22 | 17 | 24 17 | 13 | 18 |
| 9 | 0 0 | 0 | 0 | 6 27 | 53 | 23 | 15 15 | 22 | 1 | 24 27 | 13 | 12 |
| 10 | 0 0 | 0 | 0 | 6 37 | 52 | 1 | 15 25 | 21 | 46 | 24 36 | 13 | 7 |
| 11 | 0 0 | 0 | 0 | 6 47 | 50 | 39 | 15 35 | 21 | 32 | 24 46 | 13 | 1 |
| 12 | 0 0 | 0 | 0 | 6 57 | 49 | 17 | 15 45 | 21 | 17 | 24 56 | 12 | 55 |
| 13 | 0 0 | 0 | 0 | 7 7 | 48 | 9 | 15 54 | 21 | 4 | 25 5 | 12 | 49 |
| 14 | 0 0 | 0 | 0 | 7 16 | 47 | 14 | 16 3 | 20 | 52 | 25 13 | 12 | 45 |
| 15 | 0 0 | 0 | 0 | 7 25 | 46 | 19 | 16 11 | 20 | 41 | 25 22 | 12 | 40 |
| 16 | 0 0 | 0 | 0 | 7 34 | 45 | 23 | 16 20 | 20 | 29 | 25 30 | 12 | 35 |
| 17 | 0 0 | 0 | 0 | 7 43 | 44 | 28 | 16 29 | 20 | 18 | 25 39 | 12 | 30 |
| 18 | 0 0 | 0 | 0 | 7 51 | 43 | 39 | 16 37 | 20 | 7 | 25 46 | 12 | 26 |
| 19 | 0 1 | 20636 | 54 | 7 59 | 42 | 50 | 16 44 | 19 | 58 | 25 54 | 12 | 21 |
| 20 | 0 10 | 2062 | 20 | 8 7 | 42 | 10 | 16 51 | 19 | 49 | 26 1 | 12 | 19 |
| 21 | 0 17 | 1213 | 26 | 8 15 | 41 | 31 | 16 58 | 19 | 40 | 26 8 | 12 | 14 |
| 22 | 0 25 | 825 | 0 | 8 22 | 40 | 57 | 17 5 | 19 | 32 | 26 15 | 12 | 10 |
| 23 | 0 32 | 644 | 28 | 8 29 | 40 | 23 | 17 11 | 19 | 25 | 26 21 | 12 | 7 |
| 24 | 0 40 | 515 | 38 | 8 36 | 39 | 49 | 17 17 | 19 | 18 | 26 28 | 12 | 3 |
| 25 | 0 45 | 458 | 17 | 8 42 | 39 | 20 | 17 23 | 19 | 11 | 26 33 | 12 | 0 |
| 26 | 0 52 | 396 | 37 | 8 48 | 38 | 51 | 17 29 | 19 | 4 | 26 39 | 11 | 57 |
| 27 | 0 58 | 355 | 34 | 8 54 | 38 | 22 | 17 34 | 18 | 58 | 26 44 | 11 | 55 |
| 28 | 1 3 | 335 | 7 | 8 59 | 37 | 58 | 17 39 | 18 | 52 | 26 49 | 11 | 52 |
| 29 | 1 9 | 317 | 56 | 9 4 | 37 | 38 | 17 45 | 18 | 45 | 26 54 | 11 | 49 |
| 30 | 1 14 | 303 | 36 | 9 8 | 37 | 22 | 17 50 | 18 | 39 | 26 59 | 11 | 47 |
| 31 | 1 18 | 292 | 9 | 9 13 | 37 | 3 | 17 54 | 18 | 34 | 27 2 | 11 | 46 |

stature sex pedum in horis equalibus distantibus a meridie et a media graduum et

| 8 / 4 | | | 9 / 3 | | | 10 / 2 | | | 11 / 1 | | | 12 a.m. / 0 p.m. | | |
|---|---|---|---|---|---|---|---|---|---|---|---|---|---|---|
| altitudines solis | umbre hominis | | altitudines solis | umbre hominis | | altitudines solis | umbre hominis | | altitudines solis | umbre hominis | | altitudines solis | umbre hominis | |
| g. m. | pedes | partes | g. m. | pedes | partes | g. m. | pedes | partes | g. m. | pedes | partes | g. m. | pedes | partes |
| 32 9 | 9 | 33 | 40 51 | 6 | 56 | 48 24 | 5 | 20 | 53 47 | 4 | 24 | 55 45 | 4 | 5 |
| 32 21 | 9 | 28 | 41 5 | 6 | 53 | 48 39 | 5 | 17 | 54 3 | 4 | 21 | 56 2 | 4 | 3 |
| 32 34 | 9 | 24 | 41 17 | 6 | 50 | 48 51 | 5 | 15 | 54 16 | 4 | 19 | 56 16 | 4 | 1 |
| 32 44 | 9 | 20 | 41 29 | 6 | 47 | 49 3 | 5 | 12 | 54 28 | 4 | 17 | 56 30 | 3 | 59 |
| 32 56 | 9 | 15 | 41 41 | 6 | 44 | 49 18 | 5 | 10 | 54 43 | 4 | 15 | 56 46 | 3 | 56 |
| 33 7 | 9 | 12 | 41 54 | 6 | 41 | 49 32 | 5 | 7 | 54 58 | 4 | 13 | 57 2 | 3 | 54 |
| 33 18 | 9 | 8 | 42 5 | 6 | 39 | 49 44 | 5 | 5 | 55 12 | 4 | 10 | 57 16 | 3 | 52 |
| 33 29 | 9 | 4 | 42 16 | 6 | 36 | 49 54 | 5 | 3 | 55 23 | 4 | 9 | 57 28 | 3 | 50 |
| 33 39 | 9 | 1 | 42 26 | 6 | 34 | 50 6 | 5 | 1 | 55 37 | 4 | 6 | 57 42 | 3 | 48 |
| 33 49 | 8 | 57 | 42 37 | 6 | 31 | 50 18 | 4 | 59 | 55 48 | 4 | 5 | 57 55 | 3 | 46 |
| 33 59 | 8 | 54 | 42 47 | 6 | 29 | 50 29 | 4 | 57 | 56 2 | 4 | 3 | 58 8 | 3 | 44 |
| 34 9 | 8 | 51 | 42 59 | 6 | 26 | 50 41 | 4 | 55 | 56 16 | 4 | 1 | 58 23 | 3 | 42 |
| 34 17 | 8 | 48 | 43 8 | 6 | 24 | 50 51 | 4 | 53 | 56 26 | 3 | 59 | 58 34 | 3 | 40 |
| 34 27 | 8 | 45 | 43 16 | 6 | 23 | 51 0 | 4 | 51 | 56 37 | 3 | 57 | 58 44 | 3 | 38 |
| 34 35 | 8 | 42 | 43 25 | 6 | 21 | 51 11 | 4 | 50 | 56 48 | 3 | 56 | 58 55 | 3 | 37 |
| 34 44 | 8 | 40 | 43 34 | 6 | 19 | 51 21 | 4 | 48 | 56 58 | 3 | 54 | 59 6 | 3 | 36 |
| 34 52 | 8 | 37 | 43 43 | 6 | 17 | 51 30 | 4 | 46 | 57 9 | 3 | 53 | 59 17 | 3 | 34 |
| 35 0 | 8 | 34 | 43 51 | 6 | 15 | 51 40 | 4 | 45 | 57 20 | 3 | 51 | 59 28 | 3 | 33 |
| 35 7 | 8 | 32 | 43 59 | 6 | 13 | 51 48 | 4 | 43 | 57 28 | 3 | 50 | 59 37 | 3 | 32 |
| 35 14 | 8 | 30 | 44 7 | 6 | 11 | 51 56 | 4 | 42 | 57 37 | 3 | 48 | 59 47 | 3 | 30 |
| 35 21 | 8 | 27 | 44 14 | 6 | 10 | 52 4 | 4 | 40 | 57 46 | 3 | 47 | 59 56 | 3 | 29 |
| 35 28 | 8 | 25 | 44 22 | 6 | 8 | 52 13 | 4 | 39 | 57 56 | 3 | 46 | 60 6 | 3 | 27 |
| 35 35 | 8 | 23 | 44 29 | 6 | 7 | 52 21 | 4 | 38 | 58 5 | 3 | 44 | 60 16 | 3 | 26 |
| 35 41 | 8 | 21 | 44 35 | 6 | 5 | 52 27 | 4 | 37 | 58 13 | 3 | 43 | 60 24 | 3 | 25 |
| 35 47 | 8 | 19 | 44 40 | 6 | 4 | 52 33 | 4 | 36 | 58 19 | 3 | 42 | 60 30 | 3 | 24 |
| 35 52 | 8 | 18 | 44 46 | 6 | 3 | 52 39 | 4 | 35 | 58 26 | 3 | 41 | 60 38 | 3 | 23 |
| 35 58 | 8 | 16 | 44 52 | 6 | 2 | 52 46 | 4 | 33 | 58 33 | 3 | 40 | 60 45 | 3 | 22 |
| 36 4 | 8 | 14 | 44 57 | 6 | 1 | 52 52 | 4 | 32 | 58 41 | 3 | 39 | 60 53 | 3 | 21 |
| 36 8 | 8 | 13 | 45 3 | 5 | 59 | 52 57 | 4 | 32 | 58 46 | 3 | 38 | 60 58 | 3 | 20 |
| 36 12 | 8 | 11 | 45 7 | 5 | 59 | 53 3 | 4 | 31 | 58 51 | 3 | 37 | 61 4 | 3 | 19 |
| 36 16 | 8 | 10 | 45 11 | 5 | 58 | 53 6 | 4 | 30 | 58 55 | 3 | 37 | 61 8 | 3 | 19 |

# JUNIUS

| | | | | |
|---|---|---|---|---|
| 1 | | *e* | **KL** | Sancti Nichomedis martyris |
| 2 | 19 | *f* | 4 Nonas | Sanctorum Marcellini et Petri |
| 3 | 8 | *g* | 3 Nonas | |
| 4 | 16 | A | 2 Nonas | |
| 5 | 5 | *b* | Nonis | Sancti Bonefacii sociorum eius martyrum |
| 6 | | *c* | 8 Idus | |
| 7 | 13 | *d* | 7 Idus | |
| 8 | 2 | *e* | 6 Idus | Sanctorum Medardi et Gilldardi martyrum |
| 9 | | *f* | 5 Idus | |
| 10 | 10 | *g* | 4 Idus | |
| 11 | | A | 3 Idus | Sancti Barnabe apostoli |
| 12 | 18 | *b* | 2 Idus | Sanctorum Basilidis Cirini Naboris |
| | | | | |
| 13 | 7 | *c* | Idibus | |
| 14 | | *d* | 18 Kl. | Sancti Basilii episcopi et confessoris |
| 15 | 15 | *e* | 17 Kl. | Sanctorum Viti et Modesti martyrum |
| 16 | 4 | *f* | 16 Kl. | Translacio Sancti Ricardi episcopi |
| 17 | | *g* | 15 Kl. | |
| · 18 | 12 | A | 14 Kl. | |
| 19 | 1 | *b* | 13 Kl. | Sanctorum Gervasi et Prothasi |
| 20 | | *c* | 12 Kl. | |
| 21 | 9 | *d* | 11 Kl. | |
| 22 | | *e* | 10 Kl. | Sancti Albani martyris |
| 23 | 17 | *f* | 9 Kl. | |
| 24 | 6 | *g* | 8 Kl. | Nativitas Sancti Johannis Baptiste |
| 25 | | A | 7 Kl. | |
| 26 | 14 | *b* | 6 Kl. | Sanctorum Johannis et Pauli martyrum |
| 27 | 3 | *c* | 5 Kl. | |
| 28 | | *d* | 4 Kl. | Sancti Leonis pape et confessoris |
| 29 | 11 | *e* | 3 Kl. | Sanctorum Apostolorum Petri et Pauli |
| 30 | | *f* | 2 Kl. | Commemoracio Sancti Pauli |

Variant readings for this month are listed on pp. 137–38.

| Numerus dierum | Verus locus solis | | Quantitates diei artificialis | | Quantitates diei vulgaris | | Quantitates utriusque crepusculorum matutini et vespertini | |
|---|---|---|---|---|---|---|---|---|
| | g. | m. | h. | m. | h. | m. | h. | m. |
| | Gemini | | | | | | | |
| 1 | 18 | 45 | 16 | 23 | 24 | 0 | 0 | 0 |
| 2 | 19 | 42 | 16 | 24 | 24 | 0 | 0 | 0 |
| 3 | 20 | 39 | 16 | 25 | 24 | 0 | 0 | 0 |
| 4 | 21 | 36 | 16 | 26 | 24 | 0 | 0 | 0 |
| 5 | 22 | 33 | 16 | 26 | 24 | 0 | 0 | 0 |
| 6 | 23 | 30 | 16 | 27 | 24 | 0 | 0 | 0 |
| 7 | 24 | 27 | 16 | 28 | 24 | 0 | 0 | 0 |
| 8 | 25 | 24 | 16 | 28 | 24 | 0 | 0 | 0 |
| 9 | 26 | 21 | 16 | 29 | 24 | 0 | 0 | 0 |
| 10 | 27 | 18 | 16 | 29 | 24 | 0 | 0 | 0 |
| 11 | 28 | 15 | 16 | 29 | 24 | 0 | 0 | 0 |
| 12 | 29 | 12 | 16 | 29 | 24 | 0 | 0 | 0 |
| | Cancer | | | | | | | |
| 13 | 0 | 9 | 16 | 30 | 24 | 0 | 0 | 0 |
| 14 | 1 | 6 | 16 | 29 | 24 | 0 | 0 | 0 |
| 15 | 2 | 3 | 16 | 29 | 24 | 0 | 0 | 0 |
| 16 | 3 | 0 | 16 | 29 | 24 | 0 | 0 | 0 |
| 17 | 3 | 57 | 16 | 29 | 24 | 0 | 0 | 0 |
| 18 | 4 | 54 | 16 | 28 | 24 | 0 | 0 | 0 |
| 19 | 5 | 51 | 16 | 28 | 24 | 0 | 0 | 0 |
| 20 | 6 | 48 | 16 | 27 | 24 | 0 | 0 | 0 |
| 21 | 7 | 45 | 16 | 26 | 24 | 0 | 0 | 0 |
| 22 | 8 | 42 | 16 | 25 | 24 | 0 | 0 | 0 |
| 23 | 9 | 39 | 16 | 24 | 24 | 0 | 0 | 0 |
| 24 | 10 | 36 | 16 | 23 | 24 | 0 | 0 | 0 |
| 25 | 11 | 33 | 16 | 22 | 24 | 0 | 0 | 0 |
| 26 | 12 | 30 | 16 | 21 | 24 | 0 | 0 | 0 |
| 27 | 13 | 27 | 16 | 20 | 24 | 0 | 0 | 0 |
| 28 | 14 | 24 | 16 | 18 | 24 | 0 | 0 | 0 |
| 29 | 15 | 21 | 16 | 17 | 24 | 0 | 0 | 0 |
| 30 | 16 | 19 | 16 | 15 | 24 | 0 | 0 | 0 |

Translations of Latin headings are to be found in the introduction, pp. 11-25.

# JUNIUS

| Numerus dierum | Primus Ciclus | | | | Secundus Ciclus | | | | Tercius | |
|---|---|---|---|---|---|---|---|---|---|---|
| | Ciclus Conjunccionis | Tempus vere conjunccionis | Ciclus Opposicionis | Tempus vere opposicionis | Ciclus Conjunccionis | Tempus vere conjunccionis | Ciclus Opposicionis | Tempus vere opposicionis | Ciclus Conjunccionis | Tempus vere conjunccionis |
| | | h. m. | | h. m. | | h. m. | | h. m. | | h. m. |
| 1 | 16 | 14 55 | | | | | | | | |
| 2 | | | | | | | 1 | 12 8 | 5 | 17 3 |
| 3 | 5 | 18 51 | 1 | 0 37 | 5 | 8 53 | | | | |
| 4 | | | 9 | 12 10 | | | 9 | 4 54 | 13 | 11 39 |
| 5 | 13 2 | 4 42 / 11 30 | 17 | 20 36 | 13 | 0 2 | 17 | 18 14 | | |
| 6 | 10 | 21 7 | 6 | 3 54 | 2 | 12 10 | | | 2 | 11 32 |
| 7 | | | 14 | 15 8 | 10 | 18 58 | 6 | 3 29 | 10 | 19 55 |
| 8 | 18 | 10 13 | | | | | 14 | 10 48 | | |
| 9 | | | 3 | 21 46 | 18 | 3 15 | 3 | 6 4 | 18 | 2 47 |
| 10 | 7 | 19 3 | | | 7 | 2 44 | 11 | 23 54 | 7 | 14 34 |
| 11 | | | 11 | 15 55 | 15 | 21 17 | | | | |
| 12 | 15 | 12 8 | | | | | 19 | 18 33 | 15 | 5 33 |
| 13 | | | 19 | 7 28 | | | | | 4 | 15 25 |
| 14 | 4 | 4 43 | 8 | 20 18 | 4 | 1 53 | 8 | 19 21 | | |
| 15 | 12 | 11 40 | | | 12 | 12 2 | | | 12 | 6 55 |
| 16 | 1 | 22 39 | 16 | 3 7 | 1 | 18 51 | 16 | 4 2 | 1 | 19 38 |
| 17 | | | 5 | 17 27 | | | 5 | 11 9 | | |
| 18 | 9 | 13 10 | | | 9 | 4 9 | 13 | 22 3 | 9 | 2 25 |
| 19 | | | 13 | 9 41 | 17 | 16 56 | | | 17 | 10 29 |
| 20 | 17 | 6 48 | 2 | 19 18 | | | | | | |
| 21 | 6 | 14 54 | | | | | 2 | 4 7 | 6 | 9 10 |
| 22 | | | 10 | 9 28 | 6 | 1 27 | 10 | 22 25 | | |
| 23 | 14 | 3 12 | 18 | 19 59 | 14 | 18 46 | | | 14 | 3 38 |
| 24 | 3 | 11 18 | | | 3 | 12 8 | 18 | 14 17 | | |
| 25 | 11 | 19 4 | 7 | 2 55 | 11 | 19 9 | 7 | 3 46 | 3 | 8 52 |
| 26 | | | 15 | 11 54 | | | 15 | 10 34 | 11 | 19 20 |
| 27 | 19 | 5 36 | | | 19 | 2 14 | | | | |
| 28 | | | 4 | 13 38 | 8 | 19 46 | 4 | 0 13 | 19 8 | 3 7 / 11 16 |
| 29 | 8 | 11 0 | | | | | 12 | 16 9 | 16 | 23 40 |
| 30 | | | 12 | 8 19 | 16 | 13 8 | | | | |

| Ciclus Opposicionis | Tempus vere opposicionis | Ciclus Conjunccionis | Tempus vere conjunccionis | Ciclus Opposicionis | Tempus vere opposicionis | Quantitates a noctis medio ad auroram | Quantitates a noctis medio ad solis ortum | Quantitates a meridie ad solis occasum | Quantitates a meridie ad noctem obscuram |
|---|---|---|---|---|---|---|---|---|---|
| | h. m. | | h. m. | | h. m. | h. m. | h. m. | h. m. | h. m. |
| 1 | 19 48 | 16 | 10 9 | 1 | 7 6 | 0 0 | 3 49 | 8 11 | 0 0 |
| | | 5 | 2 22 | 9 | 22 29 | 0 0 | 3 48 | 8 12 | 0 0 |
| 9 | 14 25 | 13 | 19 17 | | | 0 0 | 3 48 | 8 12 | 0 0 |
| | | | | 17 | 16 33 | 0 0 | 3 47 | 8 13 | 0 0 |
| 17 | 8 21 | | | | | 0 0 | 3 47 | 8 13 | 0 0 |
| | | 2 | 4 21 | 6 | 23 27 | 0 0 | 3 47 | 8 13 | 0 0 |
| 6 | 4 1 | 10 | 17 38 | | | 0 0 | 3 46 | 8 14 | 0 0 |
| 14 | 11 24 | | | 14 | 10 52 | 0 0 | 3 46 | 8 14 | 0 0 |
| 3 | 20 27 | 18 | 3 22 | 3 | 18 17 | 0 0 | 3 46 | 8 14 | 0 0 |
| | | 7 | 10 8 | | | 0 0 | 3 46 | 8 14 | 0 0 |
| 11 | 9 36 | 15 | 19 50 | 11 | 2 35 | 0 0 | 3 46 | 8 14 | 0 0 |
| | | | | 19 | 13 58 | 0 0 | 3 46 | 8 14 | 0 0 |
| 19 | 2 13 | 4 | 23 23 | | | 0 0 | 3 45 | 8 15 | 0 0 |
| 8 | 11 34 | | | 8 | 20 47 | 0 0 | 3 46 | 8 14 | 0 0 |
| | | 12 | 18 4 | | | 0 0 | 3 46 | 8 14 | 0 0 |
| 16 | 1 15 | 1 | 18 44 | 16 | 4 53 | 0 0 | 3 46 | 8 14 | 0 0 |
| 5 | 10 59 | | | 5 | 11 21 | 0 0 | 3 46 | 8 14 | 0 0 |
| 13 | 18 10 | 9 | 3 20 | 13 | 18 54 | 0 0 | 3 46 | 8 14 | 0 0 |
| | | 17 | 10 17 | | | 0 0 | 3 46 | 8 14 | 0 0 |
| 2 | 12 38 | 6 | 21 29 | 2 | 3 31 | 0 0 | 3 47 | 8 13 | 0 0 |
| | | | | 10 | 16 19 | 0 0 | 3 47 | 8 13 | 0 0 |
| 10 | 6 16 | 14 | 12 6 | | | 0 0 | 3 48 | 8 12 | 0 0 |
| | | | | 18 | 8 40 | 0 0 | 3 48 | 8 12 | 0 0 |
| 18 | 0 57 | 3 | 21 55 | | | 0 0 | 3 49 | 8 11 | 0 0 |
| | | | | 7 | 18 13 | 0 0 | 3 49 | 8 11 | 0 0 |
| 7 | 2 31 | 11 | 13 44 | | | 0 0 | 3 50 | 8 10 | 0 0 |
| 15 | 11 26 | | | 15 | 8 15 | 0 0 | 3 50 | 8 10 | 0 0 |
| 4 | 18 24 | 19 | 1 53 | 4 | 18 28 | 0 0 | 3 51 | 8 9 | 0 0 |
| 12 | 5 0 | 8 | 9 52 | | | 0 0 | 3 52 | 8 8 | 0 0 |
| | | 16 | 17 47 | 12 1 | 1 33 19 14 | 0 0 | 3 53 | 8 7 | 0 0 |

# JUNIUS

Altitudines solis et longitudines umbrarum cuiuslibet hominis
nocte 51 graduum

| Numerus dierum | 4 / 8 altitudines solis g. m. | umbre hominis pedes | partes | 5 / 7 altitudines solis g. m. | umbre hominis pedes | partes | 6 / 6 altitudines solis g. m. | umbre hominis pedes | partes | 7 / 5 altitudines solis g. m. | umbre hominis pedes | partes |
|---|---|---|---|---|---|---|---|---|---|---|---|---|
| 1 | 1 22 | 280 | 41 | 9 16 | 36 | 51 | 17 57 | 18 | 31 | 27 5 | 11 | 44 |
| 2 | 1 26 | 269 | 14 | 9 20 | 36 | 36 | 18 1 | 18 | 26 | 27 9 | 11 | 42 |
| 3 | 1 30 | 257 | 46 | 9 23 | 36 | 24 | 18 4 | 18 | 23 | 27 12 | 11 | 41 |
| 4 | 1 34 | 246 | 18 | 9 26 | 36 | 12 | 18 7 | 18 | 20 | 27 15 | 11 | 39 |
| 5 | 1 36 | 240 | 35 | 9 29 | 36 | 1 | 18 10 | 18 | 17 | 27 17 | 11 | 38 |
| 6 | 1 38 | 234 | 51 | 9 31 | 35 | 53 | 18 12 | 18 | 15 | 27 19 | 11 | 37 |
| 7 | 1 40 | 229 | 7 | 9 34 | 35 | 42 | 18 14 | 18 | 13 | 27 21 | 11 | 36 |
| 8 | 1 42 | 223 | 23 | 9 35 | 35 | 38 | 18 15 | 18 | 12 | 27 24 | 11 | 35 |
| 9 | 1 44 | 217 | 39 | 9 37 | 35 | 30 | 18 17 | 18 | 9 | 27 25 | 11 | 34 |
| 10 | 1 45 | 214 | 47 | 9 38 | 35 | 26 | 18 18 | 18 | 8 | 27 26 | 11 | 34 |
| 11 | 1 46 | 211 | 56 | 9 39 | 35 | 22 | 18 19 | 18 | 7 | 27 27 | 11 | 33 |
| 12 | 1 47 | 209 | 4 | 9 39 | 35 | 22 | 18 19 | 18 | 7 | 27 27 | 11 | 33 |
| 13 | 1 47 | 209 | 4 | 9 39 | 35 | 22 | 18 19 | 18 | 7 | 27 27 | 11 | 33 |
| 14 | 1 47 | 209 | 4 | 9 39 | 35 | 22 | 18 19 | 18 | 7 | 27 27 | 11 | 33 |
| 15 | 1 46 | 211 | 56 | 9 39 | 35 | 22 | 18 19 | 18 | 7 | 27 27 | 11 | 33 |
| 16 | 1 45 | 214 | 47 | 9 38 | 35 | 26 | 18 18 | 18 | 8 | 27 26 | 11 | 34 |
| 17 | 1 43 | 220 | 31 | 9 36 | 35 | 34 | 18 16 | 18 | 10 | 27 24 | 11 | 35 |
| 18 | 1 42 | 223 | 23 | 9 35 | 35 | 38 | 18 15 | 18 | 12 | 27 23 | 11 | 35 |
| 19 | 1 40 | 229 | 7 | 9 33 | 35 | 45 | 18 13 | 18 | 14 | 27 21 | 11 | 36 |
| 20 | 1 38 | 234 | 51 | 9 30 | 35 | 57 | 18 11 | 18 | 16 | 27 18 | 11 | 38 |
| 21 | 1 35 | 243 | 26 | 9 28 | 36 | 5 | 18 9 | 18 | 18 | 27 16 | 11 | 39 |
| 22 | 1 33 | 249 | 10 | 9 25 | 36 | 16 | 18 6 | 18 | 21 | 27 14 | 11 | 40 |
| 23 | 1 29 | 260 | 38 | 9 22 | 36 | 28 | 18 3 | 18 | 24 | 27 12 | 11 | 41 |
| 24 | 1 25 | 272 | 6 | 9 19 | 36 | 40 | 17 59 | 18 | 29 | 27 8 | 11 | 43 |
| 25 | 1 21 | 283 | 33 | 9 15 | 36 | 55 | 17 56 | 18 | 32 | 27 4 | 11 | 45 |
| 26 | 1 17 | 295 | 1 | 9 11 | 37 | 10 | 17 52 | 18 | 37 | 27 0 | 11 | 46 |
| 27 | 1 12 | 309 | 20 | 9 7 | 37 | 26 | 17 48 | 18 | 41 | 26 57 | 11 | 48 |
| 28 | 1 7 | 323 | 40 | 9 3 | 37 | 41 | 17 43 | 18 | 47 | 26 52 | 11 | 50 |
| 29 | 1 1 | 340 | 51 | 8 57 | 38 | 8 | 17 38 | 18 | 53 | 26 48 | 11 | 52 |
| 30 | 0 55 | 374 | 57 | 8 52 | 38 | 32 | 17 33 | 18 | 59 | 26 42 | 11 | 56 |

stature sex pedum in horis equalibus distantibus a meridie et a media
et 50 minutorum

| 8 | | | 9 | | | 10 | | | 11 | | | 12 a.m. | | |
| 4 | | | 3 | | | 2 | | | 1 | | | 0 p.m. | | |
| alti-tudines solis | umbre hominis | | alti-tudines solis | umbre hominis | | alti-tudines solis | umbre hominis | | alti-tudines solis | umbre hominis | | alti-tudines solis | umbre hominis | |
| g. m. | pedes | partes | g. m. | pedes | partes | g. m. | pedes | partes | g. m. | pedes | partes | g. m. | pedes | partes |
|---|---|---|---|---|---|---|---|---|---|---|---|---|---|---|
| 36 20 | 8 | 9 | 45 15 | 5 | 57 | 53 11 | 4 | 30 | 59 0 | 3 | 36 | 61 14 | 3 | 18 |
| 36 23 | 8 | 8 | 45 18 | 5 | 56 | 53 14 | 4 | 29 | 59 4 | 3 | 36 | 61 18 | 3 | 17 |
| 36 26 | 8 | 7 | 45 22 | 5 | 56 | 53 17 | 4 | 29 | 59 8 | 3 | 35 | 61 22 | 3 | 17 |
| 36 30 | 8 | 6 | 45 25 | 5 | 55 | 53 21 | 4 | 28 | 59 11 | 3 | 35 | 61 26 | 3 | 16 |
| 36 33 | 8 | 5 | 45 27 | 5 | 55 | 53 25 | 4 | 27 | 59 15 | 3 | 34 | 61 30 | 3 | 16 |
| 36 34 | 8 | 5 | 45 29 | 5 | 54 | 53 27 | 4 | 27 | 59 17 | 3 | 34 | 61 32 | 3 | 15 |
| 36 37 | 8 | 4 | 45 31 | 5 | 54 | 53 30 | 4 | 26 | 59 21 | 3 | 34 | 61 36 | 3 | 15 |
| 36 38 | 8 | 4 | 45 34 | 5 | 53 | 53 31 | 4 | 26 | 59 22 | 3 | 34 | 61 38 | 3 | 14 |
| 36 38 | 8 | 4 | 45 34 | 5 | 53 | 53 32 | 4 | 26 | 59 23 | 3 | 33 | 61 38 | 3 | 14 |
| 36 39 | 8 | 3 | 45 35 | 5 | 53 | 53 33 | 4 | 26 | 59 24 | 3 | 33 | 61 40 | 3 | 14 |
| 36 41 | 8 | 3 | 45 37 | 5 | 53 | 53 35 | 4 | 26 | 59 26 | 3 | 33 | 61 42 | 3 | 14 |
| 36 41 | 8 | 3 | 45 37 | 5 | 53 | 53 35 | 4 | 26 | 59 26 | 3 | 33 | 61 42 | 3 | 14 |
| 36 41 | 8 | 3 | 45 38 | 5 | 52 | 53 37 | 4 | 25 | 59 28 | 3 | 33 | 61 44 | 3 | 14 |
| 36 41 | 8 | 3 | 45 37 | 5 | 53 | 53 35 | 4 | 26 | 59 26 | 3 | 33 | 61 42 | 3 | 14 |
| 36 41 | 8 | 3 | 45 37 | 5 | 53 | 53 35 | 4 | 26 | 59 26 | 3 | 33 | 61 42 | 3 | 14 |
| 36 39 | 8 | 3 | 45 35 | 5 | 53 | 53 33 | 4 | 26 | 59 24 | 3 | 33 | 61 40 | 3 | 14 |
| 36 38 | 8 | 4 | 45 34 | 5 | 53 | 53 32 | 4 | 26 | 59 23 | 3 | 33 | 61 38 | 3 | 14 |
| 36 38 | 8 | 4 | 45 33 | 5 | 53 | 53 32 | 4 | 26 | 59 23 | 3 | 33 | 61 38 | 3 | 14 |
| 36 36 | 8 | 4 | 45 31 | 5 | 54 | 53 28 | 4 | 27 | 59 19 | 3 | 34 | 61 34 | 3 | 15 |
| 36 32 | 8 | 5 | 45 27 | 5 | 55 | 53 25 | 4 | 27 | 59 15 | 3 | 34 | 61 30 | 3 | 16 |
| 36 31 | 8 | 6 | 45 26 | 5 | 55 | 53 24 | 4 | 27 | 59 13 | 3 | 35 | 61 28 | 3 | 16 |
| 36 29 | 8 | 6 | 45 25 | 5 | 55 | 53 21 | 4 | 28 | 59 11 | 3 | 35 | 61 26 | 3 | 16 |
| 36 26 | 8 | 7 | 45 21 | 5 | 56 | 53 17 | 4 | 29 | 59 8 | 3 | 35 | 61 22 | 3 | 17 |
| 36 22 | 8 | 8 | 45 16 | 5 | 57 | 53 13 | 4 | 29 | 59 2 | 3 | 36 | 61 16 | 3 | 17 |
| 36 19 | 8 | 9 | 45 14 | 5 | 57 | 53 9 | 4 | 30 | 58 58 | 3 | 36 | 61 12 | 3 | 18 |
| 36 15 | 8 | 10 | 45 8 | 5 | 58 | 53 5 | 4 | 31 | 58 53 | 3 | 37 | 61 6 | 3 | 19 |
| 36 11 | 8 | 12 | 45 5 | 5 | 59 | 53 1 | 4 | 31 | 58 49 | 3 | 38 | 61 2 | 3 | 19 |
| 36 6 | 8 | 13 | 45 0 | 6 | 0 | 52 55 | 4 | 32 | 58 44 | 3 | 38 | 60 56 | 3 | 20 |
| 36 2 | 8 | 14 | 44 56 | 6 | 1 | 52 51 | 4 | 33 | 58 39 | 3 | 39 | 60 51 | 3 | 21 |
| 35 56 | 8 | 16 | 44 51 | 6 | 2 | 52 44 | 4 | 34 | 58 32 | 3 | 40 | 60 43 | 3 | 22 |

# JULIUS

| | | | | |
|---|---|---|---|---|
| 1 | 19 | g | **KL** | Octava Sancti Johannis Baptiste |
| 2 | 8 | A | 6 Nonas | Sanctorum Processi et Martiniani martyrum |
| 3 | | b | 5 Nonas | |
| 4 | 16 | c | 4 Nonas | Translacio Sancti Martini |
| 5 | 5 | d | 3 Nonas | |
| 6 | | e | 2 Nonas | |
| 7 | 13 | f | Nonis | |
| 8 | 2 | g | 8 Idus | |
| 9 | | A | 7 Idus | |
| 10 | 10 | b | 6 Idus | Sanctorum Septem Fratrum |
| 11 | | c | 5 Idus | Translacio Sancti Benedicti |
| 12 | 18 | d | 4 Idus | |
| 13 | 7 | e | 3 Idus | |
| 14 | | f | 2 Idus | |
| 15 | 15 | g | Idibus | Translacio Sancti Swithini confessoris |
| 16 | 4 | A | 17 Kl. | |
| 17 | | b | 16 Kl. | Sancti Kenelmi regis et martyris |
| 18 | 12 | c | 15 Kl. | Sancti Arnulphi episcopi et martyris |
| 19 | 1 | d | 14 Kl. | |
| 20 | | e | 13 Kl. | Sancte Margarete virginis |
| 21 | 9 | f | 12 Kl. | Sancte Praxedis virginis non martyris |
| 22 | | g | 11 Kl. | Sancte Marie Magdelene |
| 23 | 17 | A | 10 Kl. | Sancti Apollinaris episcopi et martyris |
| 24 | 6 | b | 9 Kl. | Sancte Cristine virginis et martyris |
| 25 | | c | 8 Kl. | Sancti Jacobi apostoli |
| 26 | 14 | d | 7 Kl. | Sancte Anne matris Marie |
| 27 | 3 | e | 6 Kl. | Sanctorum Septem Dormiencium |
| 28 | | f | 5 Kl. | Sancti Sampsonis episcopi et confessoris |
| 29 | 11 | g | 4 Kl. | Sanctorum Felicis Simplicii Faustini |
| 30 | 19 | A | 3 Kl. | Sanctorum Abdon et Sennes |
| 31 | | b | 2 Kl. | Sancti Germani episcopi et confessoris |

Variant readings for this month are listed on pp. 138–39.

| Numerus dierum | Verus locus solis | | Quantitates diei artificialis | | Quantitates diei vulgaris | | Quantitates utriusque crepusculorum matutini et vespertini | |
|---|---|---|---|---|---|---|---|---|
| | g. | m. | h. | m. | h. | m. | h. | m. |
| | Cancer | | | | | | | |
| 1 | 17 | 16 | 16 | 13 | 24 | 0 | 0 | 0 |
| 2 | 18 | 13 | 16 | 12 | 24 | 0 | 0 | 0 |
| 3 | 19 | 10 | 16 | 10 | 24 | 0 | 0 | 0 |
| 4 | 20 | 7 | 16 | 8 | 24 | 0 | 0 | 0 |
| 5 | 21 | 4 | 16 | 6 | 24 | 0 | 0 | 0 |
| 6 | 22 | 1 | 16 | 4 | 24 | 0 | 0 | 0 |
| 7 | 22 | 58 | 16 | 2 | 24 | 0 | 0 | 0 |
| 8 | 23 | 55 | 16 | 0 | 24 | 0 | 0 | 0 |
| 9 | 24 | 52 | 15 | 57 | 24 | 0 | 0 | 0 |
| 10 | 25 | 50 | 15 | 55 | 24 | 0 | 0 | 0 |
| 11 | 26 | 47 | 15 | 53 | 24 | 0 | 0 | 0 |
| 12 | 27 | 44 | 15 | 50 | 24 | 0 | 0 | 0 |
| 13 | 28 | 41 | 15 | 47 | 24 | 0 | 0 | 0 |
| 14 | 29 | 8 | 15 | 45 | 24 | 0 | 0 | 0 |
| | Leo | | | | | | | |
| 15 | 0 | 36 | 15 | 42 | 23 | 32 | 3 | 55 |
| 16 | 1 | 33 | 15 | 39 | 23 | 3 | 3 | 42 |
| 17 | 2 | 30 | 15 | 37 | 22 | 43 | 3 | 33 |
| 18 | 3 | 28 | 15 | 34 | 22 | 28 | 3 | 27 |
| 19 | 4 | 25 | 15 | 31 | 22 | 15 | 3 | 22 |
| 20 | 5 | 22 | 15 | 28 | 22 | 2 | 3 | 17 |
| 21 | 6 | 20 | 15 | 25 | 21 | 51 | 3 | 13 |
| 22 | 7 | 17 | 15 | 22 | 21 | 40 | 3 | 9 |
| 23 | 8 | 15 | 15 | 19 | 21 | 29 | 3 | 5 |
| 24 | 9 | 12 | 15 | 16 | 21 | 20 | 3 | 2 |
| 25 | 10 | 10 | 15 | 13 | 21 | 11 | 2 | 59 |
| 26 | 11 | 7 | 15 | 9 | 21 | 1 | 2 | 56 |
| 27 | 12 | 5 | 15 | 6 | 20 | 54 | 2 | 54 |
| 28 | 13 | 2 | 15 | 3 | 20 | 45 | 2 | 51 |
| 29 | 14 | 0 | 14 | 59 | 20 | 37 | 2 | 49 |
| 30 | 14 | 57 | 14 | 56 | 20 | 30 | 2 | 47 |
| 31 | 15 | 55 | 14 | 53 | 20 | 21 | 2 | 44 |

Translations of Latin headings are to be found in the introduction, pp. 11-25.

# JULIUS

| Numerus dierum | Primus Ciclus | | | | Secundus Ciclus | | | | Tercius | |
|---|---|---|---|---|---|---|---|---|---|---|
| | Ciclus Conjunccionis | Tempus vere conjunccionis | Ciclus Opposicionis | Tempus vere opposicionis | Ciclus Conjunccionis | Tempus vere conjunccionis | Ciclus Opposicionis | Tempus vere opposicionis | Ciclus Conjunccionis | Tempus vere conjunccionis |
| | | h. m. | | h. m. | | h. m. | | h. m. | | h. m. |
| 1 | 16 | 5 25 | | | | | | | | |
| 2 | | | 1 | 10 54 | 5 | 21 38 | 1 | 1 55 | 5 | 7 48 |
| 3 | 5 | 3 56 | 9 | 20 13 | | | 9 | 16 26 | | |
| 4 | 13 / 2 | 11 57 / 19 42 | | | 13 | 10 19 | | | 13 | 1 25 |
| 5 | | | 17 / 6 | 3 23 / 13 11 | 2 | 18 46 | 17 | 3 16 | 2 | 19 32 |
| 6 | 10 | 7 38 | | | | | 6 | 10 21 | | |
| 7 | 18 | 23 11 | 14 | 2 58 | 10 | 2 23 | 14 | 19 5 | 10 | 2 42 |
| 8 | | | | | 18 | 12 37 | 3 | 20 4 | 18 | 9 40 |
| 9 | | | 3 | 12 23 | 7 | 17 21 | | | | |
| 10 | 7 | 9 4 | | | | | 11 | 14 44 | 7 | 2 27 |
| 11 | 15 | 23 58 | 11 | 4 58 | 15 | 11 55 | | | 15 | 19 35 |
| 12 | | | 19 | 18 3 | | | 19 | 8 32 | | |
| 13 | 4 | 11 38 | | | 4 | 11 13 | | | 4 | 4 26 |
| 14 | 12 | 18 31 | 8 | 2 59 | 12 | 19 30 | 8 | 3 37 | 12 | 17 27 |
| 15 | | | 16 | 10 26 | | | 16 | 10 56 | | |
| 16 | 1 | 10 17 | | | 1 | 2 58 | 5 | 20 13 | 1 | 2 20 |
| 17 | | | 5 | 6 18 | 9 | 14 33 | | | 9 | 9 47 |
| 18 | 9 | 3 3 | | | | | 13 | 9 44 | 17 | 19 38 |
| 19 | 17 | 21 43 | 13 | 0 18 | 17 | 5 50 | | | | |
| 20 | | | 2 | 7 32 | | | 2 | 18 56 | 6 | 23 50 |
| 21 | 6 | 1 50 | 10 | 19 11 | 6 | 15 44 | | | | |
| 22 | 14 | 11 46 | | | | | 10 | 11 48 | 14 | 18 26 |
| 23 | 3 | 18 36 | 18 | 3 42 | 14 / 3 | 7 0 / 19 14 | | | | |
| 24 | | | 7 | 10 57 | | | 18 / 7 | 1 14 / 10 37 | 3 | 18 38 |
| 25 | 11 | 4 2 | 15 | 22 4 | 11 | 2 7 | 15 | 17 56 | | |
| 26 | 19 | 17 5 | | | 19 | 10 17 | | | 11 | 3 5 |
| 27 | | | | | | | 4 | 13 3 | 19 / 8 | 9 58 / 21 32 |
| 28 | | | 4 | 4 43 | 8 | 9 42 | | | | |
| 29 | 8 | 2 1 | 12 | 22 56 | | | 12 | 6 52 | 16 | 12 34 |
| 30 | 16 | 19 11 | | | 16 | 4 19 | | | | |
| 31 | | | 1 | 19 54 | | | 1 | 14 35 | 5 | 22 29 |

# Ciclus          Quartus Ciclus

| Ciclus Opposicionis | Tempus vere opposicionis | Ciclus Conjunccionis | Tempus vere conjunccionis | Ciclus Opposicionis | Tempus vere opposicionis | Quantitates a noctis medio ad auroram | Quantitates a noctis medio ad solis ortum | Quantitates a meridie ad solis occasum | Quantitates a meridie ad noctem obscuram |
|---|---|---|---|---|---|---|---|---|---|
| | h. m. | | h. m. | | h. m. | h. m. | h. m. | h. m. | h. m. |
| 1 | 10 29 | 5 | 15 39 | | | 0 0 | 3 54 | 8 6 | 0 0 |
| | | | | 9 | 12 39 | 0 0 | 3 54 | 8 6 | 0 0 |
| 9 | 4 54 | 13 | 10 0 | | | 0 0 | 3 55 | 8 5 | 0 0 |
| 17 | 21 4 | | | 17 | 7 21 | 0 0 | 3 56 | 8 4 | 0 0 |
| | | 2 | 15 52 | | | 0 0 | 3 57 | 8 3 | 0 0 |
| 6 | 11 15 | | | 6 | 9 40 | 0 0 | 3 58 | 8 2 | 0 0 |
| 14 | 18 4 | 10 | 2 38 | 14 | 18 51 | 0 0 | 3 59 | 8 1 | 0 0 |
| | | 18 | 10 33 | | | 0 0 | 4 0 | 8 0 | 0 0 |
| 3 | 7 1 | 7 | 18 27 | 3 | 1 43 | 0 0 | 4 2 | 7 58 | 0 0 |
| 11 | 22 41 | | | 11 | 11 56 | 0 0 | 4 3 | 7 57 | 0 0 |
| | | 15 | 6 31 | | | 0 0 | 4 4 | 7 56 | 0 0 |
| 19 | 16 53 | | | 19 | 1 55 | 0 0 | 4 5 | 7 55 | 0 0 |
| 8 | 23 24 | 4 | 14 18 | | | 0 0 | 4 7 | 7 53 | 0 0 |
| | | | | 8 | 11 25 | 0 0 | 4 8 | 7 52 | 0 0 |
| 16 | 10 35 | 12 | 8 4 | | | 0 14 | 4 9 | 7 51 | 11 46 |
| 5 | 17 51 | 1 | 2 58 | 16 / 5 | 3 53 / 18 47 | 0 29 | 4 11 | 7 49 | 11 31 |
| | | 9 | 10 16 | | | 0 39 | 4 12 | 7 48 | 11 21 |
| 13 | 2 20 | 17 | 17 11 | 13 | 1 38 | 0 46 | 4 13 | 7 47 | 11 14 |
| | | 2 | 13 55 | | | 0 53 | 4 15 | 7 45 | 11 7 |
| 2 | 2 36 | 6 | 9 10 | | | 0 59 | 4 16 | 7 44 | 11 1 |
| 10 | 21 15 | | | 10 | 5 19 | 1 5 | 4 18 | 7 42 | 10 55 |
| | | 14 | 2 8 | 18 | 23 23 | 1 10 | 4 19 | 7 41 | 10 50 |
| 18 | 15 14 | | | | | 1 16 | 4 21 | 7 39 | 10 44 |
| | | 3 | 11 18 | | | 1 20 | 4 22 | 7 38 | 10 40 |
| 7 | 11 7 | | | 7 | 6 27 | 1 25 | 4 24 | 7 36 | 10 35 |
| 15 | 18 34 | 11 | 0 41 | 15 | 17 58 | 1 30 | 4 26 | 7 34 | 10 30 |
| 4 | 3 26 | 19 | 10 30 | | | 1 33 | 4 27 | 7 33 | 10 27 |
| 12 | 16 34 | 8 | 17 18 | 4 | 1 27 | 1 38 | 4 29 | 7 31 | 10 22 |
| | | | | 12 | 9 40 | 1 42 | 4 31 | 7 29 | 10 18 |
| | | 16 | 2 53 | 1 | 9 14 | 1 45 | 4 32 | 7 28 | 10 15 |
| 1 | 1 35 | 5 | 6 27 | | | 1 50 | 4 34 | 7 26 | 10 10 |

# JULIUS

Altitudines solis et longitudines umbrarum cuiuslibet hominis
nocte 51 graduum

| Numerus dierum | 4 8 | | | 5 7 | | | 6 6 | | | 7 5 | | |
|---|---|---|---|---|---|---|---|---|---|---|---|---|
| | altitudines solis | umbre hominis | | altitudines solis | umbre hominis | | altitudines solis | umbre hominis | | altitudines solis | umbre hominis | |
| | g. m. | pedes | partes | g. m. | pedes | partes | g. m. | pedes | partes | g. m. | pedes | partes |
| 1 | 0 50 | 412 | 29 | 8 46 | 39 | 1 | 17 27 | 19 | 6 | 26 37 | 11 | 58 |
| 2 | 0 43 | 479 | 36 | 8 40 | 39 | 30 | 17 21 | 19 | 13 | 26 31 | 12 | 1 |
| 3 | 0 37 | 557 | 25 | 8 34 | 39 | 59 | 17 15 | 19 | 20 | 26 25 | 12 | 5 |
| 4 | 0 30 | 687 | 33 | 8 27 | 40 | 33 | 17 9 | 19 | 27 | 26 19 | 12 | 8 |
| 5 | 0 23 | 896 | 43 | 8 20 | 41 | 7 | 17 3 | 19 | 34 | 26 13 | 12 | 11 |
| 6 | 0 15 | 1375 | 10 | 8 13 | 41 | 41 | 16 55 | 19 | 44 | 26 6 | 12 | 15 |
| 7 | 0 7 | 2945 | 24 | 8 5 | 42 | 20 | 16 48 | 19 | 53 | 25 58 | 12 | 19 |
| 8 | 0 0 | 0 | 0 | 7 57 | 43 | 2 | 16 42 | 20 | 1 | 25 51 | 12 | 23 |
| 9 | 0 0 | 0 | 0 | 7 49 | 43 | 51 | 16 34 | 20 | 11 | 25 44 | 12 | 27 |
| 10 | 0 0 | 0 | 0 | 7 41 | 44 | 41 | 16 26 | 20 | 22 | 25 36 | 12 | 32 |
| 11 | 0 0 | 0 | 0 | 7 32 | 45 | 36 | 16 17 | 20 | 33 | 25 27 | 12 | 37 |
| 12 | 0 0 | 0 | 0 | 7 22 | 46 | 37 | 16 9 | 20 | 44 | 25 19 | 12 | 41 |
| 13 | 0 0 | 0 | 0 | 7 14 | 47 | 26 | 16 0 | 20 | 55 | 25 11 | 12 | 46 |
| 14 | 0 0 | 0 | 0 | 7 4 | 48 | 27 | 15 51 | 21 | 8 | 25 2 | 12 | 51 |
| 15 | 0 0 | 0 | 0 | 6 54 | 49 | 41 | 15 42 | 21 | 21 | 24 53 | 12 | 57 |
| 16 | 0 0 | 0 | 0 | 6 44 | 51 | 3 | 15 32 | 21 | 36 | 24 43 | 13 | 3 |
| 17 | 0 0 | 0 | 0 | 6 34 | 52 | 26 | 15 22 | 21 | 51 | 24 33 | 13 | 9 |
| 18 | 0 0 | 0 | 0 | 6 23 | 53 | 56 | 15 12 | 22 | 5 | 24 23 | 13 | 15 |
| 19 | 0 0 | 0 | 0 | 6 13 | 55 | 18 | 15 1 | 22 | 22 | 24 13 | 13 | 21 |
| 20 | 0 0 | 0 | 0 | 6 2 | 56 | 49 | 14 51 | 22 | 39 | 24 3 | 13 | 27 |
| 21 | 0 0 | 0 | 0 | 5 50 | 59 | 0 | 14 40 | 22 | 57 | 23 52 | 13 | 33 |
| 22 | 0 0 | 0 | 0 | 5 39 | 61 | 7 | 14 29 | 23 | 16 | 23 41 | 13 | 41 |
| 23 | 0 0 | 0 | 0 | 5 27 | 63 | 25 | 14 17 | 23 | 36 | 23 30 | 13 | 48 |
| 24 | 0 0 | 0 | 0 | 5 15 | 65 | 43 | 14 5 | 23 | 56 | 23 18 | 13 | 56 |
| 25 | 0 0 | 0 | 0 | 5 2 | 68 | 12 | 13 54 | 24 | 16 | 23 6 | 14 | 4 |
| 26 | 0 0 | 0 | 0 | 4 49 | 71 | 45 | 13 41 | 24 | 40 | 22 53 | 14 | 13 |
| 27 | 0 0 | 0 | 0 | 4 37 | 75 | 12 | 13 29 | 25 | 3 | 22 41 | 14 | 22 |
| 28 | 0 0 | 0 | 0 | 4 24 | 78 | 57 | 13 17 | 25 | 26 | 22 29 | 14 | 30 |
| 29 | 0 0 | 0 | 0 | 4 11 | 82 | 41 | 13 4 | 25 | 51 | 22 17 | 14 | 39 |
| 30 | 0 0 | 0 | 0 | 3 57 | 87 | 17 | 12 51 | 26 | 19 | 22 4 | 14 | 48 |
| 31 | 0 0 | 0 | 0 | 3 44 | 93 | 29 | 12 38 | 26 | 48 | 21 51 | 14 | 58 |

stature sex pedum in horis equalibus distantibus a meridie et a media
et 50 minutorum

| 8 / 4 | | | 9 / 3 | | | 10 / 2 | | | 11 / 1 | | | 12 a.m. / 0 p.m. | | |
|---|---|---|---|---|---|---|---|---|---|---|---|---|---|---|
| altitudines solis | umbre hominis | | altitudines solis | umbre hominis | | altitudines solis | umbre hominis | | altitudines solis | umbre hominis | | altitudines solis | umbre hominis | |
| g. m. | pedes | partes | g. m. | pedes | partes | g. m. | pedes | partes | g. m. | pedes | partes | g. m. | pedes | partes |
| 35 50 | 8 | 18 | 44 44 | 6 | 3 | 52 38 | 4 | 35 | 58 24 | 3 | 41 | 60 36 | 3 | 23 |
| 35 44 | 8 | 20 | 44 39 | 6 | 5 | 52 31 | 4 | 36 | 58 17 | 3 | 42 | 60 28 | 3 | 24 |
| 35 38 | 8 | 22 | 44 33 | 6 | 6 | 52 24 | 4 | 37 | 58 9 | 3 | 44 | 60 20 | 3 | 25 |
| 35 32 | 8 | 24 | 44 26 | 6 | 7 | 52 17 | 4 | 38 | 58 2 | 3 | 45 | 60 12 | 3 | 26 |
| 35 27 | 8 | 25 | 44 20 | 6 | 9 | 52 11 | 4 | 39 | 57 54 | 3 | 46 | 60 4 | 3 | 27 |
| 35 19 | 8 | 28 | 44 11 | 6 | 11 | 52 0 | 4 | 41 | 57 42 | 3 | 48 | 59 52 | 3 | 29 |
| 35 12 | 8 | 30 | 44 4 | 6 | 12 | 51 53 | 4 | 42 | 57 34 | 3 | 49 | 59 43 | 3 | 30 |
| 35 5 | 8 | 32 | 43 56 | 6 | 14 | 51 45 | 4 | 44 | 57 25 | 3 | 50 | 59 34 | 3 | 32 |
| 34 58 | 8 | 35 | 43 50 | 6 | 15 | 51 38 | 4 | 45 | 57 18 | 3 | 51 | 59 26 | 3 | 33 |
| 34 49 | 8 | 38 | 43 39 | 6 | 18 | 51 27 | 4 | 47 | 57 5 | 3 | 53 | 59 13 | 3 | 35 |
| 34 41 | 8 | 40 | 43 31 | 6 | 19 | 51 17 | 4 | 49 | 56 55 | 3 | 55 | 59 2 | 3 | 36 |
| 34 32 | 8 | 43 | 43 22 | 6 | 21 | 51 8 | 4 | 50 | 56 44 | 3 | 56 | 58 51 | 3 | 37 |
| 34 23 | 8 | 46 | 43 13 | 6 | 23 | 50 57 | 4 | 52 | 56 34 | 3 | 58 | 58 41 | 3 | 39 |
| 34 15 | 8 | 49 | 43 4 | 6 | 25 | 50 48 | 4 | 53 | 56 23 | 4 | 0 | 58 30 | 3 | 41 |
| 34 6 | 8 | 51 | 42 55 | 6 | 27 | 50 36 | 4 | 55 | 56 10 | 4 | 2 | 58 17 | 3 | 42 |
| 33 56 | 8 | 55 | 42 44 | 6 | 30 | 50 26 | 4 | 57 | 55 58 | 4 | 3 | 58 4 | 3 | 44 |
| 33 46 | 8 | 58 | 42 34 | 6 | 32 | 50 15 | 4 | 59 | 55 47 | 4 | 5 | 57 51 | 3 | 46 |
| 33 36 | 9 | 2 | 42 22 | 6 | 35 | 50 2 | 5 | 2 | 55 32 | 4 | 7 | 57 37 | 3 | 48 |
| 33 26 | 9 | 5 | 42 12 | 6 | 37 | 49 51 | 5 | 4 | 55 20 | 4 | 9 | 57 25 | 3 | 50 |
| 33 15 | 9 | 9 | 42 1 | 6 | 40 | 49 40 | 5 | 6 | 55 8 | 4 | 11 | 57 12 | 3 | 52 |
| 33 4 | 9 | 13 | 41 50 | 6 | 42 | 49 27 | 5 | 8 | 54 53 | 4 | 14 | 56 56 | 3 | 55 |
| 32 52 | 9 | 17 | 41 37 | 6 | 45 | 49 13 | 5 | 11 | 54 38 | 4 | 16 | 56 41 | 3 | 57 |
| 32 41 | 9 | 21 | 41 26 | 6 | 48 | 49 0 | 5 | 13 | 54 25 | 4 | 18 | 56 26 | 3 | 59 |
| 32 30 | 9 | 25 | 41 13 | 6 | 51 | 48 47 | 5 | 15 | 54 11 | 4 | 20 | 56 11 | 4 | 1 |
| 32 18 | 9 | 29 | 41 1 | 6 | 54 | 48 34 | 5 | 18 | 53 58 | 4 | 22 | 55 57 | 4 | 3 |
| 32 5 | 9 | 34 | 40 47 | 6 | 57 | 48 20 | 5 | 20 | 53 42 | 4 | 24 | 55 40 | 4 | 6 |
| 31 52 | 9 | 39 | 40 34 | 7 | 1 | 48 6 | 5 | 23 | 53 25 | 4 | 27 | 55 23 | 4 | 9 |
| 31 40 | 9 | 44 | 40 21 | 7 | 4 | 47 51 | 5 | 26 | 53 10 | 4 | 30 | 55 8 | 4 | 11 |
| 31 28 | 9 | 48 | 40 8 | 7 | 7 | 47 37 | 5 | 29 | 52 54 | 4 | 32 | 54 52 | 4 | 14 |
| 31 15 | 9 | 53 | 39 54 | 7 | 11 | 47 22 | 5 | 32 | 52 38 | 4 | 35 | 54 35 | 4 | 16 |
| 31 2 | 9 | 58 | 39 40 | 7 | 14 | 47 7 | 5 | 35 | 52 22 | 4 | 37 | 54 19 | 4 | 19 |

# AUGUSTUS

| | | | | |
|---|---|---|---|---|
| 1 | 8 | c | **KL** | Ad vincula Sancti Petri |
| 2 | 16 | d | 4 Nonas | Sancti Stephani pape et martyris |
| 3 | 5 | e | 3 Nonas | Invencio Sancti Stephani |
| 4 | | f | 2 Nonas | |
| 5 | 13 | g | Nonis | Sancti Dominici confessoris |
| 6 | 2 | A | 8 Idus | Sanctorum Sexti Felicissimi et Agapiti |
| 7 | | b | 7 Idus | Sancti Donati episcopi et martyris |
| 8 | 10 | c | 6 Idus | Sancti Cyriaci sociorumque eius martyrum |
| 9 | | d | 5 Idus | Sancti Romani martyris |
| 10 | 18 | e | 4 Idus | Sancti Laurencii martyris |
| 11 | 7 | f | 3 Idus | Sancti Tyburcii martyris |
| 12 | | g | 2 Idus | |
| 13 | 15 | A | Idibus | Sancti Ypoliti sociorumque eius |
| 14 | 4 | b | 19 Kl. | Sancti Eusebii presbiteri |
| 15 | | c | 18 Kl. | Assumpcio Sancte Marie Virginis |
| 16 | 12 | d | 17 Kl. | |
| 17 | 1 | e | 16 Kl. | |
| 18 | | f | 15 Kl. | Sancti Agapiti martyris |
| 19 | 9 | g | 14 Kl. | Sancti Magni martyris |
| 20 | | A | 13 Kl. | |
| 21 | 17 | b | 12 Kl. | |
| 22 | 6 | c | 11 Kl. | |
| 23 | | d | 10 Kl. | Sancti Zachei episcopi |
| 24 | 14 | e | 9 Kl. | Sancti Bartholomei apostoli |
| 25 | 3 | f | 8 Kl. | |
| 26 | | g | 7 Kl. | |
| 27 | 11 | A | 6 Kl. | Sancti Rufi martyris |
| 28 | 19 | b | 5 Kl. | Sancti Augustini episcopi et doctoris |
| 29 | | c | 4 Kl. | Decollacio Sancti Johannis Baptiste |
| 30 | 8 | d | 3 Kl. | Sanctorum Felicis et Adaucti |
| 31 | | e | 2 Kl. | Sancte Wyburge virginis non |

Variant readings for this month are listed on p. 139.

| Numerus dierum | Verus locus solis | | Quantitates diei artificialis | | Quantitates diei vulgaris | | Quantitates utriusque crepusculorum matutini et vespertini | |
|---|---|---|---|---|---|---|---|---|
| | g. | m. | h. | m. | h. | m. | h. | m. |
| | Leo | | | | | | | |
| 1 | 16 | 52 | 14 | 49 | 20 | 13 | 2 | 42 |
| 2 | 17 | 50 | 14 | 46 | 20 | 6 | 2 | 40 |
| 3 | 18 | 48 | 14 | 43 | 19 | 59 | 2 | 38 |
| 4 | 19 | 45 | 14 | 39 | 19 | 51 | 2 | 36 |
| 5 | 20 | 43 | 14 | 35 | 19 | 45 | 2 | 35 |
| 6 | 21 | 41 | 14 | 32 | 19 | 38 | 2 | 33 |
| 7 | 22 | 39 | 14 | 28 | 19 | 30 | 2 | 31 |
| 8 | 23 | 36 | 14 | 25 | 19 | 25 | 2 | 30 |
| 9 | 24 | 34 | 14 | 21 | 19 | 17 | 2 | 28 |
| 10 | 25 | 32 | 14 | 17 | 19 | 11 | 2 | 27 |
| 11 | 26 | 30 | 14 | 14 | 19 | 6 | 2 | 26 |
| 12 | 27 | 28 | 14 | 10 | 18 | 58 | 2 | 24 |
| 13 | 28 | 26 | 14 | 6 | 18 | 52 | 2 | 23 |
| 14 | 29 | 24 | 14 | 3 | 18 | 47 | 2 | 22 |
| | Virgo | | | | | | | |
| 15 | 0 | 22 | 13 | 59 | 18 | 41 | 2 | 21 |
| 16 | 1 | 20 | 13 | 55 | 18 | 33 | 2 | 19 |
| 17 | 2 | 18 | 13 | 51 | 18 | 27 | 2 | 18 |
| 18 | 3 | 16 | 13 | 47 | 18 | 21 | 2 | 17 |
| 19 | 4 | 14 | 13 | 44 | 18 | 16 | 2 | 16 |
| 20 | 5 | 13 | 13 | 40 | 18 | 10 | 2 | 15 |
| 21 | 6 | 11 | 13 | 36 | 18 | 4 | 2 | 14 |
| 22 | 7 | 9 | 13 | 32 | 17 | 58 | 2 | 13 |
| 23 | 8 | 8 | 13 | 28 | 17 | 54 | 2 | 13 |
| 24 | 9 | 6 | 13 | 24 | 17 | 48 | 2 | 12 |
| 25 | 10 | 4 | 13 | 21 | 17 | 43 | 2 | 11 |
| 26 | 11 | 3 | 13 | 17 | 17 | 37 | 2 | 10 |
| 27 | 12 | 1 | 13 | 13 | 17 | 31 | 2 | 9 |
| 28 | 13 | 0 | 13 | 9 | 17 | 27 | 2 | 9 |
| 29 | 13 | 58 | 13 | 5 | 17 | 21 | 2 | 8 |
| 30 | 14 | 57 | 13 | 1 | 17 | 15 | 2 | 7 |
| 31 | 15 | 55 | 12 | 57 | 17 | 11 | 2 | 7 |

Translations of Latin headings are to be found in the introduction, pp. 11-25.

# AUGUSTUS

| | Primus Ciclus | | | | Secundus Ciclus | | | | Tercius | |
|---|---|---|---|---|---|---|---|---|---|---|
| Numerus dierum | Ciclus Conjunccionis | Tempus vere conjunccionis | Ciclus Opposicionis | Tempus vere opposicionis | Ciclus Conjunccionis | Tempus vere conjunccionis | Ciclus Opposicionis | Tempus vere opposicionis | Ciclus Conjunccionis | Tempus vere conjunccionis |
| | | h. m. | | h. m. | | h. m. | | h. m. | | h. m. |
| 1 | 5 | 12 0 | | | 5 | 9 3 | | | | |
| 2 | 13 | 18 59 | 9 | 3 35 | 13 | 19 17 | 9 | 2 35 | 13 | 14 4 |
| 3 | 2 | 5 48 | 17 | 10 25 | | | 17 | 11 20 | | |
| 4 | 10 | 20 22 | 6 | 0 34 | 2 | 2 11 | 6 | 18 24 | 2 | 2 56 |
| 5 | | | 14 | 16 52 | 10 | 11 21 | | | 10 | 9 46 |
| 6 | 18 | 14 0 | | | | | 14 | 5 14 | 18 | 17 51 |
| 7 | | | | | 18 | 0 5 | 3 | 11 21 | | |
| 8 | 7 | 22 12 | 3 | 2 35 | 7 | 8 44 | | | 7 | 16 26 |
| 9 | | | 11 | 16 52 | | | 11 | 5 44 | | |
| 10 | 15 | 10 39 | | | 15 | 2 8 | 19 | 21 42 | 15 | 10 57 |
| 11 | 4 | 18 50 | 19 | 3 29 | 4 | 19 42 | | | 4 | 16 21 |
| 12 | | | 8 | 10 29 | | | 8 | 11 21 | | |
| 13 | 12 | 2 34 | 16 | 19 23 | 12 | 2 46 | 16 | 18 11 | 12 | 2 57 |
| 14 | | | | | 1 | 13 4 | | | 1 | 9 52 |
| 15 | 1 | 0 10 | 5 | 21 9 | | | 5 | 7 42 | 9 | 18 51 |
| 16 | 9 | 18 31 | | | 9 | 3 18 | 13 | 23 45 | | |
| 17 | | | 13 | 15 56 | 17 | 20 46 | | | 17 | 7 15 |
| 18 | 17 | 13 4 | 2 | 18 41 | | | | | | |
| 19 | 6 | 11 45 | | | | | 2 | 9 45 | 6 | 15 34 |
| 20 | 14 | 19 50 | 10 | 4 3 | 6 | 5 23 | | | | |
| 21 | | | 18 | 11 18 | 14 | 18 11 | 10 | 0 14 | 14 | 9 13 |
| 22 | 3 | 3 33 | 7 | 21 3 | 3 | 2 43 | 18 / 7 | 11 11 / 18 19 | | |
| 23 | 11 | 15 30 | | | 11 | 10 23 | | | 3 | 3 31 |
| 24 | | | 15 | 10 53 | 19 | 20 34 | 15 | 3 0 | 11 | 10 43 |
| 25 | 19 | 7 12 | | | | | | | 19 | 17 45 |
| 26 | | | 4 | 20 29 | | | 4 | 4 7 | 8 | 10 29 |
| 27 | 8 | 17 12 | | | 8 | 1 28 | 12 | 22 54 | | |
| 28 | | | 12 | 13 9 | 16 | 20 7 | | | 16 | 3 46 |
| 29 | 16 | 8 13 | | | | | | | | |
| 30 | 5 | 19 55 | 1 | 4 24 | 5 | 19 34 | 1 | 2 19 | 5 | 12 43 |
| 31 | | | 9 | 11 19 | | | 9 | 11 58 | | |

Ciclus      Quartus Ciclus

| Ciclus Opposicionis | Tempus vere opposicionis h. m. | Ciclus Conjunccionis | Tempus vere conjunccionis h. m. | Ciclus Opposicionis | Tempus vere opposicionis h. m. | Quantitates a noctis medio ad auroram h. m. | Quantitates a noctis medio ad solis ortum h. m. | Quantitates a meridie ad solis occasum h. m. | Quantitates a meridie ad noctem obscuram h. m. |
|---|---|---|---|---|---|---|---|---|---|
| 9 | 18 42 | | | 9 | 3 50 | 1 54 | 4 36 | 7 24 | 10 6 |
| | | 13 | 1 8 | 17 | 22 1 | 1 57 | 4 37 | 7 23 | 10 3 |
| 17 | 8 29 | | | | | 2 1 | 4 39 | 7 21 | 9 59 |
| 6 | 18 19 | 2 | 1 59 | 6 | 18 40 | 2 5 | 4 41 | 7 19 | 9 55 |
| | | 10 | 10 43 | | | 2 8 | 4 43 | 7 17 | 9 52 |
| 14 | 1 32 | 18 | 17 41 | 14 | 2 17 | 2 11 | 4 44 | 7 16 | 9 49 |
| 3 | 19 53 | | | 3 | 10 47 | 2 15 | 4 46 | 7 14 | 9 45 |
| | | 7 | 4 43 | 11 | 23 35 | 2 18 | 4 48 | 7 12 | 9 42 |
| 11 | 13 33 | 15 | 19 22 | | | 2 22 | 4 50 | 7 10 | 9 38 |
| | | | | 19 | 16 0 | 2 25 | 4 52 | 7 8 | 9 35 |
| 19 | 8 18 | | | | | 2 27 | 4 53 | 7 7 | 9 33 |
| 8 | 10 3 | 4 | 5 19 | | | 2 31 | 4 55 | 7 5 | 9 29 |
| 16 | 19 2 | 12 | 21 13 | 8 | 1 40 | 2 34 | 4 57 | 7 3 | 9 26 |
| | | 1 | 10 42 | 16 | 15 49 | 2 37 | 4 59 | 7 1 | 9 23 |
| 5 | 2 0 | 9 | 17 34 | 5 | 2 5 | 2 40 | 5 1 | 6 59 | 9 20 |
| 13 | 12 34 | | | 13 | 9 16 | 2 44 | 5 3 | 6 57 | 9 16 |
| | | 17 | 1 28 | | | 2 47 | 5 5 | 6 55 | 9 13 |
| 2 | 18 9 | 6 | 23 20 | 2 | 2 51 | 2 50 | 5 7 | 6 53 | 9 10 |
| | | | | 10 | 20 23 | 2 52 | 5 8 | 6 52 | 9 8 |
| 10 | 12 40 | 14 | 17 47 | | | 2 55 | 5 10 | 6 50 | 9 5 |
| | | | | 18 | 15 11 | 2 58 | 5 12 | 6 48 | 9 2 |
| 18 | 4 56 | 3 | 23 45 | | | 3 1 | 5 14 | 6 46 | 8 59 |
| 7 | 19 14 | | | 7 | 17 38 | 3 3 | 5 16 | 6 44 | 8 57 |
| | | 11 | 10 39 | | | 3 6 | 5 18 | 6 42 | 8 54 |
| 15 / 4 | 2 7 / 15 2 | 19 | 18 40 | 15 | 2 54 | 3 9 | 5 20 | 6 40 | 8 51 |
| | | | | 4 | 9 46 | 3 12 | 5 22 | 6 38 | 8 48 |
| 12 | 6 49 | 8 | 2 28 | 12 | 20 4 | 3 15 | 5 24 | 6 36 | 8 45 |
| | | 16 | 14 35 | | | 3 17 | 5 26 | 6 34 | 8 43 |
| 1 | 16 48 | 5 | 22 34 | 1 | 1 7 | 3 20 | 5 28 | 6 32 | 8 40 |
| | | | | 9 | 19 45 | 3 23 | 5 30 | 6 30 | 8 37 |
| 9 | 7 45 | 13 | 16 24 | | | 3 25 | 5 32 | 6 28 | 8 35 |

# AUGUSTUS

Altitudines solis et longitudines umbrarum cuiuslibet hominis
a media nocte

| Numerus dierum | 5 / 7 alti-tudines solis g. m. | umbre hominis pedes partes | 6 / 6 alti-tudines solis g. m. | umbre hominis pedes partes | 7 / 5 alti-tudines solis g. m. | umbre hominis pedes partes | 8 / 4 alti-tudines solis g. m. | umbre hominis pedes partes |
|---|---|---|---|---|---|---|---|---|
| 1 | 3 29 | 100 39 | 12 24 | 27 20 | 21 38 | 15 8 | 30 48 | 10 4 |
| 2 | 3 15 | 107 20 | 12 11 | 27 49 | 21 24 | 15 19 | 30 34 | 10 10 |
| 3 | 3 1 | 114 0 | 11 57 | 28 21 | 21 10 | 15 30 | 30 20 | 10 15 |
| 4 | 2 47 | 126 55 | 11 43 | 28 58 | 20 57 | 15 41 | 30 6 | 10 21 |
| 5 | 2 32 | 141 15 | 11 28 | 29 38 | 20 42 | 15 53 | 29 51 | 10 27 |
| 6 | 2 16 | 156 32 | 11 14 | 30 15 | 20 28 | 16 5 | 29 37 | 10 33 |
| 7 | 2 1 | 170 52 | 10 59 | 30 56 | 20 14 | 16 17 | 29 21 | 10 41 |
| 8 | 1 47 | 209 4 | 10 45 | 31 40 | 20 0 | 16 29 | 29 7 | 10 47 |
| 9 | 1 32 | 252 2 | 10 30 | 32 27 | 19 45 | 16 43 | 28 52 | 10 54 |
| 10 | 1 16 | 297 53 | 10 15 | 33 14 | 19 29 | 16 58 | 28 37 | 11 0 |
| 11 | 1 0 | 343 43 | 9 59 | 34 5 | 19 14 | 17 12 | 28 20 | 11 8 |
| 12 | 0 44 | 468 42 | 9 44 | 35 3 | 18 59 | 17 26 | 28 5 | 11 15 |
| 13 | 0 28 | 736 39 | 9 28 | 36 5 | 18 43 | 17 43 | 27 49 | 11 23 |
| 14 | 0 12 | 1718 47 | 9 13 | 37 3 | 18 28 | 17 58 | 27 33 | 11 31 |
| 15 | 0 0 | 0 0 | 8 57 | 38 8 | 18 12 | 18 15 | 27 17 | 11 38 |
| 16 | 0 0 | 0 0 | 8 41 | 39 25 | 17 56 | 18 32 | 27 0 | 11 46 |
| 17 | 0 0 | 0 0 | 8 24 | 40 48 | 17 38 | 18 53 | 26 43 | 11 55 |
| 18 | 0 0 | 0 0 | 8 7 | 42 10 | 17 22 | 19 12 | 26 26 | 12 4 |
| 19 | 0 0 | 0 0 | 7 50 | 43 45 | 17 5 | 19 31 | 26 9 | 12 13 |
| 20 | 0 0 | 0 0 | 7 35 | 45 17 | 16 49 | 19 52 | 25 52 | 12 23 |
| 21 | 0 0 | 0 0 | 7 17 | 47 8 | 16 32 | 20 14 | 25 34 | 12 33 |
| 22 | 0 0 | 0 0 | 7 0 | 48 52 | 16 16 | 20 35 | 25 17 | 12 42 |
| 23 | 0 0 | 0 0 | 6 43 | 51 12 | 15 58 | 20 58 | 24 59 | 12 53 |
| 24 | 0 0 | 0 0 | 6 25 | 53 40 | 15 41 | 21 23 | 24 42 | 13 3 |
| 25 | 0 0 | 0 0 | 6 9 | 55 51 | 15 24 | 21 48 | 24 24 | 13 14 |
| 26 | 0 0 | 0 0 | 5 51 | 58 49 | 15 6 | 22 14 | 24 6 | 13 25 |
| 27 | 0 0 | 0 0 | 5 34 | 62 4 | 14 49 | 22 42 | 23 48 | 13 36 |
| 28 | 0 0 | 0 0 | 5 16 | 65 31 | 14 31 | 23 12 | 23 30 | 13 48 |
| 29 | 0 0 | 0 0 | 4 58 | 69 10 | 14 13 | 23 43 | 23 12 | 14 0 |
| 30 | 0 0 | 0 0 | 4 41 | 74 3 | 13 55 | 24 14 | 22 53 | 14 13 |
| 31 | 0 0 | 0 0 | 4 23 | 79 14 | 13 38 | 24 46 | 22 34 | 14 27 |

stature sex pedum in horis equalibus distantibus a meridie et
51 graduum et

| 9 | | | 10 | | | 11 | | | 12 a.m. | | |
| 3 | | | 2 | | | 1 | | | 0 p.m. | | |
| alti-tudines solis | umbre hominis | | alti-tudines solis | umbre hominis | | alti-tudines solis | umbre hominis | | alti-tudines solis | umbre hominis | |
| g. m. | pedes | partes | g. m. | pedes | partes | g. m. | pedes | partes | g. m. | pedes | partes |
|---|---|---|---|---|---|---|---|---|---|---|---|
| 39 25 | 7 | 18 | 46 51 | 5 | 38 | 52 5 | 4 | 40 | 54 2 | 4 | 21 |
| 39 10 | 7 | 22 | 46 35 | 5 | 41 | 51 48 | 4 | 43 | 53 43 | 4 | 24 |
| 38 56 | 7 | 26 | 46 30 | 5 | 44 | 51 31 | 4 | 46 | 53 25 | 4 | 27 |
| 38 42 | 7 | 29 | 46 3 | 5 | 48 | 51 14 | 4 | 49 | 53 8 | 4 | 30 |
| 38 26 | 7 | 34 | 45 46 | 5 | 51 | 50 55 | 4 | 52 | 52 49 | 4 | 33 |
| 38 11 | 7 | 38 | 45 29 | 5 | 54 | 50 36 | 4 | 55 | 52 30 | 4 | 36 |
| 37 55 | 7 | 42 | 45 12 | 5 | 58 | 50 18 | 4 | 59 | 52 11 | 4 | 39 |
| 37 39 | 7 | 46 | 44 56 | 6 | 1 | 50 0 | 5 | 2 | 51 52 | 4 | 43 |
| 37 23 | 7 | 51 | 44 39 | 6 | 5 | 49 43 | 5 | 5 | 51 34 | 4 | 46 |
| 37 7 | 7 | 55 | 44 22 | 6 | 8 | 49 24 | 5 | 9 | 51 14 | 4 | 49 |
| 36 51 | 8 | 0 | 44 4 | 6 | 12 | 49 4 | 5 | 12 | 50 54 | 4 | 52 |
| 36 35 | 8 | 5 | 43 46 | 6 | 16 | 48 46 | 5 | 16 | 50 35 | 4 | 56 |
| 36 17 | 8 | 10 | 43 27 | 6 | 20 | 48 26 | 5 | 19 | 50 14 | 4 | 59 |
| 36 0 | 8 | 15 | 43 9 | 6 | 24 | 48 7 | 5 | 23 | 49 54 | 5 | 3 |
| 35 43 | 8 | 20 | 42 52 | 6 | 28 | 47 47 | 5 | 27 | 49 36 | 5 | 6 |
| 35 25 | 8 | 26 | 42 32 | 6 | 33 | 47 26 | 5 | 31 | 49 13 | 5 | 11 |
| 35 7 | 8 | 32 | 42 12 | 6 | 37 | 47 4 | 5 | 35 | 48 51 | 5 | 15 |
| 34 49 | 8 | 38 | 41 43 | 6 | 42 | 46 44 | 5 | 39 | 48 30 | 5 | 18 |
| 34 31 | 8 | 44 | 41 34 | 6 | 46 | 46 23 | 5 | 43 | 48 9 | 5 | 22 |
| 34 14 | 8 | 49 | 41 14 | 6 | 51 | 46 3 | 5 | 47 | 47 49 | 5 | 26 |
| 33 55 | 8 | 55 | 40 54 | 6 | 56 | 45 41 | 5 | 52 | 47 26 | 5 | 31 |
| 33 37 | 9 | 2 | 40 35 | 7 | 0 | 45 20 | 5 | 56 | 47 4 | 5 | 35 |
| 33 17 | 9 | 9 | 40 15 | 7 | 5 | 44 59 | 6 | 0 | 46 42 | 5 | 40 |
| 32 59 | 9 | 14 | 39 54 | 7 | 11 | 44 38 | 6 | 5 | 46 20 | 5 | 44 |
| 32 41 | 9 | 21 | 39 35 | 7 | 16 | 44 18 | 6 | 9 | 45 59 | 5 | 48 |
| 32 22 | 9 | 28 | 39 14 | 7 | 21 | 43 55 | 6 | 14 | 45 35 | 5 | 53 |
| 32 2 | 9 | 35 | 38 54 | 7 | 26 | 43 34 | 6 | 19 | 45 14 | 5 | 57 |
| 31 42 | 9 | 43 | 38 33 | 7 | 32 | 43 12 | 6 | 23 | 44 51 | 6 | 2 |
| 31 24 | 9 | 50 | 38 13 | 7 | 37 | 42 50 | 6 | 28 | 44 30 | 6 | 7 |
| 31 5 | 9 | 57 | 37 52 | 7 | 43 | 42 28 | 6 | 33 | 44 7 | 6 | 11 |
| 30 45 | 10 | 5 | 37 30 | 7 | 49 | 42 4 | 6 | 39 | 43 43 | 6 | 17 |

# SEPTEMBER

| | | | | |
|---|---|---|---|---|
| 1 | 16 | *f* | **KL** | Sancti Egidii abbatis |
| 2 | 5 | *g* | 4 Nonas | |
| 3 | | A | 3 Nonas | |
| 4 | 13 | *b* | 2 Nonas | Translacio Sancti Cuthberti episcopi et confessoris |
| 5 | 2 | *c* | Nonis | Sancti Bertini abbatis |
| 6 | | *d* | 8 Idus | |
| 7 | 10 | *e* | 7 Idus | |
| 8 | | *f* | 6 Idus | Nativitas Sancte Marie |
| 9 | 18 | *g* | 5 Idus | Sancti Gorgonii martyris |
| 10 | 7 | A | 4 Idus | |
| 11 | | *b* | 3 Idus | Sanctorum Prothi et Jacinti martyrum |
| 12 | 15 | *c* | 2 Idus | |
| 13 | 4 | *d* | Idibus | |
| 14 | | *e* | 18 Kl. | Exaltacio Sancte Crucis |
| 15 | 12 | *f* | 17 Kl. | Octava Sancte Marie Virginis |
| 16 | 1 | *g* | 16 Kl. | Sancte Edithe virginis non martyris |
| 17 | | A | 15 Kl. | Sancti Lamberti martyris |
| 18 | 9 | *b* | 14 Kl. | |
| 19 | | *c* | 13 Kl. | |
| 20 | 17 | *d* | 12 Kl. | |
| 21 | 6 | *e* | 11 Kl. | Sancti Mathei apostoli |
| 22 | | *f* | 10 Kl. | Sancti Mauricii cum sociis eius |
| 23 | 14 | *g* | 9 Kl. | Sancte Tecle virginis et martyris |
| 24 | 3 | A | 8 Kl. | |
| 25 | | *b* | 7 Kl. | Sancti Firmini episcopi et martyris |
| 26 | 11 | *c* | 6 Kl. | |
| 27 | | *d* | 5 Kl. | Sanctorum Cosme et Damiani martyrum |
| 28 | 19 | *e* | 4 Kl. | |
| 29 | 8 | *f* | 3 Kl. | Sancti Michaelis archangeli |
| 30 | | *g* | 2 Kl. | Sancti Jeronimi doctoris |

Variant readings for this month are listed on p. 139–40.

| Numerus dierum | Verus locus solis | | Quantitates diei artificialis | | Quantitates diei vulgaris | | Quantitates utriusque crepusculorum matutini et vespertini | |
|---|---|---|---|---|---|---|---|---|
| | g. | m. | h. | m. | h. | m. | h. | m. |
| | Virgo | | | | | | | |
| 1 | 16 | 54 | 12 | 53 | 17 | 5 | 2 | 6 |
| 2 | 17 | 53 | 12 | 49 | 16 | 59 | 2 | 5 |
| 3 | 18 | 51 | 12 | 45 | 16 | 55 | 2 | 5 |
| 4 | 19 | 50 | 12 | 41 | 16 | 49 | 2 | 4 |
| 5 | 20 | 49 | 12 | 37 | 16 | 45 | 2 | 4 |
| 6 | 21 | 48 | 12 | 33 | 16 | 39 | 2 | 3 |
| 7 | 22 | 46 | 12 | 29 | 16 | 35 | 2 | 3 |
| 8 | 23 | 45 | 12 | 25 | 16 | 29 | 2 | 2 |
| 9 | 24 | 44 | 12 | 21 | 16 | 25 | 2 | 2 |
| 10 | 25 | 43 | 12 | 17 | 16 | 19 | 2 | 1 |
| 11 | 26 | 42 | 12 | 13 | 16 | 15 | 2 | 1 |
| 12 | 27 | 41 | 12 | 9 | 16 | 11 | 2 | 1 |
| 13 | 28 | 40 | 12 | 5 | 16 | 5 | 2 | 0 |
| 14 | 29 | 39 | 12 | 1 | 16 | 1 | 2 | 0 |
| | Libra | | | | | | | |
| 15 | 0 | 38 | 11 | 57 | 15 | 57 | 2 | 0 |
| 16 | 1 | 37 | 11 | 53 | 15 | 51 | 1 | 59 |
| 17 | 2 | 37 | 11 | 49 | 15 | 47 | 1 | 59 |
| 18 | 3 | 36 | 11 | 45 | 15 | 43 | 1 | 59 |
| 19 | 4 | 35 | 11 | 41 | 15 | 39 | 1 | 59 |
| 20 | 5 | 35 | 11 | 37 | 15 | 33 | 1 | 58 |
| 21 | 6 | 34 | 11 | 33 | 15 | 29 | 1 | 58 |
| 22 | 7 | 33 | 11 | 29 | 15 | 25 | 1 | 58 |
| 23 | 8 | 33 | 11 | 25 | 15 | 21 | 1 | 58 |
| 24 | 9 | 32 | 11 | 21 | 15 | 17 | 1 | 58 |
| 25 | 10 | 32 | 11 | 17 | 15 | 13 | 1 | 58 |
| 26 | 11 | 31 | 11 | 13 | 15 | 9 | 1 | 58 |
| 27 | 12 | 31 | 11 | 9 | 15 | 3 | 1 | 57 |
| 28 | 13 | 31 | 11 | 5 | 14 | 59 | 1 | 57 |
| 29 | 14 | 30 | 11 | 1 | 14 | 55 | 1 | 57 |
| 30 | 15 | 30 | 10 | 57 | 14 | 51 | 1 | 57 |

Translations of Latin headings are to be found in the introduction, pp. 11–25.

# SEPTEMBER

| Numerus dierum | Primus Ciclus | | | | Secundus Ciclus | | | | Tercius | |
|---|---|---|---|---|---|---|---|---|---|---|
| | Ciclus Conjunccionis | Tempus vere conjunccionis | Ciclus Opposicionis | Tempus vere opposicionis | Ciclus Conjunccionis | Tempus vere conjunccionis | Ciclus Opposicionis | Tempus vere opposicionis | Ciclus Conjunccionis | Tempus vere conjunccionis |
| | | h. m. | | h. m. | | h. m. | | h. m. | | h. m. |
| 1 | 13 / 2 | 2 52 / 18 40 | 17 | 18 48 | 13 | 3 49 | 17 | 19 20 | 13 | 1 50 |
| 2 | | | 6 | 14 47 | 2 | 11 17 | | | 2 | 10 45 |
| 3 | 10 | 11 36 | | | 10 | 23 0 | 6 | 4 40 | 10 | 18 14 |
| 4 | | | 14 | 8 53 | | | 14 | 18 13 | | |
| 5 | 18 | 6 20 | | | 18 | 14 21 | | | 18 | 4 13 |
| 6 | | | 3 | 16 12 | | | 3 | 3 37 | | |
| 7 | 7 | 10 30 | | | 7 | 0 26 | 11 | 20 33 | 7 | 8 33 |
| 8 | 15 | 20 33 | 11 | 3 54 | 15 | 15 45 | | | | |
| 9 | | | 19 | 12 28 | | | 19 | 10 3 | 15 | 3 17 |
| 10 | 4 | 3 22 | 8 | 19 44 | 4 | 4 3 | 8 | 19 27 | 4 | 3 27 |
| 11 | 12 | 12 55 | | | 12 | 10 58 | | | 12 | 11 55 |
| 12 | | | 16 | 7 1 | | | 16 | 2 49 | 1 | 19 13 |
| 13 | 1 | 16 23 | | | 1 | 2 5 | 5 | 22 4 | | |
| 14 | | | 5 | 13 50 | 9 | 18 50 | | | 9 | 6 36 |
| 15 | 9 | 11 12 | | | | | 13 | 16 4 | 17 | 21 47 |
| 16 | | | 13 | 8 9 | 17 | 13 33 | | | | |
| 17 | 17 / 6 | 4 26 / 21 10 | 2 | 5 5 | | | 2 | 23 51 | | |
| 18 | | | 10 | 12 48 | 6 | 18 19 | | | 6 | 7 47 |
| 19 | 14 | 4 14 | 18 | 19 43 | | | 10 | 11 52 | 14 | 23 27 |
| 20 | 3 | 15 12 | | | 14 / 3 | 4 38 / 11 31 | 18 | 20 38 | | |
| 21 | | | 7 | 10 5 | 11 | 20 50 | 7 | 3 46 | 3 | 12 17 |
| 22 | 11 | 5 54 | | | | | 15 | 14 48 | 11 | 19 11 |
| 23 | 19 | 23 44 | 15 | 2 33 | 19 | 9 44 | | | | |
| 24 | | | | | | | 4 | 21 11 | 19 | 3 18 |
| 25 | | | 4 | 12 23 | 8 | 18 36 | | | 8 | 2 16 |
| 26 | 8 | 7 59 | | | | | 12 | 15 38 | 16 | 20 55 |
| 27 | 16 | 20 26 | 12 | 2 39 | 16 | 12 4 | | | | |
| 28 | | | 1 | 13 6 | | | 1 | 13 16 | | |
| 29 | 5 | 4 34 | 9 | 20 17 | 5 | 5 28 | 9 | 21 8 | 5 | 2 16 |
| 30 | 13 | 12 30 | | | 13 | 12 35 | | | 13 | 12 48 |

## Ciclus                    Quartus Ciclus

| Ciclus Opposicionis | Tempus vere opposicionis (h. m.) | Ciclus Conjunccionis | Tempus vere conjunccionis (h. m.) | Ciclus Opposicionis | Tempus vere opposicionis (h. m.) | Quantitates a noctis medio ad auroram (h. m.) | Quantitates a noctis medio ad solis ortum (h. m.) | Quantitates a meridie ad solis occasum (h. m.) | Quantitates a meridie ad noctem obscuram (h. m.) |
|---|---|---|---|---|---|---|---|---|---|
| 17 | 19 9 | | | 17 | 12 18 | 3 28 | 5 34 | 6 26 | 8 32 |
| | | 2 | 11 24 | | | 3 31 | 5 36 | 6 24 | 8 29 |
| 6 | 2 18 | 10 | 18 45 | 6 | 3 15 | 3 33 | 5 38 | 6 22 | 8 27 |
| 14 | 10 48 | | | 14 | 10 10 | 3 36 | 5 40 | 6 20 | 8 24 |
| | | 18 | 1 44 | 3 | 22 32 | 3 38 | 5 42 | 6 18 | 8 22 |
| 3 | 11 15 | 7 | 17 50 | | | 3 41 | 5 44 | 6 16 | 8 19 |
| | | | | 11 | 14 2 | 3 43 | 5 46 | 6 14 | 8 17 |
| 11 | 6 0 | 15 | 10 55 | | | 3 46 | 5 48 | 6 12 | 8 14 |
| | | | | 19 | 8 13 | 3 48 | 5 50 | 6 10 | 8 12 |
| 19 / 8 | 0 5 / 19 58 | 4 | 2 19 | | | 3 51 | 5 52 | 6 8 | 8 9 |
| | | | | 8 | 15 20 | 3 53 | 5 54 | 6 6 | 8 7 |
| 16 | 3 28 | 12 / 1 | 9 34 / 18 53 | | | 3 55 | 5 56 | 6 4 | 8 5 |
| 5 | 12 26 | | | 16 / 5 | 2 54 / 10 24 | 3 58 | 5 58 | 6 2 | 8 2 |
| | | 9 | 2 1 | 13 | 18 43 | 4 0 | 6 0 | 6 0 | 8 0 |
| 13 | 1 42 | 17 | 12 0 | | | 4 2 | 6 2 | 5 58 | 7 58 |
| | | | | 2 | 18 31 | 4 5 | 6 4 | 5 56 | 7 55 |
| 2 | 10 53 | 6 | 15 46 | | | 4 7 | 6 6 | 5 54 | 7 53 |
| | | | | 10 | 13 14 | 4 9 | 6 8 | 5 52 | 7 51 |
| 10 | 4 4 | 14 | 10 36 | | | 4 11 | 6 10 | 5 50 | 7 49 |
| 18 | 17 53 | | | 18 | 7 30 | 4 14 | 6 12 | 5 48 | 7 46 |
| | | 3 | 11 24 | | | 4 16 | 6 14 | 5 46 | 7 44 |
| 7 | 3 41 | 11 | 20 7 | 7 | 4 5 | 4 18 | 6 16 | 5 44 | 7 42 |
| 15 | 11 0 | | | 15 | 11 44 | 4 20 | 6 18 | 5 42 | 7 40 |
| 4 | 5 34 | 19 | 3 10 | 4 | 20 23 | 4 22 | 6 20 | 5 40 | 7 38 |
| 12 | 23 27 | 8 | 14 24 | | | 4 24 | 6 22 | 5 38 | 7 36 |
| | | | | 12 | 9 22 | 4 26 | 6 24 | 5 36 | 7 34 |
| | | 16 | 5 15 | 1 | 18 19 | 4 29 | 6 26 | 5 34 | 7 31 |
| 1 | 7 37 | 5 | 15 20 | | | 4 31 | 6 28 | 5 32 | 7 29 |
| 9 | 19 56 | | | 9 | 11 43 | 4 33 | 6 30 | 5 30 | 7 27 |
| | | 13 | 7 16 | | | 4 35 | 6 32 | 5 28 | 7 25 |

# SEPTEMBER

Altitudines solis et longitudines umbrarum cuiuslibet hominis stature

| Numerus dierum | 6 6 | | | 7 5 | | | 8 4 | | |
|---|---|---|---|---|---|---|---|---|---|
| | altitudines solis | umbre hominis | | altitudines solis | umbre hominis | | altitudines solis | umbre hominis | |
| | g. m. | pedes | partes | g. m. | pedes | partes | g. m. | pedes | partes |
| 1 | 4 5 | 84 | 25 | 13 19 | 25 | 23 | 22 15 | 14 | 40 |
| 2 | 3 47 | 92 | 3 | 13 1 | 25 | 57 | 21 56 | 14 | 54 |
| 3 | 3 29 | 100 | 39 | 12 43 | 26 | 37 | 21 38 | 15 | 8 |
| 4 | 3 11 | 109 | 14 | 12 25 | 27 | 18 | 21 20 | 15 | 22 |
| 5 | 2 53 | 121 | 11 | 12 7 | 27 | 58 | 21 0 | 15 | 38 |
| 6 | 2 35 | 138 | 23 | 11 48 | 28 | 45 | 20 41 | 15 | 54 |
| 7 | 2 15 | 157 | 29 | 11 29 | 29 | 35 | 20 21 | 16 | 11 |
| 8 | 1 57 | 180 | 25 | 11 11 | 30 | 23 | 20 3 | 16 | 26 |
| 9 | 1 39 | 231 | 59 | 10 52 | 31 | 18 | 19 44 | 16 | 44 |
| 10 | 1 20 | 286 | 25 | 10 34 | 32 | 14 | 19 24 | 17 | 3 |
| 11 | 1 2 | 337 | 59 | 10 15 | 33 | 14 | 19 5 | 17 | 21 |
| 12 | 0 44 | 468 | 42 | 9 57 | 34 | 13 | 18 46 | 17 | 39 |
| 13 | 0 26 | 793 | 17 | 9 39 | 35 | 22 | 18 27 | 17 | 59 |
| 14 | 0 7 | 2945 | 24 | 9 20 | 36 | 36 | 18 7 | 18 | 20 |
| 15 | 0 0 | 0 | 0 | 9 2 | 37 | 45 | 17 48 | 18 | 41 |
| 16 | 0 0 | 0 | 0 | 8 43 | 39 | 15 | 17 27 | 19 | 6 |
| 17 | 0 0 | 0 | 0 | 8 24 | 40 | 48 | 17 8 | 19 | 28 |
| 18 | 0 0 | 0 | 0 | 8 4 | 42 | 25 | 16 48 | 19 | 53 |
| 19 | 0 0 | 0 | 0 | 7 45 | 44 | 16 | 16 29 | 20 | 18 |
| 20 | 0 0 | 0 | 0 | 7 26 | 46 | 13 | 16 10 | 20 | 42 |
| 21 | 0 0 | 0 | 0 | 7 7 | 48 | 9 | 15 50 | 21 | 10 |
| 22 | 0 0 | 0 | 0 | 6 47 | 50 | 39 | 15 30 | 21 | 39 |
| 23 | 0 0 | 0 | 0 | 6 29 | 53 | 7 | 15 10 | 22 | 8 |
| 24 | 0 0 | 0 | 0 | 6 10 | 55 | 43 | 14 50 | 22 | 40 |
| 25 | 0 0 | 0 | 0 | 5 52 | 58 | 37 | 14 32 | 23 | 11 |
| 26 | 0 0 | 0 | 0 | 5 33 | 62 | 16 | 14 12 | 23 | 44 |
| 27 | 0 0 | 0 | 0 | 5 15 | 65 | 43 | 13 52 | 24 | 19 |
| 28 | 0 0 | 0 | 0 | 4 56 | 69 | 44 | 13 34 | 24 | 54 |
| 29 | 0 0 | 0 | 0 | 4 37 | 75 | 12 | 13 13 | 25 | 34 |
| 30 | 0 0 | 0 | 0 | 4 19 | 80 | 23 | 12 54 | 26 | 13 |

sex pedum in horis equalibus distantibus a meridie et a media nocte

| 9 / 3 | | | 10 / 2 | | | 11 / 1 | | | 12 a.m. / 0 p.m. | | |
|---|---|---|---|---|---|---|---|---|---|---|---|
| altitudines solis | umbre hominis | | altitudines solis | umbre hominis | | altitudines solis | umbre hominis | | altitudines solis | umbre hominis | |
| g. m. | pedes | partes | g. m. | pedes | partes | g. m. | pedes | partes | g. m. | pedes | partes |
| 30 25 | 10 | 13 | 37 9 | 7 | 55 | 41 43 | 6 | 44 | 43 21 | 6 | 21 |
| 30 5 | 10 | 21 | 36 47 | 8 | 1 | 41 20 | 6 | 49 | 42 57 | 6 | 27 |
| 29 46 | 10 | 29 | 36 28 | 8 | 7 | 40 58 | 6 | 55 | 42 35 | 6 | 32 |
| 29 26 | 10 | 38 | 36 6 | 8 | 13 | 40 35 | 7 | 0 | 42 12 | 6 | 37 |
| 29 6 | 10 | 47 | 35 44 | 8 | 20 | 40 13 | 7 | 6 | 41 49 | 6 | 43 |
| 28 46 | 10 | 56 | 35 23 | 8 | 27 | 39 50 | 7 | 12 | 41 26 | 6 | 48 |
| 28 25 | 11 | 6 | 35 1 | 8 | 34 | 39 26 | 7 | 18 | 41 1 | 6 | 54 |
| 28 4 | 11 | 15 | 34 40 | 8 | 41 | 39 4 | 7 | 23 | 40 39 | 6 | 59 |
| 27 45 | 11 | 25 | 34 19 | 8 | 47 | 38 42 | 7 | 29 | 40 16 | 7 | 5 |
| 27 25 | 11 | 34 | 33 57 | 8 | 55 | 38 19 | 7 | 35 | 39 53 | 7 | 11 |
| 27 4 | 11 | 44 | 33 35 | 9 | 2 | 37 56 | 7 | 42 | 39 29 | 7 | 17 |
| 26 44 | 11 | 55 | 33 13 | 9 | 10 | 37 33 | 7 | 48 | 39 5 | 7 | 23 |
| 26 24 | 12 | 5 | 32 51 | 9 | 17 | 37 10 | 7 | 55 | 38 42 | 7 | 29 |
| 26 3 | 12 | 16 | 32 30 | 9 | 25 | 36 47 | 8 | 1 | 38 19 | 7 | 35 |
| 25 42 | 12 | 28 | 32 7 | 9 | 33 | 36 24 | 8 | 8 | 37 55 | 7 | 42 |
| 25 22 | 12 | 40 | 31 46 | 9 | 41 | 36 1 | 8 | 15 | 37 31 | 7 | 49 |
| 25 1 | 12 | 51 | 31 23 | 9 | 50 | 35 37 | 8 | 22 | 37 7 | 7 | 55 |
| 24 40 | 13 | 4 | 31 1 | 9 | 59 | 35 14 | 8 | 30 | 36 44 | 8 | 2 |
| 24 19 | 13 | 17 | 30 39 | 10 | 8 | 34 51 | 8 | 37 | 36 20 | 8 | 9 |
| 23 58 | 13 | 29 | 30 18 | 10 | 16 | 34 28 | 8 | 45 | 35 56 | 8 | 16 |
| 23 38 | 13 | 43 | 29 56 | 10 | 25 | 34 5 | 8 | 52 | 35 32 | 8 | 24 |
| 23 16 | 13 | 57 | 29 32 | 10 | 36 | 33 40 | 9 | 0 | 35 8 | 8 | 31 |
| 22 55 | 14 | 12 | 29 11 | 10 | 45 | 33 17 | 9 | 9 | 34 45 | 8 | 39 |
| 22 34 | 14 | 27 | 28 49 | 10 | 55 | 32 55 | 9 | 16 | 34 22 | 8 | 47 |
| 22 14 | 14 | 41 | 28 27 | 11 | 5 | 32 32 | 9 | 24 | 33 59 | 8 | 54 |
| 21 54 | 14 | 56 | 28 5 | 11 | 15 | 32 9 | 9 | 33 | 33 36 | 9 | 2 |
| 21 33 | 15 | 12 | 27 43 | 11 | 26 | 31 46 | 9 | 41 | 33 12 | 9 | 10 |
| 21 13 | 15 | 28 | 27 22 | 11 | 36 | 31 23 | 9 | 50 | 32 49 | 9 | 18 |
| 20 52 | 15 | 45 | 27 0 | 11 | 46 | 31 0 | 9 | 59 | 32 25 | 9 | 27 |
| 20 32 | 16 | 2 | 26 39 | 11 | 57 | 30 38 | 10 | 8 | 32 2 | 9 | 35 |

# OCTOBER

| | | | | |
|---|---|---|---|---|
| 1 | 16 | A | **KL** | Sanctorum Remigii Germani episcoporum |
| 2 | 5 | b | 6 Nonas | Sancti Leodegarii episcopi et martyris |
| 3 | 13 | c | 5 Nonas | |
| 4 | 2 | d | 4 Nonas | Sancti Francissi confessoris |
| 5 | | e | 3 Nonas | |
| 6 | 10 | f | 2 Nonas | Sancti Fidis virginis |
| 7 | | g | Nonis | Marci Sergii et Bachi et Epuleii |
| 8 | 18 | A | 8 Idus | |
| 9 | 7 | b | 7 Idus | Sancti Dionisii sociorumque eius martyrun |
| 10 | | c | 6 Idus | Sancti Geronis sociorumque eius martyrun |
| 11 | 15 | d | 5 Idus | Sancti Nigasii sociorumque eius martyrun |
| 12 | 4 | e | 4 Idus | |
| 13 | • | f | 3 Idus | Translacio Sancti Edwardi regis |
| 14 | 12 | g | 2 Idus | Sancti Kalixti pape et martyris |
| | | | | |
| 15 | 1 | A | Idibus | Sancti Wulfram episcopi et confessoris |
| 16 | | b | 17 Kl. | Sancti Michaelis in monte tumba |
| 17 | 9 | c | 16 Kl. | |
| 18 | | d | 15 Kl. | Sancti Luce ewangeliste |
| 19 | 17 | e | 14 Kl. | |
| 20 | 6 | f | 13 Kl. | |
| 21 | | g | 12 Kl. | Sanctarum undecim milia virginum |
| 22 | 14 | A | 11 Kl. | Sancti Marci episcopi |
| 23 | 3 | b | 10 Kl. | Sancti Romani episcopi et confessoris |
| 24 | | c | 9 Kl. | |
| 25 | 11 | d | 8 Kl. | Sanctorum Crispini et Crispiniani martyrun |
| 26 | 19 | e | 7 Kl. | |
| 27 | | f | 6 Kl. | |
| 28 | 8 | g | 5 Kl. | Sanctorum Apostolorum Symonis |
| 29 | | A | 4 Kl. | Sancti Narcissi episcopi |
| 30 | 16 | b | 3 Kl. | |
| 31 | 5 | c | 2 Kl. | Sancti Quintini martyris |

Variant readings for this month are listed on p. 140.

| Numerus dierum | Verus locus solis | | Quantitates diei artificialis | | Quantitates diei vulgaris | | Quantitates utriusque crepusculorum matutini et vespertini | |
|---|---|---|---|---|---|---|---|---|
| | g. | m. | h. | m. | h. | m. | h. | m. |
| | Libra | | | | | | | |
| 1 | 16 | 29 | 10 | 53 | 14 | 47 | 1 | 57 |
| 2 | 17 | 29 | 10 | 49 | 14 | 43 | 1 | 57 |
| 3 | 18 | 29 | 10 | 45 | 14 | 39 | 1 | 57 |
| 4 | 19 | 29 | 10 | 41 | 14 | 35 | 1 | 57 |
| 5 | 20 | 29 | 10 | 37 | 14 | 31 | 1 | 57 |
| 6 | 21 | 29 | 10 | 33 | 14 | 27 | 1 | 57 |
| 7 | 22 | 29 | 10 | 29 | 14 | 23 | 1 | 57 |
| 8 | 23 | 29 | 10 | 25 | 14 | 19 | 1 | 57 |
| 9 | 24 | 29 | 10 | 21 | 14 | 17 | 1 | 58 |
| 10 | 25 | 29 | 10 | 17 | 14 | 13 | 1 | 58 |
| 11 | 26 | 29 | 10 | 13 | 14 | 9 | 1 | 58 |
| 12 | 27 | 29 | 10 | 10 | 14 | 6 | 1 | 58 |
| 13 | 28 | 30 | 10 | 6 | 14 | 2 | 1 | 58 |
| 14 | 29 | 30 | 10 | 2 | 13 | 58 | 1 | 58 |
| | Scorpio | | | | | | | |
| 15 | 0 | 30 | 9 | 58 | 13 | 54 | 1 | 58 |
| 16 | 1 | 31 | 9 | 54 | 13 | 50 | 1 | 58 |
| 17 | 2 | 31 | 9 | 50 | 13 | 48 | 1 | 59 |
| 18 | 3 | 31 | 9 | 46 | 13 | 44 | 1 | 59 |
| 19 | 4 | 32 | 9 | 42 | 13 | 40 | 1 | 59 |
| 20 | 5 | 32 | 9 | 39 | 13 | 37 | 1 | 59 |
| 21 | 6 | 33 | 9 | 35 | 13 | 33 | 1 | 59 |
| 22 | 7 | 33 | 9 | 31 | 13 | 31 | 2 | 0 |
| 23 | 8 | 34 | 9 | 27 | 13 | 27 | 2 | 0 |
| 24 | 9 | 34 | 9 | 23 | 13 | 23 | 2 | 0 |
| 25 | 10 | 35 | 9 | 20 | 13 | 20 | 2 | 0 |
| 26 | 11 | 36 | 9 | 16 | 13 | 18 | 2 | 1 |
| 27 | 12 | 36 | 9 | 13 | 13 | 15 | 2 | 1 |
| 28 | 13 | 37 | 9 | 9 | 13 | 11 | 2 | 1 |
| 29 | 14 | 38 | 9 | 5 | 13 | 9 | 2 | 2 |
| 30 | 15 | 38 | 9 | 2 | 13 | 6 | 2 | 2 |
| 31 | 16 | 39 | 8 | 58 | 13 | 2 | 2 | 2 |

Translations of Latin headings are to be found in the introduction, pp. 11–25.

# OCTOBER

| Numerus dierum | Primus Ciclus | | | | Secundus Ciclus | | | | Tercius | |
|---|---|---|---|---|---|---|---|---|---|---|
| | Ciclus Conjunccionis | Tempus vere conjunccionis | Ciclus Opposicionis | Tempus vere opposicionis | Ciclus Conjunccionis | Tempus vere conjunccionis | Ciclus Opposicionis | Tempus vere opposicionis | Ciclus Conjunccionis | Tempus vere conjunccionis |
| | | h. m. | | h. m. | | h. m. | | h. m. | | h. m. |
| 1 | 2 | 10 23 | 17 | 5 20 | 2 | 23 8 | 17 | 4 3 | 2 | 19 47 |
| 2 | | | 6 | 7 28 | | | 6 | 17 52 | | |
| 3 | 10 | 4 55 | | | 10 | 13 33 | | | 10 | 4 56 |
| 4 | 18 | 23 32 | 14 | 2 22 | | | 14 | 10 6 | 18 | 17 31 |
| 5 | | | | | 18 | 7 13 | 3 | 20 5 | | |
| 6 | 7 | 22 2 | 3 | 4 57 | 7 | 15 51 | | | | |
| 7 | | | 11 | 14 17 | | | 11 | 10 39 | 7 | 2 8 |
| 8 | 15 | 6 3 | 19 | 21 33 | 15 | 4 34 | 19 | 21 32 | 15 | 19 48 |
| 9 | 4 | 13 58 | | | 4 | 13 0 | | | 4 | 13 51 |
| 10 | | | 8 | 7 35 | 12 | 20 46 | 8 | 4 40 | 12 | 21 4 |
| 11 | 12 | 2 9 | 16 | 21 40 | | | 16 | 13 32 | | |
| 12 | | | | | 1 | 18 5 | | | 1 | 7 14 |
| 13 | 1 | 10 16 | | | | | 5 | 15 6 | 9 | 21 23 |
| 14 | | | 5 | 7 28 | 9 | 12 31 | | | | |
| 15 | 9 | 4 11 | | | | | 13 | 10 1 | 17 | 14 53 |
| 16 | 17 | 19 6 | 13 / 2 | 0 6 / 15 4 | 17 | 7 16 | | | | |
| 17 | 6 | 6 35 | 10 | 22 1 | | | 2 | 13 11 | 6 | 23 48 |
| 18 | 14 | 13 39 | | | 6 | 6 23 | 10 | 22 44 | | |
| 19 | | | 18 | 5 40 | 14 / 3 | 14 35 / 22 16 | | | 14 | 12 49 |
| 20 | 3 | 5 53 | | | | | 18 / 7 | 6 7 / 15 46 | 3 | 21 33 |
| 21 | 11 | 23 9 | 7 | 2 10 | 11 | 10 12 | | | | |
| 22 | | | 15 | 20 29 | . | | 15 | 5 36 | 11 | 5 14 |
| 23 | 19 | 18 1 | | | 19 | 1 56 | | | 19 | 15 25 |
| 24 | | | | | | | 4 | 15 17 | 8 | 20 17 |
| 25 | 8 | 21 51 | 4 | 3 37 | 8 | 12 6 | | | | |
| 26 | | | 12 | 15 11 | | | 12 | 8 9 | 16 | 15 2 |
| 27 | 16 | 7 46 | 1 | 22 42 | 16 | 3 17 | 1 | 23 39 | | |
| 28 | 5 | 14 38 | | | 5 | 15 11 | | | 5 | 14 48 |
| 29 | | | 9 | 7 7 | 13 | 22 14 | 9 | 6 40 | 13 | 23 13 |
| 30 | 13 | 0 26 | 17 | 18 42 | | | 17 | 14 12 | | |
| 31 | 2 | 4 30 | | | 2 | 13 55 | | | 2 | 6 47 |

| Ciclus Opposicionis | Tempus vere opposicionis | Ciclus Conjunccionis | Tempus vere conjunccionis | Ciclus Opposicionis | Tempus vere opposicionis | Quantitates a noctis medio ad auroram | Quantitates a noctis medio ad solis ortum | Quantitates a meridie ad solis occasum | Quantitates a meridie ad noctem obscuram |
|---|---|---|---|---|---|---|---|---|---|
| | h. m. | | h. m. | | h. m. | h. m. | h. m. | h. m. | h. m. |
| 17 | 4 56 | 2 | 20 36 | 17 | 1 50 | 4 37 | 6 34 | 5 26 | 7 23 |
| 6 | 11 57 | | | 6 | 12 4 | 4 39 | 6 36 | 5 24 | 7 21 |
| 14 | 22 43 | 10 | 3 31 | 14 | 19 17 | 4 41 | 6 38 | 5 22 | 7 19 |
| | | 18 | 11 30 | | | 4 43 | 6 40 | 5 20 | 7 17 |
| | | | | 3 | 13 14 | 4 45 | 6 42 | 5 18 | 7 15 |
| 3 | 4 40 | 7 | 9 51 | | | 4 47 | 6 44 | 5 16 | 7 13 |
| 11 | 23 15 | | | 11 | 6 58 | 4 49 | 6 46 | 5 14 | 7 11 |
| | | 15 | 4 26 | | | 4 51 | 6 48 | 5 12 | 7 9 |
| 19 | 15 30 | | | 19 | 1 53 | 4 52 | 6 50 | 5 10 | 7 8 |
| 8 | 5 35 | 4 | 10 18 | | | 4 54 | 6 52 | 5 8 | 7 6 |
| 16 | 12 30 | 12 | 21 6 | 8 | 4 7 | 4 56 | 6 54 | 5 6 | 7 4 |
| | | 1 | 4 13 | 16 / 5 | 13 20 / 20 18 | 4 57 | 6 55 | 5 5 | 7 3 |
| 5 | 1 48 | 9 | 13 8 | | | 4 59 | 6 57 | 5 3 | 7 1 |
| 13 | 17 50 | | | 13 | 6 50 | 5 1 | 6 59 | 5 1 | 6 59 |
| | | 17 | 1 29 | | | 5 3 | 7 1 | 4 59 | 6 57 |
| | | | | 2 | 12 18 | 5 5 | 7 3 | 4 57 | 6 55 |
| 2 | 3 55 | 6 | 9 48 | | | 5 6 | 7 5 | 4 55 | 6 54 |
| 10 | 18 46 | | | 10 | 7 0 | 5 8 | 7 7 | 4 53 | 6 52 |
| | | 14 | 3 40 | 18 | 23 29 | 5 10 | 7 9 | 4 51 | 6 50 |
| 18 | 5 54 | 3 | 22 18 | | | 5 12 | 7 11 | 4 49 | 6 48 |
| 7 | 13 10 | | | 7 | 14 7 | 5 14 | 7 13 | 4 47 | 6 46 |
| 15 | 21 52 | 11 | 5 38 | 15 | 21 4 | 5 15 | 7 15 | 4 45 | 6 45 |
| 4 | 22 53 | 19 | 12 45 | | | 5 17 | 7 17 | 4 43 | 6 43 |
| | | | | 4 | 9 53 | 5 19 | 7 19 | 4 41 | 6 41 |
| 12 | 17 47 | 8 | 5 20 | | | 5 20 | 7 20 | 4 40 | 6 40 |
| | | 16 | 22 41 | 12 | 1 42 | 5 21 | 7 22 | 4 38 | 6 39 |
| 1 | 21 30 | | | 1 | 11 51 | 5 23 | 7 24 | 4 36 | 6 37 |
| | | 5 | 7 53 | | | 5 25 | 7 26 | 4 34 | 6 35 |
| 9 | 7 17 | 13 | 21 8 | 9 | 2 58 | 5 26 | 7 28 | 4 32 | 6 34 |
| 17 | 14 45 | | | 17 | 14 22 | 5 27 | 7 29 | 4 31 | 6 33 |
| | | 2 | 6 11 | 6 | 21 47 | 5 29 | 7 31 | 4 29 | 6 31 |

# OCTOBER

## Altitudines solis et longitudines umbrarum cuiuslibet

| Numerus dierum | 7 / 5 altitudines solis g. m. | umbre hominis pedes | partes | 8 / 4 altitudines solis g. m. | umbre hominis pedes | partes | 9 / 3 altitudines solis g. m. | umbre hominis pedes | partes |
|---|---|---|---|---|---|---|---|---|---|
| 1 | 4 0 | 85 | 51 | 12 35 | 26 | 55 | 20 11 | 16 | 20 |
| 2 | 3 42 | 94 | 26 | 12 16 | 27 | 38 | 19 51 | 16 | 38 |
| 3 | 3 23 | 103 | 30 | 11 57 | 28 | 21 | 19 30 | 16 | 57 |
| 4 | 3 6 | 111 | 37 | 11 37 | 29 | 14 | 19 10 | 17 | 16 |
| 5 | 2 46 | 127 | 52 | 11 18 | 30 | 4 | 18 50 | 17 | 35 |
| 6 | 2 29 | 144 | 7 | 11 0 | 30 | 52 | 18 31 | 17 | 55 |
| 7 | 2 11 | 161 | 19 | 10 41 | 31 | 52 | 18 10 | 18 | 17 |
| 8 | 1 53 | 191 | 52 | 10 22 | 32 | 52 | 17 51 | 18 | 38 |
| 9 | 1 35 | 243 | 26 | 10 3 | 33 | 52 | 17 30 | 19 | 2 |
| 10 | 1 17 | 295 | 1 | 9 45 | 34 | 59 | 17 10 | 19 | 26 |
| 11 | 1 0 | 343 | 43 | 9 26 | 36 | 12 | 16 51 | 19 | 49 |
| 12 | 0 42 | 491 | 5 | 9 9 | 37 | 18 | 16 32 | 20 | 14 |
| 13 | 0 25 | 825 | 0 | 8 50 | 38 | 42 | 16 13 | 20 | 39 |
| 14 | 0 8 | 2578 | 12 | 8 33 | 40 | 4 | 15 54 | 21 | 4 |
| 15 | 0 0 | 0 | 0 | 8 14 | 41 | 36 | 15 34 | 21 | 33 |
| 16 | 0 0 | 0 | 0 | 7 56 | 43 | 9 | 15 15 | 22 | 1 |
| 17 | 0 0 | 0 | 0 | 7 39 | 44 | 53 | 14 57 | 22 | 29 |
| 18 | 0 0 | 0 | 0 | 7 21 | 46 | 43 | 14 40 | 22 | 57 |
| 19 | 0 0 | 0 | 0 | 7 3 | 48 | 34 | 14 21 | 23 | 29 |
| 20 | 0 0 | 0 | 0 | 6 46 | 50 | 47 | 14 2 | 24 | 1 |
| 21 | 0 0 | 0 | 0 | 6 29 | 53 | 7 | 13 45 | 24 | 23 |
| 22 | 0 0 | 0 | 0 | 6 13 | 55 | 18 | 13 27 | 25 | 7 |
| 23 | 0 0 | 0 | 0 | 5 56 | 57 | 51 | 13 9 | 25 | 42 |
| 24 | 0 0 | 0 | 0 | 5 40 | 60 | 55 | 12 51 | 26 | 20 |
| 25 | 0 0 | 0 | 0 | 5 24 | 63 | 59 | 12 34 | 26 | 58 |
| 26 | 0 0 | 0 | 0 | 5 8 | 67 | 3 | 12 18 | 27 | 33 |
| 27 | 0 0 | 0 | 0 | 4 53 | 70 | 36 | 12 2 | 28 | 9 |
| 28 | 0 0 | 0 | 0 | 4 37 | 75 | 12 | 11 45 | 28 | 53 |
| 29 | 0 0 | 0 | 0 | 4 21 | 79 | 48 | 11 28 | 29 | 38 |
| 30 | 0 0 | 0 | 0 | 4 6 | 84 | 7 | 11 12 | 30 | 20 |
| 31 | 0 0 | 0 | 0 | 3 51 | 90 | 9 | 10 56 | 31 | 5 |

hominis stature sex pedum in horis de clok

| 10 2 | | | 11 1 | | | 12 a.m. 0 p.m. | | |
|---|---|---|---|---|---|---|---|---|
| altitudines solis | umbre hominis | | altitudines solis | umbre hominis | | altitudines solis | umbre hominis | |
| g. m. | pedes | partes | g. m. | pedes | partes | g. m. | pedes | partes |
| 26 16 | 12 | 9 | 30 15 | 10 | 17 | 31 39 | 9 | 44 |
| 25 55 | 12 | 21 | 29 53 | 10 | 26 | 31 17 | 9 | 52 |
| 25 33 | 12 | 33 | 29 30 | 10 | 37 | 30 53 | 10 | 2 |
| 25 12 | 12 | 45 | 29 9 | 10 | 46 | 30 31 | 10 | 11 |
| 24 50 | 12 | 58 | 28 46 | 10 | 56 | 30 8 | 10 | 20 |
| 24 29 | 13 | 11 | 28 24 | 11 | 6 | 29 46 | 10 | 29 |
| 24 8 | 13 | 24 | 28 1 | 11 | 17 | 29 22 | 10 | 40 |
| 23 48 | 13 | 36 | 27 40 | 11 | 27 | 29 1 | 10 | 50 |
| 23 26 | 13 | 51 | 27 17 | 11 | 38 | 28 38 | 11 | 0 |
| 23 5 | 14 | 5 | 26 56 | 11 | 48 | 28 16 | 11 | 10 |
| 22 44 | 14 | 19 | 26 34 | 12 | 0 | 27 55 | 11 | 20 |
| 22 23 | 14 | 35 | 26 12 | 12 | 12 | 27 32 | 11 | 31 |
| 22 3 | 14 | 49 | 25 51 | 12 | 23 | 27 11 | 11 | 41 |
| 21 43 | 15 | 4 | 25 29 | 12 | 36 | 26 49 | 11 | 52 |
| 21 23 | 15 | 20 | 25 9 | 12 | 47 | 26 28 | 12 | 3 |
| 21 3 | 15 | 36 | 24 48 | 13 | 0 | 26 6 | 12 | 15 |
| 20 43 | 15 | 52 | 24 28 | 13 | 12 | 25 46 | 12 | 26 |
| 20 24 | 16 | 9 | 24 8 | 13 | 24 | 25 26 | 12 | 37 |
| 20 5 | 16 | 25 | 23 48 | 13 | 36 | 25 5 | 12 | 49 |
| 19 46 | 16 | 43 | 23 28 | 13 | 49 | 24 45 | 13 | 1 |
| 19 27 | 17 | 0 | 23 8 | 14 | 3 | 24 25 | 13 | 13 |
| 19 8 | 17 | 18 | 22 48 | 14 | 17 | 24 5 | 13 | 25 |
| 18 49 | 17 | 36 | 22 28 | 14 | 31 | 23 46 | 13 | 37 |
| 18 31 | 17 | 55 | 22 8 | 14 | 45 | 23 26 | 13 | 51 |
| 18 13 | 18 | 14 | 21 50 | 14 | 59 | 23 5 | 14 | 5 |
| 17 55 | 18 | 33 | 21 32 | 15 | 13 | 22 47 | 14 | 17 |
| 17 37 | 18 | 54 | 21 15 | 15 | 26 | 22 29 | 14 | 30 |
| 17 19 | 19 | 15 | 20 56 | 15 | 41 | 22 10 | 14 | 44 |
| 17 2 | 19 | 35 | 20 37 | 15 | 58 | 21 52 | 14 | 57 |
| 16 46 | 19 | 56 | 20 20 | 16 | 12 | 21 35 | 15 | 11 |
| 16 30 | 20 | 17 | 20 3 | 16 | 26 | 21 18 | 15 | 24 |

# NOVEMBER

| | | | | |
|---|---|---|---|---|
| 1 | | *d* | **KL** | Festivitas omnium sanctorum |
| 2 | 13 | *e* | 4 Nonas | Commemoracio animarum |
| 3 | 2 | *f* | 3 Nonas | |
| 4 | | *g* | 2 Nonas | |
| 5 | 10 | A | Nonis | |
| 6 | | *b* | 8 Idus | Sancti Leonardi abbatis |
| 7 | 18 | *c* | 7 Idus | |
| 8 | 7 | *d* | 6 Idus | Sanctorum quatuor coronatorum |
| 9 | | *e* | 5 Idus | Sancti Theodori martyris |
| 10 | 15 | *f* | 4 Idus | Sancti Martini pape |
| 11 | 4 | *g* | 3 Idus | Sancti Martini episcopi et confessoris |
| 12 | | A | 2 Idus | |
| 13 | 12 | *b* | Idibus | Sancti Bricii episcopi |
| 14 | 1 | *c* | 18 Kl. | |
| 15 | | *d* | 17 Kl. | |
| 16 | 9 | *e* | 16 Kl. | Sancti Edmundi archiepiscopi |
| 17 | | *f* | 15 Kl. | Sancti Hugonis episcopi et confessoris |
| 18 | 17 | *g* | 14 Kl. | Octava Sancti Martini |
| 19 | 6 | A | 13 Kl. | |
| 20 | | *b* | 12 Kl. | |
| 21 | 14 | *c* | 11 Kl. | |
| 22 | 3 | *d* | 10 Kl. | Sancte Cecilie virginis et martyris |
| 23 | | *e* | 9 Kl. | Sancti Clementis |
| 24 | 11 | *f* | 8 Kl. | Sancti Grisogoni martyris |
| 25 | 19 | *g* | 7 Kl. | Sancte Katerine virginis |
| 26 | | A | 6 Kl. | Sancti Line pape et martyris |
| 27 | 8 | *b* | 5 Kl. | |
| 28 | | *c* | 4 Kl. | |
| 29 | 16 | *d* | 3 Kl. | Sancti Saturnini martyris |
| 30 | | *e* | 2 Kl. | Sancti Andree apostoli |

Variant readings for this month are listed on pp. 140–41.

| Numerus dierum | Verus locus solis | | Quantitates diei artificialis | | Quantitates diei vulgaris | | Quantitates utriusque crepusculorum matutini et vespertini | |
|---|---|---|---|---|---|---|---|---|
| | g. | m. | h. | m. | h. | m. | h. | m. |
| | Scorpio | | | | | | | |
| 1 | 17 | 40 | 8 | 55 | 12 | 59 | 2 | 2 |
| 2 | 18 | 41 | 8 | 51 | 12 | 57 | 2 | 3 |
| 3 | 19 | 42 | 8 | 48 | 12 | 54 | 2 | 3 |
| 4 | 20 | 43 | 8 | 44 | 12 | 50 | 2 | 3 |
| 5 | 21 | 44 | 8 | 41 | 12 | 49 | 2 | 4 |
| 6 | 22 | 45 | 8 | 38 | 12 | 46 | 2 | 4 |
| 7 | 23 | 46 | 8 | 35 | 12 | 43 | 2 | 4 |
| 8 | 24 | 47 | 8 | 31 | 12 | 41 | 2 | 5 |
| 9 | 25 | 48 | 8 | 28 | 12 | 38 | 2 | 5 |
| 10 | 26 | 49 | 8 | 25 | 12 | 35 | 2 | 5 |
| 11 | 27 | 50 | 8 | 22 | 12 | 34 | 2 | 6 |
| 12 | 28 | 51 | 8 | 19 | 12 | 31 | 2 | 6 |
| 13 | 29 | 52 | 8 | 17 | 12 | 29 | 2 | 6 |
| | Sagittarius | | | | | | | |
| 14 | 0 | 53 | 8 | 14 | 12 | 28 | 2 | 7 |
| 15 | 1 | 55 | 8 | 11 | 12 | 25 | 2 | 7 |
| 16 | 2 | 56 | 8 | 8 | 12 | 22 | 2 | 7 |
| 17 | 3 | 57 | 8 | 6 | 12 | 22 | 2 | 8 |
| 18 | 4 | 58 | 8 | 3 | 12 | 19 | 2 | 8 |
| 19 | 6 | 0 | 8 | 1 | 12 | 17 | 2 | 8 |
| 20 | 7 | 1 | 7 | 58 | 12 | 16 | 2 | 9 |
| 21 | 8 | 2 | 7 | 56 | 12 | 14 | 2 | 9 |
| 22 | 9 | 3 | 7 | 54 | 12 | 12 | 2 | 9 |
| 23 | 10 | 5 | 7 | 52 | 12 | 12 | 2 | 10 |
| 24 | 11 | 6 | 7 | 50 | 12 | 10 | 2 | 10 |
| 25 | 12 | 7 | 7 | 48 | 12 | 8 | 2 | 10 |
| 26 | 13 | 8 | 7 | 46 | 12 | 6 | 2 | 10 |
| 27 | 14 | 10 | 7 | 44 | 12 | 6 | 2 | 11 |
| 28 | 15 | 11 | 7 | 42 | 12 | 4 | 2 | 11 |
| 29 | 16 | 12 | 7 | 41 | 12 | 3 | 2 | 11 |
| 30 | 17 | 14 | 7 | 39 | 12 | 1 | 2 | 11 |

Translations of Latin headings are to be found in the introduction, pp. 11–25.

# NOVEMBER

| Numerus dierum | Primus Ciclus | | | | Secundus Ciclus | | | | Tercius | |
|---|---|---|---|---|---|---|---|---|---|---|
| | Ciclus Conjunccionis | Tempus vere conjunccionis h. m. | Ciclus Opposicionis | Tempus vere opposicionis h. m. | Ciclus Conjunccionis | Tempus vere conjunccionis h. m. | Ciclus Opposicionis | Tempus vere opposicionis h. m. | Ciclus Conjunccionis | Tempus vere conjunccionis h. m. |
| 1 | 10 | 23 24 | 6 | 2 0 | | | 6 | 10 7 | 10 | 18 23 |
| 2 | | | 14 | 20 18 | 10 | 6 58 | | | | |
| 3 | 18 | 16 31 | | | | | 14 | 4 29 | 18 | 9 54 |
| 4 | | | 3 | 16 43 | 18 | 1 51 | 3 | 11 50 | | |
| 5 | 7 | 8 48 | | | 7 | 6 12 | 11 | 23 40 | 7 | 20 5 |
| 6 | 15 | 15 48 | 11 | 0 22 | 15 | 16 18 | | | | |
| 7 | | | 19 | 7 21 | 4 | 23 14 | 19 | 8 18 | 15 / 4 | 11 31 / 23 53 |
| 8 | 4 | 3 18 | 8 | 22 22 | | | 8 | 15 42 | | |
| 9 | 12 | 18 23 | | | 12 | 8 50 | | | 12 | 6 54 |
| 10 | | | 16 | 15 7 | | | 16 | 2 58 | 1 | 22 7 |
| 11 | | | | | 1 | 12 24 | | | | |
| 12 | 1 | 4 32 | | | | | 5 | 9 55 | 9 | 14 56 |
| 13 | 9 | 20 22 | 5 | 0 54 | 9 | 7 18 | | | | |
| 14 | | | 13 | 14 57 | | | 13 | 4 20 | 17 | 9 47 |
| 15 | 17 / 6 | 8 36 / 16 32 | 2 | 1 2 | 17 | 0 40 | | | | |
| 16 | | | 10 | 8 20 | 6 | 17 28 | 2 | 1 21 | 6 | 14 38 |
| 17 | 14 | 0 41 | 18 | 17 44 | | | 10 | 9 7 | | |
| 18 | 3 | 23 22 | | | 14 / 3 | 0 36 / 11 39 | 18 | 16 5 | 14 | 0 57 |
| 19 | | | 7 | 20 34 | | | 7 | 6 40 | 3 | 7 55 |
| 20 | 11 | 18 6 | | | 11 | 2 31 | 15 | 23 11 | 11 | 17 25 |
| 21 | | | 15 | 15 32 | 19 | 20 24 | | | | |
| 22 | 19 | 12 38 | | | | | | | 19 | 6 24 |
| 23 | | | 4 | 17 29 | | | 4 | 9 5 | 8 | 15 23 |
| 24 | 8 | 10 24 | | | 8 | 4 44 | 12 | 23 23 | | |
| 25 | 16 | 18 22 | 12 | 2 37 | 16 | 17 9 | | | 16 | 8 52 |
| 26 | | | 1 | 9 42 | | | 1 | 9 49 | | |
| 27 | 5 | 2 39 | 9 | 20 27 | 5 | 1 17 | 9 | 17 2 | 5 | 2 10 |
| 28 | 13 | 15 12 | | | 13 | 9 18 | | | 13 | 9 19 |
| 29 | 2 | 23 44 | 17 | 10 55 | | | 17 | 2 17 | 2 | 20 9 |
| 30 | | | 6 | 20 54 | 2 | 7 26 | | | | |

Ciclus  Quartus Ciclus

| Ciclus Opposicionis | Tempus vere opposicionis | Ciclus Conjunccionis | Tempus vere conjunccionis | Ciclus Opposicionis | Tempus vere opposicionis | Quantitates a noctis medio ad auroram | Quantitates a noctis medio ad solis ortum | Quantitates a meridie ad solis occasum | Quantitates a meridie ad noctem obscuram |
|---|---|---|---|---|---|---|---|---|---|
| | h. m. | | h. m. | | h. m. | h. m. | h. m. | h. m. | h. m. |
| 6 | 0 5 | 10 | 13 47 | | | 5 31 | 7 33 | 4 27 | 6 29 |
| 14 | 13 41 | 18 | 23 44 | 14 | 6 19 | 5 32 | 7 35 | 4 25 | 6 28 |
| | | | | | | 5 33 | 7 36 | 4 24 | 6 27 |
| 3 | 23 11 | | | 3 | 6 46 | 5 35 | 7 38 | 4 22 | 6 25 |
| | | 7 | 4 7 | | | 5 36 | 7 40 | 4 20 | 6 24 |
| 11 | 16 15 | 15 | 23 0 | 11 | 1 38 | 5 37 | 7 41 | 4 19 | 6 23 |
| | | | | 19 | 19 51 | 5 39 | 7 43 | 4 17 | 6 21 |
| 19 / 8 | 5 52 / 15 21 | 4 | 23 17 | | | 5 40 | 7 45 | 4 15 | 6 20 |
| 16 | 22 48 | | | 8 | 15 53 | 5 41 | 7 46 | 4 14 | 6 19 |
| | | 12 / 1 | 7 52 / 15 8 | 16 | 23 27 | 5 43 | 7 48 | 4 12 | 6 17 |
| 5 | 18 10 | | | 5 | 8 29 | 5 43 | 7 49 | 4 11 | 6 17 |
| | | 9 | 2 40 | 13 | 21 51 | 5 45 | 7 51 | 4 9 | 6 15 |
| 13 | 12 15 | 17 | 17 57 | | | 5 46 | 7 52 | 4 8 | 6 14 |
| | | | | | | 5 46 | 7 53 | 4 7 | 6 14 |
| 2 | 20 8 | | | 2 | 7 10 | 5 48 | 7 55 | 4 5 | 6 12 |
| | | 6 | 4 10 | | | 5 49 | 7 56 | 4 4 | 6 11 |
| 10 | 8 13 | 14 | 19 51 | 10 | 0 26 | 5 49 | 7 57 | 4 3 | 6 11 |
| 18 | 17 2 | | | 18 | 14 19 | 5 51 | 7 59 | 4 1 | 6 9 |
| | | 3 | 8 40 | | | 5 52 | 8 0 | 4 0 | 6 8 |
| 7 | 0 18 | 11 | 15 39 | 7 | 0 8 | 5 52 | 8 1 | 3 59 | 6 8 |
| 15 | 11 23 | 19 | 23 55 | 15 | 7 30 | 5 53 | 8 2 | 3 58 | 6 7 |
| 4 | 17 54 | | | | | 5 54 | 8 3 | 3 57 | 6 6 |
| | | 8 | 22 59 | 4 | 2 18 | 5 54 | 8 4 | 3 56 | 6 6 |
| 12 | 12 26 | | | 12 | 20 14 | 5 55 | 8 5 | 3 55 | 6 5 |
| | | 16 | 17 45 | | | 5 56 | 8 6 | 3 54 | 6 4 |
| 1 | 10 0 | 5 | 23 4 | 1 | 4 26 | 5 57 | 8 7 | 3 53 | 6 3 |
| 9 | 17 53 | | | 9 | 16 46 | 5 57 | 8 8 | 3 52 | 6 3 |
| | | 13 | 9 37 | | | 5 58 | 8 9 | 3 51 | 6 2 |
| 17 | 0 51 | 2 | 16 37 | 17 | 1 45 | 5 59 | 8 10 | 3 50 | 6 1 |
| 6 | 14 57 | | | 6 | 8 55 | 6 0 | 8 11 | 3 49 | 6 0 |

# NOVEMBER

## Altitudines solis et longitudines umbrarum cuiuslibet

| Numerus dierum | altitudines solis (8 4) | | umbre hominis | | altitudines solis (9 3) | | umbre hominis | |
|---|---|---|---|---|---|---|---|---|
| | g. | m. | pedes | partes | g. | m. | pedes | partes |
| 1 | 3 | 37 | 96 | 50 | 10 | 41 | 31 | 52 |
| 2 | 3 | 23 | 103 | 30 | 10 | 26 | 32 | 40 |
| 3 | 3 | 9 | 110 | 11 | 10 | 11 | 33 | 27 |
| 4 | 2 | 54 | 120 | 13 | 9 | 56 | 34 | 16 |
| 5 | 2 | 41 | 132 | 39 | 9 | 42 | 35 | 11 |
| 6 | 2 | 27 | 146 | 1 | 9 | 27 | 36 | 9 |
| 7 | 2 | 14 | 158 | 27 | 9 | 14 | 36 | 59 |
| 8 | 2 | 1 | 170 | 52 | 9 | 1 | 37 | 49 |
| 9 | 1 | 49 | 203 | 20 | 8 | 48 | 38 | 51 |
| 10 | 1 | 37 | 237 | 43 | 8 | 35 | 39 | 54 |
| 11 | 1 | 25 | 272 | 6 | 8 | 22 | 40 | 57 |
| 12 | 1 | 14 | 303 | 36 | 8 | 10 | 41 | 56 |
| 13 | 1 | 3 | 335 | 7 | 7 | 58 | 42 | 56 |
| 14 | 0 | 52 | 396 | 37 | 7 | 46 | 44 | 10 |
| 15 | 0 | 41 | 503 | 33 | 7 | 35 | 45 | 17 |
| 16 | 0 | 31 | 665 | 15 | 7 | 24 | 46 | 25 |
| 17 | 0 | 21 | 982 | 4 | 7 | 14 | 47 | 26 |
| 18 | 0 | 12 | 1718 | 47 | 7 | 2 | 48 | 40 |
| 19 | 0 | 2 | 10318 | 25 | 6 | 53 | 49 | 50 |
| 20 | 0 | 0 | 0 | 0 | 6 | 44 | 51 | 3 |
| 21 | 0 | 0 | 0 | 0 | 6 | 35 | 52 | 17 |
| 22 | 0 | 0 | 0 | 0 | 6 | 25 | 53 | 40 |
| 23 | 0 | 0 | 0 | 0 | 6 | 17 | 54 | 45 |
| 24 | 0 | 0 | 0 | 0 | 6 | 10 | 55 | 43 |
| 25 | 0 | 0 | 0 | 0 | 6 | 3 | 56 | 40 |
| 26 | 0 | 0 | 0 | 0 | 5 | 56 | 57 | 51 |
| 27 | 0 | 0 | 0 | 0 | 5 | 49 | 59 | 12 |
| 28 | 0 | 0 | 0 | 0 | 5 | 42 | 60 | 32 |
| 29 | 0 | 0 | 0 | 0 | 5 | 37 | 61 | 30 |
| 30 | 0 | 0 | 0 | 0 | 5 | 32 | 62 | 27 |

hominis stature sex pedum in horis de clok

| 10 | 11 | 12 a.m. |
|---|---|---|
| 2 | 1 | 0 p.m. |

| altitudines solis | umbre hominis | | altitudines solis | umbre hominis | | altitudines solis | umbre hominis | |
|---|---|---|---|---|---|---|---|---|
| g. m. | pedes | partes | g. m. | pedes | partes | g. m. | pedes | partes |
| 16 13 | 20 | 39 | 19 46 | 16 | 43 | 21 0 | 15 | 38 |
| 15 57 | 20 | 59 | 19 29 | 16 | 58 | 20 42 | 15 | 53 |
| 15 40 | 21 | 24 | 19 12 | 17 | 14 | 20 25 | 16 | 8 |
| 15 25 | 21 | 46 | 18 56 | 17 | 29 | 20 9 | 16 | 21 |
| 15 10 | 22 | 8 | 18 41 | 17 | 45 | 19 54 | 16 | 35 |
| 14 55 | 22 | 32 | 18 25 | 18 | 1 | 19 37 | 16 | 51 |
| 14 41 | 22 | 55 | 18 10 | 18 | 17 | 19 22 | 17 | 5 |
| 14 26 | 23 | 21 | 17 54 | 18 | 34 | 19 6 | 17 | 20 |
| 14 12 | 23 | 44 | 17 39 | 18 | 52 | 18 52 | 17 | 33 |
| 13 58 | 24 | 8 | 17 25 | 19 | 8 | 18 38 | 17 | 48 |
| 13 45 | 24 | 33 | 17 11 | 19 | 25 | 18 24 | 18 | 2 |
| 13 33 | 24 | 56 | 16 59 | 19 | 39 | 18 11 | 18 | 16 |
| 13 20 | 25 | 21 | 16 46 | 19 | 56 | 17 58 | 18 | 30 |
| 13 8 | 25 | 44 | 16 34 | 20 | 11 | 17 44 | 18 | 46 |
| 12 56 | 26 | 8 | 16 22 | 20 | 27 | 17 32 | 19 | 0 |
| 12 45 | 26 | 33 | 16 10 | 20 | 42 | 17 20 | 19 | 14 |
| 12 34 | 26 | 58 | 15 58 | 20 | 58 | 17 8 | 19 | 28 |
| 12 22 | 27 | 24 | 15 45 | 21 | 17 | 16 55 | 19 | 44 |
| 12 13 | 27 | 44 | 15 35 | 21 | 32 | 16 45 | 19 | 57 |
| 12 3 | 28 | 7 | 15 25 | 21 | 46 | 16 36 | 20 | 9 |
| 11 53 | 28 | 32 | 15 15 | 22 | 1 | 16 26 | 20 | 22 |
| 11 43 | 28 | 58 | 15 5 | 22 | 16 | 16 15 | 20 | 36 |
| 11 33 | 29 | 25 | 14 55 | 22 | 32 | 16 5 | 20 | 49 |
| 11 26 | 29 | 43 | 14 47 | 22 | 45 | 15 57 | 20 | 59 |
| 11 18 | 30 | 4 | 14 41 | 22 | 55 | 15 50 | 21 | 10 |
| 11 11 | 30 | 23 | 14 33 | 23 | 9 | 15 42 | 21 | 21 |
| 11 4 | 30 | 41 | 14 25 | 23 | 22 | 15 34 | 21 | 33 |
| 10 56 | 31 | 5 | 14 17 | 23 | 36 | 15 26 | 21 | 45 |
| 10 51 | 31 | 21 | 14 11 | 23 | 46 | 15 20 | 21 | 54 |
| 10 46 | 31 | 37 | 14 6 | 23 | 54 | 15 15 | 22 | 1 |

# DECEMBER

| | | | | |
|---|---|---|---|---|
| 1 | | *f* | **KL** | |
| 2 | ¹³⁄₂ | *g* | 4 Nonas | |
| 3 | | A | 3 Nonas | |
| 4 | 10 | *b* | 2 Nonas | |
| 5 | | *c* | Nonis | |
| 6 | 18 | *d* | 8 Idus | Sancti Nicholai episcopi et confessoris |
| 7 | 7 | *e* | 7 Idus | |
| 8 | | *f* | 6 Idus | Concepcio Sancte Marie Virginis |
| 9 | 15 | *g* | 5 Idus | |
| 10 | 4 | A | 4 Idus | |
| 11 | | *b* | 3 Idus | |
| 12 | 12 | *c* | 2 Idus | |
| | | | | |
| 13 | 1 | *d* | Idibus | Sancte Lucie virginis et martyris |
| 14 | | *e* | 19 Kl. | |
| 15 | 9 | *f* | 18 Kl. | |
| 16 | | *g* | 17 Kl. | O sapiencia |
| 17 | 17 | A | 16 Kl. | |
| 18 | 6 | *b* | 15 Kl. | |
| 19 | | *c* | 14 Kl. | |
| 20 | 14 | *d* | 13 Kl. | |
| 21 | 3 | *e* | 12 Kl. | Sancti Thome apostoli |
| 22 | | *f* | 11 Kl. | |
| 23 | 11 | *g* | 10 Kl. | |
| 24 | 19 | A | 9 Kl. | |
| 25 | | *b* | 8 Kl. | Nativitas Domini Nostri Jesu Christi |
| 26 | 8 | *c* | 7 Kl. | Sancti Stephani prothomartyris |
| 27 | | *d* | 6 Kl. | Sancti Johannis apostoli et ewangeliste |
| 28 | 16 | *e* | 5 Kl. | Sanctorum Innocencium |
| 29 | 5 | *f* | 4 Kl. | Sancti Thome archiepiscopi |
| 30 | | *g* | 3 Kl. | |
| 31 | 13 | A | 2 Kl. | Sancti Silvestri pape |

Variant readings for this month are listed on p. 141.

| Numerus dierum | Verus locus solis | | Quantitates diei artificialis | | Quantitates diei vulgaris | | Quantitates utriusque crepusculorum matutini et vespertini | |
|---|---|---|---|---|---|---|---|---|
| | g. | m. | h. | m. | h. | m. | h. | m. |
| | Sagittarius | | | | | | | |
| 1 | 18 | 15 | 7 | 38 | 12 | 0 | 2 | 11 |
| 2 | 19 | 16 | 7 | 37 | 12 | 0 | 2 | 12 |
| 3 | 20 | 18 | 7 | 36 | 12 | 0 | 2 | 12 |
| 4 | 21 | 19 | 7 | 35 | 11 | 59 | 2 | 12 |
| 5 | 22 | 21 | 7 | 34 | 11 | 58 | 2 | 12 |
| 6 | 23 | 22 | 7 | 33 | 11 | 57 | 2 | 12 |
| 7 | 24 | 24 | 7 | 32 | 11 | 56 | 2 | 12 |
| 8 | 25 | 25 | 7 | 32 | 11 | 56 | 2 | 12 |
| 9 | 26 | 27 | 7 | 31 | 11 | 55 | 2 | 12 |
| 10 | 27 | 28 | 7 | 31 | 11 | 56 | 2 | 13 |
| 11 | 28 | 30 | 7 | 31 | 11 | 56 | 2 | 13 |
| 12 | 29 | 31 | 7 | 30 | 11 | 56 | 2 | 13 |
| | Capricornus | | | | | | | |
| 13 | 0 | 33 | 7 | 30 | 11 | 56 | 2 | 13 |
| 14 | 1 | 34 | 7 | 31 | 11 | 56 | 2 | 13 |
| 15 | 2 | 36 | 7 | 31 | 11 | 56 | 2 | 13 |
| 16 | 3 | 37 | 7 | 31 | 11 | 55 | 2 | 12 |
| 17 | 4 | 39 | 7 | 32 | 11 | 56 | 2 | 12 |
| 18 | 5 | 40 | 7 | 32 | 11 | 56 | 2 | 12 |
| 19 | 6 | 42 | 7 | 33 | 11 | 57 | 2 | 12 |
| 20 | 7 | 43 | 7 | 34 | 11 | 58 | 2 | 12 |
| 21 | 8 | 45 | 7 | 35 | 11 | 59 | 2 | 12 |
| 22 | 9 | 46 | 7 | 36 | 12 | 0 | 2 | 12 |
| 23 | 10 | 47 | 7 | 37 | 12 | 1 | 2 | 12 |
| 24 | 11 | 49 | 7 | 38 | 12 | 1 | 2 | 12 |
| 25 | 12 | 50 | 7 | 39 | 12 | 1 | 2 | 11 |
| 26 | 13 | 52 | 7 | 41 | 12 | 3 | 2 | 11 |
| 27 | 14 | 53 | 7 | 43 | 12 | 5 | 2 | 11 |
| 28 | 15 | 54 | 7 | 44 | 12 | 6 | 2 | 11 |
| 29 | 16 | 56 | 7 | 46 | 12 | 6 | 2 | 10 |
| 30 | 17 | 57 | 7 | 48 | 12 | 8 | 2 | 10 |
| 31 | 18 | 58 | 7 | 50 | 12 | 10 | 2 | 10 |

Translations of Latin headings are to be found in the introduction, pp. 11-25.

# DECEMBER

| Numerus dierum | Primus Ciclus | | | | Secundus Ciclus | | | | Tercius | |
|---|---|---|---|---|---|---|---|---|---|---|
| | Ciclus Conjunccionis | Tempus vere conjunccionis | Ciclus Opposicionis | Tempus vere opposicionis | Ciclus Conjunccionis | Tempus vere conjunccionis | Ciclus Opposicionis | Tempus vere opposicionis | Ciclus Conjunccionis | Tempus vere conjunccionis |
| | | h. m. | | h. m. | | h. m. | | h. m. | | h. m. |
| 1 | 10 | 17 30 | | | | | 6 | 4 35 | 10 | 10 41 |
| 2 | | | 14 | 13 17 | 10 | 2 5 | 14 | 23 33 | | |
| 3 | 18 | 8 7 | | | 18 | 20 44 | | | 18 | 4 25 |
| 4 | 7 | 19 3 | 3 | 3 33 | 7 | 19 4 | 3 | 2 2 | | |
| 5 | | | 11 | 10 31 | | | 11 | 11 21 | 7 | 13 2 |
| 6 | 15 | 2 12 | 19 | 18 23 | 15 | 3 7 | 19 | 18 37 | | |
| 7 | 4 | 19 22 | | | 4 | 11 13 | | | 15 / 4 | 1 42 / 10 5 |
| 8 | | | 8 | 15 46 | 12 | 23 35 | 8 | 4 55 | 12 | 17 59 |
| 9 | 12 | 12 49 | | | | | 16 | 19 8 | | |
| 10 | | | 16 | 10 16 | | | | | 1 | 15 34 |
| 11 | 1 | 21 52 | | | 1 | 7 47 | | | | |
| 12 | | | 5 | 16 53 | | | 5 | 5 1 | 9 | 10 8 |
| 13 | 9 | 10 58 | | | 9 | 1 43 | 13 | 21 37 | | |
| 14 | 17 | 20 30 | 13 / 2 | 4 6 / 11 24 | 17 | 16 34 | | | 17 | 4 52 |
| 15 | 6 | 3 28 | 10 | 20 11 | | | 2 | 12 22 | | |
| 16 | 14 | 13 44 | | | 6 | 3 54 | 10 | 19 21 | 6 | 3 44 |
| 17 | | | 18 | 8 12 | 14 | 11 0 | | | 14 | 11 56 |
| 18 | 3 | 18 30 | | | 3 | 3 37 | 18 / 7 | 3 5 / 23 56 | 3 | 19 50 |
| 19 | | | 7 | 16 0 | 11 | 20 55 | | | | |
| 20 | 11 | 13 19 | | | | | 15 | 18 19 | 11 | 7 58 |
| 21 | | | 15 | 10 7 | 19 | 15 51 | | | 19 | 23 44 |
| 22 | 19 | 6 11 | | | | | | | | |
| 23 | 8 | 21 36 | 4 | 5 40 | 8 | 19 28 | 4 | 1 18 | 8 | 9 56 |
| 24 | | | 12 | 13 9 | | | 12 | 12 45 | | |
| 25 | 16 | 4 38 | 1 | 22 33 | 16 | 5 16 | 1 | 20 12 | 16 | 1 1 |
| 26 | 5 | 16 53 | | | 5 | 12 12 | | | 5 | 12 45 |
| 27 | | | 9 | 12 7 | 13 | 22 14 | 9 | 4 48 | 13 | 19 46 |
| 28 | 13 | 8 17 | | | | | 17 | 16 35 | | |
| 29 | 2 | 18 30 | 17 | 5 10 | | | | | 2 | 11 53 |
| 30 | | | 6 | 14 40 | 2 | 2 31 | | | | |
| 31 | 10 | 9 58 | | | 10 | 21 24 | 6 | 0 2 | 10 | 4 59 |

Ciclus            Quartus Ciclus

| Ciclus Opposicionis | Tempus vere opposicionis | Ciclus Conjunccionis | Tempus vere conjunccionis | Ciclus Opposicionis | Tempus vere opposicionis | Quantitates a noctis medio ad auroram | Quantitates a noctis medio ad solis ortum | Quantitates a meridie ad solis occasum | Quantitates a meridie ad noctem obscuram |
|---|---|---|---|---|---|---|---|---|---|
| | h. m. | | h. m. | | h. m. | h. m. | h. m. | h. m. | h. m. |
| | | 10 | 1 56 | 14 | 19 50 | 6 0 | 8 11 | 3 49 | 6 0 |
| 14 | 7 16 | 18 | 14 42 | | | 6 0 | 8 12 | 3 48 | 6 0 |
| | | | | | | 6 0 | 8 12 | 3 48 | 6 0 |
| 3 | 17 17 | 7 | 23 24 | 3 | 1 55 | 6 1 | 8 13 | 3 47 | 5 59 |
| | | | | 11 | 20 33 | 6 1 | 8 13 | 3 47 | 5 59 |
| 11 | 7 50 | 15 | 17 5 | | | 6 2 | 8 14 | 3 46 | 5 58 |
| 19 | 18 40 | | | 19 | 12 46 | 6 2 | 8 14 | 3 46 | 5 58 |
| 8 | 1 47 | 4 | 10 56 | | | 6 2 | 8 14 | 3 46 | 5 58 |
| 16 | 10 52 | 12 | 18 12 | 8 | 2 41 | 6 3 | 8 15 | 3 45 | 5 57 |
| | | 1 | 4 35 | 16 / 5 | 9 39 / 23 17 | 6 2 | 8 15 | 3 45 | 5 58 |
| 5 | 12 40 | 9 | 18 55 | | | 6 2 | 8 15 | 3 45 | 5 58 |
| | | | | 13 | 15 24 | 6 2 | 8 15 | 3 45 | 5 58 |
| 13 | 7 37 | 17 | 12 32 | | | 6 2 | 8 15 | 3 45 | 5 58 |
| | | | | | | 6 2 | 8 15 | 3 45 | 5 58 |
| 2 | 10 36 | 6 | 21 22 | 2 | 1 31 | 6 2 | 8 15 | 3 45 | 5 58 |
| 10 | 20 6 | | | 10 | 16 18 | 6 3 | 8 15 | 3 45 | 5 57 |
| | | 14 | 10 16 | | | 6 2 | 8 14 | 3 46 | 5 58 |
| 18 | 3 27 | 3 | 18 55 | 18 | 3 21 | 6 2 | 8 14 | 3 46 | 5 58 |
| 7 | 13 25 | | | 7 | 10 34 | 6 2 | 8 14 | 3 46 | 5 58 |
| | | 11 | 2 41 | 15 | 19 28 | 6 1 | 8 13 | 3 47 | 5 59 |
| 15 | 3 24 | 19 | 13 7 | | | 6 1 | 8 13 | 3 47 | 5 59 |
| 4 | 13 9 | | | 4 | 20 45 | 6 0 | 8 12 | 3 48 | 6 0 |
| | | 8 | 18 11 | | | 6 0 | 8 12 | 3 48 | 6 0 |
| 12 | 5 56 | | | 12 | 15 42 | 6 0 | 8 11 | 3 49 | 6 0 |
| 1 | 21 10 | 16 | 12 59 | 1 | 19 9 | 6 0 | 8 11 | 3 49 | 6 0 |
| | | 5 | 12 24 | | | 5 59 | 8 10 | 3 50 | 6 1 |
| 9 | 4 10 | 13 | 20 44 | 9 | 4 51 | 5 58 | 8 9 | 3 51 | 6 2 |
| 17 | 11 47 | | | 17 | 12 16 | 5 57 | 8 8 | 3 52 | 6 3 |
| | | 2 | 4 25 | 6 | 21 54 | 5 57 | 8 7 | 3 53 | 6 3 |
| 6 | 8 5 | 10 | 16 18 | | | 5 56 | 8 6 | 3 54 | 6 4 |
| | | | | 14 | 11 39 | 5 55 | 8 5 | 3 55 | 6 5 |

# DECEMBER

## Altitudines solis et longitudines umbrarum

| Numerus dierum | 9 3 altitudines solis g. m. | 9 3 umbre hominis pedes | 9 3 umbre hominis partes | 10 2 altitudines solis g. m. | 10 2 umbre hominis pedes | 10 2 umbre hominis partes |
|---|---|---|---|---|---|---|
| 1 | 5 26 | 63 | 36 | 10 40 | 31 | 55 |
| 2 | 5 21 | 64 | 34 | 10 35 | 32 | 11 |
| 3 | 5 16 | 65 | 31 | 10 30 | 32 | 27 |
| 4 | 5 13 | 66 | 6 | 10 26 | 32 | 40 |
| 5 | 5 10 | 66 | 40 | 10 23 | 32 | 49 |
| 6 | 5 7 | 67 | 15 | 10 20 | 32 | 58 |
| 7 | 5 4 | 67 | 49 | 10 17 | 33 | 8 |
| 8 | 5 2 | 68 | 12 | 10 14 | 33 | 17 |
| 9 | 5 0 | 68 | 35 | 10 13 | 33 | 21 |
| 10 | 4 59 | 68 | 52 | 10 12 | 33 | 24 |
| 11 | 4 58 | 69 | 10 | 10 11 | 33 | 27 |
| 12 | 4 57 | 69 | 27 | 10 10 | 33 | 30 |
| 13 | 4 57 | 69 | 27 | 10 10 | 33 | 30 |
| 14 | 4 58 | 69 | 10 | 10 11 | 33 | 27 |
| 15 | 4 59 | 68 | 52 | 10 12 | 33 | 24 |
| 16 | 5 0 | 68 | 35 | 10 13 | 33 | 21 |
| 17 | 5 2 | 68 | 12 | 10 14 | 33 | 17 |
| 18 | 5 4 | 67 | 49 | 10 17 | 33 | 8 |
| 19 | 5 7 | 67 | 15 | 10 20 | 32 | 58 |
| 20 | 5 10 | 66 | 40 | 10 23 | 32 | 49 |
| 21 | 5 13 | 66 | 6 | 10 26 | 32 | 40 |
| 22 | 5 16 | 65 | 31 | 10 30 | 32 | 27 |
| 23 | 5 21 | 64 | 34 | 10 35 | 32 | 11 |
| 24 | 5 26 | 63 | 36 | 10 41 | 31 | 52 |
| 25 | 5 32 | 62 | 27 | 10 46 | 31 | 37 |
| 26 | 5 37 | 61 | 30 | 10 51 | 31 | 21 |
| 27 | 5 43 | 60 | 21 | 10 57 | 31 | 2 |
| 28 | 5 49 | 59 | 12 | 11 4 | 30 | 41 |
| 29 | 5 56 | 57 | 51 | 11 11 | 30 | 23 |
| 30 | 6 3 | 56 | 40 | 11 18 | 30 | 4 |
| 31 | 6 10 | 55 | 43 | 11 26 | 29 | 43 |

sex pedum in horis de clok

| | 11 | | | 12 a.m. | |
| | 1 | | | 0 p.m. | |
| altitudines solis | umbre hominis | | altitudines solis | umbre hominis | |
| g. m. | pedes | partes | g. m. | pedes | partes |
|---|---|---|---|---|---|
| 13 59 | 24 | 6 | 15 8 | 22 | 11 |
| 13 54 | 24 | 16 | 15 3 | 22 | 19 |
| 13 49 | 24 | 25 | 14 58 | 22 | 27 |
| 13 46 | 24 | 31 | 14 54 | 22 | 34 |
| 13 43 | 24 | 37 | 14 51 | 22 | 39 |
| 13 39 | 24 | 44 | 14 47 | 22 | 45 |
| 13 36 | 24 | 50 | 14 44 | 22 | 50 |
| 13 33 | 24 | 56 | 14 42 | 22 | 54 |
| 13 32 | 24 | 58 | 14 41 | 22 | 55 |
| 13 31 | 25 | 0 | 14 40 | 22 | 57 |
| 13 30 | 25 | 2 | 14 39 | 22 | 59 |
| 13 28 | 25 | 5 | 14 37 | 23 | 2 |
| 13 28 | 25 | 5 | 14 37 | 23 | 2 |
| 13 30 | 25 | 2 | 14 39 | 22 | 59 |
| 13 31 | 25 | 0 | 14 40 | 22 | 57 |
| 13 32 | 24 | 58 | 14 41 | 22 | 55 |
| 13 33 | 24 | 56 | 14 42 | 22 | 54 |
| 13 36 | 24 | 50 | 14 44 | 22 | 50 |
| 13 39 | 24 | 44 | 14 47 | 22 | 45 |
| 13 43 | 24 | 37 | 14 51 | 22 | 39 |
| 13 46 | 24 | 31 | 14 54 | 22 | 34 |
| 13 49 | 24 | 25 | 14 58 | 22 | 27 |
| 13 54 | 24 | 16 | 15 3 | 22 | 19 |
| 14 0 | 24 | 4 | 15 9 | 22 | 10 |
| 14 6 | 23 | 54 | 15 15 | 22 | 1 |
| 14 11 | 23 | 46 | 15 20 | 21 | 54 |
| 14 17 | 23 | 36 | 15 26 | 21 | 45 |
| 14 25 | 23 | 22 | 15 34 | 21 | 33 |
| 14 33 | 23 | 9 | 15 42 | 21 | 21 |
| 14 41 | 22 | 55 | 15 50 | 21 | 10 |
| 14 48 | 22 | 43 | 15 58 | 20 | 58 |

**1-31** *om* D. **2** *om* A². **3** *om* A²; *add* apostoli As². **4** *om* Sanctorum So; *om* A². **5** *om* S¹BAs¹A²; *om* Sancti Thome R; *add* episcopi vigilia As². **6** *om* B. **8** *om* S¹A¹BSoAs¹AdA²; Sancti Inciani sociorum que eius R; Sancti Inciani presbiteri As². **13** *add* Hillarii So; *add* et Sancti Hillarii RA²; Sancti Hillarii confessoris As¹; *add* et Hillarii As². **14** *om* confessoris A¹BSoRAs²; *add* episcopi et martyris R; *om* A²; *add* martyris As²; *om* A². **15** *om* abbatis BSo; *add* confessoris non episcopi So; *om* A². **16** *om* martyris A¹; *om* pape et martyris BSoAd; *om* pape R; *add* episcopi et martyris Ad; *om* A²; *om* et martyris As². **17** Sancti Antonii abbatis S¹BAs¹Ad; *om* A¹A²; Sancti Antonii So. **18** *om* S¹A¹A²; *om* virginis et martyris B; *om* et martyris SoAs¹RAs². **19** *om* S¹A¹BSoAs¹AdA²; *om* et confessoris As². **20** *add* martyrum As¹R; *om* A². **21** *om* virginis et martyris S¹; *om* martyris A¹; *om* et martyris BRAdAs²; *om* A². **22** *om* A². **24** Sancti Timothei episcopi S¹; Sancti Timothei episcopi et A¹; Sancti Timothei martyris B; Sancti Timothei episcopi et martyris As¹; Sancti Thimothii episcopi Ad. **25** Conversio pietatis So; *add* dies egritudinis A². **26** Sancti Policarpi martyris So. **27** *om* confessoris A¹; *om* et confessoris B; *om* SoA². **28** Sancte Agnetis secundo A¹BAs¹RAs²; *om* A². **30** *om* S¹A¹SoA²; Sancti Mathie episcopi B; Sancti Mathie episcopi et confessoris As¹Ad; *om* et virginis RAs².

**1-28** *om* D. **1** *add* et S¹A¹; Sancte Brigide virginis SoRA²; *add* et confessoris As¹; *om* Ad; Sancte Brigide virginis non martyris As². **2** Purificacio Sancte Marie S¹A¹; Purificacio Beate Marie virginis Ad. **3** *om* martyris S¹BSoAdA². **5** *om* et martyris BSoRA². **6** *add* episcoporum B; *om* SoA²; *add* episcoporum et confessorum R. **9** Sancte Appolonie virginis et S¹; Sancte Appolonie virginis A¹BAd; Sancte Appolonie virginis et martyris As¹. **10** *om* S¹AdA²; *om* martyris A¹; *om* non martyris BSoAs¹RAs². **11** Sancte Frisdewide virginis B; Sancte Frideswide virginis So. **12** Translacio Sancte Frideswide A¹. **14** *om* martyris BAdA²; *om* As¹; Sancti Valentini episcopi et martyris R. **15** Sancti Blasii episcopi et martyris So. **16** *om* S¹A¹BSoAs¹Ad; *om* et martyris RAs²; *om* virginis et A². **18** Sancti Simeonis episcopi et S¹; Sancti Symeonis episcopi et martyris As¹; Sancti Symeonis episcopi Ad. **23** Vigilia As². **24** *om* apostoli S¹.

**1-31** *om* D. **1** Sancti Albini episcopi et confessoris S¹A¹As¹; Sancti Albini episcopi BAd; *om* SoR; dies egritudinis A²; Sancti Daviti As²; Sancti Cedde episcopi A². **7** *om* virginum S¹A¹BSoAs¹RAdAs²; *om* A². **8** *om* S¹A¹BSoAs¹ RAdA²As². **11** Sanctarum quadraginta martyrum S¹; Sanctorum quadraginta martyrum A¹BAs¹Ad. **12** *om* pape S¹SoAs¹RAd; *add* episcopi et confessoris As¹; *add* et confessoris R; *add* confessoris Ad. **17** Sancte Witburge virginis B. **18** Sancti Alexandri episcopi S¹Ad; Sancti Alexandri episcopi et A¹; *om* SoA²;

Sancti Alexandri episcopi et martyris As¹.  **19** Sancti Edwardi regis S¹; Sancti Edwardi regis et martyris A¹.  **20** Sancti Cuthberti episcopi S¹BSoAdA²As²; Sancti Cuthberti episcopi et confessoris A¹R.  **21** Equinoctium A⁷.  **25** Annunciacio beate Marie BAs²; Annunciacio dominica SoAd; *om* As¹R.  **27** Resureccio domini BSoAs².  **31** Sancti Corneli As².

## APRILIS

**1-30** *om* D.  **3** *om* confessoris S¹; *om* et confessoris BAs²; *om* SoAs¹A²; *om* episcopi et confessoris R.  **4** Sancti Ambrosii episcopi et confessoris S¹As¹Ad; *add* et confessoris A¹; *om* doctoris BSo; Sancti Ambrosii episcopi RAs²; *om* A².  **6** *add* et martyris S¹A¹; *om* SoAs¹RAdA²As².  **10** dies egritudinis A².  **14** Sanctorum Tyburcii et Valeriani S¹RAdAs²; Sanctorum Tyburcii et Valeriani martyrum A¹As¹; *om* martyris So; *om* A².  **19** *om* S¹A¹SoAs¹AdA²; *om* archiepiscopi B; Sancti Alphegi episcopi RAs².  **20** dies egritudinis A².  **24** *om* S¹A¹As¹ RAdA²As²; Sancti Wilfridi archiepiscopi So.  **26** pape *expunged* S¹; *om* SoAs¹ RAdA²As².  **28** *om* A².  **29** *om* S¹SoAs¹RAdA²As²; Translacio Sancti Edmundi martyris B.  **30** Sancti Erkenwaldi As².

## MAYUS

**1** Sanctorum Philippi et Jacobi BSo.  **2** *add* et confessoris A¹DAs¹; *om* RA² As².  **3** Invencio Sancte Crucis S¹A¹DBAs¹RAdAs²; Invencio Sancte Crucis et ——orum (?) So; Invencio Sancte Crucis dies egritudinis A².  **4** *om* martyris A¹; Ierosolymarii Sancti Quiriaci episcopi D; *om* BSoRA²As²; *om* et martyris Ad.  **6** Sancti Johannis ante portam latinam S¹A¹DBSoAs¹RAdA²As².  **7** Sancti Johannis Bewirle S¹; Sancti Johannis Bcuuirlc A¹So; Sancti Johannis Beuuirlaci episcopi D; Sancti Johannis Beuuirlaci episcopi et confessoris As¹; Sancti Johannis Beuuirlay A².  **9** Transitus Nicholai As².  **10** *om* martyrum S¹A¹DB SoAdAs²; *om* et Epimachi martyrum R; *om* A².  **12** *om* martyrum S¹A¹DSoR AdAs²; *add* et Pancratis D; *om* BA².  **18** Sancti Ethelberti regis B.  **19** *add* archiepiscopi S¹A¹SoAs²; *om* DB; *add* episcopi et confessoris As¹; *add* archiepiscopi et confessoris R; *add* episcopi Ad.  **23** Pascio beati Willelmi martyris D.  **25** *om* S¹; Sanctarum Marie Jacobi et Salome A¹; Sanctarum Matronarum D; *om* pape So; *add* et martyris As¹Ad; Sancti Aldelmi episcopi et confessoris RAs²; dies egritudinis A².  **26** *om* primi Anglorum S¹; Sancti Augustini Anglorum apostoli A¹As²; Sancti Augustini episcopi et confessoris DR; Sancti Augustini episcopi B; *om* primi Anglorum archiepiscopi SoA²; Sancti Augustini Anglorum episcopi et confessoris As¹; Sancti Augustini Anglorum Ad.  **27** Sancti Germani B; Sancti Germani episcopi et confessoris RAs².  **31** Sancte Petronille virginis A¹BSoRA²As².

## JUNIUS

**1** *om* martyris A¹; Sancti Nicomedis DR; *om* SoAdA².  **2** *add* martyrum BSo.  **3** Sancti Erasmi martyris As².  **5** *om* S¹A¹DBSoAs¹; Sancti Bonefacii sociorum

Sancti Bonefacii episcopi et martyris As². **6** Sancte Juliane virginis A². **8** *om* martyrum S¹A¹DBAs¹RAdAs²; Sancti Williami Eboraci archiepiscopi So; *om* A². **9** Sanctorum Primi et Feliciani S¹A¹DSoAs¹; Translacio Sancti Edmundi archiepiscopi R; Translacio Sancti Edmundi As². **11** *om* Sancti So; *add* dies egritudinis A². **12** *om* Naboris S¹A¹As²; *om* DBA²; Sanctorum Basilidis et Cirini As¹Ad; Sanctorum Basilidis Cirini et R. **13** Sancti As². **14** *om* S¹A¹DBAs¹AdA²; *om* et confessoris SoAs². **15** *om* martyrum S¹A¹DBRAdAs²; *om* SoA². **16** *om* S¹A¹BSoA²; Sanctorum Cyrici et Julite D; Sanctorum Cirici et Julite martyrum As¹; *add* et confessoris R; *om* episcopi AdAs². **17** Sancti Botulphi abbatis DSo; Sancti Botulphi As². **18** Sanctorum Marci et Marcelliani S¹A¹DRAdAs²; Sanctorum Marci et Marcelliani martyrum So; Sanctorum Marcelli et Marcelliani As¹. **19** *om* A². **20** Translacio Sancti Edwardi regis RAs². **22** *om* S¹A¹BA²; Sancti Paulini episcopi et confessoris As¹; Sancti Albani prothomartyris As². **23** Sancte Etheldrede virginis non A¹; Ethelrede virginis Vigilia D; Sancte Etheldrede virginis SoAd; Sancte Etheldrede R; Sancte Etheldrede virginis Vigilia As². **24** *om* Nativitas A¹; *om* Baptiste D; *om* Sancti Johannis Ad. **26** *om* martyrum S¹A¹DBSoAs¹AdAs²; *om* A². **28** Sancti Leonis pape et martyris S¹Ad; *om* confessoris A¹; Vigilia D; *om* et confessoris BAs¹As²; Sancti Leonis martyris So; *om* pape R; *om* As². **29** *om* Sanctorum S¹A¹RA²; Petri et Pauli apostolorum D; Sanctorum Petri et Pauli apostolorum So; *om* Ad. **30** *om* Sancti Ad; *om* A².

## JULIUS

**1** Sctava Sancti Johannis Baptiste B; *om* Sancti So; *om* As¹. **2** *om* martyrum S¹A¹DBSoAs¹RAdAs². **4** *om* S¹A¹DBSoA²; Translacio et ordinacio Sancti Martini RAs². **5** Sancte Modwenne virginis A². **6** Octava Apostolorum Petri et Pauli S¹A¹DBSoRAs². **7** Translacio Sancti Thome Canterburigi S¹; Translacio Sancti Thome DBAs¹AdA²; T SoR; Translacio Sancti Thome martyris As². **8** Sancti Marcialis discipuli D; Sancte Witburge virginis R. **10** *add* martyrum A¹RAs²; *om* A². **11** *om* S¹A¹DBSoAs¹AdA²; *add* abbatis RAs². **13** dies egritudinis A². **15** *om* S¹A¹DBSoAs¹Ad; *om* confessoris RAs²; Sancte Edithe virginis A². **17** *om* S¹; Commemoracio solempnis Sancte Marie A¹; Commemoracio virginis gloriose D; Commemoracio beate Marie B; Commemoracio beate virginis SoAs¹; *om* et martyris A²As². **18** *om* S¹A¹DBSoAs¹AdA²; *om* et martyris As². **20** *add* martyris D; *om* virginis A². **21** *om* non martyris S¹A¹DBSoAs¹RAdAs²; *om* A². **23** *om* et martyris S¹A¹AdAs²; *om* episcopi et D; *om* BA²; *om* episcopi et martyris So. **24** *om* S¹A¹DBSoAs¹Ad; *om* et martyris R; Vigilia A²; Sancte Christine virginis Vigilia As². **25** *add* Christofori S¹A¹. **26** Sancte Anne matris domine As¹; *om* A². **27** *om* S¹A¹AdA²; Sancte Marthe ospite Christi D; Sancte Marthe hospite Christi BSo; Sancte Marthe virginis As¹; Sanctorum Septem Fratrum Martyrum Dormiencium As². **28** *om* S¹A¹DB SoAs¹AdA²; *om* et confessoris As². **29** *om* Faustini S¹A¹RAs²; Sanctorum Felicis Simplicii et D; Octava Marie Magdelene B; Sanctorum Felicis Simplicii martyrum SoAs[1]; *om* AdA[2]. **30** Sanctorum Abdon et Sennen DBSoAd; Sanctorum Abdon et Sennen martyrum As[1]; *om* A[2]. **31** *om* et confessoris DBSo.

## AUGUSTUS

**1-31** *om* So. **1** *add* dies egritudinis A[2]. **2** *om* martyris S[1]A[1]As[2]; pape *expunged* D; *om* BA[2]; *om* pape et martyris R. **3** *add* Gamalieli D; Sancti Stephani prothomartyris B; *add* sociorum eius As[1]; *add* prothomartyris R; *om* A[2]. **4** Sancti Oswaldi regis et D. **5** Sancti Oswaldi regis et martyris R; Sancti Oswaldi regis A[2]As[2]. **6** *om* S[1]A[1]BA[2]; Transfiguracio Domini DAs[1]Ad; Sanctorum Sexti et Felicissimi R; *om* et Agapiti As[2]. **7** Sancti Donati episcopi et confessoris S[1]; *om* martyris A[1]; *om* et martyris B; *om* episcopi et martyris R; *om* A[2]. **8** Sancti Cyriaci sociorum S[1]A[1]; *om* martyrum DR; *om* BA[2]; *om* sociorumque eius Ad. **9** *om* S[1]A[1]BAs[1]AdA[2]; Vigilia D; *add* Vigilia As[2]. **10** *om* martyris A[2]. **11** *om* S[1]A[2]; *om* martyris A[1]. **13** Sancti Ypoliti sociorum S[1]A[1]; Sancti Ypoliti cum sociis martyrum B; *add* martyrum As[1]As[2]; Sancti Ypoliti martyris Ad; *om* A[2]. **14** Sancti Eusebii confessoris S[1]A[1]As[1]; Sancti Eusebii confessoris Vigilia D; *om* BAdA[2]; *add* confessoris R; *add* Vigilia As[2]. **15** *om* Virginis S[1]A[1]D; Assumpcio beate Marie BRAdAs[2]; Assumpcio beate virginis As[1]; Assumpcio beate Marie virginis A[2]. **17** Octava Sancti Laurencii S[1]A[1]DRAs[2]; Sctava Sancti Laurencii B. **18** *om* martyris R; *om* A[2]. **19** *om* S[1]A[1]DBAs[1]AdA[2]; *om* martyris R. **20** Sancti Bernardi abbatis DAs[1]Ad. **22** Octava Sancte Marie virginis D; Octava Sancte Marie BRAs[2]. **23** *om* S[1]A[1]A[2]; Vigilia D; *om* episcopi B; *add* et confessoris As[1]; Sanctorum Tymothei et Appolinaris R; Sancti Tymothei et Appolinaris Vigilia As[2]. **24** *om* apostoli BA[2]. **27** *om* DAs[1]A[2]; Sancti Ruphi martyris R. **28** *om* S[1]A[2]; *om* episcopi et doctoris A[1]B; Sancti Augustini episcopi et confessoris As[1]; *om* et doctoris R; *om* episcopi et AdAs[2]. **29** *om* Baptiste S[1]A[1]DA[2]. **30** *add* martyrum As[1]; dies egritudinis A[2]. **31** *om* S[1]A[1]DBAs[1]AdA[2]; Sancte Cuthburge virginis RAs[2].

## SEPTEMBER

**1-30** *om* So. **2** Sancti Antoninii A[2]. **3** dies egritudinis A[2]. **4** *om* S[1]A[1]DBAs[1]; *om* Translacio Ad; Sancti Cuthberti confessoris A[2]; *om* episcopi et confessoris As[2]. **5** *om* S[1]A[1]DBAs[1]Ad. **6** Sancti Gorgonii martyris *expunged* A[2]. **7** Vigilia DAdAs[2]. **8** Nativitas beate Marie virginis D; Nativitas beate Marie As[1]RAd; *add* virginis A[2]. **9** *om* B. **11** Sanctorum martyrum Prothi et Jacinti S[1]A[1]; *om* martyrum DAdAs[2]. **13** Sancti Maurelii episcopi et confessoris As[1]Ad. **14** *om* Ad. **15** *om* S[1]A[2]; *om* Virginis A[1]RAs[2]; Sancti Nichomedis martyris As[1]; Sancte Eufemie virginis Ad. **16** Sancte Eufemie virginis S[1]A[1]As[1]; *om* non martyris RAs[2]; *om* AdA[2]. **17** Sancti Lamberti episcopi et confessoris S[1]; Sancti Lamberti episcopi A[1]A[2]As[2]; *om* D; Sancti Lamberti episcopi et martyris As[1]RAd. **20**

Vigilia DAdAs$^2$. **21** *add* et ewangelii S$^1$R. **22** *om* eius S$^1$A$^1$B; Sancti Mauricii sociorumque eius As$^1$RAs$^2$; Sancti Mauricii sociorum Ad; *om* cum sociis eius A$^2$. **23** *om* S$^1$A$^1$DBAs$^1$AdA$^2$; *om* et martyris R. **24** Concepcio Sancti Johannis Baptiste A$^2$. **25** *om* S$^1$A$^1$DA$^2$; Sancti Cleophe discipuli B; Sancti Cleophe discipuli martyris As$^1$; Sancti Cleophe martyris Ad; *om* et martyris As$^2$. **26** Sancti Cipriani R; Sanctorum Cypriani episcopi As$^2$. **27** *om* S$^1$A$^1$A$^2$; Sanctorum Cosme et Dameani D; *om* martyrum BRAdAs$^2$. **30** Sancti Jeromini presbiteri S$^1$A$^1$BRAd; *om* D; Sancti Jeromini confessoris As$^1$; *om* doctoris A$^2$; Sancti Jeromini presbiteri et doctoris As$^2$.

## OCTOBER

**1-31** *om* So. **1** *om* episcoporum S$^1$A$^1$As$^2$; Sanctorum Remigii et D; Sanctorum Remigii et Germani As$^1$; Sanctorum Remigii sociorumque eius R; *om* AdA$^2$. **2** *om* martyris S$^1$A$^1$; *om* episcopi et martyris D; *om* BAs$^1$A$^2$; *om* et Ad; *om* et martyris As$^2$. **3** dies egritudinis A$^2$; Sancti Thome As$^2$. **4** *om* RA$^2$As$^2$. **6** Sanctorum Patriarcharum Habrahami S$^1$, Abrahami B; *om* A$^1$DA$^2$; Sanctorum Patriarcharum Abrahami Ysaaci et Jacobi As$^1$; Sancte Fidis virginis RAs$^2$; Sanctorum Patriarcharum Ad. **7** Sanctorum Marcii Sergi et Bachi S$^1$; Sanctorum Marcii Sergi et A$^1$; Sanctorum Marci Marcelli DAd; Sanctorum Sergii et Bachi B; Sanctorum Marci et Marcelli martyrum As$^1$; Sanctorum Marci et Marcelli et Appulei R; *om* A$^2$; Sanctorum Marci et Marcelli As$^2$. **9** Sancti Dionisii cum sociis S$^1$; *om* A$^1$; *om* que eius martyrum D; Sancti Dionisii martyris BAd; *om* martyrum RAs$^2$; *om* sociorumque eius martyrum A$^2$. **10** *om* S$^1$A$^1$BAs$^1$AdA$^2$; Sancti Paulini episcopi D; *om* martyrum RAs$^2$. **11** *om* S$^1$A$^1$BA s$^1$AdA$^2$; Sancte Ethelbuge D; *om* martyrum R; Sancti Nichasii sociorumque eius As$^2$. **12** Sancti Wilfridi episcopi D. **13** *om* S$^1$A$^1$As$^1$A$^2$; Sancti Edwardi D; *om* Translacio, *add* et martyris B; *add* et martyris R; *om* Sancti Ad. **14** *om* et martyris S$^1$BAs$^2$; *om* martyris A$^1$D; pape et *expunged* D; *om* pape et martyris R; *om* A$^2$. **15** *om* S$^1$A$^1$DBAs$^1$AdA$^2$; Sancti Wulframni episcopi et confessoris R; Sancti Wulframii episcopi As$^2$. **16** *om* S$^1$A$^1$DBAs$^1$AdA$^2$; *om* Sancti R; *om* tumba As$^2$. **21** Sanctarum 11 millini virginum As$^1$; *om* Sanctarum Ad; *om* A$^2$. **22** Ierosolymarii Sancti Marci episcopi et S$^1$A$^1$; Sancti Marci martyris D; *om* As$^1$RAs$^2$; *add* et confessoris Ad; dies egritudinis A$^2$. **23** *om* S$^1$A$^1$DBAs$^1$AdA$^2$; Sancti Romani episcopi et martyris R; *om* et confessoris As$^2$. **25** Sanctorum martyrum Crispini et Crispiniani A$^1$; *om* martyrum DAs$^1$RAdAs$^2$; *om* BA$^2$. **27** Vigilia DAs$^2$. **28** Apostolorum Symonis et Jude S$^1$RAs$^2$; *add* et Jude A$^1$; *om* Sanctorum D; Sanctorum Symonis et Jude BAdA$^2$; Sanctorum Symonis et Jude apostolorum As$^1$. **29** *add* et confessoris S$^1$A$^1$Ad; Ierosolymarii Sancti Narcissi D; *om* RA$^2$As$^2$. **31** *om* martyris, *add* Vigilia D; *om* A$^2$; *add* Vigilia As$^2$.

## NOVEMBER

**1-30** *om* So. **2** *om* A$^2$. **5** dies egritudinis A$^2$. **6** *om* abbatis A$^2$. **8** *om* A$^2$. **9** *om* BA$^2$. **10** *add* et martyris S$^1$DAs$^1$Ad; *add* et A$^1$; Octava Sancti Martini pape B;

*om* $RA^2As^2$. **11** *om* confessoris $A^1$; *om* et confessoris $BAs^2$; *om* $A^2$. **13** *add* et martyris $S^1$; *add* et confessoris $A^1RAdAs^2$; *om* episcopi, *add* martyris $As^1$; *om* $A^2$. **15** Sancti Machuti episcopi et confessoris R; Sancti Machuti episcopi $As^2$. **16** Sancti Edmundi Canterburigi archiepiscopi $S^1$; *om* $A^1As^1$; Sancti Edmundi confessoris D; *add* et confessoris R; Sancti Edmunde confessoris $A^2$. **17** *om* $S^1A^1As^1AdA^2$; *om* et confessoris $BAs^2$. **18** *om* $S^1A^1As^1AdA^2$; *add* episcopi B. **20** Sancti Edmundi regis et $S^1$; Sancti Edmundi regis DB; Sancti Eadmundi regis et martyris $As^1$; Sancti Edmundi regis et martyris $RAdAs^2$; Sancti Eadmunde regis $A^2$. **21** Presentacio beate virginis $As^1$. **22** *om* et martyris $RA^2As^2$. **23** *add* pape $S^1DA^2As^2$; *add* martyris $A^1BAd$; *add* pape et martyris $As^1$. **24** *om* $A^2$. **25** *add* et $S^1A^1$; *add* et martyris $BAs^1$; *om* $A^2$. **26** Sancti Line pape et martyris $S^1A^1DBAs^1Ad$; pape *expunged* D; Sancti Lini R; *om* $A^2$. **28** dies egritudinis $A^2$. **29** Sancti Saturnini episcopi DB; Sanctorum Saturnini et Zisinnii R; *om* $A^2$; Sancti Saturnini et Sisinnii Vigilia $As^2$. **30** *om* apostoli $A^2$.


## DECEMBER

**1-31** *om* So. **1** Sancti Eligii confessoris D; Sancti Eligii episcopi et confessoris $BAs^1$. **4** Sancte Barbare virginis et martyris $S^1A^1BAs^1$; Sancte Barbare virginis DAd. **5** Sancti Sabbe abbatis $S^1A^1BAs^1Ad$. **6** *om* et confessoris $S^1A^1BAdAs^2$; *om* episcopi et confessoris $A^2$. **8** *om* Virginis $S^1A^1AdAs^2$; Concepcio Virginis gloriose D; Concepcio beate Marie $BAs^1$. **12** dies egritudinis $A^2$. **13** *om* et martyris $S^1BAs^1RAdAs^2$; *om* virginis et martyris $A^2$. **16** *om* $S^1A^1BA$ $s^1AdA^2$; Octava Sancte Marie D. **17** Sancti Lazari episcopi et confessoris $S^1A^1DAs^1$; Sancti Lazari episcopi B; Sancti Lazari Ad. **20** Vigilia D. **21** *om* B; *om* apostoli $A^2$. **22** dies egritudinis $A^2$. **24** Vigilia $BAs^2$. **25** *om* Jesu Christi D; *om* Nostri Jesu Christi $As^1A^2$; *om* Domini Nostri Ad. **26** *om* prothomartyris $As^1A^2$. **27** *om* apostoli et ewangeliste B; Sanctorum Innocencium b $As^1$; *om* apostoli et $AdA^2$. **28** Sancti Johannis apostoli a $As^1$; *add* martyrum $As^2$. **29** Sancti Thome martyris *expunged* D; Sancti Thome episcopi et martyris $As^1$; *om* archiepiscopi $RA^2$; Sancti Thome martyris $AdAs^2$. **31** pape *expunged*, *add* et martyris D; Sancti Silvestri episcopi B; *add* et confessoris $As^1RAs^2$; Sancti Silvestri episcopi et confessoris Ad; *om* pape $A^2$.

# Tabula eclipsis solis pro primo ciclo cuius principium est annus Christi 1387 finis 1396

| Ciclus | Anni Christi | Menses | Conjuncciones vise | | | | Punctus eclipsis | | | Tempus casus | | | Duracio | | |
|---|---|---|---|---|---|---|---|---|---|---|---|---|---|---|---|
| | | | d. | h. | m. | s. | pt. | m. | s. | h. | m. | s. | h. | m. | s. |
| 1 | 1387 | Junius | 16 | 22 | 3 | 40 | 1 | 30 | 18 | 0 | 30 | 9 | 1 | 0 | 18 |
| 5 | 1391 | Aprilis | 5 | 17 | 54 | 50 | 2 | 11 | 8 | 0 | 37 | 59 | 1 | 15 | 58 |
| 6 | 1392 | Marcius | 24 | 19 | 14 | 17 | 4 | 43 | 5 | 0 | 53 | 25 | 1 | 46 | 50 |
| 7 | 1393 | Augustus | 8 | 21 | 3 | 56 | 2 | 34 | 21 | 0 | 39 | 34 | 1 | 19 | 8 |
| 8 | 1394 | Julius | 29 | 2 | 19 | 50 | 0 | 16 | 58 | 0 | 14 | 33 | 0 | 29 | 6 |
| 10 | 1396 | Januarius | 11 | 23 | 43 | 40 | 6 | 42 | 1 | 0 | 55 | 54 | 1 | 51 | 48 |

# Tabula eclipsis solis pro secundo ciclo cuius principium est annus Christi 1406 finis vero 1424

| Ciclus | Anni Christi | Menses | Conjuncciones vise | | | | Punctus eclipsis | | | Tempus casus | | | Duracio | | |
|---|---|---|---|---|---|---|---|---|---|---|---|---|---|---|---|
| | | | d. | h. | m. | s. | pt. | m. | s. | h. | m. | s. | h. | m. | s. |
| 1 | 1406 | Junius | 16 | 17 | 41 | 50 | 10 | 45 | 26 | 0 | 59 | 23 | 1 | 58 | 46 |
| 3 | 1408 | October | 19 | 20 | 56 | 55 | 7 | 0 | 56 | 0 | 57 | 8 | 1 | 54 | 16 |
| 4 | 1409 | Aprilis | 16 | 2 | 32 | 47 | 11 | 23 | 52 | 1 | 5 | 8 | 2 | 10 | 16 |
| 6 | 1411 | Augustus | 20 | 5 | 55 | 58 | 11 | 12 | 15 | 1 | 4 | 4 | 2 | 8 | 8 |
| 10 | 1415 | Junius | 7 | 17 | 53 | 10 | 9 | 31 | 57 | 0 | 57 | 51 | 1 | 55 | 42 |
| 11 | 1416 | November | 20 | 3 | 3 | 1 | 1 | 7 | 44 | 0 | 28 | 56 | 0 | 57 | 52 |
| 13 | 1418 | Aprilis | 6 | 21 | 5 | 8 | 5 | 55 | 49 | 0 | 57 | 23 | 1 | 54 | 46 |
| 14 | 1419 | Marcius | 26 | 21 | 59 | 50 | 3 | 38 | 20 | 0 | 42 | 21 | 1 | 24 | 42 |
| 19 | 1424 | Junius | 27 | 2 | 55 | 27 | 11 | 11 | 50 | 0 | 59 | 39 | 1 | 59 | 18 |

Tabula eclipsis solis pro tercio ciclo cuius principium est 1425 finis vero 1440

| 1 | 1425 | November | 10 | 20 | 53 | 57 | 2 | 41 | 30 | 0 | 42 | 25 | 1 | 24 | 50 |
|---|------|----------|----|----|----|----|---|----|----|---|----|----|---|----|----|
| 7 | 1431 | Februarius | 13 | 2 | 17 | 18 | 8 | 24 | 0 | 0 | 57 | 58 | 1 | 55 | 56 |
| 9 | 1433 | Junius | 18 | 3 | 14 | 5 | 12 | 13 | 50 | 0 | 59 | 40 | 1 | 59 | 20 |
| 12 | 1436 | Aprilis | 17 | 5 | 47 | 12 | 0 | 17 | 2 | 0 | 14 | 25 | 0 | 28 | 50 |
| 13 | 1437 | Aprilis | 6 | 6 | 34 | 59 | 7 | 51 | 10 | 1 | 1 | 57 | 2 | 3 | 54 |
| 14 | 1438 | September | 19 | 22 | 25 | 30 | 5 | 38 | 50 | 0 | 54 | 46 | 1 | 49 | 32 |
| 15 | 1439 | September | 9 | 3 | 33 | 58 | 5 | 26 | 7 | 0 | 58 | 31 | 1 | 57 | 2 |
| 16 | 1440 | Februarius | 4 | 1 | 29 | 20 | 11 | 10 | 42 | 1 | 1 | 10 | 2 | 2 | 20 |

Tabula eclipsis solis pro quarto ciclo cuius principium est 1448 finis 1462

| 5 | 1448 | Augustus | 29 | 21 | 22 | 13 | 9 | 15 | 4 | 1 | 5 | 14 | 2 | 10 | 28 |
|---|------|----------|----|----|----|----|---|----|----|---|----|----|---|----|----|
| 7 | 1450 | Februarius | 13 | 2 | 17 | 7 | 0 | 58 | 22 | 0 | 24 | 27 | 0 | 48 | 54 |
| 10 | 1453 | December | 1 | 2 | 28 | 37 | 9 | 59 | 39 | 1 | 2 | 52 | 2 | 5 | 44 |
| 17 | 1460 | Julius | 18 | 15 | 42 | 0 | 0 | 2 | 47 | 0 | 56 | 47 | 1 | 53 | 34 |
| 19 | 1462 | November | 21 | 23 | 27 | 15 | 1 | 9 | 1 | 0 | 26 | 50 | 0 | 53 | 40 |

# FIGURE ECLIPSIS SOLIS

Hec est solis incipiens anno Domini 1387 in Junio a.m. ʃ qui est 16 Kl. Julii 2 h. 26 m. 29 s.

Hec est incipiens anno Domini 1391 in Aprili a.m. *d* qui est Nonis Aprilis 6 h. 43 m. 9 s.

Hec est incipiens anno Domini 1392 in Marcio a.m. ʃ qui est 9 Kl. Aprilis 5 h. 39 m. 8 s.

Hec est incipiens anno Domini 1393 in Augusto a.m. *c* qui est 6 Idus Augusti 3 h. 35 m. 38 s.

Hec est incipiens anno Domini 1394 in Julio p.m. ʃ qui est 5 Kl. Augusti 2 h. 5 m. 17 s.

Hec est incipiens anno Domini 1396 in Januario a.m. *d* qui est 3 Idus Januarii 1 h. 12 m. 14 s.

# [FIGURE ECLIPSIS SOLIS]

Hec est incipiens anno Domini 1406 in Junio a.m. ∫ qui est 16 Kl. Julii 7 h. 17 m. 33 s.

Hec est incipiens anno Domini 1408 in Octobri a.m. e qui est 14 Kl. Novembris 4 h. 0 m. 13 s.

Hec est incipiens anno Domini 1409 in Aprili p.m. g qui est 17 Kl. Mayi 1 h. 27 m. 39 s.

Hec est incipiens anno Domini 1411 in Augusto p.m. g qui est 14 Kl. Septembris 4 h. 51 m. 54 s.

Hec est incipiens anno Domini 1415 in Junio a.m. d qui est 7 Idus Junii 7 h. 4 m. 41 s.

Hec est incipiens anno Domini 1416 in Novembri p.m. a qui est 13 Kl. Decembris 2 h. 34 m. 5 s.

Hec est incipiens anno Domini 1418 in Aprili a.m. *e* qui est 8 Idus Aprilis 3 h. 52 m. & 15 s.

Hec est incipiens anno Domini 1419 in Marcio a.m. *a* qui est 7 Kl. Aprilis 2 h. 42 m. 31 s.

Hec est incipiens anno Domini 1424 in Junio p.m. *b* qui est 6 Kl. Julii 1 h. 55 m. 48 s.

Hec est incipiens anno Domini 1425 in Novembri a.m. *f* qui est 4 Idus Novembris 3 h. 48 m. 28 s.

Hec est incipiens anno Domini 1431 in Februario p.m. *a* qui est Pridie Idus Februarii 1 h. 19 m. 20 s.

Hec est incipiens anno Domini 1433 in Junio p.m. *g* qui est 15 Kl. Julii 2 h. 14 m. 25 s.

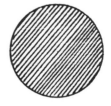

# [FIGURE ECLIPSIS SOLIS]

Hec est incipiens anno Domini 1436 in Aprili p.m. *a* qui est 16 Kl. Mayi 5 h. 32 m. 47 s.

Hec est incipiens anno Domini 1437 in Aprili p.m. *d* qui est Nonis Aprilis 5 h. 33 m. 2 s.

Hec est incipiens anno Domini 1438 in Septembri a.m. *c* qui est 13 Kl. Octobris 2 h. 29 m. 16 s.

Hec est incipiens anno Domini 1439 in Septembri p.m. *f* qui est 6 Idus Septembris 2 h. 35 m. 27 s.

Hec est incipiens anno Domini 1440 in Februario p.m. *f* qui est 3 Nonas Februarii 0 h. 28 m. 10 s.

Hec est incipiens anno Domini 1448 in Augusto a.m. *c* qui est 4 Kl. Septembris 3 h. 43 m. 1 s.

Hec est incipiens anno Domini 1450 in Februario p.m. *a* qui est Pridie Idus Februarii 1 h. 52 m. 40 s.

Hec est incipiens anno Domini 1453 in Novembri p.m. *e* qui est ultima dies Novembris 1 h. 25 m. 45 s.

Hec est incipiens anno Domini 1460 in Julio a.m. *c* qui est 15 Kl. Augusti 9 h. 14 m. 47 s.

Hec est incipiens anno Domini 1462 in Novembri a.m. *c* qui est 11 Kl. Decembris 0 h. 59 m. 35 s.

# Tabula eclipsis lune pro primo ciclo cuius principium est annus Christi 1387 finis 1405

| Ciclus | Anni Christi | Menses | Vere opposiciones d. | h. | m. | s. | Punctus eclipsis pt. | m. | s. | Tempus casus h. | m. | s. | Mora m. | s. | Duracio h. | m. | s. |
|---|---|---|---|---|---|---|---|---|---|---|---|---|---|---|---|---|---|
| 1 | 1387 | November | 26 | 9 | 42 | 18 | 0 | 38 | 50 | 0 | 27 | 21 | 0 | 0 | 0 | 54 | 42 |
| 3 | 1389 | Mayus | 11 | 6 | 52 | 52 | 15 | 16 | 58 | 1 | 11 | 16 | 38 | 21 | 3 | 39 | 14 |
| 3 | 1389 | November | 4 | 16 | 43 | 9 | 12 | 42 | 15 | 1 | 23 | 57 | 18 | 37 | 3 | 25 | 8 |
| 5 | 1391 | Marcius | 21 | 11 | 13 | 38 | 4 | 46 | 49 | 0 | 51 | 42 | 0 | 0 | 1 | 43 | 24 |
| 6 | 1392 | September | 2 | 14 | 46 | 36 | 14 | 48 | 4 | 1 | 12 | 33 | 35 | 37 | 3 | 36 | 20 |
| 7 | 1393 | Februarius | 27 | 18 | 57 | 50 | 10 | 6 | 0 | 1 | 35 | 1 | 0 | 0 | 3 | 10 | 2 |
| 9 | 1395 | December | 27 | 12 | 7 | 18 | 15 | 16 | 44 | 1 | 9 | 38 | 38 | 43 | 3 | 36 | 42 |
| 10 | 1396 | Junius | 22 | 9 | 27 | 47 | 19 | 42 | 6 | 1 | 3 | 34 | 48 | 17 | 3 | 43 | 42 |
| 10 | 1396 | December | 15 | 20 | 11 | 14 | 12 | 34 | 44 | 1 | 24 | 58 | 16 | 57 | 3 | 23 | 50 |
| 11 | 1397 | Junius | 11 | 15 | 54 | 54 | 2 | 22 | 50 | 0 | 52 | 9 | 0 | 0 | 1 | 44 | 18 |
| 12 | 1398 | October | 26 | 15 | 10 | 58 | 0 | 38 | 40 | 0 | 27 | 21 | 0 | 0 | 0 | 54 | 42 |
| 13 | 1399 | Aprilis | 21 | 7 | 49 | 42 | 13 | 10 | 59 | 1 | 20 | 9 | 24 | 12 | 3 | 28 | 42 |
| 16 | 1402 | Februarius | 18 | 17 | 4 | 19 | 3 | 2 | 44 | 0 | 57 | 39 | 0 | 0 | 1 | 55 | 18 |
| 17 | 1403 | Augustus | 3 | 10 | 25 | 17 | 17 | 57 | 57 | 1 | 5 | 13 | 46 | 26 | 3 | 43 | 18 |
| 19 | 1405 | December | 6 | 18 | 22 | 34 | 0 | 36 | 49 | 0 | 27 | 33 | 0 | 0 | 0 | 55 | 6 |

Tabula eclipsis lune pro secundo ciclo cuius principium est annus Christi 1406 finis 1424

| | | | | | | | | | | | | | | | | | |
|---|---|---|---|---|---|---|---|---|---|---|---|---|---|---|---|---|---|
| 1 | 1406 | Junius | 2 | 12 | 7 | 37 | 9 | 0 | 54 | 1 | 33 | 2 | 0 | 0 | 3 | 6 | 4 |
| 1 | 1406 | November | 26 | 9 | 48 | 42 | 15 | 21 | 50 | 1 | 11 | 2 | 36 | 53 | 3 | 35 | 50 |
| 2 | 1407 | Mayus | 22 | 13 | 21 | 48 | 17 | 9 | 38 | 1 | 6 | 59 | 45 | 6 | 3 | 44 | 10 |
| 5 | 1410 | Marcius | 21 | 12 | 4 | 9 | 16 | 40 | 13 | 1 | 7 | 3 | 42 | 59 | 3 | 40 | 4 |
| 9 | 1414 | Januarius | 6 | 20 | 21 | 42 | 15 | 11 | 10 | 1 | 11 | 7 | 37 | 12 | 3 | 36 | 38 |
| 9 | 1414 | Julius | 3 | 16 | 25 | 30 | 21 | 25 | 35 | 1 | 4 | 4 | 49 | 8 | 3 | 46 | 24 |
| 9 | 1414 | December | 27 | 4 | 48 | 25 | 12 | 43 | 29 | 1 | 24 | 7 | 17 | 58 | 3 | 24 | 10 |
| 12 | 1417 | Mayus | 1 | 14 | 59 | 45 | 11 | 44 | 25 | 1 | 40 | 48 | 0 | 0 | 3 | 21 | 36 |
| 12 | 1417 | October | 26 | 8 | 8 | 31 | 14 | 15 | 57 | 1 | 16 | 20 | 30 | 24 | 3 | 33 | 28 |
| 13 | 1418 | October | 15 | 10 | 0 | 41 | 14 | 57 | 40 | 1 | 24 | 8 | 20 | 39 | 3 | 29 | 34 |
| 16 | 1421 | Februarius | 18 | 7 | 26 | 54 | 17 | 1 | 3 | 1 | 6 | 59 | 44 | 1 | 3 | 42 | 0 |
| 16 | 1421 | Augustus | 13 | 18 | 11 | 16 | 16 | 40 | 19 | 1 | 7 | 0 | 43 | 0 | 3 | 40 | 0 |
| 17 | 1422 | Februarius | 7 | 8 | 1 | 28 | 10 | 0 | 25 | 1 | 36 | 28 | 0 | 0 | 3 | 12 | 56 |
| 17 | 1422 | Augustus | 3 | 11 | 19 | 33 | 10 | 52 | 54 | 1 | 41 | 17 | 0 | 0 | 3 | 22 | 34 |
| 19 | 1424 | December | 6 | 18 | 36 | 53 | 15 | 18 | 36 | 1 | 10 | 31 | 37 | 32 | 3 | 36 | 6 |

Tabula eclipsis lune pro tercio ciclo cuius principium est annus Christi 1425 finis 1443

| Ciclus | Anni Christi | Menses | Vere opposiciones | | | | Punctus eclipsis | | | Tempus casus | | | Mora | | Duracio | | |
|---|---|---|---|---|---|---|---|---|---|---|---|---|---|---|---|---|---|
| | | | d. | h. | m. | s. | pt. | m. | s. | h. | m. | s. | m. | s. | h. | m. | s. |
| 1 | 1425 | November | 26 | 9 | 59 | 51 | 12 | 55 | 2 | 1 | 21 | 46 | 21 | 8 | 3 | 25 | 48 |
| 4 | 1428 | September | 24 | 5 | 34 | 20 | 12 | 41 | 29 | 1 | 24 | 57 | 18 | 48 | 3 | 27 | 30 |
| 5 | 1429 | Marcius | 21 | 10 | 58 | 15 | 11 | 44 | 50 | 1 | 40 | 11 | 0 | 0 | 3 | 20 | 22 |
| 5 | 1429 | September | 13 | 12 | 26 | 16 | 14 | 22 | 40 | 1 | 12 | 36 | 33 | 2 | 3 | 31 | 16 |
| 7 | 1431 | Julius | 25 | 11 | 6 | 44 | 4 | 35 | 55 | 1 | 9 | 33 | 0 | 0 | 2 | 19 | 6 |
| 8 | 1432 | Januarius | 18 | 4 | 32 | 48 | 15 | 1 | 59 | 1 | 11 | 31 | 36 | 25 | 3 | 35 | 52 |
| 9 | 1433 | Januarius | 6 | 13 | 24 | 6 | 12 | 47 | 58 | 1 | 22 | 42 | 19 | 48 | 3 | 25 | 0 |
| 11 | 1435 | November | 6 | 16 | 14 | 53 | 13 | 51 | 57 | 1 | 16 | 18 | 29 | 41 | 3 | 31 | 58 |
| 12 | 1436 | Mayus | 1 | 11 | 1 | 27 | 16 | 39 | 6 | 1 | 7 | 2 | 43 | 1 | 3 | 40 | 6 |
| 12 | 1436 | October | 25 | 17 | 46 | 56 | 13 | 24 | 20 | 1 | 19 | 27 | 26 | 15 | 3 | 31 | 24 |
| 15 | 1439 | Marcius | 1 | 15 | 7 | 15 | 16 | 16 | 35 | 1 | 8 | 29 | 41 | 52 | 3 | 40 | 42 |
| 16 | 1440 | Februarius | 18 | 15 | 42 | 9 | 10 | 38 | 4 | 1 | 38 | 33 | 0 | 0 | 3 | 17 | 6 |
| 17 | 1441 | December | 28 | 11 | 47 | 27 | 0 | 40 | 58 | 0 | 28 | 9 | 0 | 0 | 0 | 56 | 18 |
| 18 | 1442 | December | 18 | 3 | 26 | 35 | 15 | 19 | 10 | 1 | 10 | 14 | 37 | 34 | 3 | 35 | 36 |
| 19 | 1443 | December | 7 | 18 | 39 | 48 | 12 | 57 | 3 | 1 | 21 | 16 | 21 | 28 | 3 | 25 | 28 |

| | | | | | | | | | | | | | | | | | |
|---|---|---|---|---|---|---|---|---|---|---|---|---|---|---|---|---|---|
| 1 | 1444 | 1 | 7 | 6 | 51 | 4 | 41 | 29 | 1 | 10 | 35 | 0 | 0 | 2 | 21 | 10 | Junius |
| 3 | 1446 | 5 | 13 | 14 | 2 | 11 | 52 | 34 | 1 | 41 | 34 | 0 | 0 | 3 | 23 | 8 | October |
| 4 | 1447 | 1 | 18 | 44 | 54 | 12 | 48 | 53 | 1 | 14 | 7 | 28 | 52 | 3 | 25 | 46 | Aprilis |
| 5 | 1448 | 13 | 10 | 24 | 19 | 1 | 0 | 24 | 0 | 34 | 7 | 0 | 0 | 1 | 8 | 14 | September |
| 7 | 1450 | 21 | 12 | 46 | 8 | 14 | 46 | 8 | 1 | 12 | 45 | 35 | 12 | 3 | 35 | 6 | Januarius |
| 7 | 1450 | 25 | 6 | 27 | 33 | 18 | 21 | 9 | 1 | 4 | 50 | 47 | 17 | 3 | 44 | 7 | Julius |
| 8 | 1451 | 14 | 11 | 26 | 5 | 7 | 48 | 7 | 1 | 28 | 50 | 0 | 0 | 2 | 57 | 40 | Julius |
| 12 | 1455 | 2 | 11 | 44 | 16 | 2 | 45 | 52 | 0 | 55 | 23 | 0 | 0 | 1 | 50 | 47 | Mayus |
| 13 | 1456 | 22 | 16 | 49 | 23 | 0 | 23 | 46 | 0 | 21 | 41 | 0 | 0 | 0 | 43 | 22 | Marcius |
| 14 | 1457 | 4 | 10 | 9 | 46 | 14 | 28 | 41 | 1 | 13 | 11 | 33 | 36 | 3 | 33 | 34 | September |
| 17 | 1460 | 4 | 7 | 22 | 12 | 3 | 14 | 42 | 1 | 0 | 25 | 0 | 0 | 2 | 0 | 50 | Julius |
| 17 | 1460 | 28 | 12 | 7 | 43 | 15 | 17 | 43 | 1 | 10 | 22 | 37 | 25 | 3 | 35 | 35 | December |
| 18 | 1461 | 23 | 8 | 40 | 14 | 20 | 16 | 48 | 1 | 3 | 47 | 50 | 19 | 3 | 48 | 12 | Junius |
| 18 | 1461 | 18 | 3 | 21 | 0 | 12 | 55 | 29 | 1 | 21 | 36 | 21 | 14 | 3 | 25 | 40 | December |
| 19 | 1462 | 12 | 13 | 58 | 33 | 6 | 47 | 53 | 1 | 23 | 12 | 0 | 0. | 2 | 46 | 24 | Junius |

# FIGURE ECLIPSIS LUNE

Hec est lune incipiens anno Domini 1387 in Novembri ante mediam noctem precedens *a* que est 6 Kl. Decembris 2 h. 45 m. 3 s.

Hec est lune incipiens anno Domini 1389 in Mayo ante mediam noctem precedens *e* 5 Idus Mayi 6 h. 56 m. 45 s.

Hec est incipiens anno Domini 1389 in Novembri post mediam noctem precedens *g* Pridie nonas Novembris 3 h. 0 m. 35 s.

Hec est incipiens anno Domini 1391 in Marcio ante mediam noctem precedens *c* 12 Kl. Aprilis 1 h. 38 m. 4 s.

Hec est incipiens anno Domini 1392 in Septembri post mediam noctem precedens *g* 4 Nonas Septembris 0 h. 58 m. 26 s.

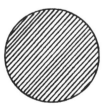

Hec est incipiens anno Domini 1393 in Februario post mediam noctem precedens *b* 3 Kl. Marcii 5 h. 22 m. 49 s.

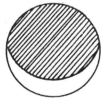

Hec est incipiens anno Domini 1395 in Decembri ante mediam noctem precedens *d* 6 Kl. Januarii 1 h. 41 m. 3 s.

Hec est incipiens anno Domini 1396 in Junio ante mediam noctem precedens *e* 10 Kl. Julii 4 h. 24 m. 4 s.

Hec est incipiens anno Domini 1396 in Decembri post mediam noctem precedens *f* 18 Kl. Januarii 6 h. 29 m. 19 s.

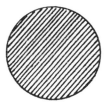

Hec est incipiens anno Domini 1397 in Junio post mediam noctem precedens *a* 3 Idus Junii 3 h. 2 m. 45 s.

Hec est incipiens anno Domini 1398 in Octobri post mediam noctem precedens *e* 7 Kl. Novembris 2 h. 43 m. 37 s.

Hec est incipiens anno Domini 1399 in Aprili ante mediam noctem precedens *f* 11 Kl. Mayi 5 h. 54 m. 39 s.

[155]

Hec est incipiens anno Domini 1402 in Februario post mediam noctem precedens *g* 12 Kl. Marcii 4 h. 6 m. 40 s.

Hec est incipiens anno Domini 1403 in Augusto ante mediam noctem precedens *e* 3 Nonas Augusti 3 h. 26 m. 22 s.

Hec est incipiens anno Domini 1405 in Decembri post mediam noctem precedens *d* 8 Idus Decembris 5 h. 55 m. 1 s.

Hec est incipiens anno Domini 1406 in Junio ante mediam noctem precedens *f* 4 Nonas Junii 1 h. 25 m. 25 s.

Hec est incipiens anno Domini 1406 in Novembri ante mediam noctem precedens *a* 6 Kl. Decembris 3 h. 59 m. 13 s.

Hec est incipiens anno Domini 1407 in Mayo ante mediam noctem precedens *b* 11 Kl. Junii 0 h. 30 m. 17 s.

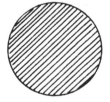

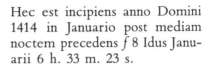

Hec est incipiens anno Domini 1410 in Marcio ante mediam noctem precedens *c* 12 Kl. Aprilis 1 h. 45 m. et 53 s.

Hec est incipiens anno Domini 1414 in Januario post mediam noctem precedens *f* 8 Idus Januarii 6 h. 33 m. 23 s.

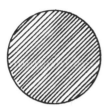

Hec est incipiens anno Domini 1414 in Julio post mediam noctem precedens *b* 5 Nonas Julii 2 h. 32 m. 18 s.

Hec est incipiens anno Domini 1414 in Decembri ante mediam noctem precedens *d* 6 Kl. Januarii 8 h. 53 m. 40 s.

Hec est incipiens anno Domini 1417 in Aprili post mediam noctem precedens *b* que est prima dies Mayi 1 h. 18 m. 57 s.

Hec est incipiens anno Domini 1417 in Octobri ante mediam noctem precedens *e* 7 Kl. Novembris 5 h. 38 m. 13 s.

Hec est incipiens anno Domini 1418 in Octobri ante mediam noctem precedens *a* Idibus Octobris 3 h. 44 m. 6 s.

Hec est incipiens anno Domini 1421 in Februario ante mediam noctem precedens *g* 12 Kl. Marcii 6 h. 24 m. 6 s.

Hec est incipiens anno Domini 1421 in Augusto post mediam noctem precedens *a* Idibus Augusti 4 h. 21 m. 16 s.

Hec est incipiens anno Domini 1422 in Februario ante mediam noctem precedens *c* 7 Idus Februarii 5 h. 35 m. 0 s.

Hec est incipiens anno Domini 1422 in Augusto ante mediam noctem precedens *e* 3 Nonas Augusti 2 h. 21 m. 44 s.

Hec est incipiens anno Domini 1424 in Decembri post mediam noctem precedens *d* 8 Idus Decembris 4 h. 48 m. 50 s.

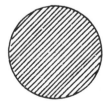

Hec est incipiens anno Domini 1425 in Novembri ante mediam noctem precedens *a* 6 Kl. Decembris 3 h. 43 m. 32 s.

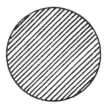

Hec est incipiens anno Domini 1428 in Septembri ante mediam noctem precedens *a* 8 Kl. Octobris 8 h. 9 m. 25 s.

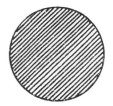

Hec est incipiens anno Domini 1429 in Marcio ante mediam noctem precedens *c* 12 Kl. Aprilis 2 h. 41 m. 56 s.

Hec est incipiens anno Domini 1429 in Septembri ante mediam noctem precedens *d* Idibus Septembris 1 h. 19 m. 22 s.

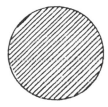

Hec est incipiens anno Domini 1431 in Julio ante mediam noctem precedens *c* 8 Kl. Augusti 2 h. 2 m. 49 s.

Hec est incipiens anno Domini 1432 in Januario ante mediam noctem precedens *d* 15 Kl. Februarii 9 h. 15 m. 8 s.

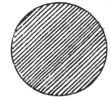

Hec est incipiens anno Domini 1433 in Januario ante mediam noctem precedens *f* 8 Idus Januarii 0 h. 18 m. 24 s.

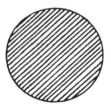

Hec est incipiens anno Domini 1435 in Novembri post mediam noctem precedens *b* 8 Idus Novembris 2 h. 28 m. 54 s.

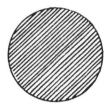

Hec est incipiens anno Domini 1436 in Mayo ante mediam noctem precedens *b* primam diem Mayi 2 h. 48 m. 36 s.

Hec est incipiens anno Domini 1436 in Octobri post mediam noctem precedens *d* 8 Kl. Novembris 4 h. 1 m. 14 s.

Hec est incipiens anno Domini 1439 in Marcio post mediam noctem precedens *d* primam diem Marcii 1 h. 16 m. 54 s.

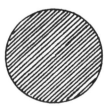

Anno Domini 1440 in Februario post mediam noctem precedens *g* 12 Kl. Marcii 2 h. 3 m. 36 s.

Hec est incipiens anno Domini 1441 in Decembri ante mediam noctem precedens *e* 5 Kl. Januarii 0 h. 42 m. 42 s.

Anno Domini 1442 in Decembri ante mediam noctem precedens *b* 15 Kl. Januarii 10 h. 21 m. 13 s.

Hec est incipiens anno Domini 1443 in Decembri post mediam noctem precedens *e* 7 Idus Decembris 4 h. 57 m. 22 s.

Anno Domini 1444 in Junio ante mediam noctem precedens *e* primam diem Junii 6 h. 3 m. 44 s.

Hec est incipiens anno Domini 1446 in Octobri ante mediam noctem precedens *e* 3 Nonas Octobris 0 h. 27 m. 32 s.

Anno Domini 1447 in Aprili post mediam noctem precedens *g* primam diem Aprilis 5 h. 2 m. 2 s. parvum ante solis ortum

Hec est incipiens anno Domini 1448 in Septembri ante mediam noctem precedens *d* Idibus Septembris 2 h. 9 m. 48 s.

Anno Domini 1450 in Januario ante mediam noctem precedens *g* 12 Kl. Februarii 1 h. 1 m. 25 s.

Hec est incipiens anno Domini 1450 in Julio ante mediam noctem precedens *c* 8 Kl. Augusti 7 h. 24 m. 30 s.

Anno Domini 1451 in Julio ante mediam noctem precedens *f* Pridie Idus Julii 2 h. 2 m. 45 s.

Hec est incipiens anno Domini 1455 in Mayo ante mediam noctem precedens *c* 6 Nonas Mayi 1 h. 11 m. 7 s.

Anno Domini 1456 in Marcio post mediam noctem precedens *d* 11 Kl. Aprilis 4 h. 27 m. 42 s.

Hec est incipiens anno Domini 1457 in Septembri ante mediam noctem precedens *b* Pridie Nonas Septembris 3 h. 3 m. 1 s.

Anno Domini 1460 in Julio ante mediam noctem precedens *c* 4 Nonas Julii 5 h. 38 m. 13 s.

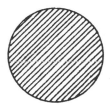

Hec est incipiens anno Domini 1460 in Decembri ante mediam noctem precedens *e* 5 Kl. Januarii 1 h. 40 m. 2 s.

Anno Domini 1461 in Junio ante mediam noctem precedens *f* 9 Kl. Julii 5 h. 13 m. 52 s.

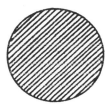

Hec est incipiens anno Domini 1461 in Decembri ante mediam noctem precedens *b* 15 Kl. Januarii 10 h. 21 m. 50 s.

Anno Domini 1462 in Junio post mediam noctem precedens *b* Pridie Idus Junii 0 h. 35 m. 21 s.

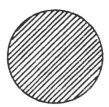

# ARIES

| Gradus ascendentis & locus solis | Ascenciones Sagittarii in circulo directo g. m. | Ascenciones Sagittarii in latitudine 51° 50′ g. m. | Equaciones domorum ad latitudinem 51 graduum et 50 minutorum | | | | |
|---|---|---|---|---|---|---|---|
| | | | II Taur. g. | III Gem. g. | IV Canc. g. | V Canc. g. | VI Leo g. |
| 1 | 90 55 | 0 25 | 3 | 3 | 1 | 30 | 29 |
| 2 | 91 50 | 0 49 | 4 | 4 | 1 | 30 | 30 |
| | | | | | | | Virgo |
| 3 | 92 45 | 1 14 | 5 | 4 | 1 | 30 | 1 |
| | | | | | | | Leo |
| 4 | 93 40 | 1 38 | 5 | 5 | 2 | 1 | 1 |
| 5 | 94 35 | 2 3 | 7 | 5 | 2 | 1 | 2 |
| 6 | 95 30 | 2 27 | 7 | 6 | 3 | 2 | 3 |
| 7 | 96 25 | 2 52 | 8 | 6 | 3 | 2 | 4 |
| 8 | 97 20 | 3 16 | 9 | 7 | 4 | 3 | 5 |
| 9 | 98 16 | 3 42 | 10 | 8 | 4 | 3 | 5 |
| 10 | 99 11 | 4 6 | 10 | 8 | 4 | 4 | 6 |
| 11 | 100 6 | 4 31 | 11 | 9 | 5 | 5 | 7 |
| 12 | 101 1 | 4 56 | 11 | 9 | 5 | 5 | 7 |
| 13 | 101 57 | 5 22 | 13 | 10 | 5 | 6 | 9 |
| 14 | 102 52 | 5 47 | 13 | 10 | 6 | 6 | 9 |
| 15 | 103 48 | 6 12 | 14 | 11 | 6 | 7 | 10 |
| 16 | 104 43 | 6 37 | 15 | 11 | 7 | 7 | 11 |
| 17 | 105 39 | 7 3 | 16 | 12 | 7 | 8 | 12 |
| 18 | 106 35 | 7 29 | 17 | 13 | 7 | 9 | 13 |
| 19 | 107 31 | 7 55 | 17 | 13 | 8 | 9 | 13 |
| 20 | 108 27 | 8 20 | 18 | 14 | 8 | 10 | 14 |
| 21 | 109 23 | 8 47 | 19 | 14 | 9 | 10 | 15 |
| 22 | 110 19 | 9 13 | 20 | 15 | 9 | 11 | 16 |
| 23 | 111 15 | 9 39 | 20 | 15 | 9 | 12 | 17 |
| 24 | 112 12 | 10 6 | 21 | 16 | 10 | 12 | 17 |
| 25 | 113 8 | 10 33 | 22 | 16 | 10 | 13 | 18 |
| 26 | 114 5 | 11 0 | 23 | 17 | 11 | 13 | 19 |
| 27 | 115 2 | 11 28 | 23 | 18 | 11 | 14 | 20 |
| 28 | 115 59 | 11 56 | 24 | 18 | 11 | 15 | 21 |
| 29 | 116 56 | 12 23 | 25 | 18 | 13 | 15 | 22 |
| 30 | 117 53 | 12 51 | 26 | 18 | 13 | 16 | 23 |

# TAURUS

| Gradus ascendentis & locus solis | Ascenciones Sagittarii in circulo directo | | Ascenciones Sagittarii in latitudine 51° 50′ | | II Taur. | III Gem. | IV Canc. | V Leo | VI Virgo |
|---|---|---|---|---|---|---|---|---|---|
| | g. | m. | g. | m. | g. | g. | g. | g. | g. |
| 1 | 118 | 50 | 13 | 19 | 26 | 18 | 14 | 16 | 24 |
| 2 | 119 | 48 | 13 | 48 | 27 | 20 | 14 | 17 | 24 |
| 3 | 120 | 46 | 14 | 17 | 28 | 20 | 15 | 18 | 25 |
| 4 | 121 | 44 | 14 | 46 | 29 | 21 | 15 | 18 | 26 |
| 5 | 122 | 42 | 15 | 16 | 30 | 21 | 15 | 19 | 27 |
| 6 | 123 | 40 | 15 | 46 | 30 | 22 | 16 | 20 | 28 |
| | | | | | Gem. | | | | |
| 7 | 124 | 38 | 16 | 16 | 1 | 23 | 16 | 20 | 29 |
| 8 | 125 | 36 | 16 | 46 | 2 | 23 | 17 | 21 | 30 |
| | | | | | | | | | Libra |
| 9 | 126 | 35 | 17 | 17 | 3 | 24 | 17 | 22 | 1 |
| 10 | 127 | 34 | 17 | 48 | 4 | 24 | 18 | 22 | 2 |
| 11 | 128 | 33 | 18 | 20 | 4 | 25 | 18 | 23 | 2 |
| 12 | 129 | 32 | 18 | 52 | 5 | 26 | 19 | 24 | 3 |
| 13 | 130 | 31 | 19 | 24 | 6 | 26 | 19 | 25 | 4 |
| 14 | 131 | 30 | 19 | 56 | 7 | 27 | 20 | 25 | 6 |
| 15 | 132 | 30 | 20 | 29 | 7 | 28 | 20 | 26 | 6 |
| 16 | 133 | 30 | 21 | 4 | 8 | 28 | 21 | 27 | 7 |
| 17 | 134 | 30 | 21 | 38 | 9 | 29 | 21 | 27 | 8 |
| 18 | 135 | 30 | 22 | 12 | 10 | 30 | 22 | 28 | 9 |
| | | | | | Canc. | | | | |
| 19 | 136 | 31 | 22 | 48 | 11 | 1 | 23 | 29 | 10 |
| 20 | 137 | 31 | 23 | 22 | 12 | 2 | 23 | 30 | 11 |
| 21 | 138 | 32 | 23 | 58 | 12 | 2 | 24 | 30 | 12 |
| | | | | | | | | Virgo | |
| 22 | 139 | 33 | 24 | 35 | 13 | 3 | 24 | 1 | 13 |
| 23 | 140 | 34 | 25 | 11 | 14 | 4 | 25 | 2 | 14 |
| 24 | 141 | 36 | 25 | 50 | 15 | 5 | 25 | 3 | 15 |
| 25 | 142 | 37 | 26 | 28 | 16 | 5 | 27 | 4 | 16 |
| 26 | 143 | 39 | 27 | 7 | 17 | 6 | 27 | 5 | 17 |
| 27 | 144 | 41 | 27 | 46 | 17 | 7 | 27 | 5 | 18 |
| 28 | 145 | 43 | 28 | 26 | 18 | 7 | 28 | 6 | 19 |
| 29 | 146 | 45 | 29 | 7 | 18 | 8 | 28 | 7 | 20 |
| 30 | 147 | 47 | 29 | 48 | 18 | 9 | 29 | 8 | 21 |

# GEMINI

| Gradus ascendentis & locus solis | Ascenciones Sagittarii in circulo directo g. m. | Ascenciones Sagittarii in latitudine 51° 50' g. m. | II Gem. g. | III Canc. g. | IV Canc. g. | V Virgo g. | VI Libra g. |
|---|---|---|---|---|---|---|---|
| 1 | 148 50 | 30 30 | 20 | 10 | 30 | 9 | 22 |
| 2 | 149 53 | 31 13 | 21 | 10 | 30 | 10 | 22 |
| 3 | 150 56 | 31 56 | 22 | 11 | 30 | 11 | 24 |
| | | | | | Leo | | |
| 4 | 151 59 | 32 40 | 22 | 13 | 1 | 11 | 24 |
| 5 | 153 2 | 33 24 | 23 | 14 | 2 | 12 | 25 |
| 6 | 154 5 | 34 9 | 24 | 14 | 2 | 13 | 26 |
| 7 | 155 9 | 34 55 | 25 | 15 | 3 | 14 | 28 |
| 8 | 156 13 | 35 43 | 26 | 16 | 4 | 15 | 29 |
| 9 | 157 17 | 36 30 | 27 | 17 | 5 | 16 | 30 |
| | | | | | | | Scorp. |
| 10 | 158 21 | 37 19 | 28 | 18 | 5 | 17 | 1 |
| 11 | 159 25 | 38 8 | 29 | 19 | 6 | 18 | 2 |
| 12 | 160 29 | 38 58 | 30 | 19 | 7 | 19 | 3 |
| | | | Canc. | | | | |
| 13 | 161 33 | 39 48 | 1 | 20 | 8 | 20 | 4 |
| 14 | 162 37 | 40 39 | 2 | 21 | 9 | 21 | 5 |
| 15 | 163 42 | 41 32 | 3 | 22 | 10 | 22 | 6 |
| 16 | 164 47 | 42 25 | 4 | 23 | 10 | 23 | 7 |
| 17 | 165 52 | 43 19 | 5 | 24 | 11 | 24 | 8 |
| 18 | 166 57 | 44 14 | 6 | 25 | 12 | 25 | 9 |
| 19 | 168 2 | 45 10 | 7 | 27 | 13 | 26 | 10 |
| 20 | 169 7 | 46 6 | 8 | 27 | 14 | 27 | 11 |
| 21 | 170 12 | 47 4 | 9 | 28 | 15 | 28 | 12 |
| 22 | 171 17 | 48 2 | 10 | 28 | 16 | 30 | 13 |
| | | | | | | Libra | |
| 23 | 172 22 | 49 1 | 11 | 29 | 17 | 1 | 14 |
| 24 | 173 27 | 50 1 | 13 | 30 | 18 | 2 | 15 |
| 25 | 174 32 | 51 1 | 14 | 30 | 19 | 3 | 16 |
| | | | | | Leo | | |
| 26 | 175 38 | 52 3 | 15 | 1 | 20 | 4 | 17 |
| 27 | 176 44 | 53 6 | 16 | 2 | 21 | 5 | 19 |
| 28 | 177 49 | 54 9 | 17 | 4 | 22 | 6 | 20 |
| 29 | 178 54 | 55 13 | 18 | 5 | 23 | 8 | 21 |
| 30 | 180 0 | 56 18 | 19 | 6 | 24 | 9 | 22 |

# CANCER

| Gradus ascendentis & locus solis | Ascenciones Sagittarii in circulo directo g. m. | Ascenciones Sagittarii in latitudine 51° 50′ g. m. | II Canc. g. | III Leo g. | IV Leo g. | V Libra g. | VI Scorp. g. |
|---|---|---|---|---|---|---|---|
| 1 | 181 0 | 57 25 | 20 | 7 | 26 | 10 | 23 |
| 2 | 182 11 | 58 31 | 21 | 8 | 27 | 11 | 24 |
| 3 | 183 16 | 59 38 | 22 | 9 | 28 | 12 | 25 |
| 4 | 184 22 | 60 47 | 23 | 10 | 29 | 14 | 26 |
| 5 | 185 28 | 61 57 | 24 | 11 | 30 | 15 | 27 |
| | | | | | *Virgo* | | |
| 6 | 186 33 | 63 7 | 25 | 12 | 2 | 16 | 28 |
| 7 | 187 38 | 64 17 | 27 | 13 | 3 | 17 | 29 |
| 8 | 188 43 | 65 28 | 27 | 15 | 4 | 18 | 30 |
| | | | | | | | *Sag.* |
| 9 | 189 48 | 66 40 | 28 | 16 | 5 | 20 | 1 |
| 10 | 190 53 | 67 52 | 29 | 16 | 6 | 20 | 2 |
| 11 | 191 58 | 69 6 | 30 | 18 | 8 | 22 | 4 |
| 12 | 193 3 | 70 20 | 30 | 19 | 9 | 23 | 5 |
| | | | *Leo* | | | | |
| 13 | 194 8 | 71 35 | 2 | 20 | 11 | 25 | 6 |
| 14 | 195 13 | 72 51 | 3 | 22 | 12 | 26 | 7 |
| 15 | 196 18 | 74 8 | 4 | 23 | 13 | 27 | 8 |
| 16 | 197 23 | 75 25 | 5 | 24 | 15 | 29 | 9 |
| 17 | 198 27 | 76 42 | 6 | 25 | 16 | 30 | 10 |
| | | | | | | *Scorp.* | |
| 18 | 199 31 | 78 0 | 7 | 27 | 17 | 1 | 11 |
| 19 | 200 35 | 79 18 | 8 | 28 | 19 | 2 | 12 |
| 20 | 201 39 | 80 37 | 9 | 29 | 20 | 4 | 13 |
| | | | *Virgo* | | | | |
| 21 | 202 43 | 81 56 | 10 | 1 | 22 | 5 | 14 |
| 22 | 203 47 | 83 17 | 12 | 2 | 23 | 6 | 15 |
| 23 | 204 51 | 84 37 | 13 | 3 | 25 | 8 | 16 |
| 24 | 205 55 | 85 59 | 14 | 5 | 26 | 9 | 18 |
| 25 | 206 58 | 87 20 | 15 | 6 | 28 | 10 | 18 |
| 26 | 208 1 | 88 42 | 16 | 7 | 29 | 11 | 18 |
| | | | | | *Libra* | | |
| 27 | 209 4 | 90 4 | 17 | 9 | 1 | 13 | 20 |
| 28 | 210 7 | 91 27 | 19 | 10 | 2 | 14 | 21 |
| 29 | 211 10 | 92 50 | 20 | 11 | 4 | 15 | 22 |
| 30 | 212 13 | 94 14 | 21 | 13 | 5 | 17 | 23 |

# LEO

| Gradus ascendentis & locus solis | Ascenciones Sagittarii in circulo directo g. m. | Ascenciones Sagittarii in latitudine 51° 50′ g. m. | II Leo g. | III Virgo g. | IV Libra g. | V Scorp. g. | VI Sag. g. |
|---|---|---|---|---|---|---|---|
| 1 | 213 15 | 95 37 | 22 | 14 | 7 | 18 | 24 |
| 2 | 214 17 | 97 0 | 23 | 15 | 8 | 19 | 25 |
| 3 | 215 19 | 98 24 | 24 | 17 | 10 | 20 | 26 |
| 4 | 216 21 | 99 49 | 26 | 18 | 11 | 22 | 27 |
| 5 | 217 23 | 101 14 | 27 | 20 | 13 | 23 | 28 |
| 6 | 218 24 | 102 38 | 28 | 21 | 14 | 24 | 29 |
| | | | | | | | Capr. |
| 7 | 219 26 | 104 3 | 29 | 22 | 16 | 25 | 1 |
| 8 | 220 27 | 105 29 · | 30 | 24 | 17 | 27 | 2 |
| | | | Virgo | | | | |
| 9 | 221 28 | 106 54 | 2 | 25 | 19 | 28 | 3 |
| 10 | 222 29 | 108 20 | 3 | 27 | 20 | 29 | 5 |
| 11 | 223 30 | 109 46 | 4 | 28 | ·22 | 30 | 6 |
| | | | | | | Sag. | |
| 12 | 224 30 | 111 12 | 5 | 29 | 23 | 2 | 7 |
| | | | Libra | | | | |
| 13 | 225 30 | 112 38 | 7 | 1 | 25 | 3 | 8 |
| 14 | 226 30 | 114 4 | 8 | 2 | 26 | 4 | 9 |
| 15 | 227 30 | 115 29 | 9 | 4 | 28 | 5 | 10 |
| 16 | 228 29 | 116 56 | 10 | 5 | 29 | 7 | 11 |
| | | | | | Scorp. | | |
| 17 | 229 28 | 118 22 | 11 | 6 | 1 | 8 | 13 |
| 18 | 230 27 | 119 48 | 13 | 8 | 2 | 9 | 14 |
| 19 | 231 26 | 121 14 | 14 | 9 | 4 | 10 | 15 |
| 20 | 232 25 | 122 40 | 16 | 11 | 5 | 11 | 16 |
| 21 | 233 24 | 124 7 | 16 | 12 | 7 | 13 | 17 |
| 22 | 234 22 | 125 34 | 18 | 13 | 8 | 14 | 18 |
| 23 | 235 20 | 127 0 | 19 | 15 | 10 | 15 | 19 |
| 24 | 236 18 | 128 26 | 20 | 16 | 11 | 16 | 20 |
| 25 | 237 16 | 129 52 | 21 | 18 | 13 | 17 | 21 |
| 26 | 238 14 | 131 18 | 22 | 19 | 14 | 18 | 22 |
| 27 | 239 13 | 132 45 | 24 | 20 | 16 | 18 | 23 |
| 28 | 240 12 | 134 12 | 25 | 22 | 17 | 20 | 24 |
| 29 | 241 10 | 135 39 | 26 | 23 | 19 | 21 | 26 |
| 30 | 242 7 | 137 5 | 27 | 24 | 20 | 22 | 27 |

# VIRGO

| Gradus ascendentis & locus solis | Ascenciones Sagittarii in circulo directo g. m. | Ascenciones Sagittarii in latitudine 51° 50′ g. m. | II Virgo g. | III Libra g. | IV Scorp. g. | V Sag. g. | VI Capr. g. |
|---|---|---|---|---|---|---|---|
| | | | Equaciones domorum ad latitudinem 51 graduum et 50 minutorum | | | | |
| 1 | 243  4 | 138 31 | 29 | 26 | 21 | 23 | 28 |
| 2 | 244  1 | 139 58 | 30 | 27 | 23 | 25 | 29 |
| | | | Libra | | | | |
| 3 | 244 58 | 141 24 | 1 | 28 | 24 | 26 | 30 |
| 4 | 245 55 | 142 50 | 2 | 30 | 26 | 27 | 30 |
| | | | | Scorp. | | | Aquar. |
| 5 | 246 52 | 144 17 | 3 | 1 | 27 | 28 | 1 |
| 6 | 247 48 | 145 42 | 5 | 2 | 28 | 29 | 2 |
| | | | | | | Capr. | |
| 7 | 248 45 | 147  9 | 6 | 4 | 30 | 1 | 3 |
| | | | | | Sag. | | |
| 8 | 249 41 | 148 35 | 7 | 5 | 1 | 3 | 4 |
| 9 | 250 37 | 150  1 | 8 | 6 | 3 | 4 | 5 |
| 10 | 251 33 | 151 26 | 9 | 8 | 4 | 5 | 6 |
| 11 | 252 29 | 152 53 | 11 | 9 | 5 | 6 | 7 |
| 12 | 253 25 | 154 19 | 12 | 10 | 7 | 7 | 8 |
| 13 | 254 21 | 155 45 | 13 | 12 | 8 | 9 | 10 |
| 14 | 255 17 | 157 11 | 14 | 13 | 9 | 10 | 11 |
| 15 | 256 12 | 158 36 | 15 | 14 | 11 | 11 | 12 |
| 16 | 257  8 | 160  3 | 17 | 15 | 12 | 13 | 13 |
| 17 | 258  3 | 161 28 | 18 | 17 | 13 | 14 | 14 |
| 18 | 258 59 | 162 54 | 19 | 18 | 15 | 15 | 15 |
| 19 | 259 54 | 164 19 | 20 | 19 | 16 | 16 | 16 |
| 20 | 260 49 | 165 44 | 21 | 20 | 17 | 17 | 17 |
| 21 | 261 44 | 167 10 | 22 | 22 | 18 | 19 | 18 |
| 22 | 262 40 | 168 36 | 24 | 23 | 18 | 20 | 19 |
| 23 | 263 35 | 170  2 | 25 | 24 | 20 | 21 | 20 |
| 24 | 264 30 | 171 27 | 26 | 25 | 22 | 22 | 22 |
| 25 | 265 25 | 172 53 | 27 | 27 | 23 | 23 | 23 |
| 26 | 266 20 | 174 18 | 28 | 28 | 24 | 25 | 24 |
| 27 | 267 15 | 175 44 | 29 | 29 | 26 | 27 | 25 |
| 28 | 268 10 | 177  9 | 30 | 30 | 27 | 27 | 26 |
| | | | Scorp. | Sag. | | | |
| 29 | 269  5 | 178 35 | 2 | 1 | 28 | 28 | 27 |
| 30 | 270  0 | 180  0 | 3 | 3 | 30 | 29 | 28 |

# LIBRA

| Gradus ascendentis & locus solis | Ascenciones Sagittarii in circulo directo g. m. | Ascenciones Sagittarii in latitudine 51° 50' g. m. | II Scorp. g. | III Sag. g. | IV Capr. g. | V Capr. g. | VI Aquar. g. |
|---|---|---|---|---|---|---|---|
| 1 | 270 55 | 181 25 | 4 | 4 | 2 | 30 | 29 |
|  |  |  |  |  |  | Aquar. | Pisc. |
| 2 | 271 50 | 182 51 | 5 | 6 | 3 | 1 | 1 |
| 3 | 272 45 | 184 16 | 6 | 6 | 4 | 2 | 2 |
| 4 | 273 40 | 185 42 | 7 | 7 | 6 | 3 | 3 |
| 5 | 274 35 | 187 7 | 8 | 9 | 7 | 4 | 4 |
| 6 | 275 30 | 188 33 | 9 | 10 | 8 | 6 | 5 |
| 7 | 276 25 | 189 58 | 11 | 11 | 10 | 7 | 6 |
| 8 | 277 20 | 191 24 | 12 | 12 | 11 | 8 | 7 |
| 9 | 278 16 | 192 50 | 13 | 13 | 13 | 9 | 9 |
| 10 | 279 11 | 194 16 | 14 | 14 | 15 | 11 | 10 |
| 11 | 280 6 | 195 41 | 15 | 16 | 16 | 12 | 11 |
| 12 | 281 1 | 197 6 | 16 | 17 | 17 | 13 | 12 |
| 13 | 281 57 | 198 32 | 17 | 18 | 19 | 14 | 13 |
| 14 | 282 52 | 199 57 | 18 | 18 | 20 | 16 | 14 |
| 15 | 283 48 | 201 24 | 19 | 18 | 21 | 17 | 16 |
| 16 | 284 43 | 202 49 | 20 | 20 | 23 | 18 | 17 |
| 17 | 285 39 | 204 15 | 21 | 22 | 24 | 19 | 18 |
| 18 | 286 35 | 205 41 | 23 | 23 | 25 | 21 | 19 |
| 19 | 287 31 | 207 7 | 24 | 24 | 27 | 22 | 20 |
| 20 | 288 27 | 208 34 | 25 | 25 | 28 | 23 | 22 |
| 21 | 289 23 | 209 59 | 26 | 26 | 29 | 25 | 23 |
| 22 | 290 19 | 211 25 | 27 | 27 | 30 | 26 | 24 |
|  |  |  |  |  | Aquar. |  |  |
| 23 | 291 15 | 212 51 | 28 | 29 | 1 | 27 | 25 |
|  |  |  |  | Capr. |  |  |  |
| 24 | 292 12 | 214 18 | 29 | 1 | 3 | 29 | 26 |
| 25 | 293 8 | 215 43 | 30 | 2 | 4 | 30 | 28 |
|  |  |  | Sag. |  |  | Pisc. |  |
| 26 | 294 5 | 217 10 | 1 | 3 | 5 | 1 | 29 |
| 27 | 295 2 | 218 36 | 2 | 4 | 7 | 3 | 30 |
|  |  |  |  |  |  |  | Aries |
| 28 | 295 59 | 220 2 | 3 | 5 | 8 | 4 | 1 |
| 29 | 296 56 | 221 29 | 4 | 7 | 10 | 5 | 2 |
| 30 | 297 53 | 222 55 | 6 | 8 | 11 | 7 | 4 |

# SCORPIO

<table>
<tr><th rowspan="2">Gradus ascendentis & locus solis</th><th>Ascenciones Sagittarii in circulo directo</th><th>Ascenciones Sagittarii in latitudine 51° 50'</th><th colspan="5">Equaciones domorum ad latitudinem 51 graduum et 50 minutorum</th></tr>
<tr><th>g. m.</th><th>g. m.</th><th>II<br>Sag.<br>g.</th><th>III<br>Capr.<br>g.</th><th>IV<br>Aquar.<br>g.</th><th>V<br>Pisc.<br>g.</th><th>VI<br>Aries<br>g.</th></tr>
<tr><td>1</td><td>298 50</td><td>224 21</td><td>6</td><td>9</td><td>12</td><td>8</td><td>5</td></tr>
<tr><td>2</td><td>299 48</td><td>225 48</td><td>7</td><td>10</td><td>14</td><td>9</td><td>6</td></tr>
<tr><td>3</td><td>300 46</td><td>227 15</td><td>9</td><td>11</td><td>15</td><td>11</td><td>7</td></tr>
<tr><td>4</td><td>301 44</td><td>228 42</td><td>10</td><td>13</td><td>17</td><td>12</td><td>9</td></tr>
<tr><td>5</td><td>302 42</td><td>230 8</td><td>11</td><td>15</td><td>18</td><td>13</td><td>10</td></tr>
<tr><td>6</td><td>303 40</td><td>231 34</td><td>12</td><td>16</td><td>20</td><td>15</td><td>11</td></tr>
<tr><td>7</td><td>304 38</td><td>233 0</td><td>13</td><td>17</td><td>21</td><td>16</td><td>12</td></tr>
<tr><td>8</td><td>305 36</td><td>234 26</td><td>14</td><td>18</td><td>23</td><td>18</td><td>13</td></tr>
<tr><td>9</td><td>306 35</td><td>235 53</td><td>15</td><td>19</td><td>24</td><td>19</td><td>15</td></tr>
<tr><td>10</td><td>307 34</td><td>237 20</td><td>16</td><td>21</td><td>26</td><td>20</td><td>16</td></tr>
<tr><td>11</td><td>308 33</td><td>238 46</td><td>17</td><td>22</td><td>27</td><td>22</td><td>17</td></tr>
<tr><td>12</td><td>309 32</td><td>240 12</td><td>18</td><td>23</td><td>28</td><td>23</td><td>18</td></tr>
<tr><td>13</td><td>310 31</td><td>241 38</td><td>18</td><td>24</td><td>30</td><td>25</td><td>20</td></tr>
<tr><td></td><td></td><td></td><td></td><td></td><td>Pisc.</td><td></td><td></td></tr>
<tr><td>14</td><td>311 30</td><td>243 4</td><td>18</td><td>25</td><td>1</td><td>26</td><td>21</td></tr>
<tr><td>15</td><td>312 30</td><td>244 31</td><td>20</td><td>27</td><td>3</td><td>27</td><td>22</td></tr>
<tr><td>16</td><td>313 30</td><td>245 56</td><td>21</td><td>28</td><td>5</td><td>29</td><td>23</td></tr>
<tr><td>17</td><td>314 30</td><td>247° 22</td><td>22</td><td>29</td><td>6</td><td>30</td><td>24</td></tr>
<tr><td></td><td></td><td></td><td></td><td></td><td></td><td>Aries</td><td></td></tr>
<tr><td>18</td><td>315 30</td><td>248 48</td><td>23</td><td>30</td><td>8</td><td>2</td><td>26</td></tr>
<tr><td></td><td></td><td></td><td></td><td>Aquar.</td><td></td><td></td><td></td></tr>
<tr><td>19</td><td>316 31</td><td>250 14</td><td>24</td><td>1</td><td>9</td><td>3</td><td>27</td></tr>
<tr><td>20</td><td>317 31</td><td>251 40</td><td>26</td><td>2</td><td>11</td><td>4</td><td>28</td></tr>
<tr><td>21</td><td>318 32</td><td>253 6</td><td>27</td><td>3</td><td>12</td><td>6</td><td>29</td></tr>
<tr><td></td><td></td><td></td><td></td><td></td><td></td><td></td><td>Taur.</td></tr>
<tr><td>22</td><td>319 33</td><td>254 31</td><td>28</td><td>4</td><td>14</td><td>7</td><td>1</td></tr>
<tr><td>23</td><td>320 34</td><td>255 57</td><td>29</td><td>6</td><td>15</td><td>9</td><td>2</td></tr>
<tr><td></td><td></td><td></td><td>Capr.</td><td></td><td></td><td></td><td></td></tr>
<tr><td>24</td><td>321 36</td><td>257 22</td><td>1</td><td>7</td><td>17</td><td>10</td><td>3</td></tr>
<tr><td>25</td><td>322 37</td><td>258 46</td><td>2</td><td>8</td><td>18</td><td>11</td><td>4</td></tr>
<tr><td>26</td><td>323 39</td><td>260 11</td><td>3</td><td>9</td><td>20</td><td>13</td><td>5</td></tr>
<tr><td>27</td><td>324 41</td><td>261 36</td><td>4</td><td>11</td><td>21</td><td>14</td><td>6</td></tr>
<tr><td>28</td><td>325 43</td><td>263 0</td><td>5</td><td>12</td><td>23</td><td>16</td><td>8</td></tr>
<tr><td>29</td><td>326 45</td><td>264 23</td><td>6</td><td>13</td><td>24</td><td>17</td><td>9</td></tr>
<tr><td>30</td><td>327 47</td><td>265 46</td><td>7</td><td>14</td><td>26</td><td>18</td><td>10</td></tr>
</table>

# SAGITTARIUS

| Gradus ascendentis & locus solis | Ascenciones Sagittarii in circulo directo | Ascenciones Sagittarii in latitudine 51° 50′ | Equaciones domorum ad latitudinem 51 graduum et 50 minutorum | | | | |
|---|---|---|---|---|---|---|---|
| | | | II Capr. | III Aquar. | IV Pisc. | V Aries | VI Taur. |
| | g.  m. | g.  m. | g. | g. | g. | g. | g. |
| 1 | 328 50 | 267 10 | 8 | 15 | 27 | 20 | 11 |
| 2 | 329 53 | 268 33 | 9 | 17 | 29 | 21 | 12 |
| 3 | 330 56 | 269 56 | 10 | 18 | 30 | 22 | 14 |
| | | | | | Aries | | |
| 4 | 331 59 | 271 18 | 11 | 20 | 2 | 24 | 15 |
| 5 | 333  2 | 272 40 | 13 | 21 | 3 | 25 | 16 |
| 6 | 334  5 | 274  1 | 14 | 22 | 5 | 26 | 17 |
| 7 | 335  9 | 275 23 | 15 | 23 | 6 | 28 | 18 |
| 8 | 336 13 | 276 43 | 16 | 25 | 8 | 29 | 19 |
| 9 | 337 17 | 278  4 | 18 | 26 | 9 | 30 | 21 |
| | | | | | | Taur. | |
| 10 | 338 21 | 279 23 | 19 | 27 | 11 | 2 | 22 |
| 11 | 339 25 | 280 42 | 20 | 29 | 12 | 3 | 23 |
| 12 | 340 29 | 282  0 | 21 | 30 | 14 | 4 | 24 |
| | | | | Pisc. | | | |
| 13 | 341 33 | 283 18 | 22 | 1 | 15 | 6 | 25 |
| 14 | 342 37 | 284 35 | 23 | 2 | 16 | 7 | 26 |
| 15 | 343 42 | 285 52 | 24 | 4 | 18 | 8 | 27 |
| 16 | 344 47 | 287  9 | 25 | 5 | 19 | 9 | 28 |
| 17 | 345 52 | 288 25 | 27 | 6 | 20 | 10 | 29 |
| | | | | | | | Gem. |
| 18 | 346 57 | 289 40 | 27 | 8 | 22 | 12 | 1 |
| 19 | 348  2 | 290 54 | 28 | 9 | 23 | 13 | 2 |
| 20 | 349  7 | 292  8 | 29 | 10 | 24 | 14 | 3 |
| 21 | 350 12 | 293 20 | 30 | 11 | 26 | 15 | 4 |
| | | | Aquar. | | | | |
| 22 | 351 17 | 294 32 | 1 | 13 | 27 | 16 | 5 |
| 23 | 352 22 | 295 43 | 2 | 14 | 28 | 18 | 6 |
| 24 | 353 27 | 296 53 | 3 | 15 | 29 | 19 | 7 |
| | | | | | Taur. | | |
| 25 | 354 32 | 298  3 | 4 | 16 | 1 | 20 | 8 |
| 26 | 355 38 | 299 13 | 5 | 17 | 2 | 21 | 9 |
| 27 | 356 44 | 300 22 | 6 | 19 | 3 | 22 | 10 |
| 28 | 357 49 | 301 29 | 7 | 20 | 4 | 23 | 11 |
| 29 | 358 54 | 302 35 | 8 | 21 | 5 | 24 | 12 |
| 30 | 360  0 | 303 42 | 9 | 22 | 7 | 25 | 13 |

# CAPRICORNUS

| Gradus ascendentis & locus solis | Ascenciones Sagittarii in circulo directo g. m. | Ascenciones Sagittarii in latitudine 51° 50' g. m. | II Aquar. g. | III Pisc. g. | IV Taur. g. | V Taur. g. | VI Gem. g. |
|---|---|---|---|---|---|---|---|
| 1 | 1 6 | 304 47 | 10 | 23 | 7 | 26 | 14 |
| 2 | 2 11 | 305 51 | 11 | 25 | 9 | 27 | 15 |
| 3 | 3 16 | 306 54 | 13 | 26 | 10 | 28 | 16 |
| 4 | 4 22 | 307 57 | 14 | 27 | 11 | 29 | 17 |
| | | | | | | Gem. | |
| 5 | 5 28 | 308 59 | 15 | 28 | 12 | 1 | 18 |
| 6 | 6 33 | 309 59 | 16 | 29 | 13 | 1 | 18 |
| 7 | 7 38 | 310 59 | 17 | 30 | 14 | 2 | 18 |
| | | | | Aries | | | |
| 8 | 8 43 | 311 58 | 18 | 1 | 15 | 3 | 20 |
| 9 | 9 48 | 312 56 | 19 | 3 | 16 | 4 | 21 |
| 10 | 10 53 | 313 54 | 20 | 4 | 17 | 5 | 22 |
| 11 | 11 58 | 314 50 | 22 | 5 | 18 | 6 | 24 |
| 12 | 13 3 | 315 46 | 22 | 6 | 19 | 7 | 24 |
| 13 | 14 8 | 316 41 | 23 | 7 | 20 | 8 | 25 |
| 14 | 15 13 | 317 35 | 24 | 8 | 21 | 9 | 26 |
| 15 | 16 18 | 318 28 | 25 | 9 | 21 | 10 | 27 |
| 16 | 17 23 | 319 21 | 26 | 10 | 22 | 11 | 28 |
| 17 | 18 27 | 320 12 | 27 | 11 | 23 | 12 | 29 |
| | | | | | | | Canc. |
| 18 | 19 31 | 321 2 | 28 | 12 | 24 | 13 | 1 |
| 19 | 20 35 | 321 52 | 29 | 13 | 25 | 13 | 1 |
| 20 | 21 39 | 322 41 | 30 | 14 | 26 | 14 | 2 |
| | | | Pisc. | | | | |
| 21 | 22 43 | 323 30 | 1 | 15 | 26 | 15 | 3 |
| 22 | 23 47 | 324 17 | 2 | 16 | 27 | 16 | 4 |
| 23 | 24 51 | 325 5 | 3 | 17 | 28 | 17 | 5 |
| 24 | 25 55 | 325 51 | 4 | 18 | 29 | 17 | 6 |
| 25 | 26 58 | 326 36 | 5 | 19 | 29 | 18 | 7 |
| 26 | 28 1 | 327 20 | 7 | 20 | 30 | 18 | 8 |
| | | | | | Gem. | | |
| 27 | 29 4 | 328 4 | 7 | 20 | 1 | 18 | 8 |
| 28 | 30 7 | 328 47 | 8 | 21 | 1 | 20 | 9 |
| 29 | 31 10 | 329 30 | 9 | 22 | 2 | 20 | 10 |
| 30 | 32 13 | 330 12 | 10 | 23 | 3 | 21 | 11 |

# AQUARIUS

| Gradus ascendentis & locus solis | Ascenciones Sagittarii in circulo directo | | Ascenciones Sagittarii in latitudine 51° 50′ | | II Pisc. | III Aries | IV Gem. | V Gem. | VI Canc. |
|---|---|---|---|---|---|---|---|---|---|
| | g. | m. | g. | m. | g. | g. | g. | g. | g. |
| 1 | 33 | 15 | 330 | 53 | 11 | 24 | 3 | 22 | 13 |
| 2 | 34 | 17 | 331 | 34 | 12 | 25 | 4 | 23 | 14 |
| 3 | 35 | 19 | 332 | 14 | 13 | 26 | 5 | 23 | 15 |
| 4 | 36 | 21 | 332 | 53 | 14 | 26 | 5 | 24 | 15 |
| 5 | 37 | 23 | 333 | 32 | 15 | 27 | 6 | 25 | 16 |
| 6 | 38 | 24 | 334 | 10 | 16 | 28 | 7 | 26 | 17 |
| 7 | 39 | 26 | 334 | 49 | 17 | 29 | 7 | 26 | 18 |
| 8 | 40 | 27 | 335 | 25 | 18 | 30 | 8 | 27 | 19 |
| 9 | 41 | 28 | 336 | 2 | 19 | 30 | 8 | 28 | 20 |
| | | | | | | Taur. | | | |
| 10 | 42 | 29 | 336 | 38 | 20 | 1 | 9 | 28 | 20 |
| 11 | 43 | 29 | 337 | 12 | 21 | 2 | 10 | 29 | 21 |
| | | | | | | | | Canc. | |
| 12 | 44 | 30 | 337 | 48 | 22 | 3 | 10 | 1 | 22 |
| 13 | 45 | 30 | 338 | 22 | 23 | 3 | 11 | 1 | 23 |
| 14 | 46 | 30 | 338 | 56 | 24 | 4 | 11 | 2 | 24 |
| 15 | 47 | 30 | 339 | 31 | 25 | 5 | 12 | 2 | 24 |
| 16 | 48 | 30 | 340 | 4 | 26 | 6 | 12 | 3 | 25 |
| 17 | 49 | 28 | 340 | 36 | 27 | 6 | 13 | 4 | 27 |
| 18 | 50 | 27 | 341 | 8 | 28 | 7 | 13 | 4 | 27 |
| 19 | 51 | 26 | 341 | 40 | 29 | 8 | 14 | 5 | 28 |
| 20 | 52 | 25 | 342 | 12 | 29 | 9 | 14 | 6 | 28 |
| 21 | 53 | 24 | 342 | 43 | 30 | 9 | 15 | 6 | 29 |
| | | | | | Aries | | | | |
| 22 | 54 | 22 | 343 | 14 | 1 | 10 | 15 | 7 | 30 |
| 23 | 55 | 20 | 343 | 44 | 2 | 11 | 16 | 7 | 30 |
| | | | | | | | | | Leo |
| 24 | 56 | 18 | 344 | 14 | 3 | 11 | 16 | 8 | 1 |
| 25 | 57 | 16 | 344 | 44 | 4 | 12 | 16 | 9 | 1 |
| 26 | 58 | 14 | 345 | 14 | 5 | 13 | 17 | 9 | 2 |
| 27 | 59 | 13 | 345 | 43 | 6 | 13 | 17 | 10 | 3 |
| 28 | 60 | 12 | 346 | 12 | 7 | 14 | 18 | 10 | 4 |
| 29 | 61 | 10 | 346 | 41 | 7 | 15 | 18 | 11 | 4 |
| 30 | 62 | 7 | 347 | 9 | 8 | 15 | 18 | 13 | 5 |

# PISCES

| Gradus ascendentis & locus solis | Ascenciones Sagittarii in circulo directo | | Ascenciones Sagittarii in latitudine 51° 50′ | | Equaciones domorum ad latitudinem 51 graduum et 50 minutorum | | | | |
|---|---|---|---|---|---|---|---|---|---|
| | | | | | II Aries | III Taur. | IV Gem. | V Canc. | VI Leo |
| | g. | m. | g. | m. | g. | g. | g. | g. | g. |
| 1 | 63 | 4 | 347 | 37 | 9 | 16 | 18 | 13 | 6 |
| 2 | 64 | 1 | 348 | 4 | 10 | 16 | 18 | 14 | 7 |
| 3 | 64 | 58 | 348 | 32 | 11 | 17 | 18 | 14 | 8 |
| 4 | 65 | 55 | 349 | 0 | 12 | 18 | 19 | 15 | 8 |
| 5 | 66 | 52 | 349 | 27 | 13 | 18 | 20 | 15 | 9 |
| 6 | 67 | 48 | 349 | 54 | 13 | 19 | 20 | 16 | 10 |
| 7 | 68 | 45 | 350 | 21 | 14 | 19 | 21 | 17 | 11 |
| 8 | 69 | 41 | 350 | 47 | 15 | 20 | 21 | 17 | 11 |
| 9 | 70 | 37 | 351 | 13 | 16 | 21 | 22 | 18 | 12 |
| 10 | 71 | 33 | 351 | 40 | 17 | 21 | 22 | 18 | 13 |
| 11 | 72 | 29 | 352 | 5 | 18 | 22 | 22 | 19 | 14 |
| 12 | 73 | 25 | 352 | 31 | 18 | 22 | 22 | 19 | 14 |
| 13 | 74 | 21 | 352 | 57 | 19 | 23 | 23 | 20 | 15 |
| 14 | 75 | 17 | 353 | 23 | 20 | 24 | 24 | 21 | 16 |
| 15 | 76 | 12 | 353 | 48 | 21 | 24 | 24 | 21 | 17 |
| 16 | 77 | 8 | 354 | 13 | 22 | 25 | 24 | 22 | 17 |
| 17 | 78 | 3 | 354 | 38 | 22 | 25 | 25 | 22 | 18 |
| 18 | 78 | 59 | 355 | 4 | 22 | 26 | 25 | 22 | 19 |
| 19 | 79 | 54 | 355 | 29 | 24 | 26 | 25 | 23 | 20 |
| 20 | 80 | 49 | 355 | 54 | 25 | 27 | 26 | 24 | 21 |
| 21 | 81 | 44 | 356 | 18 | 26 | 28 | 26 | 24 | 21 |
| 22 | 82 | 40 | 356 | 44 | 27 | 28 | 27 | 25 | 22 |
| 23 | 83 | 35 | 357 | 8 | 27 | 29 | 27 | 25 | 23 |
| 24 | 84 | 30 | 357 | 33 | 28 | 29 | 27 | 27 | 24 |
| 25 | 85 | 25 | 357 | 57 | 29 | 30 | 28 | 27 | 24 |
| 26 | 86 | 20 | 358 | 22 | 30 | 30 | 28 | 27 | 25 |
| | | | | | | Gem. | | | |
| 27 | 87 | 15 | 358 | 46 | 30 | 1 | 28 | 28 | 26 |
| | | | | | Taur. | | | | |
| 28 | 88 | 10 | 359 | 11 | 1 | 2 | 29 | 28 | 27 |
| 29 | 89 | 5 | 359 | 35 | 2 | 2 | 29 | 29 | 28 |
| 30 | 90 | 0 | 360 | 0 | 3 | 3 | 30 | 29 | 28 |

# Tabula ad sciendum pro qualibet hora diei vel noctis quis planeta regnat

| Hore | Solis | Lune | Martis | Mercurii | Jovis | Veneris | Saturni | Incipiendo diem ab ortu solis |
|---|---|---|---|---|---|---|---|---|
| 1 | Sol | Luna | Mars | Mercurius | Jupiter | Venus | Saturnus | humidus movetur. |
| 2 | Venus | Saturnus | Sol | Luna | Mars | Mercurius | Jupiter | |
| 3 | Mercurius | Jupiter | Venus | Saturnus | Sol | Luna | Mars | |
| 4 | Luna | Mars | Mercurius | Jupiter | Venus | Saturnus | Sol | Calida et sicca colera dominatur. |
| 5 | Saturnus | Sol | Luna | Mars | Mercurius | Jupiter | Venus | |
| 6 | Jupiter | Venus | Saturnus | Sol | Luna | Mars | Mercurius | |
| 7 | Mars | Mercurius | Jupiter | Venus | Saturnus | Sol | Luna | |
| 8 | Sol | Luna | Mars | Mercurius | Jupiter | Venus | Saturnus | |
| 9 | Venus | Saturnus | Sol | Luna | Mars | Mercurius | Jupiter | |
| 10 | Mercurius | Jupiter | Venus | Saturnus | Sol | Luna | Mars | Frigida et sicca melencolia regnat. |
| 11 | Luna | Mars | Mercurius | Jupiter | Venus | Saturnus | Sol | |
| 12 | Saturnus | Sol | Luna | Mars | Mercurius | Jupiter | Venus | |
| 13 | Jupiter | Venus | Saturnus | Sol | Luna | Mars | Mercurius | |
| 14 | Mars | Mercurius | Jupiter | Venus | Saturnus | Sol | Luna | |
| 15 | Sol | Luna | Mars | Mercurius | Jupiter | Venus | Saturnus | |

| | | | | | | Frigida et humida fleuma habundat. | Calidus et sanguis |
|---|---|---|---|---|---|---|---|
| 16 | Venus | Saturnus | Sol | Luna | Mars | Mercurius | Jupiter |
| 17 | Mercurius | Jupiter | Venus | Saturnus | Sol | Luna | Mars |
| 18 | Luna | Mars | Mercurius | Jupiter | Venus | Saturnus | Sol |
| 19 | Saturnus | Sol | Luna | Mars | Mercurius | Jupiter | Venus |
| 20 | Jupiter | Venus | Saturnus | Sol | Luna | Mars | Mercurius |
| 21 | Mars | Mercurius | Jupiter | Venus | Saturnus | Sol | Luna |
| 22 | Sol | Luna | Mars | Mercurius | Jupiter | Venus | Saturnus |
| 23 | Venus | Saturnus | Sol | Luna | Mars | Mercurius | Jupiter |
| 24 | Mercurius | Jupiter | Venus | Saturnus | Sol | Luna | Mars |

Jupiter atque Venus boni sunt. Saturnus Mars que maligni.
Sol et Mercurius cum Luna sunt mediocres.

| | | | |
|---|---|---|---|
| Attractive | Triplicitas | ignea | Aries Leo Sagittarius |
| Digestive | Triplicitas | aerea | Gemini Libra Aquarius |
| Retentive | Triplicitas | terrea | Taurus Virgo Capricornus |
| Expulsive | Triplicitas | aquea | Cancer Scorpio Pisces |

| Ciclus Decennovenalis | A | | | B | | | C | | | D | | |
|---|---|---|---|---|---|---|---|---|---|---|---|---|
| | Septuagesima | Pascha | Pentecoste | Septuagesima | Pascha | Pentecoste | Septuagesima | Pascha | Pentecoste | Septuagesima | Pascha | Pentecoste | Septuagesima |
| | Jan. Feb. | Mar. Apr. | May Jun. | Jan. Feb. | Mar. Apr. | May Jun. | Jan. Feb. | Mar. Apr. | May Jun. | Jan. Feb. | Mar. Apr. | May Jun. | Jan. Feb. |
| | d. | d. | d. | d. | d. | d. | d. | d. | d. | d. | d. | d. | d. |
| 1 | 5 | 9 | 28 | 6 | 10 | 29 | 7 | 11 | 30 | 8 | 12 | 31 | 2 |
| 2 | 22 | 26 | 14 | 23 | 27 | 15 | 24 | 28 | 16 | 25 | 29 | 17 | 26 |
| 3 | 12 | 16 | 4 | 13 | 17 | 5 | 14 | 18 | 6 | 15 | 19 | 7 | 16 |
| 4 | 5 | 9 | 28 | 30 | 3 | 22 | 31 | 4 | 23 | 1 | 5 | 24 | 2 |
| 5 | 22 | 26 | 14 | 23 | 27 | 15 | 24 | 28 | 16 | 25 | 29 | 17 | 19 |
| 6 | 12 | 16 | 4 | 13 | 17 | 5 | 7 | 11 | 30 | 8 | 12 | 31 | 9 |
| 7 | 29 | 2 | 21 | 30 | 3 | 22 | 31 | 4 | 23 | 1 | 5 | 24 | 2 |
| 8 | 19 | 23 | 11 | 20 | 24 | 12 | 21 | 25 | 13 | 15 | 19 | 7 | 16 |
| 9 | 5 | 9 | 28 | 6 | 10 | 29 | 7 | 11 | 30 | 8 | 12 | 31 | 9 |
| 10 | 29 | 2 | 21 | 30 | 3 | 22 | 24 | 28 | 16 | 25 | 29 | 17 | 26 |
| 11 | 12 | 16 | 4 | 13 | 17 | 5 | 14 | 18 | 6 | 15 | 19 | 7 | 16 |
| 12 | 5 | 9 | 28 | 6 | 10 | 29 | 7 | 11 | 30 | 1 | 5 | 24 | 2 |
| 13 | 22 | 26 | 14 | 23 | 27 | 15 | 24 | 28 | 16 | 25 | 29 | 17 | 26 |
| 14 | 12 | 16 | 4 | 13 | 17 | 5 | 14 | 18 | 6 | 15 | 19 | 7 | 9 |
| 15 | 29 | 2 | 21 | 30 | 3 | 22 | 31 | 4 | 23 | 1 | 5 | 24 | 2 |
| 16 | 22 | 26 | 14 | 23 | 27 | 15 | 24 | 28 | 16 | 18 | 22 | 10 | 19 |
| 17 | 12 | 16 | 4 | 6 | 10 | 29 | 7 | 11 | 30 | 8 | 12 | 31 | 9 |
| 18 | 29 | 2 | 21 | 30 | 3 | 22 | 31 | 4 | 23 | 1 | 5 | 24 | 26 |
| 19 | 19 | 23 | 11 | 20 | 24 | 12 | 14 | 18 | 6 | 15 | 19 | 7 | 16 |

Quis planeta quem humorem proicit.
Saturnus melencoliam et egritudines melencolias.
Mars coleram et egritudines coleras.
Jupiter Sol et Venus sanguinem et eius egritudines.
Luna fleuma et eius egritudines.
Mercurius omnis equaliter prout est communitus.

# duodena que mille
descende futuris

| E | | | F | | | G | |
|---|---|---|---|---|---|---|---|
| Pascha | Pentecoste | Septuagesima | Pascha | Pentecoste | Septuagesima | Pascha | Pentecoste |
| Mar. Apr. | May Jun. | Jan. Feb. | Mar. Apr. | May Jun. | Jan. Feb. | Mar. Apr. | May Jun. |
| d. | d. | d. | d. | d. | d. | d. | d. |
| 6 | 25 | 3 | 7 | 26 | 4 | 8 | 27 |
| 30 | 18 | 27 | 31 | 19 | 28 | 1 | 20 |
| 20 | 8 | 10 | 14 | 2 | 11 | 15 | 3 |
| 6 | 25 | 3 | 7 | 26 | 4 | 8 | 27 |
| 23 | 11 | 20 | 24 | 12 | 21 | 25 | 13 |
| 13 | 1 | 10 | 14 | 2 | 11 | 15 | 3 |
| 6 | 25 | 27 | 31 | 19 | 28 | 1 | 20 |
| 20 | 8 | 17 | 21 | 9 | 18 | 22 | 10 |
| 13 | 1 | 10 | 14 | 2 | 4 | 8 | 27 |
| 30 | 18 | 27 | 31 | 19 | 28 | 1 | 20 |
| 20 | 8 | 17 | 21 | 9 | 18 | 22 | 10 |
| 6 | 25 | 3 | 7 | 26 | 4 | 8 | 27 |
| 30 | 18 | 27 | 31 | 19 | 21 | 25 | 13 |
| 13 | 1 | 10 | 14 | 2 | 11 | 15 | 3 |
| 6 | 25 | 3 | 7 | 26 | 4 | 8 | 27 |
| 23 | 11 | 20 | 24 | 12 | 21 | 25 | 13 |
| 13 | 1 | 10 | 14 | 2 | 11 | 15 | 3 |
| 30 | 18 | 27 | 31 | 19 | 28 | 1 | 20 |
| 20 | 8 | 17 | 21 | 9 | 18 | 22 | 10 |

Centum quarta tenet viginti mille ve quinta. Si pro preteritis scandas descende futuris.

Hec parva subsequens tabula pro littera dominicali invenienda incipit anno Christi 1381 anno cicli solaris primo cicli vero decennovenali 14

| Ciclus solaris | | | | |
|---|---|---|---|---|
| 1 | f | e | d | c | b |
| 5 | a | g | f | e | d |
| 9 | c | b | a | g | f |
| 13 | e | d | c | b | a |
| 17 | g | f | e | d | c |
| 21 | b | a | g | f | e |
| 25 | d | c | b | a | g |

# Tabula ad inveniendum

| Signa | Domini domorum | Domini exaltacionum | | Domini triplicitatum | | | Termini | |
|-------|----------------|---------------------|---|---|---|---|---|---|
| Aries | Mars | Sol | 19 | Sol | Jupiter | Saturn. | Jupiter | 6 |
| Taur. | Venus | Luna | 3 | Venus | Luna | Mars | Venus | 8 |
| Gem. | M'curi. | Caput | 3 | Saturn. | M'curi. | Jupiter | M'curi. | 6 |
| Canc. | Luna | Jupiter | 15 | Venus | Mars | Luna | Mars | 7 |
| Leo | Sol | | | Sol | Jupiter | Saturn. | Jupiter | 6 |
| Virgo | M'curi. | M'curi. | 15 | Venus | Luna | Mars | M'curi. | 7 |
| Libra | Venus | Saturn. | 21 | Saturn. | M'curi. | Jupiter | Saturn. | 6 |
| Scorp. | Mars | | | Venus | Mars | Luna | Mars | 7 |
| Sag. | Jupiter | Cauda | 3 | Sol | Jupiter | Saturn. | Jupiter | 12 |
| Capr. | Saturn. | Mars | 28 | Venus | Luna | Mars | M'curi. | 7 |
| Aquar. | Saturn. | | | Saturn. | M'curi. | Jupiter | M'curi. | 7 |
| Pisc. | Jupiter | Venus | 27 | Venus | Mars | Luna | Venus | 12 |

# Tabula continuacionis motus solis

| Anni christi | m. | s. | Anni christi | m. | s. |
|--------------|----|----|--------------|----|----|
| 1385 | 0 | 0 | 1429 | 19 | 9 |
| 1389 | 1 | 44 | 1433 | 20 | 54 |
| 1393 | 3 | 29 | 1437 | 22 | 38 |
| 1397 | 5 | 14 | 1441 | 24 | 22 |
| 1401 | 6 | 47 | 1445 | 26 | 7 |
| 1405 | 8 | 42 | 1449 | 27 | 52 |
| 1409 | 10 | 46 | 1453 | 29 | 37 |
| 1413 | 12 | 11 | 1457 | 31 | 22 |
| 1417 | 13 | 55 | 1461 | 33 | 6 |
| 1421 | 15 | 39 | 1465 | 34 | 51 |
| 1425 | 17 | 24 | 1469 | 36 | 36 |

# dignitates planetarum in signis

| planetarum in signis secundum Egypcios et dicuntur esse hermetis | | | | | | | | Domini facierum | | |
|---|---|---|---|---|---|---|---|---|---|---|
| Venus | 6 | M'curi. | 8 | Mars | 5 | Saturn. | 5 | Mars | Sol | Venus |
| M'curi. | 6 | Jupiter | 8 | Saturn. | 5 | Mars | 3 | M'curi. | Luna | Saturn. |
| Jupiter | 6 | Venus | 5 | Mars | 7 | Saturn. | 6 | Jupiter | Mars | Sol |
| Venus | 6 | M'curi. | 6 | Jupiter | 7 | Saturn. | 4 | Venus | M'curi. | Luna |
| Venus | 5 | Saturn. | 7 | M'curi. | 6 | Mars | 6 | Saturn. | Jupiter | Mars |
| Venus | 10 | Jupiter | 4 | Mars | 7 | Saturn. | 9 | Sol | Venus | M'curi. |
| M'curi. | 8 | Jupiter | 7 | Venus | 7 | Mars | 2 | Luna | Saturn. | Jupiter |
| Venus | 4 | M'curi. | 8 | Jupiter | 5 | Saturn. | 6 | Mars | Sol | Venus |
| Venus | 5 | M'curi. | 4 | Saturn. | 5 | Mars | 4 | M'curi. | Luna | Saturn. |
| Jupiter | 7 | Venus | 8 | Saturn. | 4 | Mars | 4 | Jupiter | Mars | Sol |
| Venus | 6 | Jupiter | 7 | Mars | 5 | Saturn. | 5 | Venus | M'curi. | Luna |
| Jupiter | 4 | M'curi. | 3 | Mars | 9 | Saturn. | 2 | Saturn. | Jupiter | Mars |

# Tabula ad sciendum in quo signo et in quo gradu

| Gradus | | | | | |
|---|---|---|---|---|---|
| 1<br>2 | Aries | Taur. | Gem. | Canc. | Leo | Virgo |
| 3<br>4 | Taur. | Gem. | Canc. | Leo | Virgo | Libra |
| 5<br>6 | Gem. | Canc. | Leo | Virgo | Libra | Scorp. |
| 7<br>8<br>9 | Canc. | Leo | Virgo | Libra | Scorp. | Sag. |
| 10<br>11 | Leo | Virgo | Libra | Scorp. | Sag. | Capr. |
| 12<br>13 | Virgo | Libra | Scorp. | Sag. | Capr. | Aquar. |
| 14<br>15 | Libra | Scorp. | Sag. | Capr. | Aquar. | Pisc. |
| 16<br>17<br>18 | Scorp. | Sag. | Capr. | Aquar. | Pisc. | Aries |
| 19<br>20 | Sag. | Capr. | Aquar. | Pisc. | Aries | Taur. |
| 21<br>22 | Capr. | Aquar. | Pisc. | Aries | Taur. | Gem. |
| 23<br>24<br>25 | Aquar. | Pisc. | Aries | Taur. | Gem. | Canc. |
| 26<br>27 | Pisc. | Aries | Taur. | Gem. | Canc. | Leo |
| 28<br>29<br>30 | Aries | Taur. | Gem. | Canc. | Leo | Virgo |
| | Habet capud & faciem | Habet collum & gutturis nodum | Habet humeros brachios & manus | Habet cor pectus & pulmonem | Habet latus dorsum & stomacum | Habet epartem & intestina |

signi luna fuerit omni die secundum motum

| | | | | | | g. | m. |
|---|---|---|---|---|---|---|---|
| Libra | Scorp. | Sag. | Capr. | Aquar. | Pisc. | 13 | 10 |
| | | | | | | 26 | 20 |
| Scorp. | Sag. | Capr. | Aquar. | Pisc. | Aries | 9 | 31 |
| | | | | | | 22 | 42 |
| Sag. | Capr. | Aquar. | Pisc. | Aries | Taur. | 5 | 52 |
| | | | | | | 19 | 3 |
| Capr. | Aquar. | Pisc. | Aries | Taur. | Gem. | 2 | 14 |
| | | | | | | 15 | 24 |
| | | | | | | 28 | 35 |
| Aquar. | Pisc. | Aries | Taur. | Gem. | Canc. | 10 | 45 |
| | | | | | | 23 | 56 |
| Pisc. | Aries | Taur. | Gem. | Canc. | Leo | 8 | 6 |
| | | | | | | 21 | 17 |
| Aries | Taur. | Gem. | Canc. | Leo | Virgo | 4 | 28 |
| | | | | | | 17 | 38 |
| Taur. | Gem. | Canc. | Leo | Virgo | Libra | 0 | 49 |
| | | | | | | 13 | 59 |
| | | | | | | 27 | 10 |
| Gem. | Canc. | Leo | Virgo | Libra | Scorp. | 10 | 21 |
| | | | | | | 23 | 31 |
| Canc. | Leo | Virgo | Libra | Scorp. | Sag. | 6 | 42 |
| | | | | | | 19 | 52 |
| Leo | Virgo | Libra | Scorp. | Sag. | Capr. | 3 | 3 |
| | | | | | | 16 | 13 |
| | | | | | | 29 | 24 |
| Virgo | Libra | Scorp. | Sag. | Capr. | Aquar. | 12 | 35 |
| | | | | | | 25 | 45 |
| Libra | Scorp. | Sag. | Capr. | Aquar. | Pisc. | 8 | 56 |
| | | | | | | 22 | 6 |
| | | | | | | 5 | 17 |

| Habet lumbos renes & hancas | Habet basa semi-naria & femorem | Habet coxas & femoralia | Habet genua | Habet tibias & crura | Habet pedes |
|---|---|---|---|---|---|

[183]

To clarify further the points set out at the beginning of this calendar it should be noted: First, in order to determine the degree [in the zodiac] of the sun [one should see] that the sun in this calendar is adjusted to the year of Christ 1385, which was the first year after the leap year, and to every day of that year; and for that year, and for any of its days, the true place of the sun appears for the noon of that day in the ninth sphere according to the degree and minute in the table corresponding to the description given of the same. For the second year after the leap year 15 minutes must be deducted; for the third year, 30 minutes. And for the fourth year, which will be the leap year, 45 minutes up to the 24th day of the month of February inclusive; and the true place of the sun is established for any day of those years. On the 25th day of February in the leap year, on which day is to be celebrated the Feast of St. Matthew, 15 minutes must be added to the degrees and the minutes in that table; then the true place of the sun for that day will be evident, and the same is done for each day of that year. And then one must return to the first year after the leap year, and one must do the same again. For the sun returns once more to practically the same place, except for a small variation which will not create an error in a man's lifetime to the extent of one degree, so that in 136 years the sun is scarcely anticipated by a single degree. Nevertheless, whoever may wish to know precisely its true place should turn to the completed years of Christ in the table of the continuations of the motion of the sun found at the end of this calendar. And if he shall find precisely these years in their proper line in that table, let him add the corresponding number in the [adjacent] column to the true position of the sun as established by the means just described for establishing it, and the result is the true place of the sun on that day at noon in the city of

*Title to Canon 1 (from As¹)* om LS¹A¹DBR; Incipit canonicum de omnibus punctis precedentibus Ad; Canon kalendarii A². 1 **autem** om S¹A¹D. 1-2 **in . . . positorum** precedencium As¹RAdA². 2 **est notandum** om A². 3 ***inveniendo** (from S¹A¹DBAs¹)* inveniendus LR; inveniendum Ad. **quod sol** om As¹; quod Ad; est notandum A². 6 **eiusdem** anni illius Ad. 7 **secundum** sit secundum eius A². **gradum** om A¹As¹Ad. 10 **minuta** *(2nd)* om Ad. 12 **et** om S¹. 14-15 **Mathie** add apostoli Ad. 15 **15** 25 R. 16 **eadem** eodem A². 19 **prius** add Quantitates eciam dierum artificialium vulgarium et crepusculorum patent expresse per tabulas earum discripcionibus corespondentes A². 20 **que** quia As¹A². 21 **faciet** faceret DBAd; facit As¹A². 23-43 **Tamen . . . intentum** om As¹. 23-57 **Tamen . . . curetur** om AdA². 24 **in** om B. 25-26 **fine . . . positam** fine kalendario isto positam A¹; kalendario isto positam D. 25 **huius** om A¹. 27 **precise** precipne B. **directo** directa R. 30 **locus** add solis S¹A¹DBR. 37

Pro declaracione autem punctorum in principio huius
kalendarii positorum est notandum: Primo pro gradu
solis inveniendo quod sol in kalendario isto equatur ad
annum Christi 1385, qui erat annus primus post bisextum et ad singulos dies anni illius; et pro anno illo, et    5
quolibet die eiusdem; pro meridie illius diei patet verus
locus solis in nona spera secundum gradum et minutum
in tabula corespondente descripcioni eiusdem posita.
Pro secundo anno post bisextum minuenda sunt 15
minuta; pro tercio anno, 30 minuta. Et pro quarto anno,    10
qui erit annus bisextilis, 45 minuta usque ad 24 diem
mensis Februarii inclusive; et habetur pro quolibet die
istorum annorum verus locus solis. In 25 die Februarii in
anno bisextili, quo die celebrabitur Festum Sancti Mathie, addenda sunt 15 minuta ad gradus et minuta in    15
eadem tabula; et exurget verus locus solis pro die illo,
et sic fiat pro singulis diebus eiusdem anni. Et tunc
redeundum est ad primum annum post bisextum, et
operandum est secundum prius. Quia sol iterum rever-
titur ad eundem locum fere preter rem modicam, que in    20
vita unius hominis non faciet errorem per unum
gradum, ita quod in 136 annis sol vix per unum gradum
anticipatur. Tamen siquis eius verum locum precise
habere voluerit intret cum annis Christi perfectis in
tabulam continuacionis motus solis in fine huius kalen-    25
darii positam. Et si annos illos in linea numeri illius
tabule precise invenerit, illud quod in eorum directo
fuerit addat ad verum locum solis inventum per ea que
iam dicta sunt ad eius locum verum inveniendum, et
exurget pro die illo verus locus ad meridiem civitatis    30
Oxoniensis. Si vero numerum annorum Christi perfec-

Oxford. If, however, he does not find exactly the number of the completed years of Christ, let him then start with the closest lower number given in the table and that which was in its column; add them together. Then let him note down the next higher number and add also what is in its column. Then take the lesser from the greater and note the difference. Let him take of that difference as much as is a quarter of the excess of the completed years of Christ over the years of Christ found in the table, which part together with what was found in the column of the nearest lower years of Christ set out in the table, let him add to the true place of the sun found as before by means of his canon, and he will have achieved his objective.

## [2] CANON FOR THE LENGTHS OF THE DAYS

In addition, the lengths of the artificial [and] vulgar days and of the morning and evening twilights can be seen clearly by means of the tables corresponding to their descriptions. But it is to be noted here that the lengths of these, namely, of the artificial [and] vulgar days and the twilights set out in this calendar apply to the first year after the leap year. In other years, however, there is a slight difference. Besides, they refer specifically to the location of the city of Oxford. But in places toward the east or the west there is no difference. In places toward the south the days are longer in winter and shorter in summer. And in places to the north the opposite happens. However, such increase or diminution is not very great and is not even uniform. In consequence no account is taken here of this variation of the length of days.

accipiat *add* partes BR. 38 **annorum** *add* ut R. 41 \***fuit** (*from* S¹A¹DBR) fuit
fuit L. *Title to Canon 2* (*from* R) *om* LS¹A¹DBAs¹. 45 **matutini et vespertini**
*om* BAs¹R. **expresse** expressem S¹A¹. 46–57 **Set . . . curetur** *om* As¹. 47 **est hic**
*om* BR. **set** scilicet S¹BR; silicet A¹D. 50 **differencia** *add* ut aliquam in uno
minuto vel duobus vel in nullo unum de homino non sit cura quibus quod
modicum distat que secundo distare videtur R. 50–57 **Specialiter . . . curetur**
*om* R. 52 **vel** et B. 55 **econtra** econtrario D. **augmentacio** aumentacione D.
57 **hic non** *om* S¹; hunc non B. *Title to Canon 3* (*from* As¹) *om* LS¹A¹DBAd;

torum precise non invenerit, intret tunc cum numero
minori et propinquiori posito in tabula et illud quod in
eius directo fuerit, sumat deinde eciam intret cum
numero maiori propinquiori et sumat eciam quod in     35
eius directo fuerit; et minus de maiori demat et servet
differenciam. Et illius differencie accipiat totam quota
pars de quatuor est excessus annorum Christi perfec-
torum super annos Christi in tabula inventos, quam
partem, cum illo quod in directo annorum Christi      40
minorum propinquiorum in tabula, inventorum fuit
inventum ad verum locum solis inventum ut prius per
eius canonem addat et habebit intentum.

## [2] CANON PRO QUANTITATIBUS DIERUM

Quantitates autem dierum artificialium vulgarium et
crepusculorum matutini et vespertini patent expresse   45
per tabulas earum descripcionibus corespondentes. Set
notandum est hic quod illorum quantitates set dierum
artificialium vulgarium et crepusculorum in kalendario
isto assignate respiciunt primum annum post bisextum.
In aliis autem annis modica est differencia. Specialiter  50
eciam respiciunt locum civitatis Oxoniensis. Set in locis
versus orientem vel occidentem nulla est differencia. In
locis versus meridiem augmentantur dies hiemis et
minuuntur dies estatis. Et in locis versus septentrionem
econtra contingit. Talis autem augmentacio sive dimi-   55
nucio non est valde magna et eciam non est uniformis.
Unde de ista variacione dierum hic non curetur.

## [3] CANON OF THE TABLE FOR THE CONJUNCTIONS AND OPPOSITIONS OF THE SUN AND MOON

If somebody, however, wants to find the conjunctions and oppositions of the sun and moon with the time of the new moon, let him look in the table of conjunction if what he wants to know is the conjunction, or let him look in the table of opposition if what he wants is the opposition, under the [Metonic] cycle in which he is, taking the hours and minutes in its column, because these are the hours and fractions of hours from noon of the preceding day up to that conjunction or opposition which was being sought.

## [4] CANON FOR KNOWING THE HOURS OF THE CLOCK AT SUNRISE AND SUNSET

Now when one wishes to know clock time at dawn, let him take the hours with the minutes which he will find in the table named, "the lengths of time from midnight to dawn," in the column of the day in question, and he will have his answer. Let him do the same thing when he wants to know clock time at sunrise or sunset, and also at the end of the evening twilight, by looking in the table designed to determine the time that is sought.

## [5] CANON FOR KNOWING THE EQUAL HOURS OF THE CLOCK ON THE ARTIFICIAL DAY

Now when one may wish to know the hours of the clock and their minutes, let him take the altitude of the sun by some instrument, or take his own shadow according to the measure of six feet of the same,

Canon pro conjunccionibus et opposicionibus R; Canon conjunccionibus A². 61 **opposicionis** illam As¹Ad. 62 **minuta** add que AdA². 63 **eius** add ferunt AdA². **hore et** hores et R; *om* Ad. **horarum** *add* hore Ad. *Title to Canon 4 (from* **As¹**) *om* LA¹DBAdA²; per clok S¹; Canon pro quantitate inicii diei super clok R. 66-74 **Cum . . . ordinatam** *om* Ad. 66 **scire** *om* As¹. 68 **minutis** *add* suis A¹D. **quas invenerit** *om* As¹A². **quantitates** quantite S¹A¹; sic quantitates As¹; quantitatas R; pro quantite A². 69 **medio** *add* usque R. 71 **quantitatem** quantitatas As¹. **super . . . solis** in ortu solis super clok R. **solis** *add* si A¹A²; *add* tum eam As¹. 72 **vel** *add* a meridie As¹A². *Title to Canon 5 (from* **As¹**) *om* LA¹DBAd; Canon per clok S¹; Canon pro horis equalibus scilicet per horis de clok R; Canon per horas de clok A². 75 **eciam . . . scire** eciam scire As¹Ad; scire eciam R. **voluerit** *add* quis As¹. 76 **minuta** *add* diei artificialis As¹. 77 **secundum** per S¹; scilicet BR. 78-79 **alicuius . . . erecte** *om* As¹. 82 **et** *om* R.

188

## [3] CANON TABULE CONJUNCCIONUM ET OPPOSICIONUM SOLIS ET LUNE

Conjuncciones vero et opposiciones solis et lune siquis invenire desiderat cum numero sue primacionis, intret tabulam conjunccionis si conjunccionem habere volu- 60 erit, vel intret tabulam opposicionis si opposicionem querat, sub ciclo in quo est, accipiendo horas et minuta in directo eius, quia ille sunt hore et fracciones horarum a meridie diei precedentis usque ad illam conjunc- cionem seu opposicionem de qua fit inquisicio. 65

## [4] CANON AD SCIENDUM HORAS DE CLOK IN SOLIS ORTU ET IN OCCASU

Cum autem quis scire voluerit quantitatem temporis super clok tempore inicii aurore, accipiat horas cum minutis quas invenerit in tabula intitulata, "quantitates temporis a noctis medio ad auroram," in directo diei de quo queritur, et habebit intentum. Eodemmodo faciat 70 cum quantitatem temporis super clok in ortu solis scire voluerit vel in occasu, ac eciam in fine crepusculi vespertini, intrando tabulam ad illud tempus cogno- scendum quod queritur ordinatam.

## [5] CANON AD SCIENDUM HORAS DE CLOK CUM DIE ARTIFICIALI

Cum eciam quis scire voluerit horas de clok in earum 75 minuta, accipiat altitudinem solis per aliquod instru- mentum, vel accipiat umbram sui ipsius secundum men- suram sex pedum eiusdem, seu umbram alicuius rei

or the shadow of any object set standing perpendicularly divided into six equal parts. And let him look for a similar altitude or shadow in the table made for the hours of the clock in the column of the day in question; and what he finds at the head of the table in the first line in the column of its altitude or shadow will show him the hour of the clock if it is forenoon; and if afternoon, what he finds at the top of the table in the second line. If, however, he does not find precisely the established altitude of the sun or the shadow in his table, then let him start with the altitude found in the table immediately below that established by means of the instrument, then the altitude immediately above in the table; subtract the smaller from the larger, and note the result. Then, if it is morning, let him subtract the lower altitude found in the table from the altitude established by the instrument by means of which he had sought to enter [the table] when he could not find there what he was looking for; then multiply the result by sixty and divide the product by the difference already noted; and what will result from that division will be minutes of an hour, which minutes he should add to the hours of the clock found at the head of the table in the first line in the column of the lower altitude; and he will have the hours of the clock and the minutes of the hour. If, however, it happens to be afternoon, let him subtract the altitude established by the instrument from the next higher altitude to it found in the table and multiply the remainder by sixty, and divide the product by the difference previously found; and the result of such division will be the minutes of the hour one should add to the hours found at the top of the table in the second line in the column of the higher altitude found in the table; and one will have the hours of the clock and the minutes of the hours. However, if one prefers to work with a shadow, he should proceed in the opposite way, because if he wants to find the hours of the clock in the morning by means of someone's shadow, he should work with the shadow in the way he was taught to work with the altitude of the afternoon sun. And if he wants to find the afternoon hours of the clock

**tabule** *om* Ad.  84 **si** *om* As¹A².  86-115 **Si . . . operari** *om* Ad.  91 **servet** serve B.  93 **voluit** voluerit R.  94 **intrasse** *add* tabulam A².  **quia** quam BR.  95 **sexaginta** *om* As¹.  **et** *om* As¹A².  96 **ex** de R.  98 **tabule** tabulem S¹.  102 **proxima** prima A¹A².  105 **minuta** ad A¹.  106 **maioris** maiores S¹.  108 **hore** *add* operacio eiusdem cum umbra rei R.  **Cum** Si quis S¹.  109 **contrario** econtraverso As¹A².  **modo** in A¹R.  **horas** horam As¹A².  110 **alicuius** aliquam As¹A².  111 **secundum** *add* quia DAs¹; sicut BR.  114 **secundum** sicut

perpendiculariter erecte divise in sex partes equales. Et
consimilem altitudinem seu umbram querat in tabula 80
facta pro horis de clok in directo diei de quo queritur;
et quod in capite tabule in prima linea in directo sue
altitudinis seu umbre invenerit ostendet sibi horam de
clok si fuerit ante meridiem; vel illud quod in summitate tabule fuerit in secunda linea, si fuerit post meri- 85
diem. Si vero altitudinem solis acceptam seu umbram in
sua tabula precise non invenerit, tunc intret in eam cum
altitudine minori altitudine accepta cum instrumento
proxima tantum posita in tabula, deinde cum maiori
proxima; et tunc minorem altitudinem demat de mai- 90
ori, et servet differenciam. Postea, si fuerit ante meridiem, minuat minorem altitudinem inventam in tabula
de altitudine accepta per instrumentum cum qua voluit
intrasse quia ibi invenire non potuit, et residuum mul-
tiplicet per sexaginta et productum dividat per dif- 95
ferenciam prius servatam; et illa que exeunt ex tali
divicione erunt minuta hore, que minuta addere debet
horis de clok inventis in capite tabule in prima linea in
directo minoris altitudinis; et habebit horas de clok et
minuta hore. Si autem fuerit post meridiem, minuat 100
altitudinem acceptam per instrumentum de altitudine
maiori proxima ei inventa in tabula et residuum multi-
plicet per sexaginta, et productum dividat per differenciam prius servatam; et illa que exeunt ex tali divisione
erunt minuta hore que addere debet horis inventis in 105
summitate tabule in secunda linea in directo maioris
altitudinis invente in tabula; et habebit horas de clok et
minuta hore. Cum autem operari voluerit cum umbra,
contrario modo operetur, quia si horas de clok ante
meridiem per alicuius umbram habere voluerit, oper- 110
etur cum umbra secundum docetur operari cum altitudine solis post meridiem. Et si horas de clok post

191

with the help of somebody's shadow, let him work with it as he was taught to work with the altitude of the sun in the morning.

## [6] CANON FOR DISCOVERING AN UNEQUAL HOUR OF THE ARTIFICIAL DAY

When, however, one wishes to determine an unequal hour of the artificial day, let him take from this calendar the altitude of the meridian on the desired day; and let him place a plumb line in a quadrant over the estimated altitude and draw the plumb over the thread until it reaches the contact of the sixth hour, and let the plumb remain there without moving that day. Then let him allow the rays of the sun to pass through both apertures [of the quadrant]; and then where the plumb withdraws, it will show the unequal hour for that day. But it must be noted that the midday altitudes assigned in this calendar refer specifically to the first year after leap year and the location of the city of Oxford.

If, however, in other years one wishes to know the altitude of noon, let him see if the altitude of noon on the following day is greater, as it always is from the winter solstice up to the summer solstice. Let him then see how great is the additional amount. Let him take a quarter of this additional amount and for the second year after leap year subtract it from the noontime altitude found in the table. In the third year, let him subtract two quarters, that is to say half of the additional amount. And in the fourth, which will be leap year, let him subtract three quarters until the 24th day of the month of February inclusive. But on the 25th day of the month of February of that year, namely the leap year, on which day is to be celebrated the feast of St. Matthew, the fourth part of the additional amount is added to the noon

S¹A¹DBR. *Title to Canon 6 (from As¹) om* LA¹DBAdA²; prohora inequalitate S¹; Canon pro horis inequalibus per instrumentum R. 116-73 **Cum . . . variantur** *om* A². 116 **voluerit** *om* As¹. 117 **accipiat . . . kalendarium** per istud kalendarium accipiat As¹. 119 **consiliabilem** consimilem D; siliatem B. 122 **die** *om* As¹. **permittat** mittat B. 124-73 **Set . . . variantur** *om* As¹R. 127 **Oxoniensis** Oxonii B. 128 **meridionalem** meridianum S¹A¹Ad. 130 **secundum** sicut DB. 132 *__quartam__ (from S¹A¹DBAd) quartem L. 133 *__inventa__ (from B) inventus LS¹A¹; inventam D; inventibus Ad. 135 **scilicet** set S¹. 139 **set** scilicet S¹A¹DBAd. 144 **scilicet** *om* B. 145 **scilicet in** sive Ad. 148

meridiem mediante alicuius umbra accipere voluerit, operetur cum ea secundum cum altitudine solis ante meridiem docetur operari.

## [6] CANON AD SCIENDUM HORAM INEQUALEM DIEI ARTIFICIALIS

Cum eciam quis scire voluerit horam inequalem diei artificialis, accipiat per istud kalendarium altitudinem meridionalem illius diei de quo queritur; et ponat perpendiculum in quadrante super consiliabilem altitudinem et trahat margaritam super filum quousque perveniat ad contactum hore sexte, et maneat margarita illo die immobilis. Deinde permittat radios solares transire per ambo foramina; et tunc ubi margarita ceciderit, horam inequalem illius diei ostendet. Set notandum est quod altitudines meridionales in kalendario isto assignate specialiter respiciunt primum annum post bisextum et locum civitatis Oxoniensis. Si autem in aliis annis altitudinem meridionalem quis habere voluerit, videat si altitudo meridiana sequentis diei sit maior, secundum semper est a solsticio hyemali usque ad solsticium estivale. Tunc videat excessum. De isto igitur excessu sumat quartam partem quam ab altitudine meridiana inventa in tabula subtrahat in secundo anno post bisextum. In tercio anno, subtrahat duas quartas, scilicet mediatatem excessus. Et in quarto anno, qui erit annus bisextilis, subtrahat tres quartas usque ad quartam et vicesimam diem mensis Februarii inclusive. Set in quinta et vicesima die mensis Februarii eiusdem anni, set anni bisextilis, quo die celebrabitur festum sancti Mathie, quarta pars excessus est addenda ad altitudinem meridianam inventam in tabula, et exur-

120

125

130

135

140

193

altitude found in the table, and that gives the altitude of noon for that day; and the same procedure applies for the remaining days of that year up to the summer solstice. But from that date, namely from the summer solstice, until the winter solstice in that year, namely in leap year, the amount he was adding, namely a quarter of the additional amount of the sun's altitude, let him then subtract. In other years, however, namely in the second and third after leap year, it should be done the other way round, beause in those times, namely in the second and third year after leap year, from the winter solstice until the summer solstice, a part or parts of the additional amount of the altitude of the sun must be subtracted from the noontime altitude set out in this calendar. And from the summer solstice up to the winter solstice the parts of the additional amount are to be added. If, however, in a place other than Oxford one wishes to know the noon altitude, then let him see whether that place lies more to the north or the south. And in places to the south for each mile directly toward the south, it being understood that such a mile equals 4000 cubits, let him add one minute; and toward the north for a similar distance let him subtract an equal amount. The amount one should add or subtract can, nevertheless, be established more accurately by a table of longitude and latitude made for the regions. In places directly to the east or the west it is not necessary to add or subtract anything. But concerning the amount to be added to or subtracted from the altitude of the sun in hours of the clock in places other than Oxford toward the south or north, no certain rule is set out here nor can it be done easily. For those altitudes [of the sun] in the [clock] hours themselves increase and diminish diversely and unequally, and most of all close to sunrise and sunset. In places both directly to the east and to the west the altitudes of the sun in hours of the clock do not vary in the slightest.

**secundo** *add* anno S¹A¹DBAd.  150 **et . . . anno** anno ettercio A¹DB.  152 **subtrahende** extrahende Ad.  161 **tantum** *om* B. **tamen** cum B.  162 **debeat** debet A¹Ad. **haberi** habere S¹.  163 **de** *om* B.  166 **ab** *om* Ad.  168 **hic** *om* D. **posita** *om* A¹DAd.  169 **Nam** Quia B.  170 **et** *(1st) om* B. *Title to Canon 7 (from*

get altitudo meridiana pro die illo; et sic fiat pro residuis diebus eiusdem anni usque ad solsticium estivale. Set ex tunc, scilicet a solsticio estivali, usque ad solsticium hyemale in illo anno scilicet in anno bisextili, illud quod addebat, videlicet quartam partem excessus altitudinis solis, tunc subtrahat. In aliis vero annis, videlicet in secundo et tercio post bisextum, contrario modo operetur, quia illis temporibus, scilicet secundo et tercio anno post bisextum, a solsticio hyemali usque ad solsticium estivale, pars vel partes excessus altitudinis solis subtrahende sunt ab altitudinibus meridie positis in isto kalendario. Et a solsticio estivali usque ad solsticium hyemale partes excessus sunt addende. Si vero in alio loco ab Oxonie altitudinem meridianam habere voluerit, videat tunc utrum ille locus sit magis septentrionalis vel meridionalis. Et in locis meridionalibus pro quolibet miliari directe versus meridiem, secundum quod miliare constat ex 4000 cubitis, addat unum minutum et versus septentrionem pro consimili distancia tantum minuat. Precisius tamen quantum debeat addere vel subtrahere haberi potest per tabulam de longitudine et latitudine regionum factam. In locis directe versus orientem vel occidentem nichil oportet addere vel subtrahere. Set quo ad altitudines solis in horis de clok in aliis locis ab Oxonie versus meridiem vel septentrionem, quantum debeat addi vel subtrahi non est hic aliqua certa regula posita nec de facili esse potest. Nam altitudines ille in ipsis horis, difformiter et diversimode augmentantur et diminuuntur, et maxime prope eius ortum et occasum. In locis tamen directe versus orientem vel occidentem altitudines solis in horis dc clok in nullo variantur.

Should one wish to know the eclipse of the sun and moon, let him look
in the table of the solar eclipses, if those are what is sought, or the
tables of the eclipse of the moon with the date of the new moon and
the non-completed year of Christ, and in its column he will find the
non-completed month and day in which there will be an eclipse, with
the day beginning at noon on the preceding day. He will find also the
hours, minutes, and seconds in that column and the magnitude of the
eclipse, the time of occurrence, and the midpoint of its duration if it is
a lunar eclipse, and also its duration. The hours and fractions of hours
found [in the table] are [those of the] middle of the eclipse. Then the
start of the eclipse is determined by subtracting half the duration. It is
easier, however, to determine the beginning from the superscriptions
of the figures.

## [8] CANON FOR THE DISCOVERY OF THE ASCENDANT

When one wishes to know the ascendant degree above the horizon and
the beginnings of the other houses, he should look at the table prepared
in this calendar for the hours of the clock with the aid of the altitude of
the sun or of the shadow of someone, and see the equal hours with
their minutes, computing from midnight until the moment of his
activity, should it be for morning, or computing from noon, should it
be for afternoon; and convert those hours with their minutes into
ascensions, multiplying them with their minutes by fifteen, and the
elevated equinoctial arc will emerge, raised up to the time of his
activity, from midnight if it be morning, or from noon if it be
afternoon. And let him also add that equinoctial arc thus elevated to
the ascensions of the direct circle established with the nadir of the

**As[1])** *om* LA[1]DBAd; Per eclipses S[1]; Canon eclipsis soliset lune R; Canon
eclipsium solis et lune A[2].    174-218 **Eclipses . . . prius** *om* Ad.    174-75
**tabulam** tabulas R.    175 **eclipsis (1st)** eclipsium A[1]DRA[2]. **eclipsis (2nd)**
eclipsium A[2].    177 **et (1st)** *om* As[1]A[2]. **eius** eorum et As[1]A[2]; eorum R. **inveniet**
invenient R.    178 **eclipsis** eclipsium R.    179 **eciam** *om* A[2]. **horas** *add* et A[2].    180
**et (1st)** *om* As[1]. **eius** eorum As[1]RA[2]. **punctus** puncta BRA[2]. **eclipsis** eclipsium
A[2].    182-83 **Ille . . . eclipsis** *om* S[1].    183 **horarum** *om* As[1]RA[2]. **eclipsis** *om* A[2].
184 **eclipsis** eclipsium A[2].    185 **eclipsis** eclipsium S[1].    186 **per** sicut B. *Title to*
*Canon 8 (from* **As[1])** *om* LS[1]A[1]DBAdA[2]; Canon pro domibus planetarum R.
188-218 **Cum . . . prius** *om* A[2].    188 **ad** *om* R. **et** *add* et signorum super
orizontem R.    189 **intret** *add* in As[1]R.    190 **in** *om* S[1].    196 **multiplicando**

Eclipses solis et lune siquis scire desiderat, intret tabulam eclipsis solis, si illas querat, vel tabulas eclipsis lune 175
cum numero primacionis sue et anno Christi imper-
fecto, et in directo eius inveniet mensem et diem
imperfectos in quibus erit eclipsis, incipiendo diem in
meridie diei precedentis. Inveniet eciam horas, minu-
tos, et secundos in directo eius et punctus eclipsis, 180
tempus casus, et dimidium more si sit pro luna, ac
eciam duracionem eiusdem. Ille vero hore et fracciones
horarum invente sunt medium eclipsis. Principium
autem eclipsis habetur per subtraccionem medie duracionis a medio eclipsis; finis per addicionem medie 185
duracionis. Principium eciam facilius haberi potest per
superscripciones figurarum.

Cum ad gradum ascendentem super orizentem et reli-
quarum domorum inicia scire voluerit, intret tabulam
factam in kalendario isto pro horis de clok mediante 190
altitudine solis seu alicuius umbra, et videat horas
equales cum minutis suis, computando a media nocte
usque adinstans operacionis sue, si fuerit ante meridiem, vel computando a meridie, si fuerit post nonam;
et illas horas cum minutis suis reducat in ascenciones, 195
multiplicando eas cum minutis suis per quindecim, et
exibit arcus equinoccialis elevatus, a media nocte si
fuerit ante meridiem, vel a meridie si fuerit post nonam, usque adinstans operacionis sue. Illum vero arcum
equinoccialem sic elevatum addat super ascenciones 200
circuli directi cum nadayr gradus solis inventas, si

197

degree of the sun, if it be morning, or established with the degree of the sun, if it be afternoon. And one should seek the arc so produced among the ascensions of the oblique circle, and the equal degrees found on the side of the table toward the left with the sign written at the head of the table will show him the ascendant degree. Then, in the column of the ascendant degree in the next line after these ascensions with which he has just now discovered the ascendant degree, let him fix the beginning of the second house. Afterwards in the second line after these ascensions, let him take the beginning of the third house; in the third line, the beginning of the fourth house; in the fourth line, the beginning of the fifth house; in the fifth line, the beginning of the sixth. Then, when these houses are identified by their lowest point, the other houses are easily discovered. If, however, from the addition of any two arcs, there is an increase to an amount greater than the number of degrees in a circle, then take away 360 degrees from the calculation, and with the remainder work as before.

## [9] CANON FOR DISCOVERING THE DEGREE OF THE MOON IN THE SIGNS OF EVERY DAY

If it is desired to determine in what sign and in what degree of the sign the moon is on any day, seek first the age of the moon, next in what sign the sun was on the day of a conjunction and in what degree of that sign. Then seek the age of the moon from the left of the table, and then seek the sign of the sun on the top line where there are twelve signs, namely, from Aries to Pisces, and the sign of the moon under the sign of the sun, and opposite he will find the age of the moon and the degree of the moon at the right, opposite its age. But to these degrees of the moon found on the right he should add the degrees of the sign of the sun, namely, those in which the sun was on the day of conjunction. And if the degrees of the sun and moon taken together should be fewer

multitudo R. 207 **gradus ascendentis** post ascenciones As[1]. 208 **nunc** *om* As[1]. 211 **domus** *add* et As[1]. 212 **domus** *(1st)* *om* S[1]A[1]DBR; et As[1]. **linea** *om* As[1]. **domus** *(2nd)* et S[1]A[1]DBAs[1]R. 213 **linea** *om* As[1]. **sexte** *add* domus A[1]DBR. 215 **Si** *add* in A[1]As[1]. **aliquorum** illorum D. 217 **360** 30 S[1]. *Title to Canon 9 (from* As[1]) *om* LA[1]DAd; Pro lune S[1]; Canon pro loco lune inveniendo B; Canon scire tabulam lune R; Canon pro lune in signis A[2]. 219 **quo** *(2nd)* *om* Ad. 220 **sit** *om* S[1]A[1]; fuerunt As[1]; sunt A[2]. 220–42 **querat . . . recipit** *om* As[1]A[2]. 222 **a** *om* S[1]A[1]. 225 **Pisces** *add* et sub illo signo descendat usque in directo etatis lune BR; *add* et sub illo signo descendat usque in directo etatis Ad. 225–26 **et** *(1st)* **. . . etatem** *om* Ad. 228 **addere** *add* similis Ad. 229 **erat** et B. **et** *(2nd)* *om* RAd. 230 **simul**

fuerit ante meridiem, vel cum gradu solis inventas, si
fuerit post meridiem. Et arcum productum querat inter
ascenciones circuli obliqui, et gradus equalis inventus in
latere tabule versus sinistram cum signo scripto in       205
capite tabule ostendet sibi gradum ascendentem. Deinde, in directo gradus ascendentis in proxima linea
post istas ascenciones cum quibus nunc invenit gradum
ascendentem, accipiat principium secunde domus. Postea in secunda linea post istas ascenciones, sumat prin-   210
cipium tercie domus; in tercia linca, principium quarte
domus; in quarta linea, principium quinte domus; in
quinta linea, principium sexte. Cognitis autem hiis
domibus per earum nadayr, alie domus faciliter cog-
noscentur. Si vero ex addicione aliquorum duorum       215
arcuum, excreverit magis quam quantitas circuli, abi-
ciantur tunc 360 gradus de predicto, et cum residuo
operandum est ut prius.


[9] CANON PRO GRADU LUNE INVENIENDO
IN SIGNIS OMNI DIE

Siquis invenire voluerit in quo signo et in quo gradu
signi lune sit omni die, querat primo etatem lune,       220
postea in quo signo erat sol in die conjunccionis et in
quo gradu illius signi. Deinde querat etatem lune a
sinistris tabule, et tunc querat signum solis in supprema
linea ubi sunt duodecima signa, scilicet ab Ariete usque
ad Pisces et signum lune sub signo solis, et contra       225
etatem lune et gradum lune inveniet a dextris contra
etatem eius. Set cum illis gradibus lune que sunt a
dextris debet addere gradus signi solis, scilicet in quibus
erat sol in die conjunccionis. Et si gradus solis et lune
simul collecti fuerint pauciores triginta, tunc adhuc       230

199

than thirty, then the moon will still be in that sign which will be opposite to its age. But if the degrees exceed thirty, then the moon will be in another following sign, that is lower, and in the specific degree [of the sign] by which the number exceeds thirty; and he will have the place of the moon to the same hour as that in which the conjunction occurred. If, however, one wishes to know the degree of the moon for other hours, let him take whatever hours he may desire and always compute one degree for every two hours. But if for hours antecedent to the place of the moon, let him subtract. If for those following, add; and he will have achieved his purpose. At the foot of this table may be found for the parts of the human body which sign is related to which part.

## [10] CANON OF THE TABLE FOR THE MOVABLE FEASTS AND DOMINICAL LETTERS

To discover the movable feasts: First, the dominical letter, which is found by means of the golden table or by means of the table made for finding the dominical letter, must be sought. And, that table begins in the first year of the solar cycle [of this calendar], namely the year of Christ 1381, in which year the dominical letter was *f;* and in the next year, *e;* in the third year, *d.* In the fourth, which was leap year, *c* was the dominical letter up to the feast of Saint Matthew, and after that feast, *b;* in the fifth year, *a;* in the sixth, which is the present year and the second after leap year, *g.* And thus one should proceed until the end of the table; and when it is finished, one should return to the beginning, and the same method is to be repeated for ever. But in order to find [the dominical letter] easily for any past or future time, it should here be noted: First, that if the dominical letter should be sought for

simulis Ad. 232 **si gradus** signus Ad. **ultra** utri que D. 233 **alio** aliquo Ad. 234 **quotus** quotius Ad. **et** *om* S¹; eciam Ad. 235 *****conjunccio (*from* S¹A¹D BRAd)** conjuccio L. 236 **ad** *om* A¹. 236–40 **Si . . . intentum** *om* Ad. 237 **horas** *add* quas S¹A¹DBR. 239–240 **persequentibus** consequentibus S¹A¹DB; sequentibus R. *Title to Canon 10 (from As¹) om* LA¹DAd; Pro festis mobilibus S¹; Canon pro festis mobilibus inveniendis BR; Canon festorum mobilium A². 244 **que** et illa As¹A². **habetur . . . tabulam** habetur As¹A²; habentur pro tabula R. 244–45 **auream . . . tabulam** auream in tabula As¹A²; *om* RAd. 245–46 **Et incepit** incipiendo As¹A²; que incipit Ad. 246 **tabula illa** a As¹A². **tabula . . . ac** *om* Ad. **ac** videtur D; indebit As¹A². 247 **et** *om* As¹Ad. 248 **post** *om* AdA². **e** *add* et As¹A². **anno (2nd)** *om* S¹BAs¹RA². **d** *add* et As¹A². **quarto** *add* anno A¹DAs¹A². 248–52 **in tercio . . . procedendum** *om* Ad. 250 **festum (2nd)** *om* As¹A². 251 **sexto** *add* anno As¹A². 251–52 **qui . . . bisextum** *om* As¹A². 252 **sic** tunc B. **procedendum** *add* et cetera Ad. 253–63 **qua . . . gracia** *om* Ad. 254 **et . . . operandum** *om* As¹A². 256 **hic** *om* BAs¹A². **quod** que As¹; *om* A².

luna erit in eodem signo quod erit contra etatem eius.
Set si gradus ultra triginta excreverint, tunc luna erit in
alio signo sequenti, scilicet inferius, et in totali gradu
quotus fuerit numerus residuus ultra triginta; et habebit
locum lune ad horam consimilem qua fuït conjunccio. 235
Si autem ad alias horas gradum lune scire voluerit,
accipiat horas quas voluerit et semper pro dualibus
horis unum gradum computet. Si autem pro horis
antecedentibus a loco lune, subtrahat. Si est pro persequentibus, addat; et habebit intentum. In pede huius 240
tabule habetur de partibus corporis hominis quod signum quam partem recipit.

[10] CANON TABULE FESTORUM MOBILIUM
ET LITTERE DOMINICALIS

Ad inveniendum festa mobilia: Primo querenda est
litera dominicalis, que habetur per tabulam auream seu
tabulam factam pro litera dominicali, invenienda. Et 245
incepit tabula illa primo anno cicli solaris, ac anno
Christi 1381, in quo anno litera dominicalis erat *f;* et in
secundo anno post, *e;* in tercio anno, *d.* In quarto, qui
fuit annus bisextilis, *c* fuit litera dominicalis usque ad
festum Sancti Mathie, et post illud festum, *b;* in quinto 250
anno, *a;* in sexto, qui est annus presens et secundus post
bisextum, *g.* Et sic procedendum est usque ad finem
tabule; qua completa, recurrendum est ad principium,
et sic pro perpetuis temporibus est operandum. Set ut
faciliter habeatur pro quolibet tempore preterito sive 255
futuro, est hic notandum: Primo quod si queratur litera
dominicalis pro aliquo anno futuro, computandum est a

any future year, the calculation is to be made from the dominical letter of the year then current, working forward; and for every twentieth year or thousandth year, five letters must be calculated, and the fifth letter will be the dominical letter in the year which is sought; and for the hundredth year four should be computed, and that fourth letter will be the dominical letter. For example: should one desire the dominical letter for the thousandth year after the present year, namely 1386, let him calculate from the dominical letter *g* of the present year, which is found in the second line of the table [of the solar cycle], and going down five letters in the same [table], namely, *b, d, f, a, c;* and that letter *c* will be the dominical letter for that year. For the hundredth year, let him count out four letters, namely, *b, d, f, a;* and *a* will be the dominical letter as is evident in the verse: "The fourth [letter] holds a hundred." And should one seek to know what the dominical letter will be in 1200 years, then calculate for 1000 years five letters in the same line, and twice four for two hundred, and the question is answered. If, however, one seeks other years under those three, then for the years already mentioned work as before. And for additional years follow the method described in the first solar cycle. Thus, should one seek the dominical letter for the 105th year immediately after the present year, then calculate for one hundred years four letters from the present dominical letter, namely *b, d, f, a,* and the letter *a* will be the dominical letter in the hundredth year, as has been said. And on the line to the right five letters are to be calculated, namely, *g* for the first; *f* and *e* in the same way for the second, because it will be a leap year; next *d* for the third; *c* for the fourth; and *b* for the fifth; and that letter *b* will be the dominical letter in the year sought.

When, however, one is looking for years past, the operation is just

260 **et . . . litera** *(1st) om* BA². **litera** *(2nd) om* A². 262 **et . . . quarta** *om* BAs¹A². **litera** *(2nd) om* As¹A². 264 **millesimo** centisimo A². 265 **dominicali** dominicalis Ad. 266 **presentis** presenti R. **inventa** et inveniet D. 268 **pro** *(1st) om* D. **anno** *add* et A². 268-70 **pro** *(1st)* . . . **dominicalis** *om* Ad. 269 **anno** *add* autem S¹; autem anno DB; *om* As¹. 270 **in** *add* predicto Ad. **versu** versibus S¹. 271 **Centum . . . tenet** *om* Ad. **tenet** *om* As¹; *add* et cetera S¹BAs¹R; *add* viginti mille ne quinta Si pro preteritis scandas descende futuris A². 272 **litera** *(1st) om* B. **litera** *(2nd) om* As¹A². 272-95 **litera** *(1st)* . . . **illo** *om* Ad. 273 **in . . . linea** *om* As¹RA². **litere** littere in eadem linea As¹R; litteras in eodem linea et post A². **et** *om* A². 275 **sub illis** ab illis DAs¹R; *om* A². **pro** *om* S¹A¹. 276 **prius** *add* secundum que in As¹. 277 **secundum** sicut DBR; *add* que As¹A². **est** et D. 279 **annum** *om* B. **annis** *om* As¹A². 281 **videlicet** scilicet As¹; *om* A². **litera** *(2nd) om* As¹. 282 **secundum** sicut DB; *add* que As¹A². **Et** *add* tunc As¹A². 283 **versus** post B. 284 **pro prima** *e b d c* As¹A². **tunc** *om* R. 284-86 **f . . . quinta** *om* As¹A². 285 **deinde** *om* S¹. 286 *b (1st) om* B. **litera** *(2nd) om* As¹A². 287 **quesito** *add* Canon eiusdem pro annis preteritis R. 288 **Dum** Quando A². 289 **secundum** scilicet S¹; ut A¹D; sicut B; *add* in que A². 291 **que** qui B.

litera dominicali tunc instantis anni, descendendo; et pro quolibet vicesimo anno vel millesimo, computande sunt quinque litere, et quinta litera erit litera dominicalis in anno de quo queritur; et pro centesimo computande sunt quatuor, et illa quarta litera erit litera dominicalis. Verbi gracia: Si quis velit habere literam dominicalem pro millesimo anno post presentem annum, videlicet 1386, computet a *g* litera dominicali presentis anni, inventa in secunda linea tabule, descendendo in eadem quinque literas, videlicet, *b, d, f, a, c;* et illa litera *c* erit litera dominicalis pro illo anno. Pro centesimo anno, numeret quatuor literas, videlicet, *b, d, f, a;* et *a* erit litera dominicalis ut patet in versu: "Centum quarta tenet." Et si queratur pro 1200 que litera erit litera dominicalis, tunc pro mille computentur in eadem linea quinque litere, et bisquatuor pro ducentis, et patebit quesitum. Si vero queratur pro aliis annis sub illis tribus, tunc pro predictis annis operandum est ut prius. Et pro superadditis operandum est secundum in primo ciclo solari demonstratum est. Ut si velit habere literam dominicalem pro anno 105 proximo post presentem annum, tunc pro centesimis annis computet quatuor literas a presenti litera dominicali, videlicet, *b, d, f, a,* et *a* litera erit litera dominicalis in centesimo anno, secundum dictum est. Et in linea versus dextram computande sunt quinque litere, videlicet *g* pro prima; *f* et *e* insimul pro secunda, quia tunc erit annus bisextilis; deinde *d* pro tercia; *c* pro quarta; et *b* pro quinta; et illa litera *b* erit litera dominicalis in anno quesito.

Dum vero queritur pro annis preteritis, in omnibus operandum est secundum prius, hoc solum excep-

as before in all regards, with the sole exception that the calculation is now to be made from the current year by working backwards. For example: if one should wish to know what was the dominical letter in the year one hundred years before the present year, then from the dominical letter *g* of the present year let him compute four letters, going upwards, namely *e, c, a, f,* and that letter *f* was the dominical letter for that year. When the dominical letter has been determined, the time of the paschal moon of the year in question is to be sought, and that number is found in the table made for finding movable feasts, in the outside line of the same table toward the left, corresponding to the Metonic cycle for nineteen years. However, for other future years the computation is to be made from the paschal moon of the current year by calculating forward, and the next paschal moon [on that date] will be the paschal moon of the twentieth year following; and the fifth paschal moon [will be that] of the hundredth year; and the twelfth of the thousandth year, as is clear in the verse: "The first to twenty," etc. If, however, a search is made for past years, one must calculate by working backwards, as is clear in the same verses. When these determinations have been made, namely, the dominical letter and the time of the paschal moon, then one must look in the same table, that is, in the table made for finding movable feasts, with the number of the paschal moon, and in its column under the dominical letter which is found at the top of the table in the first line and under the description of that feast which is sought. The days of the same feast are found with red figures in the month at the top of the table in the second line written in red, or in black figures in the month at the top of the table in the third line in black writing.

291-92 **erat . . . dominicalis** erat B; litera erat dominicalis As¹; erat domini-calis A². 292 **centesimo** *om* A². 295 **erat** erit D. **dominicalis . . . illo** illo anno As¹; *add* Iam Ad. **Habita** *add* sic A². 296 **est** *om* A². 297 **in . . . pro** *om* B. 297-99 **pro . . . sinistram** *om* As¹A². 302-3 **primacio . . . primacio** prima erit primacio S¹; primacione erit primacio A¹Ad; primacione erit primacione D; primacio B. 303 **vicesimi anni** ad vicesimos annos As¹A². **sequentis** sequentur Ad. 303-4 **centesimi anni . . . duodecima** et duodecima ad As¹; centesimi anni et Ad; ad A². 304 **anni** *(2nd)* *om* As¹A². 305 **cetera** quinta centum et cetera S¹A¹D; quinta et cetera B; quinta Ad; quinta centum duodenarius mille si pro preteritis scandas A². **vero** *add* in vero B. 305-7 **Si . . . videlicet** habita Ad. 308 **numero** numerus As¹A². 309 **eandem** eadem D; *om* As¹AdA². **tabulam . . . tabulam** tabula scilicet in tabulam D; tabulam scilicet tabulam B; tabulam factam As¹AdA². 310 **inveniendis factam** inveniendis As¹A²; *om* Ad. 311-12 **in . . . tabule** *om* As¹A². 312 **linea** *add* tabule As¹A². 313

to quod tunc computandum est a tunc instanti anno 290
ascendendo. Verbi gracia: Siquis velit scire que erat
litera dominicalis anno centesimo ante presentem annum, tunc a litera dominicali *g* presentis anni computet
quatuor literas, ascendendo, videlicet, *e, c, a, f,* et illa
litera *f* erat litera dominicalis anno illo. Habita litera 295
dominicali postea, querendus est numerus primacionis
anni de quo queritur, qui numerus habetur in tabula pro
festis mobilibus inveniendis facta, in linea exteriori
eiusdem tabule versus sinistram, corespondente ciclo
decennovenali pro undevicesimis annis. Pro aliis autem 300
annis futuris computandum est a primacione anni tunc
instantis descendendo, et proxima primacio erit primacio vicesimi anni sequentis; et quinta primacio centesimi anni; et duodecima millesimi anni ut patet in versu:
"Prima viginti," et cetera. Si vero fiat inquisicio pro 305
annis preteritis, computandum est ascendendo, ut patet
in eisdem versibus. Quibus habitis videlicet litera dominicali et numero primacionis, tunc intrandum est in
eandem tabulam scilicet in tabulam pro festis mobilibus
inveniendis factam, cum numero primacionis, et in 310
directo eius sub litera dominicali que habetur in capite
tabule in prima linea et sub descripcione illius festi
quod queritur. Dies eiusdem festi cum figuris invenientur rubeis in mense in capite tabule in secunda linea
scripto cum rubeo, vel cum figuris nigris in mense in 315
capite tabule in tercia linea scripto cum nigro.

**quod** quis As¹; de quo A². **queritur** sit As¹; queritur quis A². 313–14 **figuris
invenientur** *add* in R; invenietur cum signis Ad. 314 **in mense** et sic de ceteris
Ad. **in** *(1st)* . . . **linea** *om* As¹A². 314–16 **in** *(1st)* . . . **nigro** *om* Ad. 315
\***scripto** *(from* **S¹A¹D BAs¹RA²**) scriptum L. **scripto . . . rubeo** cum scripto
rubeo in capite tabule As¹A². 315–16 **in** *(2nd)* . . . **nigro** scripto cum nigro in
capite tabule As¹. 315–565 **in** *(2nd)* . . . **Amen** subscripto nigro in capite tabule
A². 316 **tercia** tercio S¹; Secunda B. **scripto** scriptum S¹A¹. *Title to Canon 11*

Since, according to the view of Ptolemy in his *Centiloquium* and of his commentator Haly in Proposition 56, the humors of human bodies go out from the innermost parts to the exterior parts in the first and third phases of the moon, and are like rivers whose waters rise, in these phases, therefore, it is not proper to receive purges; [but] to have bloodletting done by phlebotomy or cupping, provided no other impediment exists, is very useful. In the second phase of the moon, however, and in the fourth the humors are withdrawn from the exterior parts and flow to the interior ones, and they are like rivers whose waters recede. Because of this in these phases, if every other impediment is absent, it is praiseworthy to receive purges; but to let blood does not happen without harm to the body. Also if one touches a [bodily] member with iron, the moon being in the [member's] sign, that member is extremely endangered, as Ptolemy says in the same work, Proposition 20. Haly, his commentator, offers an explanation of its cause when he says: "The moon sends the humor into the large member whenever it is in that member's sign, and one should fear to touch it with iron while [the member is] very damp, because to touch it in that way is to damage the member, and to add humidity to the wound multiplies the harm." Secondly, Campanus provides the reason, saying: "To touch that member with iron, making a wound, is the cause of pain, and the pain causes catarrh"; for which reason, he says: "In surgery one must avoid an incision into a member while the moon is in a sign that has significance for that member." Other astrologers offer a different reason, saying that the humors flow together to the

*(from* As¹) *om* LA¹D; Canon pro minucionibus faciendis et purgacionibus recipiendis S¹B; Canon pro minucionibus et purgacionibus recipiendis R; Canon pro minucionibus et purgacionibus recipiendis Fratris Nicholai de Linea Ad; Canon pro minucionibus sanguinis fugiendis S²; Canon pro minucionibus et purgacionibus recipiendis Fratris Nicholai de Lynne As³. 317 **Quia** Via M; Prima Gg. **sentenciam** sentencias S². **Tholomei** Ptolomei M. **suo** *om* M. 318 **Haly** Hali As³; *add* super M. **Proposicione 56** *add* aceciam secundum apstoiit pro de dialibus S². 319 **humores** *add* et B. 320 **secundum** sicut DBAs¹ RAdMGgAs³. 321 **quorum** *om* B. **crescunt** *add* et S². *ideo (*from* S¹A¹D BAs¹RAdMS²GgAs³)* illis L. 322 **recipere** accipere R. 323 **aliquo** *om* BAs¹RAdS²GgAs³. 323-24 **nullo . . . est** quis perutile est aliquo inpedimentis cessacionibus M. 324 *secunda (*from* S¹A¹DBMS²As³)* secundo LAs¹RAdGg. 326 **secundum** sicud D; sicut BAs¹ RAdMS²GgAs³. 331 **significanter** significante As¹MS². 332 **ut** quia AdAs³. **ibidem** idem As¹S². **Tholomeus** Ptolomeus M. 333 **20** *add* ibidem As¹MS²; 30 ibidem R; 30 Gg. **causam** *add* primo As¹RS². **Haly** Hali R. 334 **suus** *om* M. **membrum** membro DRS². **immittit** mittit As³. 335 **ipsum** *om* M. 336 **timendum** valdes periculosum Gg. 337 **et** ut M. 339-40 **cum . . . illud** membrum ferro M. 341 **reuma** fleuma R; ruina Ad. **cirurgia** cirurgiam Gg. 342 **cavendum** timendum est S²; *add* est DBAs¹RAdMAs³. 343 **significacionem** significacione S¹. 344 **Aliam** Alia Gg. **alii** *om* Gg. **dicentes** *add* quod D. 345 **confluere** confluunt D.

Quia secundum sentenciam Tholomei in suo *Centilogio*
et sui commentatoris Haly Proposicione 56, in prima
quadra lune et tercia humores corporum humanorum
exeunt ab interioribus ad exteriora, et sunt secundum      320
flumina quorum aque crescunt, ideo in illis quadris
purgaciones recipere non convenit; minuciones fieri per
fleobothomiam vel ventosiam, nullo aliquo alio impedimento existente, perutile est. In secunda vero quadra
lune et quarta retrahuntur humores ab exterioribus et      325
concurrunt ad interiora, et sunt secundum flumina
quorum aque recedunt. Propter quod in istis quadris,
alio impedimento cessante, purgaciones recipere laudabile est; minuere vero sanguinem sine detrimento corporis non contingit. Tangere eciam membrum ferro,         330
luna existente in signo, ipsum membrum significanter
periculosum est, ut dicit ibidem Tholomeus, Proposicione 20. Cuius causam assignat Haly commentator
suus, dicens: "Luna in membrum magnum immittit
humorem cum in signo illius membri fuerit, et ipsum       335
valde humidum ferro tangere timendum est eo, quod sic
tangere est membrum vulnerare, et addere vulneri
humiditatem multiplicat nocumenta." Secundo Campanus assignat causam, dicens: "Tangere cum ferro
membrum illud, vulnerando, est causativum doloris, et     340
dolor causat reuma"; propter quod inquit: "In cirurgia
cavendum ab incisione in membro, luna existente in
signo significacionem habente super illud membrum."
Aliam causam assignant alii astrologi dicentes humores
confluere ad locum dolorosum ad confortandum natu-         345

207

painful place in order to strengthen the nature of the member [which is] suffering the pain, and when they come together, they dull the pain if they cannot get out; and because they stand outside the natural state, they fester and corrupt the painful place. If, however, they get out, the patient often dies, because the humors are the subject of the heat; when they are expelled, the heat is expelled, without which the member is not able to be recalled to its pristine state. And this is the reason why, from a blow of a stone or a stick which does not break the skin, a tumor is engendered, namely, on account of the flowing of the humors. Thus Campanus says that he saw a man inexperienced in the stars who was in danger of quinsy bleed himself in the arm, the moon being in Gemini, which sign is dominant over the arms; and without any sign of the disease except a little swelling of the arm, died on the seventh day. He also knew a man, as he asserts, suffering from an ulcer on the tip of his penis, and [he said that] it was incised while the moon was in Scorpio, the sign which dominates that part of the body, and at the very hour of the incision he died in the hands of those supporting him, with no other additional cause.

### [12] CANON FOR GIVING AND RECEIVING MEDICINE

In order to know what time a laxative medicine should be given, or any other no matter what kind it might be, it is to be noted that in a man's body there are four natural powers, namely attraction, retention, digestion, and expulsion. Now the power of attraction flourishes with heat and dryness, and for that reason those things that strengthen it should be given when the moon is in a hot and dry sign without impediment. And similarly, those which strengthen retention should be given when the moon is in a cold and dry sign, because that power flourishes in coldness and dryness. Those things that strengthen diges-

---

**confortandum** confortandi Gg. 347 **si** que S¹; quod A¹. **stant** statim As¹S². 350 **quod** que RAs³. 351 **in** et Ad. 354 **narrat** *add (in margin)* non narrat Gg. 356 **sibi** *add* sanguini S². 359 **inflacione** in fleobotomacionis Gg. 363 **et** *add* in B. 364 **obiit** *om* S². **alia** *om* RS². **concurrente** *add* obiit S². ***Title to Canon 12 (from As¹)*** *om* LS¹A¹DRAdMS²GgAs³; Canon pro medicinis recipiendis BS². 365–565 **Ad . . . Amen** *om* RAs³. 365 **dari** dare As¹. 365–66 **medicina laxativa** medicinam laxativam A¹Ad; medicina sive laxativa D. 366 **quecumque** quamcumque A¹. **quecumque . . . notandum** otandum Gg. **fuerit** *om* S¹A¹DBAs¹AdMS². **quod** que S¹A¹. 367 **sunt** *om* Ad. **virtutes** *add* cardinales D; *add* quecumque Gg. 367–68 **videlicet** scilicet A¹DAd. 368 **et** *add* ista S². 369 **autem** *om* MGg. **siccum** siccitatem Gg. 370 **propter . . . ipsum** *illegible* S¹. **illa** ista S². **confortant** confortabit Ad. 371–565 **et** *(1st)* . . . **Amen** *om* S¹. 373 **in . . . frigido** frigido signo Gg. **ipsa** ipsam As¹M. 374 **Que confortant** Qui

ram membri dolorem pacientis, qui congregati obtundunt calorem si non possunt exire; et quia stant sine regimine nature, putrescunt et inficiunt locum dolorosum. Si vero exeant, frequenter moritur paciens, eo quod humores sunt subjectum caloris; quibus expulsis, expellitur calor, sine quo membrum non potest in statum pristinum revocari. Et hec est causa quare, ex ictu lapidis vel baculi non frangentis cutem, generatur tumor, videlicet propter fluxum humorum. Item narrat Campanus se vidisse hominem imperitum in astris qui in periculo squinancie minuerat sibi de brachio, luna existente in Geminis, quod signum dominatur super brachia; et absque ulla manifesta egritudine excepta modica brachii inflacione, die septimo mortuus est. Novit eciam quemdam, ut asserit, pacientem fistulam in capite membri virilis, et ipsum fuisse inscisum luna existente in Scorpione, quod signum dominatur super illam partem corporis, et eadem hora incisionis in manibus tenencium obiit, nulla alia causa concurrente.

## [12] CANON PRO MEDICINIS DANDIS ET RECIPIENDIS

Ad sciendum quo tempore debet dari medicina laxativa, sive alia quecumque fuerit, est notandum quod in corpore hominis sunt quatuor virtutes naturales, videlicet Attractiva, Retentiva, Digestiva, et Expulsiva. Virtus autem Attractiva viget per calidum et siccum, propter quod illa que ipsum confortant dari debent luna existente in signo calido et sicco non inpedita. Et conformiter que confortant Retentivam dari debent luna existente in signo frigido et sicco, eo quod ipsa virtus viget frigiditate et siccitate. Que confortant

tion [should be given] when the moon is in a hot and wet sign. But those things that strengthen the power of expulsion should be given when the moon is in a cold and wet sign. And if a physician should neglect to look at these things when giving medicine, he will be deprived very often of the effect necessary for a cure, because the power of heaven will work to the contrary. Thus, if anyone tries to help expulsion by giving a laxative medicine, the power of heaven occasionally will operate through the influence of the moon to strengthen the retentive power, and the same is true for other [powers]. For that reason, if any physician wishes by his art to improve retention, he should choose a time when the moon is in a cold and dry sign, such as Taurus or Virgo. Let him take care, also, that the ascending sign should be of the same complexion. In addition, to make it more useful, let the preparation of such medicine take place in a similar constellation, the reason being that it will work more efficaciously and better because of the power it receives at the time of preparation from the heavenly influence. For, as Thebith says, images and sculptures are made in stones so that they might receive the worth of precious stones from the influence of heaven. However, they do not have the power except from the aspect of the planets at the time when they were sculpted, the reason being that the substance of these images is dry and made of earth or metal, which is not able to stamp any such power on these sculptures. But the supercelestial power gives them the power they possess. And the same applies to whatever mixtures are compounded by physicians. But they have nearly as much power from the time of composition as they have from the material from which they were compounded. If, therefore, anyone wishes to strengthen expulsion, he should give his medicine when the moon is in a sign that is cold and wet, or at least wet, as when the moon is in Cancer, Scorpio, or

conforto Gg. 375 **Digestivam** *add* debent dari M; Digestiva debent dari Gg. **existente** viget A¹. 377 **in** *om* Gg. 378 **respicere** perspicere Gg. 379 **curacionis** *add* deficiet M. **multociens** *om* As¹S². **privabitur** *om* M. 380 **celi** *om* S²Gg. **siquis** *add* multam M. 381 **affectat** affectet Gg. 382 **interdum** *om* As¹S². **ad** *om* S². 383 **fortificandum** fortificandam As¹; *om* M; fortitudinem S². **quod** *om* As¹. 385 **tempus** tempore B. 386 **secundum** sicut A¹DBAs¹AdMS². 388 **simili** consimili A¹DAdM. 390 **quam** quicumqui A¹AdGg; quicum S². **tempore** *om* M. **confeccionis** confectio M. 391 **secundum** sicut A¹DBA s¹AdMS²Gg. **Thebyth** Thebith A¹DBAs¹AdM; Thebit Gg. 392 **ut** et Gg. 393 **celi** *om* As¹; quod Ad. **influencia** *add* celi As¹. 393-94 **autem** tamen S². 395 **ymaginum** ymagini Ad. 396 **et** *om* BAs¹MS²Gg. 397 **istam** illam As¹S². 398 **quam** quilibet Ad. 400 **Set** quod A¹DAs¹ AdMS²Gg; quia B. **ex** quod Ad; *om* Gg. 401 **ex . . . de** de materia ex BAs¹S². 402 **igitur** ergo D; vero S². 403 **det** debet M. **suam** *add* in Gg. 404 **vel . . . humido** conficionis et sic et M. 404-5

Digestivam luna existente in signo calido et humido. 375
Illa vero que confortant virtutem Expulsivam dare
convenit luna existente in signo frigido et humido. Et si
medicus ista respicere neclexerit dando medicinam, ab
effectu curacionis necessario multociens privabitur,
quia virtus celi contrarium operabitur. Ut siquis Expul- 380
sivam confortare affectat dando medicinam laxativam,
virtus celi interdum per influenciam lune operabitur ad
Retentivam fortificandum, et ita in aliis. Propter quod
siquis medicorum velit sua arte confortare Retentivam,
eligat tempus quo luna fuerit in signo frigido et sicco, 385
secundum in Tauro vel Virgine. Respiciat eciam quod
ascendens sit signum eiusdem complexionis. Necnon
pro utiliori, fiat confeccio talis medicine in simili con-
stellacione, eo quod tanto efficacius et melius operabitur pro virtute quam recipit tempore confeccionis ex 390
influencia supercelesti. Nam secundum dicit Thebyth,
ymagines et sculpture fiunt in lapidibus ut virtutem
Geminarum ex celi influencia recipiant. Virtutem autem non habent nisi ex aspectu planetarum in tempore
quo artificiantur, eo quod materia illarum ymaginum 395
siccea est et terrea seu metallina, que nullam talem
virtutem ipsis sculpturis imprimere potest. Set istam
quam habent virtus supercelestis eisdem administrat. Et
sic est de confeccionibus quibuscumque a medicis com-
positis. Set fere tantam habent virtutem ex tempore 400
composicionis quantam habent ex materia de qua com-
ponuntur. Si quis igitur velit virtutem Expulsivam
confortare, det medicinam suam luna existente in signo
frigido et humido, vel saltem humido, ut quando luna

Pisces. And let him see to it that such a sign is ascending, that is to say, the cold and wet sign. And besides that, such mixtures should be prepared in a similar constellation, as has been said. And because different planets refer to different humors, when a certain humor ought to be discharged, a time should be chosen in which a planet referring to [the humor] is located in a bad position or is weakened, and then let the physician take action to evacuate that humor because then the effect of the planet does not resist the effect of the medicine. Thus, when one wishes to get rid of melancholy, let Saturn be weakened; if choler, Mars; if blood, the sun, Jupiter, or Venus; if phlegm, let the moon be weakened. In addition it is to be noted that according to Ptolemy in his *Centiloquium,* in Proposition 19, no one should take purging medicine when the moon is visible with Jupiter. Haly explains the reason for this in the commentary, saying: "The effect," he says, "of medicine is not natural to the body, that is to say that by attracting humors it overcomes the natural powers [of the body] by its own force; and thus the effect of corporeal nature, which is natural to the body, is contrary to the effect of medicine." And thus whatever promotes strength in one weakens the strength of the other, just as is evident with two contestants in a fight. According to the astrologers, therefore, since Jupiter strengthens natural things because he is a friend to all nature, the one who wishes to evacuate a humor when the nature of the humor is strengthened by the influence of Jupiter himself, has his work cut short and his effect minimized. Haly gives an example, saying: "Pleasant odors," he says, "strengthen nature and for that reason in the very impact of the medicine weaken its effect, and this is why the constituents that are fetid to the nose and bitter are to be included in many medicines."

**ut . . . respiciat** *om* M.  405 **vel** *add* in S². **quod** que M.  406 **scilicet . . . humidum** *om* M. **humidum** humiditem Gg.  407 **quod** quidem Ad; *om* Gg. **confecciones** confeccionas M. **consimili** simili Gg.  408 **diversi** diverse BAd. 410 **humor** humorem Gg. **tempus** tempore B.  411 **habeat** habuerit D. **aut** ut Ad.  412 **illum** istum S². **eo** *om* D. **pro** *om* Gg.  413 **planete . . . resistit** p resistet n D.  414 **malencoliam** *add* resistare et Gg. **velit** *om* B. **Saturnus** Saturnum M.  415 **Mars** Martem M. **sol . . . Venus** solem Jovem et Venerem M.  416 **notandum est** est medium notandum Gg.  417 **secundum** sicut B. **Tholomeum** Tholomeus A¹; Ptholomeum M.  418 **19** 10 As¹; decam S². **cum** in Ad.  419 **nullus** ullus BAs¹.  420 **Effectus** *add* planete *expunged* As¹. **inquit** *om* M. **non** *om* M.  423 **qui** quo S². **est** *(1st) add* corporalis Gg.  424 **confortat fortitudinem** confortitudinem B.  425 **secundum** sicut A¹BAdGg; et prohibet eius effectum sicut D; et prohibebit effectui eius sicut As¹S².  425–26 **secundum . . . pugnam** *om* M.  426 **duobus** *add* sunt Gg. **Cum** *om* Ad.  426–27 **secundum** scilicet M.  427 **Jupiter** Jubiter AdS²Gg.  428 **est** es Ad; *om* Gg. **nature** *om* As¹.  429 **humoris** *add* qui fortificatur scilicet natura humoris Gg. 430–31 **minuitur** *add* et M.  431 **ponit** ponat Ad. **Haly dicens** *om* M.  432 **in** *om* Gg.  433 **hinc** hunc Ad. **est** *om* B. **in** *om* Ad.  434 **amara** *add* ferinacien planetis

est in Cancro, Scorpione, vel Pisce. Et respiciat quod 405
tale signum sit ascendens scilicet frigidum et humidum.
Ac eciam quod confecciones tales in consimili constel-
lacione conficiantur, ut dictum est. Et quia diversi
planete diversos humores respiciunt, quando aliquis
humor debet eici, eligatur tempus in quo planeta ipsum 410
respiciens male se habeat aut debilitetur, et tunc agat
medicus ad evacuandum illum humorem eo quod pro
tunc effectus planete effectui medicine non resistit. Ut
dum malencoliam velit, evacuare debilitetur Saturnus;
si coleram, Mars; si sanguinem, sol, Jupiter, vel Venus; 415
si flemma, debilitetur luna. Insuper notandum est quod
secundum Tholomeum in suo *Centilogio,* Proposicione
19, medicinam purgantem luna cum Jove existente
nullus sumere debet. Causam huius assignat Haly in
commento, dicens: "Effectus inquit medicine non est 420
naturalis corpori, set attrahendo humores superat virtutes naturales impetu suo; et sic effectus nature corporalis, qui est naturalis corpori, est contrarius effectui
medicine." Et sic quicquid confortat fortitudinem unius
debilitat fortitudinem alterius, secundum apparet de 425
duobus congredientibus ad pugnam. Cum igitur secundum astrologos Jupiter confortat res naturales, eo quod
amicus est omni nature, qui vult evacuare humorem
quando fortificatur natura humoris per influenciam
ipsius Jovis abreviatur, opus eius et eius effectus minui- 430
tur. Exemplum ponit Haly, dicens: "Odorifera inquit
confortant naturam et ideo in ipso impetu medicine
debilitant effectum eius, et hinc est quod in multis
medicinis applicanda sunt naribus fetida et amara."

Ptolemy, also, in Proposition 21 of his *Centiloquium* teaches that taking starches while the moon is in Cancer, Scorpio, or Pisces, provided that the approach of the ascendant planet is beneath the earth, will be praiseworthy. But if the ascendant lord should be approaching, with the planet in the middle of the sky, one will suffer nausea and vomit medicine. Haly assigns the cause of this in the same place in the commentary, saying: "A triple wet and watery disposition, such as Cancer, Scorpio, and Pisces, is entirely useful to every potion of a soluble medicine," the reason being that when the medicine enters the body it finds moisture in the members, which [moisture] obstructs [the body's natural] strength. And for that reason when the ascendant lord happens to be joined to a planet located under the earth, it will move material to the lower parts of the body in spite of the intrinsic strength of the body, and thus its action will be useful. But if at the time of giving medicine the ascendant lord is conjoined to a planet located above the earth, it will move that [material] to the upper parts of the body to such an extent that the person receiving it will suffer nausea frequently. Here is the reason for that. The ascendant and its lord are the part of heaven which most presides over the medical potion, the nature of which is to move downward. When, therefore, the lord of the middle of the sky has with it an ascendant lord who is at that time the lord of medicine, it draws that [lord] to itself, that is to say, to a higher level, just as the sun attracts vapors. And thus the medicine will go out through vomiting against its nature or it will stay because of the rule of nature, and it will putrify or will go out by evacuation against the motion of the lord of the ascendant, any one of which [results] is not to be commended and is harmful to nature. In addition, it should be noted that when the moon is in Leo it is not good to give an emetic, inasmuch as the medicine then harms the stomach and throat and makes one vomit blood. Even phlebotomy is not then suitable, nor even when the moon is in the combust way, just

Gg. 435 **Tholomeus** Ptholomeus M. **suo** *om* M; *add* propter Gg. 436 **farinacie** ferinacien Gg. 437 **vel** et Ad; *add* vel Gg. **ascendentis** ascendent Ad. **planete** *om* S². 438 **applicatus** applicato DAs¹MS². **laudabilis** laudabit B; laudabile S². **erit** est BMS². **Set** Sic BAdS². 440 **causam** *om* Gg. 441 **Haly** Aly Gg. **ibidem** *om* M. 445 **fortitudini** fortitudinem As¹AdS². **ideo** *om* Gg. **cum** quando A¹DBAs¹AdMS²; quod Gg. 446 **existenti** assistenti B. 447 *ad (from A¹DBA s¹AdMS²Gg)* ab L. **inferiora** inferio Gg. 448 **eius** *om* M. 449 **Set** Scilicet Ad. **dacionis** acceptionis M; dacionie Gg. 450 **planete** planeti Ad. 451 **illam** illa Gg. 452 **Cuius** Eius Ad. 453 **Ascendens** Ascendes Ad. **dominus** *om* B. 454 **movere** vomere Ad. 455 **igitur** ergo S². 455–56 **dominum ascendentem** dominos ascendentes Ad. 456 **protunc** pro tempore S². 457 **secundum** sicut A¹DBAs¹AdMS². 458–60 **per . . . vel** *om* As¹. 461 **ascendentis** ascendentem Gg. **illaudabile et** *om* M. 462 *Insuper (from A¹DBAs¹AdMS²Gg)* Susuper L. **quod** quia A¹DAdM. 463–64 **eo . . . medicina** *om* Ad; eo quia medicinam M. 464 *facit (from A¹DBAs¹ AdMS²Gg)* ficit L. 465 **Fleobothomia** Fleuobotomi As¹; Fleomatici S². **eciam** et S². 465–66 **tunc . . . convenit** non

Tholomeus eciam in *Centilogio* suo Proposicione 21 435
docet quod accepcio farinacie, luna existente in Cancro, Scorpione, vel Pisce, dummodo ascendentis planete
applicatus sub terra, laudabilis erit. Set si dominus
ascendens fuerit applicatus, cum planeta in medio celi,
nauseam pacietur et evomet medicinam. Cuius causam 440
assignat Haly ibidem in commento, dicens: "Triplicitas
humida et aquatica, ut Cancer, Scorpio, et Piscis, tota
prodest pocioni medicine solubilis," eo quod medicina
cum ingreditur corpus reperit in membris humiditatem,
que obstat fortitudini eius. Et ideo cum domus ascen- 445
dens planete existenti sub terra conjunctus fuerit, movebit materiam ad inferiora corporis non obstante
fortitudine corporali intrinseca, et ita erit eius actus
utilis. Set si in tempore dacionis medicine conjunctus
fuerit dominus ascendens planete existenti super ter- 450
ram, movebit illam ad superiora in tantum quod accipiens frequenter nauseam pacietur. Cuius racio est hec.
Ascendens et eius dominus est pars celi que magis preest
pocioni medicine, cuius natura est movere inferius.
Cum igitur dominus medii celi habet secum dominum 455
ascendentem qui est protunc dominus medicine, trahit
ipsam ad se scilicet superius, secundum sol attrahit
vapores. Et sic medicina exhibit per vomitum contra
sui naturam vel stabit propter regimen nature, et putre-
fiet vel exibit per secessum contra motum dominum 460
ascendentis, quorum quodlibet est illaudabile et nature
nociuum. Insuper notandum est quod luna existente in
Leone non est bonum dare medicinam vomitinam, eo
quod medicina tunc nocet stomaco et gutturi et facit
vomere sanguinem. Fleobothomia eciam tunc non con- 465
venit, nec eciam quando luna est in via combustionis,

as it is at the end of Libra and in the beginning of Scorpio, in both cases through a range of fifteen degrees. Also, when the moon is in Aries, Taurus, or Capricorn, the person who takes medicine at once vomits it, and that is why withdrawing medicine should not then be given, but an emetic. To sum up, then, it should be known that the choice time for giving medicine is [the time] when the moon and the ascendant lord are free from evil and not impeded by it, and the tenth house is well disposed; and one must above all beware of giving medicine while the moon is in a bad aspect with Saturn or Mars, and one must above all choose [the time] when the moon is in Pisces and not impeded by equals. If, however, the moon at the start of the sickness should be in a moving sign, the sickness is quickly changeable; if in a stable sign, it is permanent; while if in an average sign, it is average.

If, however, one has an almanac and wants to get closer to the truth, one should correlate all the planets at the hour of the beginning of the illness, and when they are correlated, locate them in the appropriate houses; and when he has done this he should study at least seven: first, namely, the place of the moon in the figure; second the ascendant and its lord; third the middle of the sky, which is the tenth house; fourth the angle of the earth, which is the fourth house and its lord; fifth the sixth house and its lord; sixth the eighth house and its lord; seventh the birthday of the patient and his lord. If for [the patient] at the beginning a bad [lord] should have been ascendant, and his lord [now] bad or seen by some chance with an evil aspect, and should be in conjunction with something evil or with the sun, because the sun through conjunction signifies evil although through its aspect it signifies good, the patient will do himself harm. But if [the lord] were there good, let him on the contrary indicate good. And the reason for this is that the part of the sky which is called the ascendant has a relation to the patient. And similarly if in the tenth house [the

convenit tunc M.  467 **secundum** sicut A¹DBAs¹AdMS²Gg. **Libre** Libri Gg. **in** *(2nd) om* A¹DBAdMGg.  468 **quindecim** duodecim Ad.  469 **Ariete** *add* vel in Gg. **vel** *add* in Gg.  470 **statim** *om* M. **evomet** evomit A¹Ad. **illam** illas S². 471 **set** scilicet A¹BAs¹Ad. **vomica** vomitiva S².  472 **sciendum** sciendi Gg. 474 **impediti** impedita Ad. **non . . . et** quando M.  475 **est** *om* Gg. **medicinam** medicinas S².  476 **dum** *om* M. **est** existente M. **aspectu** aspectum As¹. **vel** et Ad.  477 **quando . . . in** *om* S². **in** *om* Gg. **cum** ceteris M.  480 **in** *(2nd) om* S². **est** *add* et cetera Gg.  482–565 **Siquis . . . Amen** *om* As¹S²Gg.  483 **accedere** *add* attendum M.  484 **eosque** eos BM. **equatos** *om* M.  485 **adequatis** *om* M.  486 **scilicet** *om* M. **in figura** *om* M.  488 **que . . . domus** *om* M.  488–89 **que** *(2nd)* **. . . domus** *om* M.  489 **eius** *om* Ad.  489–90 **quinto . . . eius** *om* M.  490 **octavam** igitur Ad; sextam M.  493 **et** *om* B. **aliqua** eum M.  494 **fortuna** forma A¹DBAd; *om* M.  495 **sit conjunctus** *om* M.  497 **sibimet** sibi ipse A¹DBAdM. **vero** *om* D. **dicat** dicit D.  498 **rei** *om* M. **pars** per que M.  499–501

secundum in fine Libre et in principio Scorpionis, in utroque per quindecim gradus. Item quando luna fuerit in Ariete, Tauro, vel Capricorno, accipiens medicinam statim evomet illam, et hinc est quod medicina secessiva tunc non est danda, set vomica. Sentencialiter autem sciendum est quod tempus electum ad dandam medicinam est quando luna et dominus ascendens sunt liberi a malo et non impediti ab eo, et decima domus est bene disposita; et summe cavendum est dare medicinam dum luna est in malo aspectu cum Saturno vel Marte, et summe eligendum est quando luna est in Piscibus cum paribus non impedita. Si autem luna in principio egritudinis fuerit in signo mobili, ipsa egritudo cito mutabilis est; si in signo stabili, permanens est; in mediocri vero, mediocris est.

Siquis autem habuerit almanak et magis ad unitatem accedere voluerit, ad horam inicii egritudinis planetas omnes adequare debet, eosque equatos, in domibus adequatis constituere; quo facto, ad septem adminus respicere debet: primo scilicet locum lune in figura; secundo ascenciones et dominum eius; tercio medium celi, que est decima domus; quarto angulum terre, que est quarta domus et dominum eius; quinto sextam domum et dominum eius; sexto octavam domum et dominum eius; septimo nativitatem pacientis et dominum eius. Quo ad primum si malus fuerit in ascencione et dominus eius malus vel aspectu malivolo aliqua fortuna aspiciatur, et conjunctus fuerit alicui malo sive soli sit conjunctus, quia sol per conjunccionem significat malum licet per aspectum significat bonum, ipse paciens sibimet nocebit. Si vero ibi fuerit bonus, dicat bonum econtra. Et causa huius rei est quia illa pars celi que vocatur ascendens habet aspectum ad pacientem. Et similiter si in decima domo fuerit bonus vel dominus

ascendant] was good or its lord good, the doctor will perform well for him. But if it were bad there, then the patient would be hurt by the doctor and the reason is this: a part of the sky is related to the doctor and his operations. Similarly, should there be good luck in the sixth house, the patient will be cured quickly, and if an evil [lord], the opposite will result. For usually such lords move from sickness to sickness, and the reason is that this house concerns sickness. The same thing is to be said that if in the fourth house there were good luck or its lord were properly disposed and not impeded, the medicine that is given will help the patient. And if there was bad [luck] there, without doubt it will harm him, and the reason is that this part of the sky regards all kinds of medicines that are given to the patient. Let him also check if the ascendant should be a mobile sign and if the moon were in a mobile sign and the ascendant lord also, the sickness without doubt will quickly end either in a good way or in a bad way, especially, nevertheless, if the moon were moving fast in its course and the ascendant lord and the sixth lord and, according to others, the seventh lord were prone to advance, that is, direct; but if it were to happen the opposite way, they will signify a length of illness, especially when they happen to be in a fixed sign. And when he will thus see the lord of the ascendant good or well disposed, that is, free from evils and joined to good things, and see the same of the moon, the end of the sickness will be good, especially if they were not joined bodily or by an aspect with the lord of the house of death, which is the eighth [house], since that part of the sky and its lord have an aspect for every kind of death. Moreover, if the ascendant lord and either the moon or the lord of illness, which is the sixth [house], were in combust or retrograde, or if the ascendant lord were in the house of death joined

Et . . . medicus *om* Ad. 501 **sibi** ibi B. **vero** *om* B. 502 **et . . . hec** et huius quia illa M. **est** *add* quia D. 504 **fortuna** forma A¹DBAd. 504-5 **domo . . . cito** domo cito paciens erit curatus A¹DBAd; cito erit bitunc paciens M. 506 **et . . . est** *om* M. 507 **hec** sexta M. 508 **domo** *om* M. **fortuna** forma A¹DBAdM. **fuerit** *om* M. 509 **non** *om* B. **ministrata** *om* M. 510 **si** *om* M. 510-14 **infortunium . . . ascendens** malus vel dominus eius fuerit infortunatus proculdubio nocebit quia quod respicit omne genus medicine que pacienti eatunc Respiciat eciam ut supra si luna fuerit in signo mobili vel ascendens an sit signorum mobile et an dominus ascendens planetarum sit in signo mobili M. 516 **tamen** *om* M. **in** *om* M. 517 **sextus** primus M. 517-18 **et (2nd) . . . septimus** *om* M. 518-19 **processivi id est** *om* M. 519 **acciderit** *om* M. 520 **in . . . fuerint** fuerint in signo fixo M. 521 **cum** *om* M. **viderit** *add* et M. **seu** *om* M. 523 **viderit** *om* M. **hoc** hec M. 524 **non** *om* M. 524-25 **conjuncti . . . cum** liberi a M. 525 **que** *om* B. 525-27 **que . . . Adhuc** *om* M. 527 **si** *add* aut M. 528 **ascendens** *add* aut M. **infirmitatis . . . est** *om* M. 529

eius bonus, bene proficiet sibi medicus. Si vero ibi fuerit
malus tunc, ledetur paciens a medico et causa est hec:
Pars celi respicit medicum et operaciones eius. Similiter
si fuerit fortuna in sexta domo, paciens erit curatus
cito, et si malus contrarium eveniet. Solent enim tales    505
transire ab egritudine in egritudinem, et causa est quia
hec domus respicit egritudinem. Hoc idem dicatur si in
quarta domo fuerit fortuna vel eius dominus fuerit
formatus et non impeditus, medicina ministrata juvabit
pacientem. Et si ibi fuerit infortunium, proculdubio       510
nocebit ei, et causa est quia ista pars celi respicit omne
genus medicinarum que pacientibus poriguntur. Respiciat eciam si ascendens fuerit signum mobile et luna
fuerit in signo mobili et dominus ascendens similiter,
proculdubio egritudo cito terminabitur sive ad bonum       515
sive ad malum precipue, tamen si luna fuerit in cursu
velox et dominus ascendens et dominus sextus et, secundum alios, dominus septimus fuerint processivi, id
est directi; set si econtra acciderit, significabunt egritudinis longitudinem, precipue cum in signo fixo fuerint.    520
Et cum ita viderit dominum ascendentem bonum seu
formatum, id est liberum a malis et conjunctum bonis,
et viderit hoc idem de luna, bona erit terminacio
egritudinis, precipue si non sint conjuncti corporaliter
vel per aspectum cum domino domus mortis, que est        525
octava, quoniam ipsa pars celi et dominus eius habent
aspectum ad omne genus mortis. Adhuc si dominus
ascendens et luna aut dominus infirmitatis, que est
sexta, fuerint combusti sive retrogradi, aut dominus
ascendens fuerit in domo mortis conjunctus Marti aut       530

in conjunction bodily with Mars or Saturn, or at least through an evil aspect, it is not reasonable to hope for life. But if he should see a waxing moon and one increased in its light, and if it should be joined to a lord ascending and both were well disposed, he would quickly see a cure of the sickness. But if the moon were in some impediment joined by the lord of the house of death, the patient will die. And there is a universal rule that it is always good to have in mind, because all the wise among astronomers are in agreement on it: that generally when the moon and the ascendant lord are impeded, the sign is troublesome, because one should always fear death or a relapse, but when they are fortunate and with many strengths, the sign is praiseworthy and toward life. To this rule, however, it joins to another, not less universal nor useful, with which none of the wise has disagreed, that whenever someone sees evil, let him say evil, and where good, let him say good. And there is an example that if one sees evil in the ascendant, it will be evil concerning the patient. For this is his house, and let him check through all the other things in the same way. Because if through the whole or in the greater part, the evil [lords] are conquering, it is evil universally, and if the opposite, the opposite will appear. Nevertheless, anyone who might have seen many of the aforesaid signs, let him nonetheless not mention [them] unless he has seen well how that planet which dominated at the hour of the birth of the patient was located at the hour of the beginning of his illness, because the significance thereof, whether good or bad, is very great. It is helpful if it is joined with others. In addition, we should note diligently what the physical condition of the patient may be, namely whether he keeps himself appropriately conditioned to receive the celestial impressions; because if this [point] is not taken into account, the evaluation would

**sexta** *add* domus D. **retrogradi** introgradi B. **dominus** *om* B. 531 **saltem** *om* M. 533 **et** *(1st) om* M. **in** *om* M. *****lumine** *(from* DBAdM) *add* in LA[1]. **fuerit** numero M. **juncta** junctam M. 534 **ascendente** *om* A[1]DAd. **ambo . . . formati** ambos fortunatos M. 535 **fuerit** *om* M. 536 **juncta** *add* fuerit M. 537-38 **quam . . . ea** inquia M. 539 **quod** quodam Ad. **generaliter** *om* M. 540-41 **signum . . . quia** *om* M. 541 **timetur** dubitatur M. **de** *(2nd) om* M. 542 **fortunati** formati A[1]DBAd. 543 **Isti** Iste BAd. 544 **non . . . utilem** *om* M. 545 **est** *om* M. 547 **Et . . . siquis** ut si M. **quod** quodam B. 548 **hic** hec D. 548-52 **hic . . . viderit** sit de singularis M. 549 **et** *om* Ad. 550 **maiori parte** maiorem partem D. 553 **tamen** *add* est facillime M. **indicet** indicandum M. **bene** quis M. **quomodo** qui D. 553-54 **quomodo . . . egritudinis** locum nativitatis et dominum eius M. 554-56 **ille . . . adjungatur** *om* M. 554 **qui** que B. 556 **Juvat** *add* et B. 557 **advertere . . . diligenter** advertendum est M. 558 **se . . . ad** habeat A[1]DBAdM. **disposicionem** digestionem M. 559 **inpressiones** disposiciones M. 559-60 **quia . . . hoc** alias enim M. 560 **de** *(1st)*

Saturno, corporaliter vel saltem per aspectum malivo-
lum, non oportet de vita sperare. Set si viderit lunam
processivam et auctam in lumine suo, et fuerit juncta
domino ascendente et ambo sint formati, cito videbit
curam egritudinis. Set si luna fuerit in aliquo impedi- 535
mento juncta domino domus mortis, paciens morietur.
Et adhuc est una regula universalis quam semper bonum
est habere in mente, quia in ea concordati sunt omnes
sapientes astronomorum: quod generaliter quando luna
et dominus ascendens fuerint inpediti, signum est mo- 540
lestum, quia semper timetur de morte aut de recidivo,
set quando fortunati sunt et cum pluribus fortitudini-
bus, signum est laudabile et ad vitam. Isti autem regule
adjungat aliam, non minus universalem nec utilem, in
qua nullus sapientum discordatus est, quod ubicumque 545
quis viderit, malum dicat malum, et ubi bonum, dicat
bonum. Et est exemplum quod siquis viderit malum in
ascendente, malum erit ex parte pacientis. Quia hic est
domus eius, et ita discurrat per omnia alia. Quod si per
totum vel maiori parte, mali vincant, malum est univ- 550
ersaliter, et si econtra, econtra apparebit. Verumpta-
men quamquam multa de predictis signis quis viderit,
non tamen indicet nisi bene viderit quomodo se habet in
hora inicii egritudinis ille planeta qui dominabatur hora
nativitatis pacientis, quia significacio ex isto, sive bona 555
sive mala, multum. Juvat si cum aliis adjungatur. Insuper advertere debemus diligenter que sit habitudo pacientis utrum, scilicet se habeat ad disposicionem
materie ad recipiendum inpressiones celestes; quia si
non respiceretur hoc, idem esset judicium de sanis et de 560

be the same for those who are well and those who are ill, since in the same hour when Sortes began to grow ill, both Plato and Socrates were healthy, although there was no change in the heavenly pattern. But in fact the heavenly influence is impressed on those who are ill, not however on those who are healthy, the reason being that the physical condition is differently disposed in the one case and in the other. The end. Amen.

... **et** in sanis M. 561 **egris** egrotis M. 562 **et** *(1st) om* M. **Socrates** Socpates D. 563 **celesti** celestis D. 564 **est** *om* M. 565 **Explicit Amen** Expliciunt canones super kalendarium A¹D; Expliciunt canones super kalendarium fratris Nicholai de Linnea ordinis carmelitarum DEUS NOS ADJUVET ASCENDERE AD CELUM B; Expliciunt canones super kalendarium Fratris Nicholai de Linnea Ad; Et sic est finis annus deo 1470 M; *add* Aries calidum et siccum minucio bona Taurus

egris, quia eadem hora qua incepit Sortes egrotare, et Plato et Socrates erant sani, non mutata figura celesti. Set celestis influencia in egris inprimitur, in sanis vero non, quia aliter et aliter est materia disposita hic et ibi. Explicit. Amen.                    565

frigidum et siccum minucio mala  Gemini calidum et humidum minucio mala Cancer frigidum et humidum minucio media  Leo calidum et siccum minucio mala  Virgo frigidum et siccum minucio mala  Libra calidum et humidum minucio bona  Scorpio frigidum et humidum minucio media  Sagittarius calidum et (*om* A¹) siccum minucio bona  Capricornus frigidum et (*om* A¹Ad) siccum minucio mala  Aquarius calidum et (*om* A¹) minucio bona  Pisces frigidum et (*om* A¹) humidum minucio media A¹DAd.

# APPENDICES

# APPENDIX A

## COMPARISONS OF SHADOW LENGTHS
## AT LOW SOLAR ALTITUDES

Appendix A shows the contrast between the various lengths of the shadows of a six-foot man when the sun is at an altitude of less than one degree. Certain manuscripts (LS¹A¹DB), as explained in the introduction, undoubtedly give the lengths of the shadows as Nicholas of Lynn wrote them. Other manuscripts (SoAs¹RAdA2As²) give what appear to be approximations of Nicholas's figures. Appendix A shows for each month except December, when no solar altitudes below one degree are recorded, the figures for the presumably accurate manuscripts, the figures for the presumably approximate manuscripts, and the figures for the actual lengths of the shadows, given Nicholas's solar altitudes.

# JANUARIUS

## Comparison of MSS. and actual shadows
## at very low solar altitudes

Numerus dierum

| | 8 LS¹A¹B | 8 SoAs¹RAdA²As² | 8 actual a.m. |
|---|---|---|---|
| | 4 LS¹A¹B | 4 SoAs¹RAdA²As² | 4 actual p.m. |

8 LS$^1$A$^1$B  8 SoAs$^1$RAdA$^2$As$^2$  8 actual a.m.
4 LS$^1$A$^1$B  4 SoAs$^1$RAdA$^2$As$^2$  4 actual p.m.

| Numerus dierum | altitudines solis g. m. | umbre hominis pedes | partes | altitudines solis g. m. | umbre hominis pedes | partes | altitudines solis g. m. | umbre hominis pedes | partes |
|---|---|---|---|---|---|---|---|---|---|
| 5 | 0 6 | 3439 | 26 | 0 6 | 3600 | 0 | 0 6 | 3529 | 25 |
| 6 | 0 15 | 1375 | 10 | 0 15 | 1350 | 0 | 0 15 | 1363 | 38 |
| 7 | 0 25 | 825 | 0 | 0 25 | 830 | 46 | 0 25 | 821 | 55 |
| 8 | 0 35 | 589 | 15 | 0 35 | 600 | 0 | 0 35 | 588 | 14 |
| 9 | 0 45 | 458 | 17 | 0 45 | 459 | 34 | 0 45 | 458 | 1 |
| 10 | 0 56 | 368 | 15 | 0 56 | 366 | 0 | 0 56 | 368 | 6 |

# FEBRUARIUS

## Comparison of MSS. and actual shadows
## at very low solar altitudes

7 LS$^1$A$^1$B  7 SoAs$^1$RAdA$^2$As$^2$  7 actual a.m.
5 LS$^1$A$^1$B  5 SoAs$^1$RAdA$^2$As$^2$  5 actual p.m.

| Numerus dierum | g. m. | pedes | partes | g. m. | pedes | partes | g. m. | pedes | partes |
|---|---|---|---|---|---|---|---|---|---|
| 10 | 0 13 | 1586 | 38 | 0 13 | 1661 | 32 | 0 13 | 1578 | 57 |
| 11 | 0 31 | 665 | 15 | 0 31 | 675 | 0 | 0 31 | 666 | 40 |
| 12 | 0 48 | 429 | 39 | 0 48 | 431 | 53 | 0 48 | 428 | 34 |

# MARCIUS

## Comparison of MSS. and actual shadows
## at very low solar altitudes

6 LS$^1$A$^1$B  6 SoAs$^1$RAdA$^2$As$^2$  6 actual a.m.
6 LS$^1$A$^1$B  6 SoAs$^1$RAdA$^2$As$^2$  6 actual p.m.

| Numerus dierum | g. m. | pedes | partes | g. m. | pedes | partes | g. m. | pedes | partes |
|---|---|---|---|---|---|---|---|---|---|
| 12 | 0 13 | 1586 | 38 | 0 13 | 1661 | 32 | 0 13 | 1578 | 57 |
| 13 | 0 31 | 665 | 15 | 0 31 | 675 | 0 | 0 31 | 666 | 40 |
| 14 | 0 49 | 420 | 54 | 0 49 | 423 | 25 | 0 49 | 419 | 35 |

## APRILIS

### Comparison of MSS. and actual shadows at very low solar altitudes

5 LS¹A¹DB — 5 SoAs¹RAdA²As² — 5 actual a.m.
7 LS¹A¹DB — 7 SoAs¹RAdA²As² — 7 actual p.m.

| Numerus dierum | altitudines solis g. m. | umbre hominis pedes | partes | altitudines solis g. m. | umbre hominis pedes | partes | altitudines solis g. m. | umbre hominis pedes | partes |
|---|---|---|---|---|---|---|---|---|---|
| 12 | 0 16 | 1289 | 15 | 0 16 | 1270 | 35 | 0 16 | 1276 | 36 |
| 13 | 0 34 | 606 | 35 | 0 34 | 617 | 9 | 0 34 | 606 | 4 |
| 14 | 0 49 | 420 | 54 | 0 49 | 423 | 25 | 0 49 | 419 | 35 |

## MAYUS

### Comparison of MSS. and actual shadows at very low solar altitudes

4 LS¹A¹DB — 4 SoAs¹RAdA²As² — 4 actual a.m.
8 LS¹A¹DB — 8 SoAs¹RAdA²As² — 8 actual p.m.

| | g. m. | pedes | partes | g. m. | pedes | partes | g. m. | pedes | partes |
|---|---|---|---|---|---|---|---|---|---|
| 19 | 0  1 | 20636 | 54 | 0  1 | 21600 | 0 | 0  1 | 20000 | 0 |
| 20 | 0 10 | 2062 | 20 | 0 10 | 2160 | 0 | 0 10 | 2068 | 58 |
| 21 | 0 17 | 1213 | 26 | 0 17 | 1200 | 0 | 0 17 | 1224 | 29 |
| 22 | 0 25 | 825 | 0 | 0 25 | 830 | 46 | 0 25 | 821 | 55 |
| 23 | 0 32 | 644 | 28 | 0 32 | 654 | 33 | 0 32 | 645 | 10 |
| 24 | 0 40 | 515 | 38 | 0 40 | 514 | 17 | 0 40 | 517 | 14 |
| 25 | 0 45 | 458 | 17 | 0 45 | 459 | 34 | 0 45 | 458 | 1 |
| 26 | 0 52 | 396 | 37 | 0 52 | 399 | 53 | 0 52 | 397 | 21 |
| 27 | 0 58 | 355 | 34 | 0 58 | 354 | 0 | 0 58 | 355 | 3 |

## JUNIUS

### Comparison of MSS. and actual shadows at very low solar altitudes

4 LS¹A¹DB — 4 SoAs¹RAdA²As² — 4 actual a.m.
8 LS¹A¹DB — 8 SoAs¹RAdA²As² — 8 actual p.m.

| | g. m. | pedes | partes | g. m. | pedes | partes | g. m. | pedes | partes |
|---|---|---|---|---|---|---|---|---|---|
| 30 | 0 55 | 374 | 57 | 0 55 | 372 | 19 | 0 55 | 375 | 0 |

# JULIUS

## Comparison of MSS. and actual shadows
## at very low solar altitudes

| Numerus dierum | 4 LS¹A¹DB / 8 LS¹A¹DB | | | 4 SoAs¹RAdA²As² / 8 SoAs¹RAdA²As² | | | 4 actual a.m. / 8 actual p.m. | | |
|---|---|---|---|---|---|---|---|---|---|
| | altitudines solis g. m. | umbre hominis pedes | partes | altitudines solis g. m. | umbre hominis pedes | partes | altitudines solis g. m. | umbre hominis pedes | partes |
| 1 | 0 50 | 412 | 29 | 0 50 | 415 | 16 | 0 50 | 413 | 48 |
| 2 | 0 43 | 479 | 36 | 0 43 | 480 | 0 | 0 43 | 480 | 0 |
| 3 | 0 37 | 557 | 25 | 0 37 | 568 | 25 | 0 37 | 555 | 33 |
| 4 | 0 30 | 687 | 33 | 0 30 | 696 | 46 | 0 30 | 689 | 39 |
| 5 | 0 23 | 896 | 43 | 0 23 | 900 | 0 | 0 23 | 895 | 31 |
| 6 | 0 15 | 1375 | 10 | 0 15 | 1350 | 0 | 0 15 | 1363 | 38 |
| 7 | 0 7 | 2945 | 24 | 0 7 | 3085 | 43 | 0 7 | 3000 | 0 |

# AUGUSTUS

## Comparison of MSS. and actual shadows
## at very low solar altitudes

| Numerus dierum | 5 LS¹A¹DB / 7 LS¹A¹DB | | 5 As¹RAdA²As² / 7 As¹RAdA²As² | | 5 actual a.m. / 7 actual p.m. | |
|---|---|---|---|---|---|---|
| 12 | 0 44 | 468 42 | 0 44 | 469 34 | 0 44 | 468 45 |
| 13 | 0 28 | 736 39 | 0 28 | 744 50 | 0 28 | 740 44 |
| 14 | 0 12 | 1718 47 | 0 12 | 1661 32 | 0 12 | 1714 17 |

# SEPTEMBER

## Comparison of MSS. and actual shadows
## at very low solar altitudes

| Numerus dierum | 6 LS¹A¹DB / 6 LS¹A¹DB | | 6 As¹RAdA²As² / 6 As¹RAdA²As² | | 6 actual a.m. / 6 actual p.m. | |
|---|---|---|---|---|---|---|
| 12 | 0 44 | 468 42 | 0 44 | 469 34 | 0 44 | 468 45 |
| 13 | 0 26 | 793 17 | 0 26 | 800 0 | 0 26 | 789 28 |
| 14 | 0 7 | 2945 24 | 0 7 | 3085 43 | 0 7 | 3000 0 |

# OCTOBER

## Comparison of MSS. and actual shadows
### at very low solar altitudes

| | 7 LS¹A¹DB | | | 7 As¹RAdA²As² | | | 7 actual a.m. | | |
| | 5 LS¹A¹DB | | | 7 As¹RAdA²As² | | | 5 actual p.m. | | |

| Numerus dierum | altitudines solis (g. m.) | umbre hominis (pedes) | (partes) | altitudines solis (g. m.) | umbre hominis (pedes) | (partes) | altitudines solis (g. m.) | umbre hominis (pedes) | (partes) |
|---|---|---|---|---|---|---|---|---|---|
| 12 | 0 42 | 491 | 5 | 0 42 | 490 | 55 | 0 42 | 491 | 48 |
| 13 | 0 25 | 825 | 0 | 0 25 | 830 | 46 | 0 25 | 821 | 55 |
| 14 | 0 8 | 2578 | 12 | 0 8 | 2700 | 0 | 0 8 | 2608 | 42 |

# NOVEMBER

## Comparison of MSS. and actual shadows
### at very low solar altitudes

| | 8 LS¹A¹DB | | | 8 As¹RAdA²As² | | | 8 actual a.m. | | |
| | 4 LS¹A¹DB | | | 4 As¹RAdA²As² | | | 4 actual p.m. | | |

| Numerus dierum | altitudines solis (g. m.) | umbre hominis (pedes) | (partes) | altitudines solis (g. m.) | umbre hominis (pedes) | (partes) | altitudines solis (g. m.) | umbre hominis (pedes) | (partes) |
|---|---|---|---|---|---|---|---|---|---|
| 14 | 0 52 | 396 | 37 | 0 52 | 399 | 53 | 0 52 | 397 | 21 |
| 15 | 0 41 | 503 | 33 | 0 41 | 502 | 20 | 0 41 | 504 | 12 |
| 16 | 0 31 | 665 | 15 | 0 31 | 675 | 0 | 0 31 | 666 | 40 |
| 17 | 0 21 | 982 | 4 | 0 21 | 981 | 49 | 0 21 | 983 | 36 |
| 18 | 0 12 | 1718 | 47 | 0 12 | 1661 | 32 | 0 12 | 1714 | 17 |
| 19 | 0 2 | 10318 | 25 | 0 2 | 10800 | 0 | 0 2 | 10000 | 0 |

# APPENDIX B

## COMPARISONS OF NICHOLAS'S ECLIPSES
## WITH ACTUAL ECLIPSES

Appendix B is based on the two tables by Nicholas of Lynn entitled *Tabula Eclipsis Solis* and *Tabula Eclipsis Lune*. The tables in Appendix B, however, show in the manner of Nicholas the actual solar and lunar eclipses visible from Oxford between 1387 and 1462 inclusive.

Certain observations about the eclipses may be made. The conjunction of the sun with the moon in the solar eclipse on 26 April 1446 occurred three minutes before sunrise. Lunar eclipses on 26 November 1406, 3 September 1411, 14 July 1413, 26 October 1417, 21 April 1418, 18 February 1421, 26 November 1425, 24 September 1428, and 13 June 1443, began before moonrise. Lunar eclipses on 27 February 1393, 3 July 1395, 9 April 1400, 13 August 1421, 12 June 1424, 1 June 1425, 6 November 1435, 25 October 1436, 13 August 1440, and 1 April 1447, ended after moonset.

One may compare these tables with the corresponding tables in the *Kalendarium* of Nicholas to see the difference between the prediction of eclipses made by Nicholas and the actual occurrences of the eclipses.

Tabula eclipsis solis pro primo ciclo cuius principium est annus Christi 1387 finis 1399

| Ciclus | Anni Christi | Menses | Conjuncciones vise | | | | Punctus eclipsis | | | Tempus casus | | | Duracio | | |
|---|---|---|---|---|---|---|---|---|---|---|---|---|---|---|---|
| | | | d. | h. | m. | s. | pt. | m. | s. | h. | m. | s. | h. | m. | s. |
| 1 | 1387 | Junius | 16 | 22 | 23 | 24 | 1 | 40 | 48 | 0 | 42 | 0 | 1 | 24 | 0 |
| 5 | 1391 | Aprilis | 5 | 18 | 24 | 0 | 1 | 33 | 36 | 0 | 33 | 18 | 1 | 6 | 36 |
| 6 | 1392 | Marcius | 24 | 19 | 10 | 12 | 6 | 0 | 0 | 1 | 4 | 12 | 2 | 8 | 24 |
| 7 | 1393 | Augustus | 8 | 21 | 47 | 24 | 2 | 31 | 12 | 0 | 50 | 24 | 1 | 40 | 48 |
| 10 | 1396 | Januarius | 11 | 23 | 25 | 48 | 7 | 12 | 0 | 1 | 12 | 18 | 2 | 24 | 36 |
| 13 | 1399 | October | 30 | 0 | 15 | 36 | 9 | 21 | 36 | 1 | 23 | 6 | 2 | 46 | 12 |

Tabula eclipsis solis pro secundo ciclo cuius principium est annus Christi 1406 finis vero 1424

| Ciclus | Anni Christi | Menses | Conjuncciones vise | | | | Punctus eclipsis | | | Tempus casus | | | Duracio | | |
|---|---|---|---|---|---|---|---|---|---|---|---|---|---|---|---|
| | | | d. | h. | m. | s. | pt. | m. | s. | h. | m. | s. | h. | m. | s. |
| 1 | 1406 | Junius | 16 | 18 | 10 | 12 | 11 | 31 | 12 | 0 | 55 | 30 | 1 | 51 | 0 |
| 3 | 1408 | October | 19 | 21 | 3 | 36 | 7 | 12 | 0 | 1 | 4 | 12 | 2 | 8 | 24 |
| 4 | 1409 | Aprilis | 16 | 3 | 11 | 24 | 11 | 31 | 12 | 1 | 22 | 48 | 2 | 45 | 36 |
| 6 | 1411 | Augustus | 20 | 6 | 22 | 12 | 10 | 55 | 12 | 0 | 46 | 12 | 1 | 32 | 24 |
| 10 | 1415 | Junius | 7 | 18 | 13 | 12 | 10 | 19 | 12 | 0 | 54 | 54 | 1 | 49 | 48 |
| 13 | 1418 | Aprilis | 6 | 21 | 15 | 0 | 5 | 38 | 24 | 1 | 12 | 54 | 2 | 25 | 48 |
| 14 | 1419 | Marcius | 26 | 21 | 35 | 24 | 2 | 2 | 24 | 0 | 49 | 30 | 1 | 39 | 0 |
| 19 | 1424 | Junius | 27 | 2 | 20 | 24 | 10 | 26 | 24 | 1 | 6 | 36 | 2 | 13 | 12 |

Tabula eclipsis solis pro tercio ciclo cuius principium est annus Christi 1425 finis vero 1440

| | | | | | | | | | | | | | | | |
|---|---|---|---|---|---|---|---|---|---|---|---|---|---|---|---|
| 1 | 1425 | November | 10 | 20 | 51 | 36 | 1 | 48 | 0 | 0 | 42 | 0 | 1 | 24 | 0 |
| 7 | 1431 | Februarius | 13 | 2 | 22 | 12 | 8 | 24 | 0 | 1 | 3 | 18 | 2 | 6 | 36 |
| 9 | 1433 | Junius | 18 | 3 | 27 | 36 | 11 | 31 | 12 | 1 | 4 | 30 | 2 | 9 | 0 |
| 12 | 1436 | Aprilis | 17 | 6 | 18 | 36 | 0 | 43 | 12 | 0 | 22 | 48 | 0 | 45 | 36 |
| 13 | 1437 | Aprilis | 6 | 6 | 22 | 48 | 7 | 56 | 0 | 0 | 46 | 12 | 1 | 32 | 24 |
| 14 | 1438 | September | 19 | 22 | 56 | 24 | 4 | 55 | 12 | 1 | 9 | 0 | 2 | 18 | 0 |
| 15 | 1439 | September | 9 | 4 | 26 | 24 | 6 | 28 | 48 | 1 | 8 | 6 | 2 | 16 | 12 |
| 16 | 1440 | Februarius | 4 | 1 | 6 | 36 | 10 | 19 | 12 | 1 | 13 | 30 | 2 | 27 | 0 |

Tabula eclipsis solis pro quarto ciclo cuius principium est annus Christi 1446 finis 1462

| | | | | | | | | | | | | | | | |
|---|---|---|---|---|---|---|---|---|---|---|---|---|---|---|---|
| 3 | 1446 | Aprilis | 26 | 16 | 30 | 0 | 4 | 19 | 12 | 0 | 10 | 30 | 0 | 21 | 0 |
| 5 | 1448 | Augustus | 29 | 21 | 49 | 12 | 8 | 45 | 36 | 1 | 25 | 48 | 2 | 51 | 36 |
| 7 | 1450 | Februarius | 13 | 1 | 45 | 0 | 1 | 40 | 48 | 0 | 37 | 30 | 1 | 15 | 0 |
| 10 | 1453 | December | 1 | 2 | 34 | 48 | 10 | 4 | 48 | 1 | 16 | 12 | 2 | 32 | 24 |
| 17 | 1460 | Julius | 18 | 16 | 15 | 36 | 6 | 36 | 0 | 0 | 24 | 18 | 0 | 48 | 36 |
| 19 | 1462 | November | 21 | 23 | 12 | 36 | 1 | 40 | 48 | 0 | 25 | 12 | 1 | 20 | 24 |

ACTUAL LUNAR ECLIPSES CALCULATED IN THE MANNER OF NICHOLAS OF LYNN

Tabula eclipsis lune pro primo ciclo cuius principium est annus Christi 1387 finis 1405

| Ciclus | Anni Christi | Menses | Vere opposiciones | | | | Punctus eclipsis | | | Tempus casus | | | Mora | | Duracio | | |
|---|---|---|---|---|---|---|---|---|---|---|---|---|---|---|---|---|---|
| | | | d. | h. | m. | s. | pt. | m. | s. | h. | m. | s. | m. | s. | h. | m. | s. |
| 1 | 1387 | November | 26 | 9 | 52 | 48 | 0 | 28 | 48 | 0 | 22 | 12 | 0 | 0 | 0 | 44 | 24 |
| 2 | 1388 | Mayus | 22 | 6 | 13 | 48 | 11 | 9 | 36 | 1 | 42 | 0 | 0 | 0 | 3 | 24 | 0 |
| 3 | 1389 | Mayus | 11 | 6 | 49 | 12 | 16 | 4 | 48 | 1 | 10 | 12 | 43 | 12 | 3 | 46 | 48 |
| 5 | 1391 | Marcius | 21 | 11 | 37 | 48 | 2 | 16 | 48 | 0 | 46 | 48 | 0 | 0 | 1 | 33 | 36 |
| 6 | 1392 | September | 2 | 14 | 48 | 36 | 14 | 45 | 36 | 1 | 13 | 24 | 36 | 36 | 3 | 39 | 0 |
| 7 | 1393 | Februarius | 27 | 18 | 47 | 24 | 11 | 16 | 48 | 1 | 34 | 48 | 0 | 0 | 3 | 9 | 36 |
| 9 | 1395 | Julius | 3 | 20 | 18 | 0 | 7 | 48 | 0 | 1 | 21 | 0 | 0 | 0 | 2 | 42 | 0 |
| 9 | 1395 | December | 27 | 11 | 49 | 48 | 15 | 15 | 48 | 1 | 10 | 48 | 37 | 12 | 3 | 36 | 0 |
| 10 | 1396 | Junius | 22 | 9 | 51 | 0 | 20 | 38 | 24 | 1 | 0 | 0 | 51 | 0 | 3 | 42 | 0 |
| 11 | 1397 | Junius | 11 | 16 | 29 | 24 | 2 | 31 | 12 | 0 | 54 | 0 | 0 | 0 | 1 | 48 | 0 |
| 12 | 1398 | October | 26 | 15 | 1 | 12 | 0 | 28 | 48 | 0 | 21 | 36 | 0 | 0 | 0 | 43 | 12 |
| 13 | 1399 | Aprilis | 21 | 7 | 52 | 12 | 13 | 26 | 24 | 1 | 16 | 48 | 26 | 24 | 3 | 26 | 24 |
| 14 | 1400 | Aprilis | 9 | 20 | 4 | 48 | 14 | 38 | 24 | 1 | 7 | 12 | 33 | 36 | 3 | 21 | 36 |
| 16 | 1402 | Februarius | 18 | 16 | 57 | 36 | 2 | 38 | 24 | 0 | 52 | 12 | 0 | 0 | 1 | 44 | 24 |
| 17 | 1403 | Augustus | 3 | 10 | 34 | 24 | 18 | 50 | 24 | 0 | 58 | 12 | 46 | 48 | 3 | 30 | 0 |
| 18 | 1404 | Julius | 23 | 3 | 39 | 0 | 10 | 26 | 24 | 1 | 29 | 24 | 0 | 0 | 2 | 58 | 48 |

## Tabula eclipsis lune pro secundo ciclo cuius principium est annus Christi 1406 finis 1424

| | | | | | | | | | | | | | | | | | |
|---|---|---|---|---|---|---|---|---|---|---|---|---|---|---|---|---|---|
| 1 | 1406 | Junius | 2 | 12 | 43 | 12 | 9 | 14 | 24 | 1 | 35 | 24 | 0 | 0 | 3 | 10 | 48 |
| 1 | 1406 | November | 26 | 9 | 42 | 0 | 15 | 43 | 12 | 1 | 3 | 0 | 37 | 12 | 3 | 20 | 24 |
| 2 | 1407 | Mayus | 22 | 13 | 19 | 48 | 17 | 52 | 48 | 1 | 6 | 36 | 48 | 48 | 3 | 50 | 24 |
| 3 | 1408 | Mayus | 5 | 17 | 15 | 0 | 1 | 40 | 48 | 0 | 43 | 12 | 0 | 0 | 1 | 26 | 24 |
| 5 | 1410 | Marcius | 21 | 12 | 12 | 0 | 17 | 2 | 24 | 1 | 0 | 36 | 42 | 0 | 3 | 25 | 12 |
| 6 | 1411 | September | 3 | 4 | 49 | 12 | 14 | 2 | 24 | 1 | 12 | 0 | 30 | 12 | 3 | 25 | 12 |
| 8 | 1413 | Julius | 14 | 3 | 41 | 24 | 6 | 7 | 12 | 1 | 13 | 48 | 0 | 0 | 2 | 27 | 36 |
| 9 | 1414 | Julius | 3 | 16 | 49 | 48 | 22 | 51 | 36 | 1 | 0 | 0 | 51 | 36 | 3 | 43 | 12 |
| 12 | 1417 | Mayus | 1 | 15 | 5 | 24 | 12 | 0 | 0 | 1 | 35 | 24 | 1 | 0 | 3 | 18 | 0 |
| 12 | 1417 | October | 26 | 8 | 27 | 36 | 14 | 38 | 24 | 1 | 12 | 36 | 34 | 48 | 3 | 34 | 48 |
| 13 | 1418 | Aprilis | 21 | 3 | 48 | 0 | 15 | 57 | 36 | 1 | 0 | 18 | 39 | 36 | 3 | 25 | 12 |
| 13 | 1418 | October | 15 | 10 | 22 | 24 | 13 | 33 | 36 | 1 | 20 | 24 | 28 | 12 | 3 | 37 | 12 |
| 16 | 1421 | Februarius | 18 | 7 | 31 | 12 | 17 | 2 | 24 | 1 | 7 | 12 | 45 | 36 | 3 | 45 | 36 |
| 16 | 1421 | Augustus | 13 | 18 | 18 | 36 | 17 | 24 | 0 | 0 | 59 | 24 | 43 | 48 | 3 | 26 | 24 |
| 17 | 1422 | Februarius | 7 | 7 | 40 | 12 | 11 | 2 | 24 | 1 | 42 | 36 | 0 | 0 | 3 | 25 | 12 |
| 17 | 1422 | Augustus | 3 | 11 | 14 | 24 | 11 | 52 | 48 | 1 | 33 | 36 | 0 | 0 | 3 | 7 | 12 |
| 19 | 1424 | Junius | 12 | 19 | 9 | 0 | 7 | 19 | 12 | 1 | 27 | 36 | 0 | 0 | 2 | 55 | 12 |

ACTUAL LUNAR ECLIPSES CALCULATED IN THE MANNER OF NICHOLAS OF LYNN

Tabula eclipsis lune pro tercio ciclo cuius principium est annus Christi 1425 finis 1443

| Ciclus | Anni Christi | Menses | Vere opposiciones | | | | Punctus eclipsis | | | Tempus casus | | | Mora | | Duracio | | |
|---|---|---|---|---|---|---|---|---|---|---|---|---|---|---|---|---|---|
| | | | d. | h. | m. | s. | pt. | m. | s. | h. | m. | s. | m. | s. | h. | m. | s. |
| 1 | 1425 | Junius | 1 | 19 | 48 | 0 | 19 | 48 | 0 | 1 | 4 | 48 | 52 | 12 | 3 | 54 | 0 |
| 1 | 1425 | November | 26 | 9 | 38 | 24 | 14 | 24 | 0 | 1 | 8 | 24 | 31 | 48 | 3 | 20 | 24 |
| 4 | 1428 | September | 24 | 5 | 37 | 48 | 12 | 48 | 0 | 1 | 26 | 24 | 18 | 0 | 3 | 28 | 48 |
| 5 | 1429 | Marcius | 21 | 10 | 55 | 12 | 12 | 50 | 24 | 1 | 18 | 48 | 20 | 24 | 3 | 18 | 0 |
| 5 | 1429 | September | 13 | 12 | 36 | 0 | 15 | 7 | 12 | 1 | 7 | 48 | 36 | 36 | 3 | 28 | 48 |
| 7 | 1431 | Julius | 25 | 11 | 9 | 0 | 4 | 33 | 48 | 1 | 4 | 48 | 0 | 0 | 2 | 9 | 36 |
| 9 | 1433 | Januarius | 6 | 13 | 28 | 48 | 13 | 55 | 12 | 1 | 11 | 24 | 28 | 48 | 3 | 20 | 24 |
| 9 | 1433 | Julius | 3 | 5 | 30 | 0 | 6 | 7 | 12 | 1 | 21 | 36 | 0 | 0 | 2 | 43 | 12 |
| 11 | 1435 | November | 6 | 16 | 31 | 48 | 14 | 9 | 36 | 1 | 14 | 24 | 32 | 24 | 3 | 33 | 36 |
| 12 | 1436 | Mayus | 1 | 11 | 25 | 48 | 17 | 24 | 0 | 1 | 0 | 36 | 43 | 48 | 3 | 28 | 48 |
| 12 | 1436 | October | 25 | 18 | 3 | 36 | 14 | 2 | 24 | 1 | 17 | 24 | 32 | 24 | 3 | 37 | 12 |
| 14 | 1438 | Marcius | 12 | 9 | 6 | 36 | 1 | 12 | 0 | 0 | 35 | 24 | 0 | 0 | 1 | 10 | 48 |
| 15 | 1439 | Marcius | 1 | 15 | 14 | 24 | 16 | 19 | 12 | 1 | 9 | 0 | 43 | 12 | 3 | 44 | 24 |
| 16 | 1440 | Februarius | 18 | 15 | 19 | 48 | 11 | 45 | 36 | 1 | 44 | 24 | 0 | 0 | 3 | 28 | 48 |
| 16 | 1440 | Augustus | 13 | 18 | 56 | 24 | 1 | 6 | 0 | 1 | 14 | 24 | 22 | 48 | 3 | 14 | 24 |
| 17 | 1441 | December | 28 | 11 | 55 | 48 | 0 | 28 | 48 | 0 | 21 | 0 | 0 | 0 | 0 | 42 | 0 |
| 19 | 1443 | Junius | 13 | 2 | 13 | 48 | 21 | 50 | 24 | 1 | 3 | 36 | 53 | 24 | 3 | 54 | 0 |

Tabula eclipsis lune pro quarto ciclo cuius principium est annus Christi 1444 finis 1462

| | | | | | | | | | | | | | | | | | |
|---|---|---|---|---|---|---|---|---|---|---|---|---|---|---|---|---|---|
| 1 | 1444 | Junius | 1 | 7 | 4 | 48 | 5 | 16 | 48 | 1 | 12 | 36 | 0 | 0 | 2 | 25 | 12 |
| 3 | 1446 | Aprilis | 12 | 4 | 13 | 12 | 14 | 52 | 48 | 1 | 6 | 0 | 33 | 36 | 3 | 19 | 12 |
| 3 | 1446 | October | 5 | 13 | 16 | 12 | 11 | 52 | 48 | 1 | 42 | 0 | 0 | 0 | 3 | 24 | 0 |
| 4 | 1447 | Aprilis | 1 | 18 | 44 | 24 | 13 | 55 | 12 | 1 | 12 | 0 | 29 | 24 | 3 | 22 | 48 |
| 5 | 1448 | September | 13 | 10 | 25 | 48 | 1 | 4 | 48 | 0 | 32 | 24 | 0 | 0 | 1 | 4 | 48 |
| 6 | 1449 | Augustus | 4 | 18 | 40 | 48 | 3 | 0 | 0 | 0 | 54 | 0 | 0 | 0 | 1 | 48 | 0 |
| 7 | 1450 | Januarius | 28 | 12 | 27 | 0 | 14 | 38 | 24 | 1 | 12 | 0 | 34 | 8 | 3 | 33 | 24 |
| 7 | 1450 | Julius | 25 | 6 | 52 | 48 | 18 | 57 | 24 | 1 | 1 | 48 | 49 | 12 | 3 | 42 | 0 |
| 8 | 1451 | Julius | 14 | 12 | 1 | 12 | 7 | 55 | 12 | 1 | 30 | 0 | 0 | 0 | 3 | 0 | 0 |
| 10 | 1453 | Mayus | 23 | 5 | 19 | 48 | 9 | 0 | 0 | 1 | 21 | 36 | 0 | 0 | 2 | 43 | 12 |
| 11 | 1454 | Mayus | 12 | 18 | 57 | 36 | 18 | 57 | 36 | 0 | 58 | 12 | 47 | 24 | 3 | 31 | 12 |
| 12 | 1455 | Mayus | 2 | 11 | 55 | 48 | 3 | 0 | 0 | 0 | 52 | 48 | 0 | 0 | 1 | 45 | 36 |
| 13 | 1456 | Marcius | 22 | 16 | 57 | 0 | 0 | 12 | 0 | 0 | 13 | 36 | 0 | 0 | 0 | 27 | 36 |
| 14 | 1457 | September | 4 | 10 | 10 | 12 | 15 | 7 | 12 | 1 | 4 | 48 | 34 | 48 | 3 | 19 | 12 |
| 17 | 1460 | Julius | 4 | 7 | 57 | 12 | 3 | 21 | 36 | 1 | 3 | 0 | 0 | 0 | 2 | 6 | 0 |
| 17 | 1460 | December | 28 | 12 | 5 | 24 | 15 | 28 | 48 | 1 | 3 | 36 | 36 | 36 | 3 | 20 | 24 |
| 18 | 1461 | Junius | 23 | 8 | 40 | 12 | 20 | 16 | 48 | 1 | 4 | 12 | 52 | 12 | 3 | 52 | 48 |
| 19 | 1462 | Junius | 12 | 13 | 58 | 12 | 7 | 4 | 48 | 1 | 22 | 12 | 0 | 0 | 2 | 44 | 24 |

# TEXTUAL NOTES

# NOTES TO THE TEXT

## PROLOGUE

The prologue to the *Kalendarium* appears in L (the base MS.) and the following: S¹A¹SoAs¹RAdA². S¹A¹SoR follow L fairly closely. Aside from one major hiatus recorded in the corpus of variants, so does Ad. As¹A² have a prologue comprised of bits and pieces of Nicholas's text as reconstructed in this edition rearranged to fit the purposes of the scribes of As¹A². Using the line numbers I have given to the prologue in this edition, I offer the rearrangement of As¹A² in the following manner. As¹: 1-40, 41-44, 61-62, 59-61, 57-59, 55-57, 40-41, 63-67; A²: 1-44, 61-62, 59-61, 57-59.

## THE CALENDAR

FEBRUARY. The Metonic order shown on the beginning page of February contains two errors. For 15 February the number 17 replaces the correct 7; for 18 February the number 14 replaces the correct 4. This error is unique to L and has been emended to the correct numbers.

In L the third cycle of the new moon for 26 February shows "3 23 30," meaning that in the third year of the third cycle (1427) the new moon was on 26 February at 23 hours, 30 minutes, or at 11:30 A.M. on 26 February by modern computation. This edition is here emended to be consistent with S¹BSoAs¹A²As², which show the time to be 23 hours, 21 minutes. The other manuscripts do not show this cycle. Actually the time of the new moon was 12:02 on 27 February 1427, or 0 hours, 2 minutes by Nicholas's method of computation.

In L the fourth cycle of the full moon for 3 February shows "12 4 35," meaning that in the twelfth year of the fourth cycle (1455) the full moon was on 3 February at 4 hours, 35 minutes, or 2 February at 4:35 P.M. by modern computation. BSoAdA²As² show the time at 5 hours, 34 minutes. S¹A¹DAs¹R do not show this cycle. In spite of the preponderance of manuscripts stating the time of this full moon to be 5 hours, 34 minutes, I have judged no emendation to be necessary because the actual time of the full moon on 3 February 1455, by Nicholas's method of computation, was 4 hours, 15 minutes, somewhat closer to the 4 hours, 35 minutes of L than to the time offered in the other manuscripts.

MARCH. Under *Quantitates diei artificialis* for 3 March, L offers 11° 24', and this figure has been emended in this edition to 11° 27', as it is in S¹A¹BSoAs¹RAdA² As². Apparently L is in error here.

The altitudes of the sun at 9/3 on 28, 29, 30 March are given in L as 13° 30', 31° 49', 32° 8'. BSoAs¹RAdA²As² agree with L. S¹A¹, however, give the same figures as 31° 31', 31° 51', 32° 11'. On the same page at 11/1 the minutes of the degree for the altitude of the sun on 28 March is given as 50 by S¹A¹. The other manuscripts agree with L that the figure is 56 minutes, and no emendation is necessary. This page offers two of a number of examples in which S¹A¹ have comparable figures differing from the majority of the manuscripts.

Another such example appears on the very next page. The altitude of the sun at 12/0 on 20 March is given as 41° 36′ in $S^1A^1$. $LBSoAs^1RAdA^2As^2$ give the figures as 41° 34′.

APRIL. On the first page of April in L the name *Aries* by 20° 14′ of *Verus locus solis* and the name *Taurus* by 0° 54′ of *Verus locus solis* do not appear, although they would normally do so. In addition certain other numbers do not appear on this page of L, although they should: 8, 16, and 5 under the lunar scale; 4, 3, and 2 preceding *Nonas;* and 8, 7, 6, 5, and 4 preceding *Idus.* All of these have been supplied from $S^1$.

MAY. 1 May: The Saints Philip and James were transferred in modern times to 11 May.

3 May: *Sancti Blasii episcopi et martyris* is an error repeating the entry of 3 February. The proper notation for this date is *Invencio Sancte Crucis.* See corpus of variants of listed saints, p. 137.

In L the third cycle of the new moon for 13 May shows "15 16 50," meaning that in the fifteenth year of the third cycle (1439) the new moon was on 13 May at 16 hours, 50 minutes, or 13 May at 4:50 A.M. by modern computation. $BSoAs^1As^2$ agree. $S^1D$ offer "15 15 50." The true time of the new moon on 13 May 1439 was 5:17 A.M., or "15 17 17," as Nicholas would write it. Thus L and those like it are closer to the true new moon than $S^1D$, and no emendation is necessary.

AUGUST. In the third cycle of August in L the full moon for the eighteenth year (1442) is given as the 4th hour and 56th minute on 22 August. This information also appears in $S^1D$. In $BAs^1RAdA^2As^2$ the date is given as 21 August. The hour in $BAs^1AdA^2$ is 22, although the minutes remain the same. In R the time is 8 hours, 53 minutes; and in $A^2$ the time is 11 hours, 18 minutes. The true time, as Nicholas reckons time, for the August full moon in 1442 was 22 August at 11 hours, 3 minutes. Thus $LS^1D$ are far closer to the accurate time, while the other manuscripts are about a full day or more in error. No emendation is necessary.

In $S^1$ in the third cycle of the August full moon the scribe has miscopied the numbers, placing each into the column where the number above it should be. Thus the column begins and ends with a 9 instead of a 1.

OCTOBER. 6 October: *Sancti* is an error for *Sancte.* This error is unique to L and does not appear in $RAs^2$, which also list St. Faith for this date.

28 October: Obviously the scribe planned to list more apostles than just St. Simon. St. Jude was listed with St. Simon in $S^1A^1BAs^1RAdA^2As^2$.

In the shadow scale for 12/0 the altitude of the sun for 5 October is given as 20° 8′ in L. This is an error. All of the other manuscripts and the logic of the figures demand that the correct altitude is 30° 8′, and accordingly I have placed such an emendation in this edition.

NOVEMBER. 26 November: *Line* is an error for *Lini.*

DECEMBER. On the first page of December the scribe for L omitted the letter *A* to indicate the dominical letter for 31 December. $S^1A^1DBAs^1RAdA^2As^2$ contain no such omission, nor does this edition.

16 December: During the last seven days of Advent, 17 to 23 December, antiphons are sung beginning with *O:* The antiphon for 17 December begins with the words *O sapiencia.* Because each day in this *Kalendarium* begins at noon on the previous day, LR have listed *O sapiencia* for 16 December.

TABULA ECLIPSIS SOLIS. The date 1 November 1453 appears in L and is an error. The actual date, 1 December 1453, appears in S¹A¹DBAs¹, and therefore an emendation is justified. Ad, which presents the same information in the manner of John Somer and does not on this chart begin the astronomical day at noon on the previous day, offers 30 November 1453.

FIGURE ECLIPSIS SOLIS. The time of the beginning of the eclipse in March 1392 reads 5 hours, 39 minutes, 9 seconds before noon in L. This edition is emended here to be consistent with S¹A¹BAs¹A², which read 5 hours, 39 minutes, 8 seconds before noon, a figure which coincides with the information provided in the *Tabula eclipsis solis.* The actual time of the beginning of this eclipse is 5 hours, 54 minutes, 0 seconds before noon (i.e., 6:06 A.M. by modern computation). In a like manner L offers 4 hours, 0 minutes, 14 seconds before noon for the eclipse of October 1408, where the other manuscripts and the *Tabula eclipsis solis* offer 4 hours, 0 minutes, 13 seconds before noon. Accordingly the 14 in L is emended to the 13 in this edition. The actual time of the beginning of that eclipse was 4 hours, 0 minutes, 36 seconds before noon (i.e., 7:59:24 A.M. by modern computation).

TABULA ECLIPSIS LUNE. The eclipse of March 1391 in L shows a *Tempus casus* of "0 51 52." S¹A¹BAs¹ show "0 51 42," and Ad shows "0 51 41." The scribe of L appears to be in error, and this edition is emended to "0 51 42." The actual *Tempus casus* of this eclipse is "0 46 48."

The date 1 April 1417 appears in L and is an error. The actual date, 1 May 1417, appears in S¹A¹BAs¹ and, accordingly, in this edition. Ad, for reasons described in the note to the *Tabula eclipsis solis,* offers 30 April 1417.

The *Duracio* of the lunar eclipse in July 1431 is given by LA¹ as "2 19 6." This figure is correct because it is twice the sum of the *Tempus casus,* which is "1 9 33," and the *Mora,* which is "0 0." No emendation is necessary. Nevertheless, S¹BAs¹Ad give the initial number as 3 instead of 2. Apparently an early scribe, copying a column of almost all 3's, put a 3 where a 2 belongs.

The lunar eclipse in January 1450 is given as 21 January in LS¹BAs¹As². Ad, for reasons explained in the note to the *Tabula eclipsis solis,* offers 20 January. The correct day is 28 January. (See Appendix B.) Because the error is common to Nicholas of Lynn and to John Somer, as may be seen in the information presented in Ad, I suggest it appeared in their common source. Interestingly enough, A¹ gives the correct date of 28 January. The error, as it appears in LS¹BAs¹As²Ad, is carried over to the *Figure eclipsis lune* (except for L, which lacks this folio), as is the correct date in A¹. Because the error is consistently in all manuscripts (including presumably the one Chaucer held in his hand), no emendation is necessary.

FIGURE ECLIPSIS LUNE. In As¹AdA² the duration and the year within the cycle are given for each eclipse figure.

In the description of the lunar eclipse of January 1432, the scribe of L writes the year as 14, leaving off the last two digits of the number. The emendation here to 1432 is consistent with the other manuscripts.

Certain descriptions of lunar eclipses in S[1] eliminate the words *Hec est incipiens* and begin instead with the words *Anno domini.* These eclipses are those for October 1436, February 1440, December 1442, June 1444, April 1447, January 1450, July 1451, March 1456, July 1460, June 1461, and June 1462.

Beginning with the lunar eclipse in March 1439, and lasting through the lunar eclipse of June 1462, the drawings of the eclipses are taken from A[1] because the artist of A[1] more accurately portrays each *punctus eclipsis,* or magnitude, than does the artist of S[1]. The text which surrounds each drawing, however, is taken from S[1] because the information given conforms more closely to the eclipse tables of L than does the information in A[1]. Beginning with *ARIES Equaciones domorum* and lasting through *TAURUS Equaciones domorum,* the material is taken from S[1]. L has a complete folio missing here. See introduction, p. 47.

In the eclipse of January 1450, the date *12 Kl* is an error for the actual *5 Kl.* See note concerning the lunar eclipse of January 1450. Because the error is consistently in all manuscripts except L, which lacks this folio, and A[1], which contains the correct and presumably altered information, no emendation is necessary.

ARIES. In S[1]A[1] the equation of the fourth house begins with Taurus, an error. The proper beginning is Cancer, which follows the end of Gemini in the fourth house of Pisces. The proper information appears in BAs[1], and this edition is so emended. The other manuscripts do not have this page.

GEMINI. The material again follows L.

In L the notation *Scorp.* after Libra 30° in the Sixth House is missing, although present in S[1]A[1]DBAs[1]. The notation is added in this edition.

LEO. After Sagittarius 29° in the Sixth House the notation in L is *Aquar.,* indicating the beginning of Aquarius. Because Capricorn and not Aquarius begins at this point, the notation is incorrect and is accordingly emended. This error also appears in S[1]A[1]D. The correct notation appears in BAs[1].

VIRGO. The same error as above occurs in L after Sagittarius 29° in the Fifth House of Virgo. The notation *Aquar.* should be *Capr.* and is so emended. Again the error appears in S[1]A[1]D but not in BAs[1].

B reverses the headings LIBRA and SAGITTARIUS and also reverses the headings SCORPIO and CAPRICORN.

PISCES. At Pisces 22° the ascension in the direct circle is given at 82° 20′ in LS[1]D. The correct figure, 82° 40′, appears in A[1]BAs[1] and is so emended in this edition.

TABULA . . . QUIS PLANETA REGNAT. In L the title to the table on this page is given as *Tabula ad cognoscendum pro qualibet hora diei vel noctis quis planeta regnat.* One word in the title, *cognoscendum,* is unique to L; it appears in all other manuscripts as *sciendum,* and is so emended in this edition. Also unique to L are the headings of the last four days of the week. These appear in the nominative case instead of the customary genitive. Therefore they indicate planets and not days of the week. In this edition they are emended from the nominative to the genitive in accordance with the equivalent material in A¹. The words *confortacio virtutis* appear to the left of the material at the bottom of the page in S¹A¹DBR. S¹ in the box that contains the words *calidus et* offers the words *calida et sicca,* an error. As¹ makes the same error. AdAs³ eliminate all of the material at the bottom of the page. A² eliminates both the material at the bottom of the page and the chart to the right of the page. The separation between the words *Mars* and *que* under the chart, although not conventional Latin, is consistent to all manuscripts which offer these words.

PRIMA VIGINTI QUINTA CENTUM DUODENA QUE MILLE. The word *preteritis* in the second line of the heading is misspelled as *preteris* in L. The correct spelling appears in S¹A¹DBAs¹RAdA² and is so emended in this edition. The date for Easter in the First Cycle, dominical letter *g,* is 8 April. The 8 has been blotted out in L but appears in S¹A¹DBAs¹RAdA² and is added here. The date for Septuagesima Sunday in the Seventh Cycle, dominical letter *c,* is given incorrectly as 21 January in L. The correct date, 31 January, appears in S¹A¹DBAs¹ RAdA² and in this edition. The matter was not, one may presume, of great concern to Nicholas and his contemporaries. The first occurrence of the Seventh Cycle with dominical letter *g* after the 1387 composition of the *Kalendarium* was in 1507.

THE FINAL TABLE IN THE CALENDAR. The various headings for this lunar table are as follows: *Tabula ad sciendum locum lune quolibet die et mora eius sub quolibet signo,* S¹A¹B; *Tabula ad sciendum locum lune quolibet die et moram eius sub quolibet signo,* D As²; *Tabula ad sciendum in quo signo fuerit luna quolibet die quondam ad medium motum,* As¹; *Tabula ad cognoscendum in quo signo et in gradu fuerit luna,* Ad; *Tabula ad sciendum in quo signo fuerit luna quolibet die anni,* A². R does not have this table.

## THE CANONS

Line 3. Following the *d* in *inveniend-,* L and R show the small loop which customarily indicates a *-us* ending. Ad shows two minims with a line over them, indicating a *-um* ending. The word agrees with *gradu* and requires an ablative. I have accordingly emended it for this edition.

Lines 41–42. L reads as follows: *inventorum fuit fuit inventum* although only one use of the word *fuit* appears in S¹A¹DBR. As¹AdA² do not have this passage. Apparently the doubling of the word *fuit* was an error, and the scribe of L expunged the first use of the word by underlining it. Accordingly, this edition is emended to eliminate the first use of *fuit.*

Line 59. The word *primacio* means the first appearance of the new moon.

Line 132. Apparently the scribe of L thought that *quartam* should have the same suffix as the word *partem,* which follows.

Line 133. LS¹A¹ give the ending of the word which is reproduced in this text as *inventa* as a high small curve, an abbreviation that in fourteenth-century manuscript usage customarily means *-us*. Nevertheless, the word *inventus* would not agree with *altitudine meridiana,* which it modifies. Therefore, the word is emended from B to *inventa,* a correct feminine ablative singular. D reads *inventam,* and Ad has *inventibus,* both, I believe, being errors. As[1]RA[2] do not have this passage.

Lines 158–59. The words *miliari* and *miliare* are two forms of a neuter i-stem noun of the third declension and according to this context mean "mile." See R. E. Latham, M. A., *Revised Medieval Latin Word-List from British and Irish Sources* (London: Oxford University Press, 1965), p. 299.

Line 226. An extra *inveniet* is placed in the margin of L here (folio 39r, line 31). The handwriting is not that of the L scribe, although the abbreviations are consistent with the time the scribe was writing.

Line 237. The word *quas* was not originally in L but is inserted lightly in another hand. Both the ink and the width of the pen differ from those in L. The word *quas* appears normally in all the other manuscripts which have this passage.

Line 313–16. As it is impossible in this edition to reproduce Nicholas's red figures, a means for determining Easter using only black figures is offered in the introduction, p. 20.

Line 324. The word *secunda* is emended from *secundo* of L. The error was apparently caused by a scribe who thought that *secunda* modified *vero* and not *quadra.* See the corpus of variants, where the expanse of this error is indicated.

Line 341. The word *inquit* is spelled with a final *t* both in this line and in line 420, although the scribes of LS[1]A[1]Ad always abbreviate the word. Late Latin *inquio,* meaning "say," is a third conjugation *-io* verb with a normal present third person singular ending of *-it.* Although very late manuscripts such as S[2]GgAs[3] spell the word *inquid,* I find no obligation to follow such a spelling unless there is absolute evidence that the scribe of L favored it, which there is not. On this line DBAs[1]RM have a visible *t* at the end of the word.

Line 420. *inquit.* See note to line 341.

Line 442. Apparently Haly considered *Piscis* to be a single fish.

Line 465. The word *non* appears above the line in L as an insertion written with a very light ink and a thin pen. It appears conventionally in A[1]DBA s[1]AdMS[2]Gg.

Line 466. The *via combustionis* is the combust way, which is defined by the *Oxford English Dictionary* (Oxford: The Clarendon Press, 1971) as "The space in the second half of Libra and through the whole sign of Scorpio." There seems to be no question here that *combustionis* is spelled with a *t* instead of the expected *c.* The *t* is consistent in all manuscripts.

Line 512. The spelling *poriguntur* is unique to L; other manuscripts have the proper *porriguntur,* except M, where the text here is completely different.

Line 529. The word *house* is placed in brackets in the translation because the adjective *sixth* in Latin is feminine and must refer to the assumed word *house.* Furthermore, in D the word *domus* appears after the word *sexta.*

Line 533. The redundancy *in lumine in suo* is limited to La[1].

Line 561. The word *Sortes* is a standard medieval abbreviation for "Socrates," as John Burrow points out in the *Times Literary Supplement* (21 May 1976), p. 615. See this usage in William Langland, *Piers Plowman,* ed. W. W. Skeat, I (London: Oxford Univ. Press, 1886, rpt. 1965), 1:383, text C, passus XV, line 193: "Ne of Sortes, ne of Salamon · no scripture can telle." See also vol. 2, p. 187 for Skeat's explanation. The abbreviation *sorti* is listed for *Socrati* in A. Cappelli, *Dizionario de Abbreviature latine ed italiano,* 6th ed. (Milan: Ulrico Hoepli, 1967), p. 357. Professor Morton W. Bloomfield of Harvard University graciously explained to me that in medieval logic the name *Sortes* came to mean not just "Socrates" but "someone" or "anyone." That is, *Sortes currit* might be translated as "Someone runs." Because Socrates' name appears five words after *Sortes* in this passage and because an obvious contrast is implied, I believe that in the mind of Nicholas *Sortes, Socrates,* and *Plato* are three distinct Greek names used here to mean, as Professor Richard C. Jensen of the Classics Department of the University of Arizona kindly suggested to me, merely A, B, and C.

# NOTES TO CORPUS OF VARIANTS

## THE CALENDAR

FEBRUARY. The saint noted for 11 February in B, *Frisdewide virginis,* is an error and misspelling for St. Frideswide, the patron saint of Oxford, whose saint's day, according to Herbert Thurston, S. J., and Donald Attwater, eds., *Butler's Lives of the Saints,* revised edition (New York: P. J. Kenedy & Sons, 1963), 4: 150f., and according to DAd, is celebrated on 19 October, and whose translation, according to A[1], is 12 February.

APRIL. The saint noted in So for 24 April is either St. Wilfrid, Bishop of York, who died in 709, and whose saint's day was customarily celebrated on 12 October, or St. Wilfrid the Younger, also Bishop of York, who died in 744, and whose saint's day was celebrated on 29 April. Neither Wilfrid was known to be an archbishop.

MAY. The added variant for So on 3 May, although clearly a second declension genitive plural, is otherwise illegible.

Note that As[2]'s notation for 9 May does not say, as is customary, *Translacio.* Cf. Vulg., Exod. 12:11: "Est enim phase id est transitus dominis." *Translacio* translates as "translation," or the simple transference of the remains of a saint. *Transitus* translates as "passing over," with the implication that a threat thereby is being avoided. The relics of St. Nicholas were moved from Myra in Asia Minor to Bari, Italy, on 9 May 1087, just before the Saracens captured Myra.

JUNE. As[2]'s notation for 3 June is an error for 2 June.

JULY. A[2]'s notation for 5 July is an error for 6 July.

AUGUST. D's notation for 4 August is an error for 5 August.

SEPTEMBER. A[2]'s notation for 6 September is a corrected error for 9 September. Ad's notation for 15 September is an error for 16 September.

OCTOBER. D's notation for 11 October is an error for *Sancte Ethelburge,* whose saint's day is celebrated on 12 October.

DECEMBER. Apparently the scribe of As[1] reversed the notations for 27 and 28 December and then either he or another corrected the error with the notations *.b.* and *.a.*

Line 413. In D (folio 88r, lines 16–17) the words which appear in the other manuscripts as *planete effectui medicine non resistit* are written in the margin with only the *p* of *planete* and the *n* of *non* remaining on the surviving vellum.

Line 420. The word *planete* was written in As[1] (folio 42r, line 14) following the word *effectus*. However, the scribe of As[1] or another person crossed out *planete*.

Line 425. In D (folio 88r, line 26) the words *eius effectum sicut* appear in the margin.